PERSIAN NATIVITIES

VOLUME II:
'Umar al-Tabarī & Abū Bakr

TRANSLATED AND EDITED BY
BENJAMIN N. DYKES, PHD

The Cazimi Press
Minneapolis, Minnesota
2010

Published and printed in the United States of America
by The Cazimi Press, Minneapolis, MN 55414

© 2010 by Benjamin N. Dykes, Ph.D.

All rights reserved. No part of this publication may be reproduced, stored in or introduced into a retrieval system, or transmitted, in any form or by any means (electronic, mechanical, photocopying, recording or otherwise), without the prior written permission of both the copyright owner and the above publisher of this book.

The scanning, uploading, and distribution of this book via the Internet or via any other means without the permission of the publisher is illegal and punishable by law. Please purchase only authorized electronic editions and do not participate in or encourage electronic piracy of copyrighted materials. Your support of the author's rights is appreciated.

Library of Congress Control Number: 2009913705

ISBN-13: 978-1-934586-04-4

Acknowledgments

I would like to thank Frank Clifford, Andy Gehrz, and Christopher Warnock for making this book possible.

TABLE OF CONTENTS

Book Abbreviations ix
Table of Figures..x
INTRODUCTION xi
'UMAR AL-TABARĪ: *THREE BOOKS ON NATIVITIES* ..1
  BOOK I: BIRTH AND LONGEVITY...1
    Chapter I.1: The planetary months of gestation.........................1
    Chapter I.2: Determining an unknown birth Ascendant 2
    Chapter I.3: Rearing and the determinations of births...............3
    Chapter I.4: On the *hīlāj* and *kadukhudhāh*.............................7
  BOOK II: ANNUAL METHODS...23
    Chapter II.1: Annual direction of the *hīlāj* 23
    Chapter II.2: The direction of the Ascendant, and its *jārbakhtār*........27
    Chapter II.3: How mundane directions differ from the revolutions of
      nativities 30
    Chapter II.4: 'Umar's method of profections.............................32
    Chapter II.5: The general, greater, and lesser conditions of the native
      and his parents 33
    Chapter II.6: Examples of directions and profections for the native...35
    Chapter II.7: Ptolemy's annual directions 43
    Chapter II.8: Rejection of alternative methods 44
  BOOK III: TOPICS..46
    Chapter III.1: Social Status and Prosperity 46
    Chapter III.2: Wealth...52
    Chapter III.3: Siblings...53
    Chapter III.4: Parents 55
    Chapter III.5: Marriage 59
    Chapter III.6: Children 62
    Chapter III.7: Infirmities 64
    Chapter III.8: Travel 67
    Chapter III.9: Work and Mastery...68
    Chapter III.10: Friends 71
    Chapter III.11: Enemies 74
    Chapter III.12: Faith 76
    Chapter III.13: Death 77
ABŪ BAKR: *ON NATIVITIES*..79
  BOOK I: OVERVIEW, PREGNANCY, LONGEVITY...........................79
    Chapter I.1.0: What is proper to know for him who wishes to establish
      the judgments of nativities..79
    Chapter I.1.2: The native's body, mind, and topics of life 81
    Chapter I.1.3: Prediction, the *hīlāj*, *kadukhudhāh*, and primary
      directions 84

Chapter I.2: On the projection of seed into the womb 85
Chapter I.3: On the native's stay in the mother's womb 89
Chapter I.4: On knowing the *namūdār*, and the hour of the projection of seed into the womb..91
Chapter I.5: Detailed planetary dispositions of the months..................93
Chapter I.6: Whether the birth is legitimate or from adultery 101
Chapter I.7: On the native's progression out of the mother's belly, whether it was quick or slow 102
Chapter I.8: On the types of the native, and of what nature he will be, and whether he will be a man or a brute animal................103
Chapter I.9: On the native's face 107
Chapter I.10.1: On the colors of the planets 109
Chapter I.10.2: On the colors of the signs 111
Chapter I.11: On the one to whom the boy will be likened: namely to the father or mother, paternal uncle or maternal uncle 112
Chapter I.12: On the nourishing of boys..113
Chapter I.13: On the abandonment of the native...............................124
Chapter I.14: On the beauty of the native's nourishment 124
Chapter I.15: On the knowledge of the *hīlāj* and the *kadukhudhāh*...125
Chapter I.16: On the years of the planets which the sages used in the distribution of the nativity 133
Chapter I.17: On the knowledge of the distributors or distribution of the native's years..135
BOOK II: TOPICS...139
Chapter II.1.0: On the native's morals and his nature 139
Chapter II.1.1: On him who has anxiety 143
Chapter II.1.2: On the native's quickness to wars and rage 143
Chapter II.1.3: On the native's humbleness..144
Chapter II.1.4: On the shamelessness of the native 144
Chapter II.1.5: On the native's shame 145
Chapter II.1.6: On the beauty of the native's morals 145
Chapter II.1.7: On the native's lies 145
Chapter II.1.8: On the native's truth...146
Chapter II.1.9: On the native's religion 146
Chapter II.1.10: On the native's pretended sanctity 148
Chapter II.1.11: On the native's idolatry 149
Chapter II.1.12: On the native's knowledge 150
Chapter II.1.13: On the native's memory...153
Chapter II.1.14: On the native's bad intellect 154
Chapter II.1.15: On the native's good and quick intellect 154
Chapter II.1.16: On the native's stupidity 155
Chapter II.1.17: On those born actors 155
Chapter II.1.18: On the native's faithfulness 156
Chapter II.1.19: On those born wicked, and their unfaithfulness.......157

Chapter II.1.20: On those born robbers 157
Chapter II.1.21: On natives' liberality 158
Chapter II.1.22: On the native's greed 158
Chapter II.1.23: On the native's envy 159
Chapter II.1.24: On the conceit and magnanimity of the native 159
Chapter II.1.25: On the cheerfulness of the native's face 159
Chapter II.1.26: On the native's joyfulness 160
Chapter II.1.27: On the native's sorrow and weakness 160
Chapter II.1.28: On the native's eagerness when eating 161
Chapter II.1.29: On natives sowing discord among men 162
Chapter II.1.30: On the native's bad thinking 162
Chapter II.1.31: On the native's beauty 162
Chapter II.1.32: On the dignified or serious and calm [nature] of natives 162
Chapter II.1.33: On the native's hastiness 163
Chapter II.2.0: Prosperity and Eminence 164
Chapter II.2.1: On natives who are kings, and their fortune 165
Chapter II.2.2: On the dominions of natives, and their fortune in them 167
Chapter II.2.3: On the native's middling fortune 168
Chapter II.2.4: On the native's misery and labor 170
Chapter II.2.5: On natives returned to servitude 171
Chapter II.2.6: On natives who will be incarcerated 172
Chapter II.2.7: On natives who are beggars 173
Chapter II.2.8: On natives who come down from riches to poverty . 175
Chapter II.2.9: On natives who are raised up from out of poverty to riches 177
Chapter II.2.10: On natives who are greater than their own parents . 179
Chapter II.3.0: Wealth 181
Chapter II.3.1: Indications of great wealth 181
Chapter II.3.2: On the administrators of kings, and their fortune 183
Chapter II.3.3: On natives who are wise, and their fortune 184
Chapter II.3.4: On the native's fortune from commerce 185
Chapter II.3.5: On the native's fortune from slaves and servants 187
Chapter II.3.6: On the native's fortune from beasts 188
Chapter II.3.7: On masters of soldiers, and their fortune 189
Chapter II.3.8: On natives who are soldiers, and their fortune 191
Chapter II.3.9: On the native's fortune on the occasion of money in the earth or found elsewhere 192
Chapter II.3.10: On the native's fortune coming about from the inheritances of the dead 192
Chapter II.3.11: On the native's fortune from fields and gardens 194
Chapter II.4.0: Siblings 196
Chapter II.4.1: Multiple siblings 196

Chapter II.4.2: On the scarcity of siblings...198
Chapter II.4.3: On the native's fortune with the siblings 199
Chapter II.4.4: On the siblings' enmity..200
Chapter II.4.5: On the misfortune and fall of the siblings 201
Chapter II.5.0: Parents..204
Chapter II.5.1: On the parents' exaltation..204
Chapter II.5.2: On the parents' fall or being pressed down.................205
Chapter II.5.3: On the native's friendship and enmity with the parents
....207
Chapter 157: On the native's fortune with the parents........................209
Chapter II.5.5: On natives squandering the parents' money...............209
Chapter II.5.6: On the fortune of the native's parents.........................210
Chapter II.5.7: On the labor and impediment of the native's parents 211
Chapter II.5.8: On the death of the native's parents 213
Chapter II.5.9: Primary directions for the parents]..............................215
Chapter II.5.10: The father, according to 'Umar al-Tabarī..................216
Chapter II.5.11: The mother, according to 'Umar al-Tabarī................217
Chapter II.5.12: The method of pseudo-Ptolemy................................219
Chapter II.5.13: The method of Dorotheus..220
Chapter II.5.14: Comment on 'Umar's method 222
Chapter II.6.0: Children..223
Chapter II.6.1: Multiple children..223
Chapter II.6.2: On natives lacking children, or having few children ..225
Chapter II.6.3: On sterile natives 226
Chapter II.6.4: On the number of children..227
Chapter II.6.5: On the hour or time in which the native will have
    children...228
Chapter II.6.6: On the native's happiness with children......................228
Chapter II.6.7: On the native's labor with a child or children 229
Chapter II.6.8: On the fortune of the native's children 230
Chapter II.6.9: On the labor of the native's children 231
Chapter II.6.10: On the death of the children.....................................232
Chapter II.7.0: Illness..234
Chapter II.7.1: Illnesses according to planetary signification...............235
Chapter II.7.2: Chronic illness...236
Chapter II.7.3: On blindness and illnesses of the eyes.........................237
Chapter II.7.4: On the loss of one eye..239
Chapter II.7.5: On cloudiness in the eyes...239
Chapter II.7.6: On one-eyed people or squinting eyes........................240
Chapter II.7.7: On dark eyes...240
Chapter II.7.8: On weak vision 241
Chapter II.7.9: On illnesses of the ears...242
Chapter II.7.10: On the native's speech..242
Chapter II.7.11: On hunchbacked natives..243

Chapter II.7.12: On leprous natives 244
Chapter II.7.13: On natives having white morphew 244
Chapter II.7.14: On those born lunatics, fools, or one-eyed 245
Chapter II.7.15: On epileptic natives 246
Chapter II.7.16: On paralytic natives 247
Chapter II.7.17: On natives with heart problems 247
Chapter II.7.18: On natives with liver problems..................................248
Chapter II.7.19: On natives with spleen problems 248
Chapter II.7.20: On natives with lung problems..................................249
Chapter II.7.21: On natives with stomach problems 249
Chapter II.7.22: On natives having pain in the belly and intestines ...250
Chapter II.7.23: On illnesses of the genitals 250
Chapter II.7.24: On stones and grains of sand......................................251
Chapter II.7.25: On natives having much sexual intercourse 251
Chapter II.7.26: On natives having little sexual intercourse..............252
Chapter II.7.27: On natives [who are] eunuchs and hermaphrodites.253
Chapter II.7.28: On the illness of the anus 253
Chapter II.7.29: On natives of short stature 254
Chapter II.7.30: On natives of tall and even stature...........................255
Chapter II.7.31: On natives with weak bodies.....................................255
Chapter II.7.32: On bald natives..255
Chapter II.7.33: On natives having a sparse beard 256
Chapter II.7.34: On natives having sweat and stinking breath 256
Chapter II.7.35: On the illness of the joints, and the breaking of limbs
257
Chapter II.7.36: On illnesses of the hands and feet.............................257
Chapter II.7.37: In what part of the body the illness will be...............258
Chapter II.7.37: On the time of illness 259
Chapter II.7.38: On the greatness of the native's testicles 259
Chapter II.8.0: Slaves 260
Chapter II.9.0: Marriage 261
Chapter II.9.1: Good and bad sexuality..261
Chapter II.9.2: On natives who will not be loved by women 262
Chapter II.9.3: On natives lacking a wife 262
Chapter II.9.4: On marriage with charming and good women...........263
Chapter II.9.5: On marriage to wicked women and prostitutes 264
Chapter II.9.6: On the native's marriage with little old women, foul
 ones, or sterile ones 265
Chapter II.9.7: On the native's marriage-union with slave-girls..........266
Chapter II.9.8: On natives marrying against the law, or lying with
 prohibited women 266
Chapter II.9.9: On natives' fornication...268
Chapter II.9.10: On the sodomy of male and female natives 269

Chapter II.9.11: On the innocence of natives, or the prohibition of sodomy 271
Chapter II.9.12: On the womanliness of natives 271
Chapter II.9.13: On the native's fortune regarding women 272
Chapter II.9.14: On the native's misfortune regarding women..........273
Chapter II.9.15: On natives who fornicate secretly with women........274
Chapter II.9.16: On natives whose wives die first 274
Chapter II.9.17: On the number of the native's wives 275
Chapter II.9.18: On the time at which the native will take a wife.......276
Chapter II.10.0: Death 277
Chapter II.10.1: Types of death 277
Chapter II.10.2: Death according to an Ascendant template...............278
Chapter II.10.3: On natives fearing death 279
Chapter II.10.4: On natives who will die by some illness.....................279
Chapter II.10.5: On natives who will die a bad death 279
Chapter II.10.6: On natives who will die a sudden death.....................280
Chapter II.10.7: On natives who will die in water 281
Chapter II.10.8: On natives who will die by fire 281
Chapter II.10.9: On natives who will die by falling from high places 282
Chapter II.10.10: On natives who will die by a poison or toxin...........282
Chapter II.10.11: On natives who will be eaten or killed by beasts 283
Chapter II.10.12: On natives who will die by the sword or be hung..283
Chapter II.10.13: On natives who kill themselves 285
Chapter II.10.14: On natives who will die on the occasion of women
285
Chapter II.10.15: On natives whose death will be secret......................286
Chapter II.10.16: On natives who will die in their own land or homeland 286
Chapter II.10.17: On natives who will die outside their homeland, or in a foreign place 287
Chapter II.11.0: Travel..289
Chapter II.11.1: Successful travel...289
Chapter II.11.2: On natives who will die on their journeys, or never come back from them 290
Chapter II.11.3: On natives who come back on their journeys...........291
Chapter II.11.4: On natives who incur losses and misfortunes on the occasion of journeys 291
Chapter II.12.0: Dominion and mastery...293
Chapter II.12.1: Indications of lasting dominion 293
Chapter II.12.2: On the native's mastery...294
Chapter II.12.3: Fortune and misfortune in masteries 296
Chapter II.12.4: Masteries by type of sign..298
Chapter II.12.5: Venus, Mars, and Mercury as significators................299
Chapter II.12.6: Other points to look at for the mastery.......................301

Chapter II.12.7: The Moon with other planets signifying masteries...301
Chapter II.12.8: Other points to consider...304
Chapter II.12.9: On natives who are weavers...304
Chapter II.12.10: On native who are sewers...305
Chapter II.12.11: On natives who are common laborers or tawyers..305
Chapter II.11.12: On natives who are carpenters...305
Chapter II.12.13: On natives who are painters and sculptors...306
Chapter II.12.14: On natives who are dyers...307
Chapter II.12.15: On natives who are diggers...307
Chapter II.12.16: On natives who are sailors...308
Chapter II.12.17: On natives who are craftsmen...308
Chapter II.12.18: On natives who are jokers...309
Chapter II.12.19: On natives who are medical doctors and surgeons309
Chapter II.12.20: On natives who are fishermen or trappers or hunters...310
Chapter II.12.21: On natives who are ropemakers...310
Chapter II.12.22: On natives who sell good-smelling commodities...311
Chapter II.12.23: On natives who are shopkeepers...311
Chapter II.12.24: On merchants of fruits...312
Chapter II.12.25: On merchants of herbs or roots, and of seeds...312
Chapter II.12.26: On natives who are farmers...312
Chapter II.12.27: On merchants of *rethau* and of things smelling nice...313
Chapter II.12.28: On merchants of cloths of linen or silk...313
Chapter II.12.29: On merchants of wool...314
Chapter II.12.30: On merchants of bread-grains and of other seeds.314
Chapter II.12.31: On merchants of leather [or hide]...315
Chapter II.12.32: On the merchants of slaves...315
Chapter II.12.33: On merchants of quadrupeds...316
Chapter II.12.34: On merchants of birds...316
Chapter II.12.35: On merchants of fish...317
Chapter II.12.36: On natives who are potters...317
Chapter II.12.37: On those turning and putting together bowls...318
Chapter II.12.38: On merchants or preparers of pearls...318
Chapter II.12.39: On natives who are moneychangers...319
Chapter II.12.40: On natives who are butchers and bakers...319
Chapter II.12.41: On merchants of dates and apples [and] olives...320
Chapter II.12.42: On merchants of bread and wine...320
Chapter II.12.43: On merchants of sugarcane, arrows, spears, or lumber...321
Chapter II.12.44: On natives who are heralds...321
Chapter II.12.45: On diverse masteries of natives...322
Chapter II.12.46: In order to find the lord of the mastery...323
Chapter II.13.0: Friends...325

Chapter II.13.1: On the friendship of kings or lofty men toward the native 325
Chapter II.13.2: On the friendship of bad and low-class men, and of certain others, toward the native 326
Chapter II.13.3: On the native's faithful and good friendship..............327
Chapter II.13.4: On natives who will have discord with friends..........328
Chapter II.13.5: On natives who will receive evil from their friends .329
Chapter II.14.0: Enemies..330
Chapter II.14.1: Good and bad fortune with enemies 330
Chapter II.14.2: On natives who have their enemies in their own power 332

Appendix A: Miscellaneous 'Umar Excerpts 334
Appendix B: Alternative Text for the Firdāriyyāt of the Nodes 338
Appendix C: The Trutine of Hermes (Abū Bakr I.4.1)............................339
BIBLIOGRAPHY 342
INDEX..345

BOOK ABBREVIATIONS

Abū 'Ali al-Khayyāt:	*The Judgments of Nativities*	*JN*
Abū Ma'shar:	*Liber Introductorii Maioris ad Scientiam Iudiciorum Astrorum (Great Introduction to the Knowledge of the Judgments of the Stars)*	*Gr. Intr.*
	On the Revolutions of Nativities	*On Rev. Nat.*
Bonatti, Guido	*Book of Astronomy*	*BOA*
Dorotheus of Sidon:	*Carmen Astrologicum*	*Carmen*
Māshā'allāh:	*Book of Nativities*	*Nativities*
	Book of Aristotle	*BA*
Ptolemy	*Tetrabiblos*	*Tet.*
Sahl bin Bishr:	*The Introduction*	*Introduct.*
'Umar al-Tabarī	*Three Books on Nativities*	*TBN*
Vettius Valens:	*The Anthology*	*Anth.*

TABLE OF FIGURES

Figure 1: Direction of the *hīlāj* #1 19
Figure 2: Direction of the *hīlāj* #1 24
Figure 3: The "lesser" condition of the native 36
Figure 4: The "greater" condition of the native 39
Figure 5: The "general" condition of the native 41
Figure 6: Monstrous birth #1 105
Figure 7: Monstrous birth #2 106

INTRODUCTION

Persian Nativities is part of a cycle of translations which will define the contours of medieval astrology for modern students, using the most important Latin texts, astrologers, and parts of the medieval period: primarily the Latin translations of the Persian and Arab astrologers of the 8th-10th Centuries.[1] In *Persian Nativities II* I present translations of 'Umar al-Tabari's *Three Books on Nativities* (TBN) and Abū Bakr's *On Nativities*, both important natal works which had lasting influence in the Latin West up through the time of William Lilly. *Persian Nativities III* (forthcoming, 2010) will present a new translation of Abū Ma'shar's *On the Revolutions of the Nativity* as a stand-alone volume, containing annual techniques such as profections, solar revolutions, primary directions through the bounds, the *firdāriyyāt* (sing. *firdāriyyah*), and more. Barring new discoveries,[2] after *Persian Nativities III* I will consider the natal portion of the cycle complete and definitive.

In the next few years I will release other installments in this cycle, featuring first-time translations of horary, electional, and mundane material, with additional volumes acting as invitations and introductions to the whole project. Within five years, students interested in traditional and particularly medieval astrology will enjoy a complete learning experience in all branches of astrology, from basic concepts to delineation, numerous predictive techniques, and a traditional philosophical outlook. Of course students may also supplement their reading with Hellenistic works such as the *Carmen* of Dorotheus, Ptolemy's *Tetrabiblos*, or Rhetorius, and also by later Renaissance and early modern works. On my own site at www.bendykes.com, I have begun to issue free study guides for students, and more will appear throughout the cycle.

§1: New insights: prosperity, the mubtazz

One benefit of comparing all four texts in *Persian Nativities I-II* is that one may get a richer view of how topics were handled and conceived. For one thing, both *BA* and Abū Bakr provide lists of individual questions to ask

---

[1] Original Pahlavi works are largely lost, and there are few astrologers in the Western tradition who can read Arabic.
[2] Pingree has claimed that an edition of the *Book on Nativities* by a so-called Zaradusht will be published, but I do not currently know its status. Zaradusht also wrote several works on mundane astrology.

about topics such as marriage or siblings.[3] For another, the treatments of topics such as wealth and prosperity shed light on how the Persians reconceived the Hellenistic material. If we take Abū Bakr as our example, the Persians first seem to have distinguished several categories of prosperity, from those who will always enjoy high status, to middling or low status, and even those who will go from high to low or from low to high prosperity.[4] This overlapped with but was not identical to, financial wealth. In a related way, they also distinguished those who have well-defined leading roles in the society as a whole (which normally confers lasting wealth and prosperity) from those who work at a trade (which can fluctuate in wealth). Thus in the leading roles we have kings, politicians and governmental functionaries, military leaders, and what we might now call captains of industry: these are handled alongside the prosperity material, or at least separately from the trades. In the category of trades or "masteries" (professions) people are distinguished by practical skills such as being a carpenter, but with *no* indications as to the inherent level of wealth. Thus the Persian delineation of prosperity, wealth, and profession is handled in terms of a realistic understanding of social structure and functions. But these distinctions are not made at all clear in Bonatti, appear in a disorganized, piecemeal way in Dorotheus, and were obscured in Holden's translation of *JN*. Only by taking these works together can we see a coherent approach and set of delineation instructions.

These texts also provide the closest answer yet to the issue of the "weighted" *mubtazz* and who invented it. *Mubtazz* (often spelled *almuten*) means "winner," and is nothing more than a planet which—among a set of competing options—is authoritative enough to act as the chief planet to represent some topic. This idea is common enough in Hellenistic longevity techniques, when identifying the "predominator" (Gr. *epikratētor*) or in medieval astrology the *hīlāj* (or *hyleg*). And Ptolemy himself[5] provides a method for finding a *mubtazz* or ruling planet, in which the rulers of different dignities in some place each receive one point or count: the one with the most points is the most authoritative planet to work with.

But at some point in the Perso-Arabic period, a weighted approach to the *mubtazz* was adopted. Instead of the Lords of dignities receiving one point

---

[3] See throughout *BA* III, and Abū Bakr I.1.2.
[4] See for instance *BA* III.2.0, *JN* Ch. 7, *TBN* III.1, and Abū Bakr II.2.0.
[5] *Tet.* III.5.

apiece, the domicile Lord of a place received 5, the exalted Lord (if there was one) received 4, the primary triplicity Lord 3, the bound Lord 2, and the face or decan Lord 1. Again, the one with the most points was the *mubtazz*. But this method was not universally adopted. It is not found in Sahl or Māshā'allāh or Abū 'Alī's *JN*. 'Umar himself seems to follow Ptolemy, but in one place (*TBN* III.4.2) he refers to the luminary of the sect as being a *mubtazz*, showing that it did not always have a consistent technical meaning. But by about 850 AD, the weighted *mubtazz* was straightforwardly endorsed by al-Kindī[6] and later by al-Qabīsī,[7] whose book was so popular in the Latin West that Bonatti simply repeats al-Qabīsī's account.[8] What happened between the 790s and approximately 850 AD?

We may now know. In his material on parents, Abū Bakr makes a few statements explaining his connections to 'Umar and his texts. First (II.5.9), he describes a day on which a then-famous poet and astrologer, Abū al-'Anbas al-Saimari,[9] helped him delineate a client's chart (thus establishing al-'Anbas as a more experienced mentor). Next (II.5.10), he describes how his own father used to watch 'Umar work. Finally (II.5.14), he mentions in passing that al-'Anbas[10] told him how "he had found the *mubtazz* according to what 'Umar said, by giving 5 dignities to the Lord of the domicile, 4 to the Lord of the exaltation," and so on. But Abū Bakr does not explicitly endorse or reject this approach, which indicates that it was not a commonly-accepted view.

Let me say a few words about this al-'Anbas, because more research needs to be done on him.[11] He was a poet, raunchy satirist, polemicist, and astronomer-astrologer. Sources agree he was originally from Kufa and died in 888 AD, but his birth year is unclear. Sezgin claims that the usual date of 828 AD is suspect, and I agree. For Abū Bakr says (II.5.9) that either he or al-

---

[6] *The Forty Chapters* §137.
[7] Al-Qabīsī I.77.
[8] *BOA* pp. 145-46.
[9] Al-'Anbas seems to mean "the talker," which does match his reputation (see below).
[10] The 1540 edition and Jag. seem to differ on this. 1540 unequivocally names al-'Anbas, but Jag. attributes a different statement to him, then attributes the weighted *mubtazz* to something like Azemczael, who is probably al-Hasan bin Sahl, an astrologer and vizier to Caliph al-Ma'mūn (r. 813-833), whose dates are 782-851. But this al-Hasan bin Sahl is probably not the inventor of the weighted *mubtazz*, as he was part of the Pahlavi-to-Arabic translation movement and so would probably would have followed the source material which did not contain such a weighted *mubtazz*. He should also have been able to ask 'Umar personally about his *mubtazz*, instead of having to invent a weighting system.
[11] See Sezgin pp. 152-53, and Bosley pp. 30-31.

'Anbas was twenty-three when they were together in 844 AD: if al-'Anbas were born in 828, this would have made him sixteen when he mentored Abū Bakr (which is unlikely); but if Abū Bakr was twenty-three, then al-'Anbas's birth is would have been somewhat earlier, putting Abū Bakr's own birth at about 821 AD. This latter option makes more sense to me.

Al-'Anbas befriended famous poets of the day, was for a while a magistrate, and lived at the courts of Caliphs al-Mutawakkil (r. in Samarra 847-861) and al-Mu'tamid (r. in Baghdad 870-892). He was interested in a life of vagrancy and the social underworld, wrote bawdy works whose titles should probably not be repeated here, a *Refutation of the Astrologers* (in which he probably posed as a critic), and much more. Astrologically speaking, he wrote several works which survive in Arabic, including a *Book of Nativities* and an introductory work on astrology which—according to critics—he plagiarized from his contemporary Abū Ma'shar. In fact it seems that accusations of plagiarism followed him in several areas, and I get the impression that there was something of the moocher and con man to him. However, his works deserve to be examined, because I suspect that he would be rather vocal about having invented the weighted *mubtazz*.

Thus, Abū Bakr had a connection to one of the more famous early astrologers of the period through a family member, which increases his credibility regarding 'Umar's practice. He identifies a bombastic astrologer and poet as inventing the weighted *mubtazz*. It further suggests that as people learned this Persian astrology now in Arabic, they struggled with some of the techniques: the weighted *mubtazz* must have been part of this attempt at understanding, but it was a particular response to a particular passage and not conclusive or generalizable in any way. From this we should conclude that the real and dubious influence of al-'Anbas was to have invented this weighted *mubtazz* sometime between the death of 'Umar in 815 and his mentorship of Abū Bakr in 844 AD, bequeathing it thereafter to notable contemporaries such as al-Kindī. The rest, as they say, is history. But these facts also support the argument that the weighted *mubtazz* is misguided and artificial. Those who use it, from the *mubtazz* of the chart as found in Abraham ibn Ezra,[12] to the elaborate numeric grids in Lilly's *Christian Astrology*, must wonder if and when it is justified.

---

[12] See ibn Ezra, pp. 13-14.

§2: Between the Persians and the Latins: medieval changes and trajectories

Based on the above facts and some of the trends I noted in my introduction to *Persian Nativities I*, I would like to summarize a few important changes which took place in medieval astrology, which affects our understanding of it today.

First, the readability of John of Spain's translations influenced what works were favored in the Latin West, and what vocabulary astrologers still use. Difficult, fussy translations by people like Hugo of Santalla (such as the *Book of Aristotle*, with its Hellenistic techniques) were more readily ignored, while easier works written by John or in his style (such as Abū Bakr, *JN*, *TBN*) were more popular and used as the basis for works like Bonatti's *Book of Astronomy*. Thus also, we say "exaltation" because of John's use of *exaltatio*; we do not follow Hugo and speak of a planet's "kingdom" or "supremacy" (*regnum*).

Second, the timing and length of certain translations also affected what texts and techniques were used. For example, Abū Ma'shar's *On Rev. Nat.* seems to have been translated into Latin too late (1268) for Bonatti to have used it. Thus, early and shortish introductory works like al-Qabīsī's, which uses a weighted *mubtazz* but has only minimal information on the annual predictive techniques, enjoyed great popularity—thus passing on the weighted *mubtazz* but not the extensive annual methods. This too, affected how astrologers worked.

Third, one clear feature of the astrology of the very popular 'Umar and Abū 'Ali is the use of methods akin to horary in delineating natal matters. Abū 'Ali clearly draws on the older 'Umar, looking at the relationship between the most powerful planet ruling the matters of the native, and the one ruling the matters of some topic (such as parents). This would have been familiar to people practicing horary, for which 'Umar was well known. But the delineation material in *JN* and *TBN* which supplies the remaining details (based on Hellenistic-era texts) is disorganized and thin compared with the parallel and fuller accounts in the *Book of Aristotle*. Thus the horary contribution to astrology began to blend into much natal practice.

Based on these trends and this new discovery in Abū Bakr, I would like to propose that there was a divergence of "lineage" in natal astrology. The first stream or lineage is the more traditional one based on Hellenistic techniques. It runs from sources in Valens, Dorotheus and Rhetorius, through

Māshā'allāh and Sahl.[13] It does not use a weighted *mubtazz*, continued to rely more on whole-sign houses, and borrowed little from horary technique. But it did not predominate in the Latin West and so was largely lost after the 13th Century. The second stream or lineage draws less on the delineation details of Dorotheus and others, and runs through 'Umar, al-'Anbas, al-Kindī, and others. This stream began to adopt the weighted *mubtazz*, tended towards quadrant-based houses, and applied horary technique to nativities. It was more popular and so became favored. Not every astrologer fits neatly into one of these two categories, and some (such as Abū 'Ali) straddle both. But I think this basic distinction is helpful in trying to understand the nature of medieval natal practice in the West.

§4: 'Umar al-Tabarī's Three Books of Nativities

'Umar bin al-Farrukhān al-Tabarī[14] was one of the earliest and most famous Persian astrologers writing in Arabic. Like Māshā'allāh, he was one of the members of the largely Persian team to have established the election chart for the founding of Baghdad (July 31, 762). Apart from *TBN*, he wrote a work on the Persian theory of conjunctions and mundane revolutions, a work of 138 chapters on horary (which must be the basis for his prominence in the Latin *Book of the Nine Judges*), another work of 136 chapters which seems to be on horary and perhaps elections, and another on "reading thoughts," a work which must have been on consultation charts, and which recalls Māshā'allāh's *On the Interpretation of Cognition*.[15] Sezgin lists other possible works which still need to be verified. Perhaps his most important contribution was a translation of Dorotheus's *Carmen* from its Pahlavi edition into Arabic, the most complete surviving version of that book in any language. Māshā'allāh had also made his own translation, but it exists only in small bits. The fact that these two colleagues made their own translations, and that *TBN* mentions Māshā'allāh only to criticize him, suggests that they may not have been on good terms. 'Umar died in about 815 AD.

This is the second translation of *TBN*, replacing the Project Hindsight edition of 1997. At the time, there were few known texts explaining the Persian annual methods: 'Umar himself omits some elements such as the

---

[13] It may also be picked up by Abū Ma'shar in his work on nativities, which is still only in Arabic.
[14] See Sezgin, pp. 111-13.
[15] See my *Works of Sahl & Māshā'allāh* (2008).

firdāriyyāt, only a few people even knew of the existence of the *Book of Aristotle* or its model in the work of al-Andarzaghar, and no one has yet translated Abū Bakr's own work on the revolutions of nativities. Moreover, as I mentioned earlier, Bonatti's and al-Qabīsī's treatments are rather brief and not well informative. On top of this, *TBN* Books I-II were badly organized: as a result, they appeared to be a nightmare jumble of theories and techniques.[16]

All of these problems have now disappeared, and readers of this edition of *TBN* will find it very reader-friendly and easy to understand. It is now evident that the formerly jumbled appearance (with insertions from other authors) actually disguised a kind of organization followed by Abū Bakr, borrowed in turn from 'Umar. Using *BA* and Abū Bakr as partial models, I have for the most part simply rearranged individual paragraphs to form a virtually seamless and logical progression of ideas and techniques. Otherwise, I have deleted the insertions from other works (now in Appendix A), and added some bracketed section titles and added bracketed numbers to itemize certain lists of significators and topics in order to make *TBN*'s relation to contemporary Persian treatments explicit. Following are some highlights of this edition:

Book I: Organization. This book is now wholly devoted to general questions about life: conception, gestation, rearing or nourishment, and longevity. Several paragraphs on these topics have been brought up from the end of the Latin Book III, while others were put into Appendix A: it seems that some editor inserted four horary questions about pregnancy and birth based on works of 'Umar, since two of them bear a resemblance to questions in the *Book of the Nine Judges*.

Book I: Four types of nativities. 'Umar's four-part division of births is based on Dorotheus's material on rearing, which Māshā'allāh handled in only a very general way in *BA* III.1.2-3. Abū Bakr clearly bases his own division on 'Umar, and like 'Umar has a similar (but greatly expanded) treatment of pregnancy.

Book II: Organization. This book is devoted entirely to annual methods, and needed the most reorganization. 'Umar's methods include directions, the *jārbakhtār* method of directing through the bounds, directions in the solar revolution, and profections.

---

[16] Also, being mislead by later texts, Hand and Schmidt believed that 'Umar used a compound weighted *mubtazz* (pp. *vi, viii*).

Book II: Three predictive "conditions." As part of his annual methods, 'Umar introduces three terms for predicting the life and condition of the native and his parents (II.4-6). The "general" condition of the native and parents uses primary directions in the nativity; the "greater" condition uses profections in the nativity; the "lesser" condition uses primary directions in the solar revolution, directing various points around the entire circle over the course of one year. For parents, the points to be directed differ based on what condition is sought.

Book II: 30° increment profections. 'Umar's profection method departs from the usual approach. In Hellenistic astrology and as found in *BA*, profections are done sign-by-sign. But 'Umar profects in 30° increments from whatever point he is interested in, and treats that increment as a compacted year: thus every 2.5° of a 30° increment is equivalent to one month, and shows by the positions of planets or their rays when some effect should come about.

Book II: 7th Century charts. 'Umar's charts illustrating the three conditions of the native suggest an intriguing possibility: that his annual techniques are based on a Sassanian original, perhaps by al-Andarzaghar himself. For the charts can all be dated to between 614 and 642 AD, shortly before the Muslim invasions: since al-Andarzaghar seems to be Māshā'allāh's and Abū Ma'shar's main sources, could these charts provide evidence of his rough dates?[17]

Book III: Horary-style delineations. As mentioned above, 'Umar did rely primarily on works like *Carmen* and *Tet.* for his material on rearing and longevity, and presumably material based on al-Andarzaghar for his annual methods. But his distinctive approach to delineation is largely a combination of a Ptolemy-style *mubtazz* to determine primary significators, and a horary-style comparison between them. In fact it is striking how little material Hellenistic material available to him (especially as a translator of *Carmen*) he actually used in topical delineations such as siblings and wealth—which is one reason why his chapters are so short when compared with the other works in *Persian Nativities*. This does not make his focus on horary-style combinations illegitimate, but it is something to note when comparing him to his contemporaries.

---

[17] We must also consider Abū Ma'shar's chart in *On Rev. Nat.*, which can be dated to August 19, 550 AD JC. This chart would have been cast around the time of the revisions to many Pahlavi texts and the influx of philosophers and astrologers from the Byzantine Empire.

Relation to JN. In *Persian Nativities I*, I pointed out that Abū 'Alī's *JN* was a *pastiche* of different works, with the middle portions based on *BA* and *TBN*, and the beginning and final chapters comprised of works by Māshā'allāh. I still maintain this view, but would like to add a few more details. While there is a close connection between *JN* and *TBN* (such as the initial lists of significators and their horary-style combinations), the text still shows that Abū 'Alī either had access to fuller editions of works like *Carmen* or else relied on Māshā'allāh—and yet kept to a very pared-down treatment of topics. For example, in the material on travel, almost all of 'Umar's treatment (III.8) is reflected virtually verbatim in *JN* Ch. 27. Abū 'Alī then goes on to include material such as the days of the Moon after birth, which comes right out of the fuller edition of *Carmen* which Māshā'allāh had (see *BA* III.9.2). But Abū 'Alī omits the rest of the *Carmen* material we can see reflected in *BA* III.9.2. For the topic of friends, *JN*'s description of the quadruplicities of the significators (pp. 301-02) provides a more complete account than *TBN*'s, which only includes the movable signs. But rather than use *BA*'s additional descriptions of synastry with the Lot of Friends (*BA* III.12), he sticks to 'Umar's horary-style structure.

Thus, while *JN* is reader-friendly and good for beginners, it is a *pastiche* whose motivations for particular contents is puzzling. It uses some of *BA* or *Carmen* to supplement *TBN* (travel) but neglects other, obvious material. It fills in some gaps in *TBN* (friends), suggesting that perhaps there was a fuller version of *TBN* available, but then does not use all of 'Umar's material. And when other approaches to topics are available, Abū 'Alī prefers 'Umar's simplified horary structure. *JN* probably represents an attempt both to compose a handy textbook for Abū 'Alī's personal use, and a general attempt to confront and synthesize the different lineages or streams which were forming during the Arabic period, as I mentioned above.

§5: *Abū Bakr's On Nativities*

Abū Bakr al-Ḥasan bin al-Khaṣībī al-Kūfī was an astrologer and possibly a physician living in the 9th Century, and very influential on astrologers such as William Lilly. His exact dates are unknown, but as I explained above he was most likely born in 821 AD. "Al-Khaṣīb" refers to calculation and arithmetic, indicating that his father was a mathematician and—according to his report in II.5.10—an observer of 'Umar's own astrological practice. As also mentioned, a mentor of his was the bombastic astrologer and poet, al-'Anbas al-Saimari. Abū Bakr wrote a large work on astrology in four parts, of which his *On Nativities* is the third part: the first two parts were an introduction to astronomy/astrology and on predicting with mundane revolutions. The fourth part, which also exists in a Latin translation by Salio of Padua, was on natal solar revolutions.[18] This is the first English translation of Abū Bakr's *On Nativities*.

My translation was made primarily from the 1540 printed edition by Johannes Petreius (hereafter 1540), but about six weeks before publication I was alerted to a digital copy in MS. BJ 793 III (dated 1458-1459) at the Biblioteka Jagiellońska in Krakow, Poland. Publication was delayed while I compared virtually every sentence in the manuscript (hereafter Jag.) with 1540. While not perfect, Jag. was invaluable in correcting some mistakes and unclarity in 1540, as well as suggesting yet more of the editorial interference I found in the editions of Bonatti's *Book of Astronomy*. Jag. is hard to read but has lovely multicolored text, with pleasant capital letter design. Its language is very terse, but sometimes more complete in basic content: for example, in several places it was clear that 1540 had taken the first part of one sentence and the last part of the next sentence from its own source, while Jag. preserved both sentences intact. Jag. also has delineation material not found in 1540 at all (and *vice versa*). In terms of editorial interference, Jag. usually speaks of "signs" to indicate whole-sign houses, but 1540 frequently says "houses," thus muddying the waters on house systems. In my own edition, I have not mentioned every single correction based on Jag., preferring to notify readers by footnote when I correct instances of sentence-truncation as just described, or when adding or subtracting words such as "not," when it changes the meaning of the delineation. Wholesale insertions of complete sentences are usually not footnoted but made obvious by brackets. Ultimately it would be worthwhile to have a critical edition of the complete four-part work from the Arabic.

As already mentioned, Abū Bakr clearly comes from the 'Umar-based lineage, both through his father and al-'Anbas, but textually as well. One obvious sign of this is his use of the four-part division of births from *TBN*. Perhaps also in accordance with his background as a physician, he greatly expands 'Umar's brief comments about planetary rulership during gestation.

---

[18] My own copy of this is badly photographed and in difficult handwriting. It is shortish and does not really offer anything that *BA* IV or Abū Ma'shar's *On Rev. Nat.* does not already have. Any translation of it would have to be compared with other manuscript copies.

There are even some minor but striking textual details, such as when Abū Bakr copies 'Umar's mistake in saying that this "same" Ptolemy allowed the *hīlāj* for longevity to be below the earth.[19] In one place Abū Bakr even allows us to correct omissions or mistakes in *TBN*,[20] or offers more plausible versions of material in *TBN*.

Abū Bakr's book is very valuable on a number of fronts, but one general benefit is his use of *multiple, specific* configurations to illustrate various delineations, many of whose sources are completely unknown at this time. Some may be drawn from his own personal practice. But even if they are particular to some client, they at least allow one to meditate on the *reasons for* such configurations and delineations—much more than the very general lists of indications which most astrologers provide. In other words, Abū Bakr's delineations act as models for the *types* of things to look for in charts. Following are some of the more notable contributions:

Gestation. Perhaps drawing on his background as a physician, Abū Bakr provides detailed information on how to look at planetary transits during gestation to predict matters of character and illness.

Illnesses. Abū Bakr has the most complete astrological account of illness I have seen in contemporary literature, from determining leprosy and liver disease to bad breath and oversized testicles. To be honest, I wonder if some of this material comes from decumbiture or horary charts during the Sassanian period, rather than from works on nativities. But it should prove a significant contribution to traditional medical astrology.

Character. Likewise, Abū Bakr includes many character delineations, from the native's timidity or boldness to his truthfulness and tendency towards calmness or hastiness. This too is something I have not seen in contemporary material, and should be useful for astrologers wanting to show that traditional astrology has plenty of tools for determining character.

Profession. Again, the list of trades and professions is very lengthy, even distinguishing merchants of different kinds of cloth or fruits. I cannot vouch for these fine-grained distinctions, but it should prove valuable for research.

There is however one area of profession and trades which stands out: the applications of the Moon. This is important because traditional texts emphasize the positions and configurations of Mercury, Venus, and Mars for

---

[19] *TBN* I.4.1, Abū Bakr I.15.
[20] For example, the list of significators for fathers in *TBN* III.4 (from Abū Bakr II.5.10 and II.5.14).

the trades. We are also advised to look at the next application of the Moon, often at the nativity but sometimes after the pre-natal lunation, but with no other information or means of prioritizing the Moon over the other planets. Here however, Abū Bakr tells us when the Moon's application *replaces* the usual considerations: either when she is in the tenth sign (and in her own domicile or exaltation) or by being aspected by one of the three planets normally signifying mastery (Mercury, Venus, Mars). In these cases, Abū Bakr first presents the aspect of the Moon with some other primary planet, the latter providing the fundamental type of mastery. Then the text lists more specific masteries if one of the other planets in turn is also aspecting. For example, the Moon aspecting Saturn signifies a profession related to construction. But if Venus is also aspecting, it has to do with construction involving beautiful design.

The question is, whom must this secondary planet aspect: the Moon or the primary planet? Would Venus have to aspect the Moon, or Saturn? The 1540 edition insists on the Moon, while Jag. rarely uses any pronoun, preferring constructions such as: "if it will be planet X instead of planet Y." I believe that this secondary planet must aspect the primary planet: thus for example Venus would have to aspect Saturn, thereby modifying the type of construction he already signifies by himself. But because the two editions disagree, I have not forced the text to obey my interpretation. The reader should read and think it through for himself or herself.

There are some other points to note about Abū Bakr which affect the nature of his delineations. Frequently, 1540 contains conditions which intensify a situation or present an extreme case, compared with Jag. For example, Jag. might say, "if Saturn is in the sixth," while 1540 will say, "if Saturn *is peregrine and made unfortunate* in the sixth." My sense is that Jag. represents a more faithful version of Abū Bakr, but as of now I cannot prove it. The reader should be aware of this and view it in light of Abū Bakr's general approach of providing ideal *types* of planetary combinations.

Lot of Spirit. Abū Bakr calls the Lot of Spirit the "Lot of Absence." This might seem very odd were it not for the fact that the Lot of Spirit was anciently used in connection with travel, i.e., being absent from home (*Anth.* II.30). However, Abū Bakr offers a number of delineations relative to religion and especially spiritual sincerity, in II.1.10. I have not seen these types of delineations before.

Fixed Stars. It is evident that Abū Bakr relies on *BA* for his stars. For Rhetorius does not have the stars with the Sun or Moon in his version, but Māshā'allāh clearly does (*BA* III.2.0-2.1). Moreover, Abū Bakr's stars injurious to the eyes (II.7.3) are very close to *BA* III.6.2: in fact the stars in Leo are identical between Abū Bakr and Māshā'allāh, whereas the account in Dorotheus and Sahl (who copied Māshā'allāh) were somewhat different. Using *BA* I have also been able to correct the natures of, and identify, certain stars described by Abū Bakr: see for example II.1.7.

Binding, pushing, possessing. Abū Bakr not only uses the "pushing" language familiar to readers of Sahl[21] and Abū Ma'shar[22] and elsewhere,[23] but frequently adopts the language of "gluing" or "binding" which appear in Hellenistic astrology (Gr. *kollēsis*, see Schmidt 2009, pp. 161ff). I do not know whether Abū Bakr prefers the Hellenistic 3° orb for aspects or conjunctions, but a translation of his introductory work to astrology from Arabic should provide the answer. Readers should also know that the Latin Abū Bakr occasionally uses the term "possess" with respect to planets and places. As in *BA*, this does not mean that a planet owns or rules a sign/place, but rather that it is in it and occupies it.

§3: *Translator's Notes*

Finally, I would simply like to point out a couple of features of my translation. First of all, the Latin Abū Bakr frequently speaks of a planet's or a person's *dominium*. This word means "dominion, rulership," and so on, and it is tempting to suppose that it refers to some kind of *mubtazz* or simply to a domicile Lord. I have usually translated this as "dominion," and left it open to interpretation.

Second, these authors sometimes speak about their predecessors and refer to what the *universitas* or the *universi* thought about some topic. These words can indeed mean that something was "universally" believed, i.e., without exception. But they also simply refer to a "generality" of things or people. I have favored "generality, generally," and so on. If one thing is certain, there is almost no method that is absolutely agreed upon without exception among the ancient authors.

---

[21] *Introduct.* §5.12-13, in Dykes 2008.
[22] *Abbr.* III.30-34.
[23] Al-Qabīsī III.17-19.

THREE BOOKS ON NATIVITIES
'UMAR AL-TABARĪ

BOOK I: [BIRTH AND LONGEVITY]

[Chapter I.1: The planetary months of gestation][24]

When the seed falls into the vulva in the first month, it comes to be in the disposition of Saturn, and he disposes [the fetus] through cold. And in the second month Jupiter disposes it, and the Lord projects spirit in it, and it disposes it by a certain mixture.[25] In the third month it is disposed by Mars, and blood comes to be. But in the fourth month the Sun disposes it, and God infuses[26] the breath[27] of life (that is, the living being)[28] in it, and therefore He grants a portion to him in relation to the *hīlāj*.[29] Do you not see that when the Sun comes along into a sign, it moves the weather, and conveys a likeness of the nature of his sign to the earth? But if he were changed from the sign, the work of that sign which comes to be recedes, because [it is like] a body without a soul. [In] the fifth it is disposed by Venus, and God puts together the masculine or feminine sex into it. [In] the sixth [it is disposed] by Mercury, [who] operates the tongue in it. In the seventh the Moon, and its image is perfected in it. Which if he were born in the disposition of the Moon, he will pass [safely] through. But if he were born in the eighth, the disposition for it returns to Saturn, and he will die. And if he were born in the ninth month, the disposition reverts to Jupiter and he will live, if God wills.

---

[24] This chapter originally fell at the end of Book III, but belongs here. Cf. Abū Bakr I.2-3, I.5.
[25] *Temperamento*.
[26] That is, by breathing (*inspirat*), as in *Genesis* 2:7.
[27] *Spiraculum*.
[28] Reading *animationem* for *animatum*.
[29] Hand reads this as though it pertains to the Lot of the *Hīlāj*.

[Chapter I.2: Determining an unknown birth Ascendant][30]

If therefore you wished to know the degrees of an unknown Ascendant, put down the figure of that same ascension, and of the planets[31] in their places in the signs. After this, know whether it is conjunctional or preventional, and you will verify it (that is, the conjunction or prevention) by its degree and minute. Which if it were conjunctional, look at the planet which will be in charge of the degree of the conjunction. If it were preventional, you will look at the degree of the luminary which was above the earth.

After this you should look at the planet which, above the rest, has more dignities (of the domicile or exaltation, triplicity or bound) in the degree of the conjunction or[32] prevention, [and] you will give an aspect a part of the strength. For example, if a planet were the Lord of a domicile, and it aspected the degree of the conjunction or prevention, and another were the Lord of the exaltation [but did not] aspect, from thence the one aspecting will be more worthy.[33] And you will understand the strengths of these from their places.

But if two or more planets agreed [in strength], you will look at those closer than the rest from a foundation, [and] you will establish [them] as models.[34] And the one closer than the rest in terms of a foundation is that you should look at the planets to see if there were, in an angle, one who was closer to the degree of the angle. And if they were oriental, the one which was closer to the Sun. And if they were in the bounds, the one which was closer to the bound. But if the dignity of each of the planets, and the aspect, were equal, you will set up as the model the one which was closer by aspect. After this, you will look at this model to see whether it is closer to the degree of the Ascendant or to the degree of the Midheaven (and its nadir). Which if it were closer to the degree of the Ascendant and its nadir, cast away the degree of the [imprecise] Ascendant (that is, dismiss it), and make the Ascendant to be like the degree of the planet and its minute. But if it were

---

[30] According to Ptolemy, *Tet.* III.3; cf. Bonatti pp. 1116-18. This chapter originally fell at the end of Book III, but belongs here. Cf. Abū Bakr I.4, which uses different methods.
[31] Reading *planetarum* for *planetae*.
[32] Reading *aut* for *a*.
[33] Reading ...*[non vero] aspexerit, inde aspiciens dignior erit* for ...*inde aspexerit aspiciens digniorque erit*.
[34] *Auctores.* That is, the planet which will act as the standard for establishing the correct Ascendant.

closer to the degree of the Midheaven and [its] nadir, make the degree of the Midheaven just like the degree of the planet and its minute. Then know how many hours will be ascending, in what hour those degrees ascend, through the operation of extracting the Ascendant from the Midheaven: and what came out for you in terms of hours, establish the planets upon that, and this will be the time in the hour of the native, if God wills.

[For][35] the knowledge of the Ascendant from the Midheaven, look from the first minute of Capricorn up to the minute of the Midheaven by the ascensions of the right circle. After this, project this from the first minute of Aries by the ascensions which I have explained to you; and where it reached, turn that into equal degrees, and that will be the Ascendant.

[Chapter I.3: Rearing and the determinations of births][36]

'Umar bin al-Farrukhān al-Tabarī[37] said: Know that there are four determinations of nativities for nourishment, namely [1] one of them: those who do not taste food, nor do their souls have life. [2] The second of them: those who taste food and are not nourished. [3] The third of them: those who taste food and are nourished, but do not reach long life. [4] The fourth of them: those who are nourished and reach long life (that is, to old age).

[3.1: The first determination of births]

[1] But now we must speak of the first determination, namely about those who neither taste nor are nourished, so that you should look at [1a] the degree of the Ascendant, and at [1b] the angles, also [1c] the degrees of the luminaries, and [1d] the Lords of all these, and at [1e] all three Lords of the triplicity of the Ascendant, and at [1f] the Lot of Fortune, and at [1g] its Lord, even at [1h] the Lord of the conjunction or prevention which was before the native's nativity.

---

[35] This instruction is based on the practice of assigning a value of 0° RA to 0° Capricorn. Since by definition the oblique ascension of the Ascendant is 90° in RA from the RA of the Midheaven, the distance of the Midheaven in RA from 0° Capricorn will be the distance which the Ascendant's oblique ascension has from 90° RA (or 0° Aries). Most modern astrologers will simply find it easier to use a Table of Houses or a computer program to generate the Ascendant from the Midheaven.
[36] Cf. Abū Bakr I.12.
[37] Lat. *Omar Belnalfargdiani Tiberiadis.*

After these things, you should look at [1i] the *mubtazz* over these places: that is, at that planet which had dominion in these places, whether it were one or two or three. Which if it were one, and you found it cadent and impeded from out of the degrees of some bad one (that is, so that it would be with a bad one in one degree), or the degree of the ascending sign were impeded, then he will taste nothing until he dies. And if the degrees of the shining ones were impeded in any way, and [also] the degree of the Ascendant, he will not taste anything, if God wills. Ptolemy also said:[38] because if the luminary whose authority it was were impeded, and [also] the degree of the Ascendant, and the Lord of the shining ones receded from the angles, he will not taste food until he dies. And the same hour of this matter [will be] when the luminaries arrived at a bad one.

But the generality of the ancients said:[39] because if all three Lords of the triplicity of the Ascendant receded from the angles, and the luminaries and their Lords receded, and the conjunction or prevention and its Lord receded, then the native will not taste anything (if God wills), or that native will not be a man, or he will be of those who are born with some signs like apes, or those who are said by the rustics to be "changed": that is, he will be born a monster or a brute animal. If however he were a brute animal, it would be with the receding of these which I have said, being impeded by the bad ones, and, were the bad ones in charge of them,[40] the animal itself will be an impeding wolf, who will not be united with men. But if [both] bad ones and good ones were in charge (especially if Mercury had some dignity in these places), he will be an animal of those who are joined with men, and with whom they play.

[3.2: The second determination of births]

[2] The second determination is that you should look at [2a] the Ascendant and [2b] the angles and [2c] the degrees of the luminaries, and at [2d] their Lords; also [2e] the three Lords of the triplicity of the Ascendant, and at [2f] the Lot of Fortune, and [2g] its Lord, even at [2h] the conjunction or prevention, and also [2i] the Lord of the conjunction or prevention which was before the native's nativity.

---

[38] Based on *Tet.* III.10, pp. 26-28.
[39] Perhaps referring to a version of *Tet.* III.9. Cf. Abū Bakr I.8.
[40] *Praefuerint.* Bonatti reads this as though "the *mubtazz* itself were a malefic" (*BOA* p. 1124).

If [2j] the *mubtazz* which has dominion in these places were cadent from the angles, and the bad ones were in charge of them, and there were some distance in degrees between the *mubtazz* [and the bad ones], it signifies that he would taste and be nourished, until the *mubtazz* arrived at the bad ones by body or by rays: then it signifies that he will perish when it reached the bad ones, by days or months or years, according to the quantity of their degrees, if God wills. And likewise if there were bad ones in the angles, and the *mubtazz* cadent, and the degree of the Ascendant joined to a bad one, or the degree of a bad one to the Moon, then the native will perish at [so many] years or months or days, according to the quantity of those degrees which were between them, if God wills. And if all of these or many of them fell from the angles, he will taste food and will not be nourished.

But if you wished to know the hour, direct from the degree of the Ascendant to the bodies of the bad ones, and to their square aspects or oppositions, [giving] to every sign a month by equal degrees—which if a year passed, turn the profections by giving a year to every 30°:[41] and then the native will perish, if God wills. Look even, for the hour, at certain good ones (if they were in the angles or in an optimal place, namely in their own dignities), or a planet which was more worthy in the degree of the Ascendant and [in the] year[42] and the Lot of Fortune, who signifies here (according to the quantity of its strength and weakness) that in terms of life [the native] will reach months according to the quantity of the donation of that same planet from out of its own lesser and greater years, and perhaps they will be days according to the quantity of its condition in weakness and strength.

But according to what Dorotheus thinks,[43] if the first and second Lords of the triplicity of the Ascendant were cadent, it signifies that the native would not be nourished, especially if Saturn were in an angle in nativities of the night, and Mars in nativities of the day. And the hour of his death will be when the profection of some other year[44] reached the angles: because if a bad one were in an angle, the year will not come to some one of the angles unless the light of the square aspect of a bad one is there, or its opposition, or the body of the bad one—if he were not dead in the first year.

---

[41] Māshā'allāh in *Nativities* gives a month for every degree by primary directions (p. 395).
[42] *Anno*. Precise role unclear here, unless perhaps it means the profected sign or Lord of the Year.
[43] Probably *Carmen* I.7.9ff.
[44] This might mean the profection of the Ascendant in a future year. Cf. Abū Bakr I.12.2 and below, I.4.5.

And it is thought in the *Book of Likenesses*[45] [that] if there were two *mubtazz*es, and one of them were impeded, the native will die, and the other one would not be able to suffice. Likewise if there were three lords,[46] and one of them were impeded and two strong, the infant will last, but his life will not be prolonged. But if two[47] were impeded and one were useful, the native will not remain (if God wills); likewise [if there were] four,[48] and one or two of them were impeded, and the rest were life-giving, the boy will remain, but his life will not be prolonged, if God wills.

[3.3: The third determination of births]

[3] The third determination is that the native does not have a *hīlāj* nor a *kadukhudhāh*, but [3a] the luminaries and [3b] their Lords, also [3c] the Lord of the Ascendant, were free from the bad ones, and from retrogradation or burning up, or [they were] cadent [but] free from the degrees of the bad ones and [from] their opposition or conjunction, also from the dominion of the bad ones over them.

For[49] if the nativities were of this kind, the native will be nourished but he will not reach long life (if God wills), and perhaps his life will be destroyed within twelve years. For if the nativities were according to what we have said, we defer speaking about those nativities on account of the falling of the significators, until the Ascendant runs through one orb—this is twelve years, namely [by giving] one year to every sign. For whenever the orb arrives from the Ascendant to the bodies of the bad ones or to their square aspects or oppositions, it will be feared concerning him, until the Ascendant runs through one orb. And when one orb has passed, we direct for him from the Ascendant, [by giving] one year for every degree, by the ascensions of that same clime in which he was born, until such time as it would reach the bad ones, if God wills.

---

[45] Unknown to me at this time.

[46] That is, *mubtazz*es.

[47] Reading *duo* for *tres*.

[48] This kind of statement suggests that 'Umar's *mubtazz* might not even have been determined by a counting mechanism at all—or at least definitely not from one weighted by dignity.

[49] Cf. Abū Bakr I.12.2.

[3.4: The fourth determination of birth]

[4] But the fourth determination is of those who have a *hīlāj* and *kadukhudhāh*, and the lords of nourishment which we stated in the first heading were free, if God wills.

[Chapter I.4: On the *hīlāj* and *kadukhudhāh*]

[4.1: The hīlāj]

The knowledge of the *hīlāj* [is that] you will look at the Sun in nativities of the day. If he were in the Ascendant or in the 11th or the Midheaven, he will be the *hīlāj* in whatever sign he was, whether a feminine or masculine one. But if he were in the 8th or 9th and the sign were masculine, he will be the *hīlāj*. And know that the Sun (or the rest of the places which are used for the *hīlāj*) would not be able to be the *hīlāj* unless the Lord of his domicile would be aspecting him, or the Lord of the bound or exaltation or triplicity. Because if he were the *hīlāj* and one of the aforesaid who are the Lords of his dignities (in which he is) did not aspect him, his[50] *hīlāj* will be annulled. Likewise the Moon in the night and day, and the Lot of Fortune, and the degree of the conjunction or prevention, and also the degree of the Ascendant.

If however the Sun were not the *hīlāj*, look at the Moon: which if she were in an angle or a succeedent to an angle in a feminine sign, and some one of the aforesaid four aspected her, she will be the *hīlāj*.

But if did not befit the Moon that she should be the *hīlāj*, and the nativity were preventional, begin from the Lot of Fortune and seek the *hīlāj* from it, in the way it was shown to you. But if the nativity were conjunctional, begin from the Ascendant, seeking the *hīlāj* from the same, and prefer it to the Lot of Fortune. And know, just as we have said before, it could not be the *hīlāj* unless some one of the aforesaid four would be aspecting it. Which if one of the four did not aspect it, its *hīlāj* will be destroyed.

And if you passed over[51] the Ascendant, and it was not agreeable that it should be the *hīlāj*, after this seek the *hīlāj* from the Lot of Fortune. Which if this could not be the *hīlāj*, seek the *hīlāj* from the degree of the

---

[50] That is, the Sun's: his *role as the releaser* is annulled.
[51] Reading *praetermiseris* for *praemiseris*.

conjunction which was before the nativity (namely, for a conjunction from the degree of the conjunction, and for a prevention from the degree of the Moon at the hour of the prevention). But if one of the four did not aspect this, it will be rejected just as we have said before, if God wills.

And if all four aspected the *hīlāj*, the one which was closer to the degree of the *hīlāj* by the number of degrees in front or behind (and were it stronger in place) will be the *kadukhudhāh*, if each of them had one authority.[52] But if some one of them had two authorities or three, that one will be in charge, whether its aspect were closer or farther, just so long as it would aspect the sign,[53] if God wills.

And if you knew the *hīlāj* and the *kadukhudhāh*, know that the *kadukhudhāh* signifies the years of the native's life and its dangers, but the *hīlāj* signifies the native's life [itself], if God wills. If however the *hīlāj* arrived (according to the years established by the degrees of ascensions, namely a year to every degree) to the bodies of the bad ones and their rays, and to the Tail, and also to the square aspect of the Moon, and to her degree or the opposition of her degree, and those years themselves were equal to the years of the *kadukhudhāh* (or [were] near them), and a fortune did not project rays to that bound itself in which the *hīlāj* reached a bad one, the native will perish then. And if it reached a bad one, and the years were not quite similar to the years of the *kadukhudhāh*, he will be endangered by a danger like death, and he will escape, if God wills. This is the disposition of the method of the *hīlāj*.[54]

And[55] know that "*hīlāj*" expresses a name which in Latin can be said as "wife," and likewise "*kadukhudhāh*" expresses "husband" from this signification, because just as a woman cannot manage her home well without the assistance of a man, so the *hīlāj* without the authority of a *kadukhudhāh* does not suffice for you to signify the years of life, even though certain astronomers use the *hīlāj* alone, and they do not care about the *kadukhudhāh*. Otherwise, the *hīlāj* is called the "place of life," because from

---

[52] That is, "dignity."
[53] This is a helpful point.
[54] See also I.4.5-8 below.
[55] Based on the strange translation of *hīlāj* and the statement at the end of the paragraph about returning to the book, I believe this comment is by the medieval translator. The Middle Persian word which in Arabic is *hīlāj*, simply means "releaser," like the Gr. *apheta*. At any rate, the image is striking and may be worth something. *Kadukhudhāh*, though, does mean "domicile master" or "house manager."

it should be sought the status of the life; and the *kadukhudhāh* is [also] said to be the "giver" or "significator" of years; but let us return to the book.

The generality of them thought about the *hīlāj* [as] Dorotheus did:[56] that the Sun is not the *hīlāj* in the 8th or 7th unless he is in a masculine sign; which if he were in these places in feminine signs, he will be feminized and his strength is weakened and it will be unequal (that is, [in]temperate).

But Ptolemy thought[57] that the Sun would not be the *hīlāj* in the 8th because this place is turbid and dark, and no light of the Ascendant is in it; and he praised the ninth because it is in a triplicity just like [that of] the Ascendant, and of its same kind. It is also the place of the Sun's joy, which is his foundation; and since the Sun would be more temperate in it, a good life will be effected in it and will last, if God wills. The same Ptolemy thought[58] that if it were the authority of the Sun in the night, in the investigation of the *hīlāj*, and he were in the opposition of these places under the earth, he will be the *hīlāj*. But Dorotheus even said:[59] because if he were in the opposition of these places in the night (in which we said he could become the *hīlāj* in the day), he will be the *hīlāj* unless he is in masculine signs.

If however the Sun were not in these places in the day, he would not be able to be the *hīlāj*: then seek the *hīlāj* from the Moon. Which if she were in an angle or a succeedent of the angles, she will be the *hīlāj* without examining the masculine or feminine signs. But more useful is that she be in feminine signs in the nativities of women, and in masculine signs in the nativities of males. But all thought that the Moon would be the *hīlāj* in the third, because it is the place of her joy and foundation. But concerning the ninth, Dorotheus thought that the Moon will be impeded if she were in this place. Ptolemy however did not deny that the Moon could become the *hīlāj* in the ninth, but he assigned her the Sun's rule.[60]

---

[56] *Carmen* III.1.15-18, which is a little ambiguous. It seems to describe only whether the bound Lord of the Sun in this situation can be the *kadukhudhāh*, but evidently 'Umar and Abū Bakr believed it referred to the Sun's ability to be the *hīlāj*.
[57] *Tet.* III.11 pp. 32-33, although the description of darkness actually describes the twelfth place.
[58] Ptolemy did not allow the *hīlāj* to be below the earth. Since 'Umar is among the earliest Arabic writers in astrology, this attribution probably comes from earlier Persian commentaries.
[59] Cf. *Carmen* III.1.19.
[60] That is, he treated her the same.

Which if the Moon were not in these places, and she fell,[61] the *hīlāj* will be sought from the degree of the native's Ascendant (namely if the nativity were conjunctional). But if the nativity were preventional, you will begin from the Lot of Fortune, which is the Ascendant of the Moon.[62] And they put the degree of the Ascendant after [that], and therefore they preferred the Lot of Fortune in the prevention, because then the Moon is full, having the power of the night with her perfection.[63] And they started from the Ascendant in conjunctional nativities because the Moon is without light in the conjunction, and then the whole light will belong namely to the Ascendant of the Sun.

If however you began from the Lot of Fortune, and it were in the angles or in the succeedents of the angles, it will be made fit to be the *hīlāj*, and [no other] will be sought, whether the signs are masculine or feminine. And if you began from the Ascendant, it will wholly be the *hīlāj* (unless the Lot of Fortune is there or [the Ascendant] were impeded)—and one does not consider whether it would be cadent from the angles, because it is in it. And any [other] need not be sought, because what is feared for the *hīlāj* in the condition of the other places in terms of success or [failure does not matter in this case]:[64] for it is possible that the aforesaid places would [not] be in successful places, but the Ascendant does not cease to be in a successful [place].[65]

But if the Sun and the Moon and the Lot of Fortune or the Ascendant were not appropriate for [being] the *hīlāj*, look at the conjunction or prevention which was before the nativity, and [make sure one of its Lords aspected it]: if it is in an angle or the succeedent to an angle, it will be the *hīlāj*, and the nature of the sign and its sex (whether it is masculine or feminine) need not be considered.

[4.2: The kadukhudhāh]

And if you knew the *hīlāj* and you wished to know the distributor [or] *kadukhudhāh* according to the statements of Dorotheus, look at the Lord of

---

[61] *Ceciderit*. Probably identical to being cadent. Cf. *Anth*. III.1 p. 30.
[62] This derives from *Tet*. III.11 p. 35.
[63] By "perfection," 'Umar means her being filled by the Sun's light.
[64] Omitting superfluous *in profectu*.
[65] This could be the rationale for 'Umar, Abū Bakr, and Abū Ma'shar directing the bound lord of the Ascendant as the *jārbakhtār* in preference to the bound Lord of the *hīlāj*. Cf. below, II.2, Abū Bakr I.17, and *On Rev. Nat*. III.

the domicile and the Lord of the bound, and the Lord of the exaltation or the triplicity; and, of them, you will begin from the Lord of the bound: which if it projected its own rays to that bound, aspecting it, it will be the *kadukhudhāh*. But if it did not project its own rays to that bound, and the Lord of the domicile or of the exaltation or of the triplicity projected, [then] the one of them which projected its rays will be the *kadukhudhāh* if there were one dignity of them—that is, if it were of one dignity.

If however one of them had [more] dignities and it projected its own rays to the bound, this one will be the *kadukhudhāh*. Likewise a lord of three dignities which was stronger in place [is] more worthy. But if the place [of two candidate *kadukhudhāh*s] were the same or very similar, the one which was closer to the point[66] in the angle (or to the Sun, if it were in [its] arising) will be stronger.

And this is the explanation of their condition (that is, of a [potential] *kadukhudhāh*) in a point:[67] if at any rate the planets were in the angles or in the succeedents of the angles, the one which was closer to the degree of the angles or to the succeedents of the angles will be stronger; and if one of them were peregrine and the other in its own domicile, [the latter] will be stronger. But if they were oriental, the one which was closer to the Sun will be stronger.

And[68] commingle the planet which was in the Ascendant or the Midheaven with the *hīlāj*. And its commingling is that you should look at the planet which was in the Ascendant or the Midheaven, [to see] if it had some dignity (of domicile or exaltation or triplicity or bound) in [the place of] the *hīlāj*: it will be called the partner, that is it will be just like it, and it will be held [to be] more worthy than one which had [only] one portion (that is, one dignity).

What Dorotheus said:[69] that if Saturn and Jupiter and Mars were oriental or with the Sun in one degree, or in some one of the stations, or before these places or after them by seven days, provided that from thence they had some testimony in the *hīlāj*, it moderates or perhaps will be in charge of the *hīlāj* or *kadukhudhāh*.

---

[66] *Cuspide*. Note that this Latin word is an equivalent to Gr. *kentron*, so that the Sun is understood to be the basis of a set of angles.
[67] *In cuspide*. That is, relative to the axial degrees of the angles or *kentra* or pivots.
[68] This paragraph offers another candidate for the *kadukhudhāh*.
[69] Yet another candidate for the *kadukhudhāh*, from *Carmen* III.1.1-6.

But better and more worthy is the Lord of the bound of the *hīlāj*, if it projected its own rays to the bound of the *hīlāj*. But if many were strong, and their portions were equal, and they all aspected the *hīlāj*, the one which was closer to the *hīlāj* than the rest by aspect will be in charge of the *hīlāj*.

Ptolemy,[70] however, named an aspect itself as though [it were] one of the other worthy portions. He said:[71] and if one looks at the Lords of the dignities of the *hīlāj* (of the domicile and exaltation or triplicity[72] and bound), the one which had more dignity with an aspect will be the *kadukhudhāh* [and] be in charge. If however there were a planet having one dignity in the [place of the] *hīlāj*, and it aspected, and there were another having three dignities, and the Lord of [those] three dignities did not aspect, [the former] will be in charge. And he even said that that planet is more worthy to be in charge which had more dignity in the Ascendant and [in the places of] the luminaries, and in the Lot of Fortune, or in the degree of the conjunction or prevention which was before the nativity. Which if there were a planet having dignity in three or four places, or in two of these places (namely of the above-stated ones), we should establish it as a *mubtazz*[73] which is in charge of (that is, which has dominion over) the nativity.[74]

---

[70] *Tet.* III.3.

[71] The rest of this paragraph is a misunderstanding of *Tet.* III.11 p. 35, which discusses how to find the planetary *hīlāj* if neither the Sun nor Moon can be it. It is not relevant to finding a *kadukhudhāh*, especially since Ptolemy did not use a *kadukhudhāh*. But the Persians may have been mislead by Ptolemy's talk of rulership here, and assumed that he was talking about the planet ruling over the *hīlāj*, viz. the *kadukhudhāh*. Or perhaps they simply adopted this passage as being similar to the longevity treatments in Dorotheus and Valens.

[72] Reading *triplicitatis* for *triplici*.

[73] This planet is a *mubtazz* simply because it happened to be best suited to be the *kadukhudhāh*. But if it is the bound Lord of the *hīlāj*, then it will also act as a (or the) *jārbakhtār* (see Book II below, where 'Umar prefers that the bound Lord of the Ascendant be the *jārbakhtār*).

[74] At the end of Book I appeared the following sentences, which do pertain to the matter of the *kadukhudhāh*, but only rehash longer statements in the preceding material. I am not certain they are meant to stand alone, but note their similarity to *JN* Ch. 3 p. 233. If Abū 'Ali and 'Umar were drawing on the same source, then perhaps they come from an alternate Persian commentary tradition, or else from a lost bit of Dorotheus: "But concerning the diversity of the *kadukhudhāh*, Dorotheus said: because if one planet had three dignities, and another had one, and the Lord of the one did aspect, but the Lord of three did not aspect, the one which aspected would have been more worthy. But Ptolemy says the one which had more dignity will be more worthy and [deserves] more attention, whether it aspects or not."

[4.3: The years of the kadukhudhāh]

After these things, we will look to the place of this planetary *mubtazz* for knowing the years [of the native]: which if it were oriental and in an angle, and in addition it were in its own *ḥayyiz* (that is, a masculine planet in the day in a masculine sign above the earth, and so on),[75] and it were in its own dignity (like in the domicile and exaltation, in the triplicity and the bound), and it came about that it is in [its own] *ḥayyiz* and in the angles which are the Ascendant and the Midheaven, it will give its own greater years. But if it were oriental in its own dignity and in the followers of the angles, and especially in [its own] *ḥayyiz*, if it were not in the degrees of the angle,[76] free, it will signify its own middle years. And if it were free in the same way which we have said, but it were cadent from an angle, it signifies its own lesser years. But if [this] happened to it with fall, retrogradation, and peregrination, or descension,[77] it will signify hours according to the number of its own lesser years.

If therefore you knew the authority,[78] and you wished to know what the planets will increase for it or take away from the years, look thusly: if a fortune aspected it, it will increase [for] it its own lesser years, unless it is retrograde or burned up (because then it will add months to it, according to the number of its own lesser years). But if a bad one aspected it by a square aspect or the opposition, or it were conjoined (that is, with it in one degree or sign), it will take away from it according to the lesser years. And if Mercury were with the fortunes and those giving, he will give his own lesser years. But if he were with the bad ones and those taking away, he will likewise take away his own lesser years.

---

[75] The conflation of gender with sect membership seems to have been common in the Perso-Arabic literature. According to *Gr. Intr.* VII.6, *ḥayyiz* "is like if a masculine planet is in a masculine sign and masculine degrees in the day above the earth, and in the night below the earth, and a feminine one in a feminine sign and feminine degrees in the day below the earth and in the night above the earth." Al-Qabīsī distinguishes *ḥayyiz* from a lesser condition called *ḥalb*: *ḥalb* is when (a) a diurnal planet is above the earth by day but below it by night, while a nocturnal planet is below the earth by day but above it by night, and *ḥayyiz* is when a planet in *ḥalb* is also in a sign of the same gender as itself.

[76] This must mean "in any of the degrees of the angular house," whether this is construed according to whole-sign or quadrant houses.

[77] This might pertain to the descending portion of its circle of the *awj*.

[78] That is, the *kadukhudhāh*.

Again,[79] the years of life are from the *kadukhudhāh*, according to what I will describe to you. You should look at the planet which was in charge of the *hīlāj*:

Which if it were in its own domicile or exaltation or its own triplicity, in the Midheaven or in the Ascendant or in the 11th (if it were diurnal, that is, in the figure of the day),[80] and in such a strength in the fourth and in the fifth (in the night),[81] it signifies its own greater[82] years.

And if it were peregrine and occidental in these places, it signifies its own lesser years.

And know that peregrination and setting[83] and retrogradation or burning up does not harm the higher planets so much as it does the inferior planets. But if the higher planets were impeded by a serious impediment, it signifies months or days according to the number of its own lesser years.

But if the *kadukhudhāh* were outside (that is, [outside] the domicile and the rest of these places), in the angles or the succeedents of the angles, it signifies its own years whether it were peregrine or whatever its condition was—unless it were burned up, because burning up signifies a scarcity of life.

And if the *kadukhudhāh* were in the cadents from the angles, it signifies its own lesser years. And in whatever kind of way it signified the years, there will be days or months according to the quantity of its years. But if it were burned up, it signifies days or hours by the number of its own years, and certain ones of them die and will not taste life. And especially if the *kadukhudhāh* itself and the Ascendant were impeded by some impediment, that is, if they were impeded by the bad

---

[79] The remaining paragraphs in this section originally appeared near the beginning of Book II, but I have put them in their appropriate place here.
[80] 'Umar seems to be describing a maximally good situation, but has left out the sect status of the *kadukhudhāh*.
[81] Moving "in such a strength" to the nocturnal condition.
[82] Reading *maiores* for *minores*.
[83] *Occasus*, referring to the occidentality in the previous sentence.

ones and the Moon were impeded by the bad ones in the angles or outside the angles.

[4.4: Adding to and subtracting from the years of the kadukhudhāh]

Know[84] that if fortunes aspected the *kadukhudhāh*, and it were not under the rays of the Sun, they will increase for it, and they will give it their own lesser years.

And know that if the *kadukhudhāh* were burned up, and [therefore] it signified nothing, and Venus and Jupiter (or one of them) were in the Ascendant or in the Midheaven in the nativity, there will be hope of life for the native according to the lesser years of Venus or Jupiter.

Which if the good ones gave something to the *kadukhudhāh* by means of an aspect, [the good one] will increase for it [by] months or days according to its own lesser years, if [the good one] were impeded or seized.[85]

Know that the fortunes, if they aspected from out of a square aspect or the opposition, or they were with the *kadukhudhāh*, they do not cut off anything from him—that is, it does not take away from it, but they increase the lesser years if they were not retrograde or burned up or impeded by the bad ones.

If the *kadukhudhāh* were in the angles, oriental or not oriental (if, however, not retrograde nor burned up), it will give its own greater years, by the command of God. But if it were not in a condition like this and it were cadent, it will give its own lesser years.

And if a fortune aspected the *kadukhudhāh*, it will increase its own lesser years for it—if it were [not] retrograde nor burned up. But if it were retrograde or burned up, it will give months [according to] the number of its own lesser years.

---

[84] The paragraphs in this section continue the long passage I have replaced here from Book II.
[85] Hand is probably right to understand this as besiegement.

And if the bad ones aspected the *kadukhudhāh* from out of the opposition or the square aspect, or were[86] with it in one sign, they will subtract from it according to their own lesser years, whether they received it or not. If however a bad one aspected the *kadukhudhāh* by a trine or sextile aspect, and they seized it[87] without the aspect of the fortunes, then the bad one which was so [placed] will subtract according to its own lesser years.

If the *kadukhudhāh* were with the Tail, and it were a bad one, and there were 12° or less between it and the Tail, it will subtract one-fourth of the years which were put [down] for the *kadukhudhāh*. But if the Head were with the *kadukhudhāh*, and the *kadukhudhāh* were a good one, and there were 12° [or less] between it and the *kadukhudhāh*, it will increase one-fourth of the years upon the years of the *kadukhudhāh*.

However, [there is] a circumstance[88] which enters into the granting of the lesser or greater or middle years: you must consider your method [not only as to] which planets have impediments apart from fall and retrogradation and burning up, but [also] from the opposition of the bad ones and their square and conjunction. I have even indicated to you in what way they impede it, and how retrogradation will take away one step from the rank [of the type of years],[89] and likewise burning up [will take] another. Again, if retrogradation or burning up were conjoined upon it[90] (without fall), he will not taste anything until he dies.

If the Sun were with the *kadukhudhāh* by conjunction or opposition and the square aspect, he likewise cuts off [according to the number of] his lesser years. If he aspected the *kadukhudhāh* from out of a trine or sextile, he adds his own lesser years to it. And if he were conjoined to or opposite it, or he were in its square aspect, and there were reception in the same place, he will subtract months or days [according to] a like [number] of his own lesser years, if God wills.

---

[86] Reading *fuerint* for *non fuerit*.
[87] Again, this is probably besiegement.
[88] *Accidens*.
[89] One would think this means that it takes the greater years down to the middle years, but 'Umar has not yet used the middle years. At any rate, in some sense it takes the types of years down a notch.
[90] That is, if both of these conditions pertain to the *kadukhudhāh*.

If the disposition with respect to the *kadukhudhāh* were [that it is] under the rays, it will be practically blind: it would not be able to receive increase from the fortunes, because it does not look at them nor do they look at it, unless it is with the Sun in one degree (that is, under the Sun in one degree): because in that same place it is a stronger fortune than it could [otherwise] be, whether the *kadukhudhāh* were a bad one or a fortune.[91] Also, if a planet were covered up,[92] it will not increase the *kadukhudhāh* unless it is a middling [amount]. But the Moon is received by the Sun, because she receives light from him from out of every domicile; but when she is received by the opposition, she loses one-half of the reception. But if she received [the Sun's light] in her own domicile or exaltation, there will be two receptions.

More than that, the Sun subtracts years [from] the *kadukhudhāh*, whether [the *kadukhudhāh*] were oriental or occidental.

But if a malefic were in the angles or in the succedents, in its own exaltation or bound or its own triplicity, it signifies its own greater years, because it is of [a good] substance, [whether] oriental or occidental.[93]

If a fortune aspected the *kadukhudhāh* from the opposition and it were retrograde and weak from an impediment of the bad ones, it would not be able to add, by the command of God, unless it was months according to the number of its own lesser years, if God wills.

[4.5: Directing the hīlāj for longevity]

And if you knew the native's years from the years of the significations of the *kadukhudhāh*, you will direct the *hīlāj* for him to the rays of the bad ones from the square aspect or the opposition, and [from] the conjunction of one sign, also from the one-third[94] or sextile aspect, through the degrees of the ascension of his region, [giving] a year to every degree.[95]

And if it reached a bad one without the projection of a fortune's rays to that degree, and the years were like the years of the *kadukhudhāh*, that will be the year itself in which the native will perish, and especially if the native's

---

[91] Reading *fortuna* (sing.) for *fortunae* (pl.).
[92] Reading *opertus* for *operatus*, referring to being under the rays.
[93] Reading as *quia est ex [bona] substantia [vel] orientalis vel occidentalis*. Hand suggests that *substantia* should probably read *esse* (which I tend to translate as "condition").
[94] I.e., from the trine.
[95] Again, these are the ascensional directions featured below and in *BA* II.17, Abū Bakr, Rhetorius, Dorotheus, etc.

year and the Lord of the Ascendant[96] of that same year, and also the Lord of its profection, [were] impeded by that bad one.

And know, whenever the profection[97] of the *hīlāj* reached the rays or body of a bad one (that is, to the degrees where bad ones were, and of their rays) in the root of the nativity,[98] or it projected its own rays to that degree,[99] it will be a year of danger and cutting-off by the bad ones ([for] the cutters are the bad ones); and worse than this if the bad one in [its] course were in the degree of the *hīlāj* in height and declination: because Dorotheus thought that, were the *hīlāj* conjoined to a bad one from the square aspect or the opposition, and the bad one were removed from the journey of the *hīlāj* (that is, running up[100] toward the north and south in latitude), it will not kill the master of the nativity,[101] but it will make danger for him.

And you should not make a direction without an awareness of the planet's latitude: that is, you should not direct the *hīlāj* or any such thing unless you use the latitude of the planets and fixed stars. After these things you should know, in the non-right circle,[102] [to] whose degree the bad planet goes, from the course of the circle of signs. And if you knew [that], you will project its rays from that same degree: then when the *hīlāj* reaches the rays of its trine or sextile or square or the aspect of opposition, or to its body, it will kill, if God wills.

[4.6: Example: directing the hīlāj for the native's life][103]

Moreover, the direction of the degree if the *hīlāj*, for knowing the matters of life, by the command of God. For you will direct from the degree of the *hīlāj* to the bodies of the fortunes, the bad ones, and their rays, and you will put a year for every degree which was between the *hīlāj* and the rays or

---

[96] Reading *ascendentis* for *ascensionis*: that is, the calculated Ascendant of the year or "east of the year" (*BA* IV).
[97] This may originally have referred to primary directions, but since 'Umar uses degree-based profections, he probably adapted it to his own uses.
[98] Omitting extra *ad corpus mali*.
[99] Omitting "or not."
[100] Reading *accurrens* for *accipiens*. Hand and Schmidt speculate that *accipiens* may have translated an Arabic translation of *anairetos*, but this does not make much sense to me. There are other Latin words which are more likely as well, such as *accrescens* ("increasing").
[101] I.e., the native himself.
[102] This probably refers to oblique ascensions, as Hand thinks.
[103] This example originally appeared near the end of Book II, but belongs here.

bodies of the bad ones, by degrees of ascensions. Of which an example is this:[104]

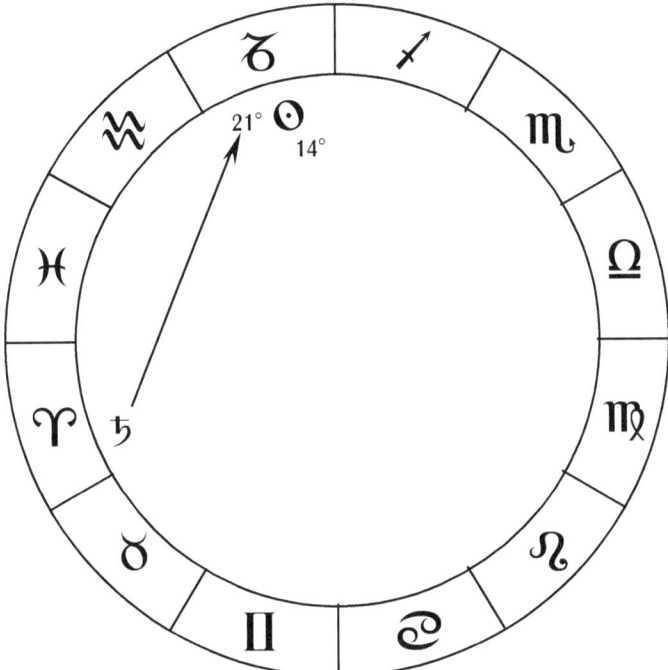

Figure 1: Direction of the *hīlāj* #1

The Sun was the *hīlāj*, and he was in the Midheaven in Capricorn, in the fifteenth degree; and the rays of the square aspect of Saturn in the twenty-second degree. We put the degrees of the Sun [as] ascensions, and they were 14°. We also put the degrees of Saturn [as] ascensions, and they were 20° 29'.[105] After this we took the degrees of the Sun away from the rays of Saturn, and 6° 30'[106] by ascensions remained. We say that the Sun thrives [up to] the square aspect of Saturn by four years and half [of that again], and one-

---

[104] Diagram not in text. I have partly followed Hand's reasoning in looking at and amending the values below. My solution is roughly this. The chart is cast for 29°-30° N. The Sun is in 14° Capricorn, which equates to roughly 14° of ascensions. The square from Saturn (who is in Aries or Libra) is cast into 21° Capricorn, which equates to roughly 20° 29' in ascensions. Thus there are about 6° 30' degrees in ascensions between the two, which gives the Sun about 6.5 years until the square of Saturn hits it.
[105] Reading for "nineteen" in order to make the math work.
[106] Reading for "7° 30'."

tenth of [four years]:[107] and then the native would suffer in his feet from cold and dryness, and [would suffer] a pain of the knees, and gout:[108] which [would be] thus far [until] the space of life crossed that bound, by the command of God.

Moreover, for knowing the native's [general] condition[109] you will direct the degree of the Ascendant by ascensions, always to the rays of the bad ones and good ones, whether or not the Ascendant were the *hīlāj*, if God wills.

[4.7: Which bodies or points are malefic][110]

And know that the bad ones cannot be more than six:

[1-2] The two bad ones, namely Saturn and Mars;

[3] And Mercury, if he were with them or in their nature by aspect.

[4] And the fourth [is] the Sun, especially if he were with Mars, either in his square aspect or his conjunction or opposition, or in the sextile or trine aspect of an infortune[111] to them: for then he becomes a similar bad one [when he is] with Saturn.[112]

[5-6] But the fifth of the bad ones is the Head, and the sixth is the Tail.[113]

And know that the bad ones are necessarily six. For two are naturally bad (Saturn and Mars), and two accidentally so (Mercury and the Sun), but two by place (the Head and Tail). Know[114] that all of these, if they were just as I

---

[107] 4 plus one-half of 4 (2) plus one-tenth of 4 (.4) = 6.4, which is very close to the 6.5 years mentioned above.
[108] Probably because Capricorn rules the knees.
[109] See II.5 and II.6.3 below.
[110] This section originally appeared below, after I.2.9.
[111] Reading *infortunae* for *fortunae*.
[112] The Latin here is a bit confusing. The point simply seems to be that both the Sun and Mercury can be malefic if they are in the angles (conjunction, square, opposition) of the malefics, and also (perhaps) by sextile and trine.
[113] Bonatti (p. 1147) specifies this as the Head with malefics, the Tail with benefics.
[114] The rest of this paragraph seems to derive from *Carmen* IV.1.129-34 (cf. also *BA* III.6.6), and does not really fit here. A tamed-down version appears below in the chapter on infirmities.

told you before, and if these six were assembled over Venus without the aspect of a fortune, the native will be a eunuch; which if the first Lord of the triplicity of Venus were strong, this will profit him. But lacking this, in addition to what he suffered he would be full of labor, lacking food for his belly all the days of his life.

[4.8: The killers in hīlāj-directions][115]

But the killers are:

[1-3] Saturn and Mars and the Sun, from the opposition and the square aspect and conjunction.

[4] Also, the Moon kills if it were from the square aspect of the Sun, however the *hīlāj* were joined to it.[116] And likewise if the same Moon were in his[117] opposition. [And] when the degree of the sign of the Ascendant is joined to her through her own body (if it were the *hīlāj*) it kills, and also if she is being joined to the degree of the Ascendant (if she herself were the *hīlāj*), it kills: because the Moon is an enemy of the Ascendant. Likewise the Ascendant is even inimical to [her] on account of the diversity of their substances, because the Ascendant is of the substance of the day, that is, of the substance of the heat and the Sun. But the Moon [is] of the nature[118] of night and cold, and they are enemies and contraries to each other.

[5] Even the cloudy and dark places[119] of the circle kill, [if] the *hīlāj* is conjoined with them.

---

[115] This section originally appeared below, but I have moved it here as more appropriate.
[116] Translation uncertain as to how the *hīlāj* fits in here. *Tet.* III.11 p. 39 has the body of the Sun killing when the Moon is the *hīlāj*, but Bonatti (p. 1141) has the Moon killing if she is in the angles of the Sun, "whether she is the *hīlāj* or not." In fact this whole paragraph seems to be an incongruous combination of Dorotheus, Ptolemy, and possibly Valens, though perhaps based on earlier Persian material.
[117] Reading *eius* with Bonatti.
[118] Reading *natura* for *calore* ("heat").
[119] This must refer to various nebulae. Bonatti takes these to be the cusps of the 12th, 6th, or 8th quadrant houses (p. 1142).

[6-7] For *Cor Scorpionis*[120] and *Cor Tauri*[121] kill if the *hīlāj* is joined [to them], because of their excessive and overflowing heat.

[8] Also Mercury kills if he were with the bad ones (namely in their square aspect or the opposition or in the sextile or trine aspect), namely with an assault by the bad ones without the aspect of the good ones,[122] and he were joined to the degree of the body of the *hīlāj*, or its sextile or trine or square aspect or its opposition. But if it were to the contrary of what I have said, he does not kill.

[9] If the *hīlāj* or the Moon (or whatever you directed to it) is joined even to the setting degree, that is to the seventh, it kills.

[10] And if the direction were completed at the end of a sign with half of the lesser or middle or greater years of the *kadukhudhāh*, it kills.[123]

And if the disposition of the *hīlāj* is changed from out of a bad one's bound into a bad one's bound, by that entrance of some bad one,[124] [it kills]; and if it does not kill, what has already lasted for a long time concerning that bound will be feared for him.

---

[120] Antares.
[121] Aldebaran.
[122] Reading *bonorum* for *eorum*.
[123] I do not know the source of this statement. It must be a minority Persian doctrine, but it does bear resemblance to Hellenistic teachings about using halves of the planetary years in prediction. The "direction" here may be one of 'Umar's 30° profections.
[124] This means that the *hīlāj* is being directed out of a malefic's bound into another malefic's bound, with a malefic aspecting or occupying that bound itself—though whether this must be by the nativity or at the revolution is unclear.

BOOK II: [ANNUAL METHODS]

Concerning the direction of the degree of the *hīlāj* and the degree of the Ascendant, namely in the revolution of nativities and of their years, and everything else which is necessary for them in terms of directions.

[Chapter II.1: Annual direction of the *hīlāj*]

[1.1:] The knowledge of the projection of the rays [of the hīlāj]

If[125] you wished to know the native's life and his condition by the distribution of his life, it is necessary for you to begin the work of the projection of the planets' rays from [the *hīlāj*].[126]

And of the two methods from the sayings of the ancients, one of them is that through which virtually all [of those] distributing the ray[127] take and work: which is the work of Dorotheus.[128] Of which this is the beginning step: look at the place of the planet, and [direct] it through equal degrees and minutes [in the zodiac]. After this, know its sextile or square or opposite aspect, because it will project its own rays to them through like equal degrees and minutes; and turn them into the degrees of the ascensions of the same sign, and these will be the rays of the planet. And in its own sign you will look at the degrees of the same, and turn them into ascensions, and you will write them [down], and this is the degree of its body.[129] And you will do the Ascendant likewise, and the twelve places, through degrees of ascensions:[130] this is the work which the ancients used, and this is an example:

---

[125] Omitting a partial sentence which was misplaced here by a scribe or typesetter, but which appears properly below ("Know that the *hīlāj* (the Sun and Moon or any other").
[126] Reading *hīlāj* for *eis*.
[127] Reading *dividentes radium* for *dividimus radium*.
[128] *Carmen* III.1-2.
[129] This method uses "ascensional aspects," which are described rather briefly and clearly in II.1.2 below, and in the Appendices. Ascensional directions are less precise than Ptolemy's proportional semi-arc directions.
[130] This puzzling remark could simply mean that we will ultimately need the ascensions for all of the places, and not just for that of the Ascendant or the *hīlāj*. It may also be a later interpolation, which is why it sounds like a direction of cusps.

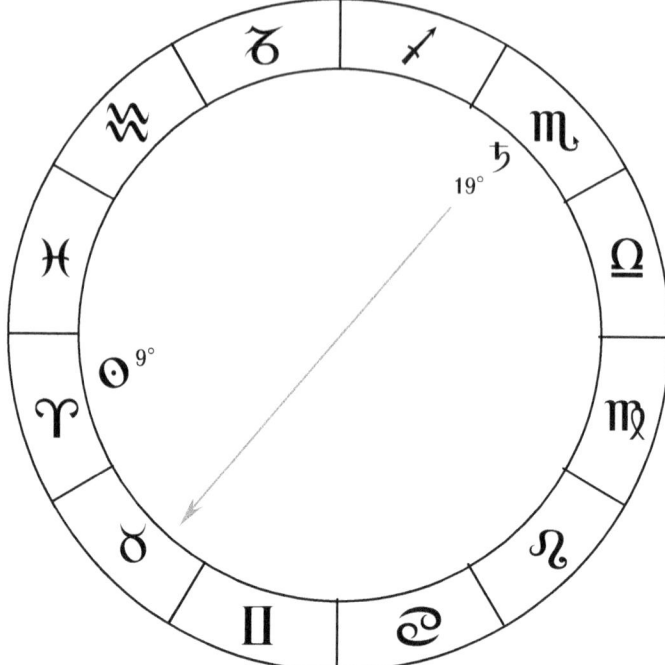

Figure 2: Direction of the *hīlāj* #1

If the *hīlāj* had been in the tenth degree of Aries, and the bad one to which we wanted to direct [were] in the twentieth degree of Scorpio, we direct from the place of the *hīlāj* in the degree of Aries to the rays of the bad one [in] Taurus.[131] But we will direct as above by subtracting the ascensions which are in the straight line of the *hīlāj* from the ascensions which are in the straight line of the twenty degrees of Taurus: and what remained, those namely will be the degrees of the direction, to the number of which we should give years, and so on.

But Ptolemy[132] worked in another way, and he used to say[133] that all the rays would be assembled in a point, that is in the point of the earth, and they

---

[131] Omitting *et* and adding *Ariete*.
[132] This is the "second" method above, but 'Umar has made its application here confusing. The ostensible purpose of this section is to describe the direction of the *hīlāj* through the bounds: an annual method to be used throughout life. But 'Umar is opposing the ascensional method for directing through bounds, to Ptolemy's proportional semi-arc method for directing the *hīlāj* for *longevity*. Thus the key distinction between ascensional directing and Ptolemy's method (which can also be used for annual methods or longevity) is being obscured. In addition, Ptolemy wants to direct *hīlāj*es on the western side of the Midheaven toward the Descendant, i.e. in a direction opposite that used for annual

were one thing. And he said that it is necessary for us to know the diversity of the rays according to the position of the place.

For you will begin to attend to the rays by the distance[134] of the planets from the angles, and by the ascensions of the city in which you were, just as you have worked in this chapter. And when you have put the place of the planets in order, you will direct the *hīlāj* and the degree of the Ascendant according to these distances in the way I have told you. And when it reached the bad ones, [it signifies] evil according to [its] condition and strengths, if God wills.

Know that if the *hīlāj* (the Sun and Moon or any other) were in these places which are between the Midheaven and the setting degree, it will be directed backwards, that is, toward the seventh (against the succession of signs), and by means of the degree falling in front of the Ascendant, taking [it] backwards from the starting-degree of the Ascendant,[135] through the ascensions of the clime, and according to the light of the degrees which were between them, through the ascensions, a year for every degree, and it kills. And this direction is well laid out in the book of introductions by al-Qabīsī and Abū Ma'shar.[136]

---

methods: thus again 'Umar confusingly seems to oppose "direct" directions to "converse" directions.
[133] *Tet.* I.24 p. 48.
[134] *Longitudinem.*
[135] A somewhat confused passage, amending the text from "and by means of" to here, in order to match roughly the basic idea expressed in al-Qabīsī IV.12 (mentioned immediately below). A planet directed to the Descendant needs to be calculated using oblique descensions, but this is the same as using the oblique ascensions of the opposite degree, which will therefore fall in front of the Ascendant. Suppose a planet were in the 8th, and we directed it to the Descendant: this would be the same as directing a degree which lies "in front of" the Ascendant in a later degree to the Ascendant itself, and we would take the difference between the oblique ascension of the Ascendant and that of this opposite degree. This also seems to be the meaning implied by Bonatti (p. 1145). The original text reads ...*et gradu cadente qui prae ascendentis accipiens retrorsum a capite gradu ascendentis*. Hand reads this somewhat differently.
[136] See e.g. al-Qabīsī IV.12. This is an obvious clue that there are some later interpolations in these books.

But[137] if the direction were to the Tail, direct from the degree of the Tail by means of the degree of ascension, and it will be years according to the number of degrees which was between them.

If however [it were] for a *hīlāj* [placed] here between the Midheaven and the west, and you directed to it, direct backwards against the succession of the signs toward the west, just as I have told you before.[138]

[1.2: Directing the hīlāj for the native's condition][139]

And if you wished to know the native's life, and his condition in the distribution of his life, it is necessary for you to begin to work with the projections of the planets' rays. After this you will direct his *hīlāj* (that is, the degrees) according to the work of these[140] in longitude, according to what was said in his work.[141]

And if you wished to direct the *hīlāj* to some degree of the bad ones or to their rays, take what there was between the *hīlāj* and the degree of the bad one by means of the ascensions in the city in which the boy was born, in terms of degrees and minutes, and [for] what came out, put a year for every degree. The work of which [is] that you take [it] from the first minute of the sign of Aries up to the degree and minute in which the *hīlāj* was, by means of the ascensions of that city. Again, you will take [it] from the first minute of Aries up to the degree and minute in which the bad one was and his rays, and you will take the difference[142] which was between them (that is, you will take away the lesser from the greater), and what remained from that is the distance which was between them, and you will put a year for each degree. And this is the work of the *hīlāj*.

---

[137] My sense is that this derives from Persian practice.
[138] Section I.2.7 on the number of malefics originally appeared at this point.
[139] This section originally appeared at the end of Book I.
[140] That is, the *hīlāj* and the other planets.
[141] I take this to refer to Dorotheus.
[142] Lit., "overflow" (*superfluum*).

[Chapter II.2: The direction of the Ascendant, and its *jārbakhtār*][143]

There are also three manners of direction[144] which it is good for you to know (whether it were good or bad), seeing as judgments are fit in them:

> The first is the distributor which is called the *jārbakhtār* (which is the Lord of the bound of the Ascendant, whether it aspected the Ascendant or not).[145] It will be the distributor, which does not leave off disposing [matters] until the degree of its bound of the sign is finished. After this [comes the next *jārbakhtā*], the distributor of the second bound which succeeds it, which will not cease to be the distributor until the degree of its bound would be finished by ascensions, a year to every degree. You will do likewise up to the end of the native's life, if God wills.

> The second is the lord of the rays, which you should know from the first of the planets [which was] from the degree of the distribution,[146] whether that planet were quicker in the course of the distribution or slower: for it is necessary for the distribution that [the Ascendant] should go through to its rays and be joined to them. And when [the Ascendant] reached its rays, if it were a fortune, it signifies the enlargement of life, and acquisition and success[147] in the substance of that same planet, and in those things which pertain to it in terms of the houses of the circle, with the health[148] of the body and the evenness of its complexion. But if it were a bad one, it signifies preoccupation and infirmity, and disease from the substance of the planet, and in those things which pertain to it in terms of the houses of the circle: that is, if

---

[143] Replacing the nonsensical introductory heading, "The knowledge of the three rays."
[144] Reading *directionis* for *directioni*. In my translation, these three are simply as follows: the *jārbakhtār* or bound Lord of the directed Ascendant; any planet in or casting rays there; and the *jārbakhtār* or bound Lord of the following bound, understood as making things better (benefic) or worse (malefic) than in the previous one.
[145] In *BA*, the *jārbakhtār* is the bound Lord of the directed *hīlāj*, not the Ascendant.
[146] Reading *divisionis* for *divisoris* here and below, which changes the whole tone of the paragraph. The text and Hand's translation make it seem that the "lord of the rays" is a planet which stands in relation to the *jārbakhtār* itself, either in zodiacal order or by transit. But it is simply a planet casting rays into the bound of the directed Ascendant, a standard part of the Persian annual procedure. See *On Rev. Nat.*
[147] Reading *profectum* for *profectu*.
[148] Omitting *qui*.

it were the Lord of the house of substance, he will suffer in his substance; and if it were the Lord of the house of children, his child will die; but if it were the [Lord of the] royal house, the king will impede him. Know this for all houses.

But the third [manner] is the receiver (that is, the one which receives the distribution), and even the change from planet to planet.[149] Which if the distributor were a bad one, and its disposition is perfected, [then] if the one who receives the disposition from it were [also] a bad one, it signifies evil because it is being changed from bad one to a bad one.

And [if] the distributor distributed in the rays of a bad one, and it were changed to the rays of another [bad one] even after the completion of the rays of that [first] bad one, and if [the native's] life were not yet [completed], perhaps it will kill in this way. For the ancients judged he was going to die if all four [of these] were bad ones. But if all four [were fortunes], it signifies the enlargement of life and of [his] bearing beyond means, and the greatest resources, if God wills. If however three were bad and one a fortune, there will be more evil. But if three were fortunes [and] one bad, there will be more good. And if the fortunes and bad ones were equal, [it signifies] the goods and evils are equal. Know this.

And now we make mention of the explanation of these four [to which we just alluded]:

> The first is the one whose distribution was before the second one, and this comes to be in the middles of signs (that is, within a sign), but it will be the beginning of the disposition because the first distributor from the degrees of the Ascendant is the Lord of the bound [itself]. Therefore there [is] not one earlier than [this] first one, because it is the same one.

> But in the middles of the signs will be the disposition of the second distributor after the first distributor: and that [first] one is the one who pushed (that is, who committed) disposition to [the second one]. The

---

[149] In other words, the "receiver" is the Lord of the following bound of the directed Ascendant.

second one [is the one] which receives the disposition from the [first] distributor.

But the third one is the lord of the rays, and [it is] he who commits disposition to the [fourth] distributor, [the next lord of the rays].[150]

Moreover,[151] [there are] four [planets] in which there is trust,[152] namely: [1] the distributor, and [2] the Lord of the Year, and [3] the Lord of the rays, and the [4] receiver who receives from the distributor. And the sign of the profection will be commingled with these: because, were[153] it in signs in which there were the bodies or the square aspects of the bad ones, or their oppositions, it increases evil and quickens betrayal and death. And if [the sign of the profection] were in signs in which, in the root, the bodies of the fortunes were, or their rays, and the bad ones did not aspect it, it will be a wholesome and profitable year, by the command of God. (And in the disposition of the days, many dread giving the disposition to the sign, and they give it [instead] to the planets in the revolution of the year of the nativity, and that of interrogations and beginnings).[154]

And for knowing the condition of the parents,[155] you will [likewise] give the first distributor and the disposition to the Lord of the bound, just as we have told you before in the advancement of nativities, if God wills. For there are two directions from the revolution of the year:[156] namely, one for

---

[150] No fourth planet is clearly identified here. But due to the description of two successive planets casting rays into the bounds, Hand plausibly believes that the third and fourth planets represent the planet from whose rays the Ascendant comes, and the one to whose rays it goes. Thus I have inserted the missing phrases in brackets.

[151] Now 'Umar lists a slightly different set of four planets, omitting the hypothetical second lord of the rays, and inserting the profected Lord of the Year.

[152] Omitting *ii*.

[153] Omitting *non*.

[154] This is something of a misleading statement, unless 'Umar is separating himself from standard Persian practice (see e.g., *BA* IV). Normally one *also* looks at the transits of the planets at the moment of the revolution, *in addition* to the natal positions; in fact, one can also track the transits of the Lord of the year through the angular whole signs from the profected sign. So by noting that some people *only* use the transits, he is either saying we should not use the transits at all (which would put him in the minority), or else that we must use both, and that these unnamed people are wrong to exclude the natal positions.

[155] Omitting *sit*.

[156] As Māshā'allāh makes clear in *BA* IV, interpreting the "revolution/cycle of the year" requires *both* the annual profection (the "greater condition") *and* the calculated Ascendant, subsequent directions and transits at the time of the revolution itself (the "lesser condition").

knowing the lesser condition, every day up to the completion of the year, and the other for [knowing] the greater condition, and [whether] it were perhaps one condition or two or more: and this [greater condition] is known from the sign of the profection. And I will explain these ways to you, if God wills:

In the direction of the Ascendant for knowing the [native's lesser] condition, you will always direct from the degree of the Ascendant [of the revolution] to the rays of the bad ones and the fortunes, up to the completion of 360°, until it turns back to the degree of the Ascendant, a day for every 59' and 8" by equal degrees. And when it reached the fortunes and the giving planets and the ones who receive from bad ones, we will say that he will find substance and acquire, and he will be sound in that same disposition, and there will be success and the acquisition of substance from the substance of the planet and the substance of the sign pertaining to the planet from the circle (that is, of the house in which it is) [at the time] when it disposed, if God wills. And the planet which was projecting its own rays to the degree and minute of the Ascendant [at the time of the revolution], [its] disposition will be in the beginning of the matter. But if it did not project its own rays to the degree of the Ascendant, we will grant the disposition to the degree of the Ascendant until it would apply to a planet or to the rays of a planet, and we will say that the judgment in this will be [related to] the Lord of the Ascendant, whether it aspected the Ascendant or did not aspect, were it present or absent. After this, you will give the disposition to the lord of the rays to which the disposition was applied, just as we have said before.[157]

[Chapter II.3: How mundane directions differ from the revolutions of nativities][158]

The direction for knowing the condition of the king, and for knowing for how long he will be in charge of the kingdom, and for [knowing] the revolution of the year of the world or of the year of the native:

---

[157] Thus the direction of the Ascendant of the year has its own set of daily bounds, *jārbakhtār* and aspecting "lords of the rays," mirroring the direction of the natal Ascendant.

[158] All of the indented items below are repeated virtually verbatim in al-Qabīsī IV.13. Since there are clearly also interpolated comments, the issue is who is taking from whom. Although most of this material pertains to mundane revolutions, I have retained it because it has comments and a brief disagreement about how these compare with directions in the revolutions for nativities.

For, [with] either the direction of the king or the wealthy, you will direct for them from the degree of the Midheaven by means of the ascensions of the right circle, one day for every 59' 8", until it reaches the bad ones or the fortunes.

And for knowing the condition of the king's body, in the soundness and infirmity of it,[159] you will direct likewise from the degree of the Ascendant to the bad ones [and] the fortunes.

And [for knowing the condition] of the vulgar and the rustics, in the revolution of the world you will direct from the degree of the Ascendant to the bad ones and the fortunes, one day for every 59' 8".

And for knowing the condition of the king, you will direct from the degree of the Midheaven to the fortunes and the bad ones, [one day] for every 59' 8".

And for knowing the condition of the native's years in the revolution of the years of nativities, you will direct from the degree of the Ascendant to the fortunes and the bad ones, one day for every 59' 8".

And when the advancement reached the good ones of the sign, [it signifies] soundness and prosperity and success. And when it reached the bad ones, it signifies infirmity and loss and the commingling of his condition, if God wills.

[But][160] 'Uthmān bin 'Affān,[161] who was the [third] emperor of the Saracens, [used to direct for the common people] from the rays of the Moon from the Midheaven, within the Midheaven—against whom we have said: since the work of these years in the revolution of a year of the world [is] for

---

[159] Omitting *corporis*.

[160] This paragraph originally appeared at the end of Book II, but I have placed it here because it pertains to directions for kings.

[161] Lat. *Othmen filii Affen*. 'Uthmān was the third Caliph of the Islamic empire, and personally known to Muhammad. His reign (644-656 AD) coincides with the Muslim conquest of the Sassanian Persians, who for centuries had practiced and preserved the astrological material which Māshā'allāh and 'Umar were now translating into Arabic for the first time. 'Umar may be suggesting that 'Uthmān had also hired his own Persian astrologers, who used the method described here (the context suggests that it was used in mundane revolutions).

[knowing] the diversity of the vulgar, it is necessary that [for the vulgar] there be a direction of the Ascendant, and for the native's *mastery* from the Midheaven.

[Chapter II.4: 'Umar's method of profections]

In terms of the profection in the revolution of the native's years, [he says] that you should look from the degree to which the profection arrived from the Ascendant, one year for every 30°. After this, you will put it from the degree to which the year arrived up to the completion of 30° [more], and to every year you will give 30°.[162]

Then you will look to see how many degrees there are between the degree to which the year arrived, and the degree of a fortune or bad one [within that 30° interval], and you will take the difference[163] which was between them, and you will multiply it by 12 and 1/6[164] of a full degree, and you will take it in terms of days according to the quantity of those degrees.[165] And when there was the conjunction of a degree with a bad one, there will be duress and an evil condition from life; and when it reached fortunes according to the quantity of the same number (having been multiplied by 12 1/6), it signifies[166] the bounty and [great] extent of his condition, and an evenness of complexion, and his soundness, according to the quantity of the nature of that fortune in the circle: that is, if [the fortune] were the Lord of substance, it signifies substance; and if it were the Lord of the royal house, it signifies a kingdom or a house from the king.[167]

---

[162] Omitting *et universo anno, id est.*
[163] Lit. "overflow" (*superfluum*).
[164] Here, the text reads "one-seventh," but I have used "one-sixth" just as it reads below.
[165] A whole year of 365 days must be allotted to the current 30° increment. Since 365 days / 30° = 12.166 or 12 1/6 days, every degree of the 30° for the year represents 12 1/6 days. Later, 'Umar offers a more exact value, multiplying the distance by 12 and dividing by the Sun's mean daily motion (59' 08"): thus 1° x 12 / 59' 08" = 12.17587 days per degree. This is closer to the actual value, since a more exact year of 365.2425 days / 30° = 12.17475 days per degree.
[166] Reading *significat* for *signi*.
[167] At this point two separate and unrelated passages originally appeared in the text. The first passage discusses some electional or revolutional material from Māshā'allāh, and the second passage returns to the subject of the *kadukhudhāh*. I have moved the Māshā'allāh material to Appendix A, and the *kadukhudhāh* material to I.4.3 above.

[Chapter II.5: The general, greater, and lesser conditions of the native and his parents][168]

For the [general condition of the] native, you will direct the degree of the [natal] Ascendant (whether it were the *hīlāj* or [not]), [giving] a year to every degree by means of ascensions, up to the rays of the bad ones or of the fortunes in the root of the nativity.

And for knowing the greater condition of the native, you will direct from the sign of the advancement.[169] And know that the sign of the advancement is always like the degree of the Ascendant, because every 30° are one year. For it is like the Ascendant of the root, an example of which is this: if the Ascendant of the root were the tenth degree of the sign of Aries, the sign of the advancement in the second year will be the same degree of Taurus. Likewise, [you will] always [give] one sign to every year, if God wills. Likewise if you wished to know [the native's] greater condition [to the day], multiply the degrees of the sign of the profection and the rays of the bad ones and the fortunes. That is, multiply the degrees which are between the degree of the sign of the profection and the rays [of the planet] by 12 1/6,[170] and on that number of days, the native's condition will be changed from good into evil, or from evil into good, according to the nature of the Lord of the rays, whether it were a fortune or a bad one.

And for knowing [the native's] [lesser] condition in the revolution of the year, direct the degree of the Ascendant [of the revolution] by equal degrees[171] to the rays of the fortunes and the bad ones, [and] to the Lords[172] of the places, and you will put an entire day[173] for every 59' 8", if God wills.

For knowing [the general condition of] the life [of the parents], the Lot of the Father and [the Lot] of the Mother are directed by means of ascensions in terms of the number of degrees to the bodies of the bad ones and [to]

---

[168] In this section, 'Umar introduces three types of direction and profection, with some new vocabulary. I have rearranged the paragraphs so that the parents and native are not mixed together as in the text. The "general" condition of the native and parents is found by directing points in the nativity; the "greater" condition is found through the 30° profections described above; the "lesser" condition is found by directing a point around the circle within the native's solar revolution.
[169] *Provectione.* That is, the profection. See also below.
[170] Reading as above in the first explanation of this method. The text reads: *septem gradus...et sextam partem unius.*
[171] That is, ecliptical degrees.
[172] Reading *dominos* for *domos.*
[173] Reading "day" for "degree," with Hand.

their rays, namely a year for every degree, or [until] some one of the four actors[174] aspected them: that is, [the Lord] of the domicile or bound or exaltation and triplicity.

(And[175] [it was] Māshā'allāh [who] said you will direct from the ray of the Lord of the exaltation of the Ascendant (or of the Lord of the triplicity or of the bound of the same Ascendant), namely from the rays of the one whose aspect [into the rising sign] was closer to the degree of the Ascendant. Granted, [this] opinion is not valid, since it can come about that some one of these four does not aspect the Ascendant or the Lot of the Father or of the Mother, and the house of fathers, or the degrees of these places. And it is necessary for us to direct from them, if God wills: [therefore] you will direct from the sign of the profection [of the Ascendant] up to the completion of the year, for knowing the greater condition [of the native]; and for the greater condition of the father and mother,[176] from the profection of the Lot [for each], if God wills.)

And for knowing the greater condition of the father [to the day], you will direct from the sign of the profection—that is, from the Lot of the Father,[177] from the number of all 30°. For you will direct what there was between the aforesaid and the rays of the bad ones and the fortunes, and you will multiply those degrees[178] by 12 1/6,[179] and what it reached will be the number of the days which will signify the happening of the evils or goods[180] according to the nature of the Lord of the rays, and those things of the places pertaining to it.

And for knowing the [lesser] condition of the father every day, you will direct from the degree of fathers [in the revolution] (that is, from the degree of the 4th house) to the bodies of the fortunes, the bad ones, and their rays, and you will put one day for every 59' 8". And in what befalls [him], it will be described according to the quantity of the bad ones and the good ones, and

---

[174] *Actorum*. I have not seen this term before.
[175] The rest of this paragraph originally appeared below, after the first example. But it is clearly 'Umar's or an interpolator's criticism of the view just expressed. 'Umar wants us to direct and profect to whatever body or aspect comes next, and not to these three or four Lords in particular. See also below, II.8.
[176] Omitting an extra *partis/patris*.
[177] Omitting "the house of the father." 'Umar makes it clear below that one profects the Lots for the greater condition of the parents.
[178] Omitting a redundant "which were between the aforesaid and the rays of the bad ones and the good ones."
[179] Reading as before, for *xii gradibus ex x minutis*.
[180] Reading *bonorum* for *malorum*.

the fortunes in which they were, and [according to] the places in which they were, and what pertains to their places[181] through [their] rulership of the twelve signs: because each planet conveys the nature of its own sign, provided that it aspects the sign.[182] But one which did not aspect the sign [does not convey] the likeness of its nature by vision and desire and thought,[183] if God wills.

And for knowing [the mother's] life [in general], you will direct from the Lot of the Mother in the root of the nativity to the rays of the fortunes or the bad ones, and every degree will be a year by means of ascensions.[184]

But for the greater condition of the same mother, you will direct it[185] in the root of the nativity, a year for every 30°, in just the way you do [it for the life] of the father for [his] greater condition.

For the [lesser condition of the] mother, you will direct the degree of the Moon [in the revolution], an entire day for every 59° and 8".[186]

[Chapter II.6: Examples of directions and profections for the native]

And I have already repeated for you many times in this book, for knowing the native's [general] condition, that in nativities you should always direct the degree of the Ascendant, because [the bound Lord of the Ascendant] is the distributor which is called the *jārbakhtār*. After this you would look at what remained to it, until it completes its own bound, in terms of degrees and minutes; and you will put [down] for them a year for every degree by means of the ascensions. Then, when the bound is completed, look from the Lord of the second bound [and] how many degrees it has: because you will even

---

[181] *Et pertinentia locorum.*
[182] Translating somewhat loosely from: *planeta quodcunque, id est, ex suis propriis signorum aspexerit, affert eius signi naturam.*
[183] The reason for 'Umar's expressing things this way is unclear to me. But the basic point is clear: we can only be confident of certain significations if the natal planet to which the profection arrives is able to aspect its own domicile. Hand's confusion in this paragraph was due to two things. First, he read *affert* ("conveys") as *aufert* ("bears away"). Second, in the 1990s it was not very clear that traditional astrologers insisted on the importance of aspecting one's own domicile: thus Hand did not see the sign itself as the object of the aspecting. See the Introduction to my *Works of Sahl & Māshā'allāh.*
[184] Omitting *in vita.*
[185] *Eum.* If correct, this could mean the house of mothers (i.e., the degree of the Midheaven); but it might also mean the Lot of the Mother (*eam*), as with the father's greater condition above.
[186] Reading *lix* for *xxx.*

put those down by means of the ascensions, since it will distribute[187] years according to the number of their degrees. And if the distribution were in the rays of a fortune and the distributor were a good one, he will be in tranquility and abundance in those years, or the bounty of life; and it will extend to the end of those things which it signified in terms of the good, when the degree arrives at the degree of a good one, if God wills. You will do likewise until the work of life would be perfected.

[6.1: The native's lesser condition]

Now I will put [down] an example for you through which you will direct, and always [so] that you will go step-by-step:

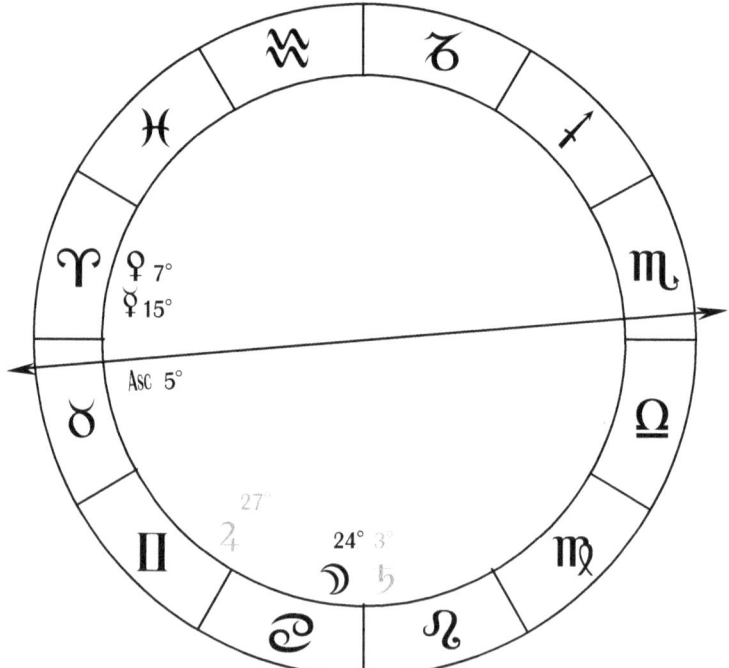

Figure 3: The "lesser" condition of the native

---

[187] Reading *dividet* for *dimittet*.

I looked at the directions of this [revolution of the] nativity.[188] And the Ascendant was the fifth degree of Taurus, and none of the planets was in it, nor were [any of] their rays more than 5°, except for the Moon's.

But she was in the sextile aspect of the Ascendant,[189] namely in Cancer in 24°.[190] I took away the 5° of the Ascendant from 24° of the rays of the Moon in the Ascendant, and there remained 19°. And we said that the Ascendant would have disposed 19 days[191] up to where it reached the disposition of the Moon, through the rays of her sextile aspect.

After this, the Moon will manage [from] the completion of 30° from the Ascendant, and, of the second [sign], two complete degrees, up to where it reached the light of the rays of Saturn's sextile aspect, [making] nine [degrees total].[192]

Then Saturn will receive the disposition up to[193] the light of the sextile aspect of Venus, because the closer of the planets to the rays of Saturn, after Saturn, was Venus. And so we subtracted the degrees of Saturn from Venus, and there remained 4°. And we said that Saturn will dispose four days.

After that we subtracted [the degree of the sextile of Venus][194] from [the sextile of][195] Mercury, and there remained eight days.

---

[188] Diagram mine. The date may be approximately March 28, 614 AD GC (with some allowances for incorrect values for Mercury and Venus), except that Mars is in Taurus (which would have put him directly in the middle of the direction). I have put a gray Jupiter and Saturn in the signs they occupied on that date, with the degrees given in the text.
[189] Note that 'Umar is using whole-sign configurations in this statement.
[190] There is confusion in the text between cardinal and ordinal numbers.
[191] 'Umar should be multiplying by 59' 08", but perhaps the values will often be so close to 1°, he feels entitled to simplify matters for the example.
[192] The Moon's sextile aspect was really in the 24th degree of Taurus, or 23°. The sextile of Saturn falls at 2° Gemini. Thus she disposed the remaining 7° of Taurus and the first 2° of Gemini, making 9° total.
[193] Reading *usque* for *per*.
[194] Reading for *minimusve est*.
[195] Mercury must be in Aries, else he would already have been in or cast his ray to degrees already covered.

Then we subtracted Mercury from Jupiter, and there remained thirteen,[196] and we said that Mercury would dispose thirteen days.

After this, we took the 27° of Jupiter away from the thirty, and there remained three days of Gemini. Let it happen likewise up to the completion of the twelve houses.

And if some planet aspected the degree of the Ascendant from a like degree, the Ascendant would have had no disposition, but the planet would have had the disposition because the planet would have been occupying the ascending minute.

[If you] revolved the year from the Ascendant, work it in this way up until the Ascendant [of the revolution] even returns [to the place it was in at the revolution], if God wills: and you will do thusly for knowing the [native's lesser] condition, and in this way you will direct from the degree according to the house of fathers for the father, and for the mother from the degree of the Moon for knowing her lesser condition.

---

[196] In order for the numbering to work, this should be "twelve."

[6.2: *The native's greater condition*]

Moreover, I looked at another figure:[197]

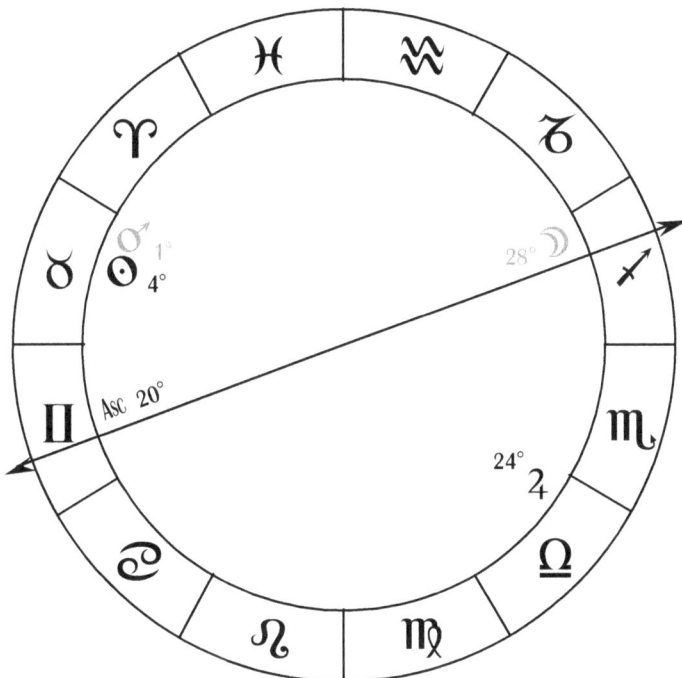

Figure 4: The "greater" condition of the native

And the Ascendant of the nativity in the root was the 20° of the sign of Gemini; and the sign of the profection in the fifth year arrived at Libra, 20°. We want, with God helping, to know his condition in that same year from that number, [such that] 30° are given to one year through the rays. We subtract the lesser from the greater, [and] afterwards we multiplied by twelve, and there was one day for every 59' and 8" [of that product].

For[198] we subtracted the [degrees] of the sign of the profection (which were 20° of the sign of Libra) from Jupiter, and there remained 4; we

---

[197] Diagram mine. This chart dates to approximately April 27, 642 AD GC. On this date Mars was several degrees after the Sun, not before him. I have put a gray Mars and Moon in the signs they occupied on that date, but with the degrees given in the text.

multiplied the 4 which remained, by 12, and 48° came out. And we said [the Ascendant] will dispose the least amount of these days through [to the] the light of Jupiter's conjunction, and [this was] 48 days; [and from there], up to the Moon's sextile aspect.

Then we subtract Jupiter from the [sextile of the] Moon, and 5° came out between them, which we multiplied by 12: this reached 60°, and [so] we said that Jupiter will dispose 60 days, through [to] the sextile aspect of the Moon.

After this, we subtract the Moon's degrees (which were 28)[199] from the sign of the profection, and 1 remained. Then we looked at the next sign, and behold, Mars was projecting light into it, the second degree. And we took the degree which remained in the sign of the profection, and we multiplied [it and] the 2° of the [next] sign [making 3° total] by 12, and 36 days came out, and it was the Moon's disposition.

After this we subtract Mars, who is [a certain number of] degrees from the [opposition of the] Sun, and 3° remained, which we multiplied by 12, and 36 days came out. We said that Mars would dispose these days through [to] the light of the Sun's opposition.[200]

Again we multiplied the 15°[201] which remained from out of the sign of the profection (from out of a profection of 30°) by 12,[202] and 180 came out. Therefore we said that the Sun will dispose up to 180 completed days.

---

[198] Throughout this section I have added clarifying material in brackets and corrected some of the numbers: for example, immediately below the text reads "four" days when it should read "forty-eight," and "degrees" when it should read "days." Note also that 'Umar now simply multiplies by 12 for simplicity's sake, instead of then dividing by 59' 08" as he has advised.

[199] This should actually read "29."

[200] At this point the year would end, since the Sun in this example is at 5° Scorpio, completing the 30° increment of the year. But now 'Umar seems to want to continue into the next year, although he is presenting it as though we are still dealing with the current year. I will do my best to present his multiplication accurately, but the planetary positions seem to break down again.

[201] Or, "16."

[202] This must mean that another planet or aspect is at 20° Scorpio.

And if the Sun had been in 15°, and we had subtracted Mars from it, 13 would have remained.[203] And if the year had ended at 15°, we would project three, and multiply 15 by 12, and the disposition would belong to Mars through to the light of the Sun's opposition, until the year ended, if God wills.

[6.3: The native's general condition]

Therefore look here: because you will do thusly through the root of the nativity until the life would be ended, [giving] a year to every degree by ascensions. In this way you will even do the following for the father and mother [using their Lots], though we have directed the *Ascendant* by ascensions in this way for knowing the *native's* [general] condition. If you wished to know the native's condition you will do [it] by a general knowledge [of this kind], by the command of God: you will always direct the ascending degree and not from another.

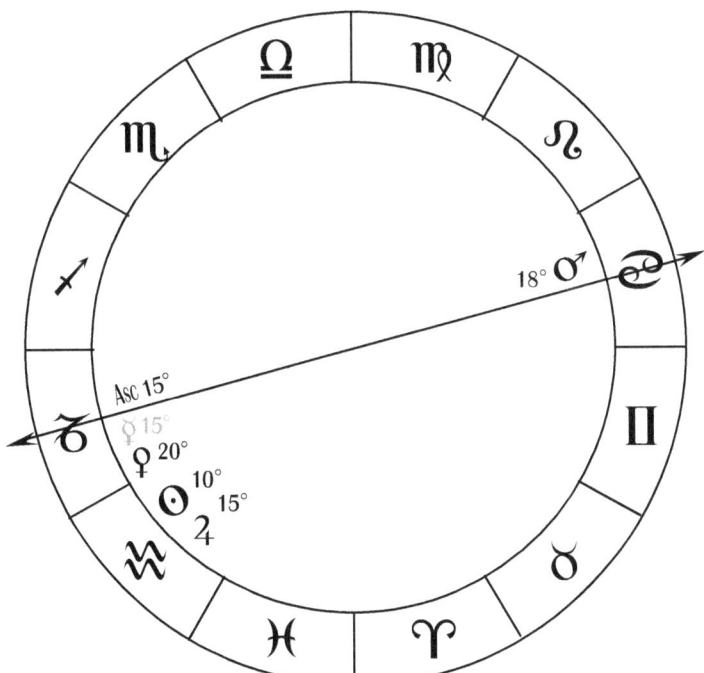

Figure 5: The "general" condition of the native

---

[203] Reading *xiii* for *xviii*.

Therefore[204] we looked, and 15° of Capricorn was ascending, and Mercury [in] that degree, by degree—that is, in the same ascending degree. And we directed the degree of Mercury because the Ascendant had no work.[205] (Likewise in every place if you saw [something] like this.)

And we looked to see which of the planets was closer to Mercury, of those who were closer to him and were in more degrees: and [the opposition of] Mars had 18°. Therefore we subtracted Mercury from Mars, and 3° came out. And we said that Mercury would dispose three years up to the light of the opposition of Mars.

Then we took Mars from Venus (who was in 20°), and two came out. [Therefore] we said that Mars would dispose (that is, [for two] years) up to the light of the conjunction of Venus.

After this, we subtracted Venus from the [end of the] ascending sign, [and] 10° of the ascending sign remained, and it reached the Sun in the next sign, at 10°. And we said that Venus will dispose ten years through her own nature, and ten [more] years up to the nature of the Sun.

Then we subtracted the Sun from Jupiter and 5° remained, and we said the Sun would dispose five years through to the nature of Jupiter.

You will always do [it] in this way until it is finished—that is, he speaks [in this way] regarding [the native's general] condition, [giving] a year to every degree by ascensions, if God wills.

Moreover, look regarding the Lord of the bound of the Ascendant, because it is the *jārbakhtār*, that is, the distributor. That is, look to see what remained of its bound in terms of degrees and minutes until it completes it, and put it [as] ascensions, and turn the equal degrees of the bound into

---

[204] This chart can be dated to approximately January 30, 622 AD GC, but Mercury is in Capricorn, and Jupiter in Aquarius (as he is below at the end of the instructions): therefore I read *Mercurius* for *Iuppiter* throughout this first part of the direction and have replaced this first instance of Jupiter with a grayed-out Mercury in the diagram as well. Unfortunately this date also puts the opposition of Saturn from Cancer next to Venus, unmentioned by 'Umar. Note again that 'Umar ignores the ascensional values and simplifies things by giving a year to every ecliptical degree.

[205] Since Mercury was already in the rising degree, the Ascendant did not have to assume the role of the dispositor as it did in previous examples.

degrees of ascensions, and put a year for every degree, and they [are] in the distribution of that same planet. After this, look at the Lord of the following bound and [see] how many degrees of [the bound] there are, and even put down those ascensions as above (since it will be in the distribution of that same planet), a year for every degree. Which if that planet were a fortune, [and if][206] it will distribute in the rays of fortunes, they will be in tranquility and a broad extent, and prosperity. But if it were otherwise, speak to the contrary. But if they were good ones and bad ones, his condition will be in the middle. Do likewise for the third bound, and the fourth and fifth, until his life is ended, if God wills.

And know that a planet which signifies the detriment of a limb and the distresses of life, and grief also, and the danger of the body, will come with its own signification when it distributes, by the command of God; likewise a planet which signifies a king[dom] (that is, an honor), and so on.

[Chapter II.7: Ptolemy's annual directions]

And know that it seemed to Ptolemy[207] that the Moon should always be directed to the rays of the bad ones and of the good ones for knowing the condition of the body in soundness or infirmity, and for the condition of the mother; and the Lot of Fortune for knowing a man's acquisitions (namely riches) and his poverty; and [the direction of] the Sun for knowing the condition of the father and [the native's] kingdom and mastery. It also seemed to him that the direction of the degree of the Midheaven [should be] by means of the ascensions of the right circle.

On the other hand, it seemed to him and others generally[208] that it should be directed from the degree of the Ascendant for knowing his condition, [by means of] the distributions of the bounds to the rays of the bad ones and the fortunes:

---

[206] The text is ambiguous as to what planet is a fortune, so I have added this clarification. 'Umar is stating an ideal condition: if the bound Lord is a benefic, as well as benefics casting rays into that bound.

[207] Perhaps referring to *Tet.* IV.10 p. 45, 47. But there Ptolemy connects the Ascendant to the body, not the Moon.

[208] Abū Ma'shar greatly emphasizes the direction of the Ascendant, but Ptolemy does not. Cf. *Tet.* IV.10 pp. 49-50.

In the same way,[209] if it came about that the distributor [were] a bad one, and the distribution were involved in the rays of the bad ones, one should pronounce distresses and a bad bearing in this; also an infirmity of the body and a corruption of the complexion according to the quantity of the nature of the bad one.

But if the distributor were a bad one and the rays were of a good one, his condition will be dual:[210] that is, infirmity with health, and poverty with abundance.

But if the distributor were a fortune and likewise the rays were of a good one, if someone of those born were of the children of paupers, and with the bearing of middling [people] in [his] condition, he will likewise be mediocre in the distribution, he will be mediocre in his condition and in his bearing, if God wills.

[Chapter II.8: Rejection of alternative methods]

[But] when Māshā'allāh used to direct for knowing the native's condition from the Ascendant, [he used to do it] from that degree [in the rising sign] to which the Lord of the Ascendant is projecting rays, and he used to give disposition of the same condition to the Lord of the Ascendant, just as it is directed in the year.[211]

However,[212] it is possible that the Lord of the Ascendant does not aspect the Ascendant, nor the Lord of the Midheaven the Midheaven. Which if he said that it will be directed from the degree of the Lord of the Ascendant in the Ascendant by the degrees of his rays in the Ascendant (which if he were not there, [then] from the Lord of the triplicity and its degrees in the Ascendant), we will say that it will be possible that these four do not aspect the Ascendant. And [therefore] it is altogether necessary to direct from the Ascendant, and through this their opinion is broken: that is, their explanation

---

[209] Adding *modo*.
[210] *Communis*.
[211] I have not seen this in *BA*, but it may have been Māshā'allāh's way of interpreting the Persian method. I am doubtful.
[212] Reading *autem* for *et*.

of those things which we told you in the beginning of the work.[213] Because he who makes a direction, it is necessary for him that he direct from the degree of the Ascendant.

But in the year of a profection, the native's year reaches the next number, [such] that 30° is given for each year to the sign of the profection, to a like degree and minute of the Ascendant.[214] Therefore, if you wished to know the [native's] greater condition, we will take [it] from these degrees, up to the completion of 30° in[215] the next sign, by equal degrees. That is, we will take [it] up to that degree itself in which the rays of the fortunes or bad ones are projected, and we will multiply them by 12 1/6. Which if [all] 30° were multiplied [by 12 1/6], they would be 365, which are the days of the year. And you will put down that disposition [as being] through the rays of that planet. If the planet were a fortune, the days will be fortunate in the disposition of its planet; but if it were a bad one, it signifies according to what I told you first—that is, whether it were bad one or good one, it signifies[216] according to its own substance, if God wills.

---

[213] That is, the earlier view regarding Lords not aspecting.
[214] Reading *minutum* for *neuter*, with Hand.
[215] Reading *in* for *ex*.
[216] Reading *significat* for *signi*.

BOOK III: [TOPICS][217]

[Chapter III.1: Social Status and Prosperity]

If you ordered the matter of the native with respect to nourishing and life (with God ratifying), and [his] condition in the direction of the degree of the Ascendant from the perspective[218] of the distributor and the conversion of the degrees of the bound of the distributor into ascensions, and by their direction to the rays of the bad ones and the fortunes, a year for every degree; and [if] by the command of God you wished to know his accidents and dignities, begin, and know of what stock and dignity the native is.

[1.1: Delineating prosperity]

[1] The knowledge of which is that you should look (by the command of God) at the statements of Ptolemy[219] in accordance with the *dustūriyyah* of the diurnal planets from the Sun, and the *dustūriyyah* of the nocturnal planets from the Moon; and the explanation of *dustūriyyah* is "security" or "rightness."[220] But this happens if the planets were oriental from the Sun in the day, and occidental from the Moon in the night. If therefore the superior planets were oriental from the Sun, in their own domiciles or own exaltations, and with the Sun in his own domicile or exaltation, and the place were an angle, and they aspected each other, the native will be a king or prince similar to a king; and if they were in their own domiciles or exaltations, and they were not all in angles, or [at least] one of them [was], the native will be a duke or a great prince, if God wills. And if they were cadent and peregrine, the native will be from middling house[holds], [from] men of

---

[217] The Latin subtitle read: "On natural things according to their quantity and their fortune" (reading *fortunium* for *fortunarum*).
[218] *Ex parte*.
[219] 'Umar is relying on *Tet.* IV.3 for his ranking of different levels of *dustūriyyah*, but not so much for its content. The very garbled content (note for instance the confusion between superior and diurnal planets) is ultimately dependent on Rhetorius Ch. 23 (and originally on Antiochus), but mixes elements from all three types of *dustūriyyah*. Cf. *BA* II.12 and *JN* Ch. 6 p. 240.
[220] *Dexteratio*. The origin of the notion of *dustūriyyah* (Gr. *doruphoria*) is indeed that or bodyguarding: see *Persian Nativities* I p. *xl*. The notion of "rightness" comes from the fact that *dustūriyyah* Types 2 and 3 refer to planets on the right of, or rising before, the Sun. See *BA* II.12 and Schmidt's reconstruction of this concept (2009, pp. 247-265).

good bearing, and [he will be] respectable among his associates. But if there were not a *dustūriyyah* to the luminary from superior planets which were in their own *ḥayyiz*,[221] the native will be of low-class people, of no memory,[222] and unknown in his own rank.

[2] But according to Dorotheus,[223] in diurnal nativities it is looked at from the Lord of the Sun's triplicity (that is, the sign where [it is]): and firstly the Sun in the day, and firstly from the Lord of the Moon's triplicity in the night. After [this], you will look at the condition of the planets out of the twelve places, and you will take the degrees which are between the degree of the planet and the degree of the angle, and where it arrived in terms of degrees: if the planet were in the first 15°, the native will be a prince or like a king; and if it were in the next 15°, he will be a noble prince of high memory; but if it were in the third 15°, the native will be of middling men; and if it added [degrees] on top of this, he will be hard at labor, miserable, and low-class.

[3] But the third way in the knowledge of this matter springs up in the opinion of rational things from the *Book of Allegories*.[224] For the philosopher said that there are four types of nativities:

[3.1] Certain people are born who will be kings, and they persist in a kingdom.

[3.2] And certain people are born who will be full of labor, and they persist in labor and trouble.

[3.3] And certain ones of those born were first paupers and full of labor, after this they are made kings or rich.[225]

[3.4] But others were first kings or rich, afterwards they are made to be full of labor and paupers.

[3.1] Certain people are born kings, and they will last in a kingdom—these are those in the nativity of whom the Lord of the Ascendant and the Moon

---

[221] See footnote in I.4.3 above.
[222] That is, they have little record of their lineage, or are ignored by their contemporaries.
[223] *Carmen* I.26.2-4. Cf. also *JN* Ch. 7 pp. 240-41 and *BA* III.2.1 p. 82.
[224] Unknown at this time, but the following division of topics is closely related to *BA* III.2.0.
[225] Omitting a redundant *postea efficiuntur laboriosi*, which belongs with the next type.

were in the angles, and each are being joined to planets[226] in the angles or to the Lords of the angles, or the luminaries and the Lords of the angles are being joined to the Lord of the Ascendant, and [the Lord of the Ascendant] itself was received in the angles: this signifies that he is going to be born a king or rich, and he will persist in the kingdom and in riches.

[3.2] And if the Moon and the Lord of the Ascendant were cadent, and were joined to cadent planets, and they themselves were the Lords of places which are called cadent, or the Lords of the cadents are being joined to them, the native will be miserable and full of labor, of the children of low people, and he will persist in his labor.

[3.3] But[227] if the Lord of the Ascendant and the Moon and the Sun were cadent or in their own descensions, and they were joined to fortunes in the angles (or to bad ones who will receive them in the angles), and they themselves were Lords of angles, they will be born in the houses of people full of labor, and of those who were in distress and life's affliction. And at first they will paupers,[228] [but] after this they are made lofty, and they will be respectable according to what we told you.

[3.4] And if the Lord of the Ascendant and the Moon and the Sun and the Lords of the angles were in angles, and they were joined to cadent and receding planets, and to bad planets [or] the Head, [and][229] bad ones were the Lords of cadent houses, the native will be a king of great power, and he will fall from his fortune, and his kingdom will be taken away, and he will arrive at labor and poverty, and certain ones of them are captured [and] subjected to servitude.

[4] Also, Dorotheus[230] and Hermes[231] thought that one should look, after the native's nativity, first at the planet which proceeds[232] to the degree of the Moon, or to the degree of the Ascendant[233] apart from the degree of the Moon, because that planet signifies the native's dignity and his fortune:

---

[226] Reading *planetis* for *plures*.
[227] This paragraph originally appeared after the following one [3.4], but I have put it here in order to conform to the list above.
[228] Reading *pauperes* for *principes*.
[229] Somewhat conjectural, as some small words and case endings are missing and wrong: *et planetis malis capiti mali fuerunt*. Hand reads this as: "and the lords of the angles are malefics seized by malefic planets."
[230] *Carmen* I.12.
[231] Source unknown at this time.
[232] *Profiscitur*. I am not sure if this is by transit or direction, or even by profection.
[233] In the next paragraph this seems to be the first degree of the rising sign, not necessarily the axial degree.

which if it were a fortune and the place were appropriate to it, he will be a well-fortunate king or wealthy man, by the command of God. If there were not a bad one impeded in the same places (which are the place of the Moon's degree and the degree of the Ascendant), the native will be falling and full of labor, if God wills.

[5] Hermes[234] thought that the planet which first changed its figure in the revolution of the year of the world[235] (that is, through its own change from a sign into the next sign, or from an eastern degree to the west, or through its arrival to the Moon's degree or [to] the degree of the ascending sign apart from the Moon), it itself will be the Lord of the Year, and the significator of the matter of the year.

[6] And the generality [of the sages] thought that when the Moon proceeds from her own average course to her faster course, the native will be noble and rich. and when she proceeds from her own greater course to her average course, he will be of a middling condition below the nobles. And if she is changed from the average course to the lesser course, the native will be unfortunate and they said [he would be] of a bad condition.

[7] Which if the Moon were joined to none of the planets, nor separated from one in nativities, the native will be a wild man, of the sects of the desert. It will especially increase evil if she were in the nature of bad ones and in a bad place.

[1.2: Three methods of prediction]

The knowledge of [the native's] condition in nativities: and this comes to be in many ways from the sayings of the ancients.

[The first way is:] look at the Lords of the triplicity of the luminary whose authority or power it is. For you are looking at the first age from the first Lord of the triplicity of the Sun, and [the condition] of the second age from the second Lord of the triplicity of the Sun, and [the condition] of the third one from the third Lord of the triplicity of the Sun—in the day. Whatever one of them were of a better[236] place, and more sound, that same age will be better and more worthy. Likewise look in the night from the Lords of the triplicity of the Moon, just as you look for the Sun.

---

[234] Source unknown at this time, but cf. Sahl's *On Times* pp. 223-24.
[235] This should probably be a revolution of the year of the nativity.
[236] Reading *melioris* for *mediocris*.

The second way [of knowing the] condition is according to Ptolemy[237] and the generality [of the sages]:

That you should look for the middle of the first [part of] life from the Ascendant, and its beginning from the twelfth, [and] the end of the first [part of] life from the second.

And you should look for the middle of the middle [part of] life from the Midheaven, the beginning[238] of the middle [part of] life from the ninth, but the termination of that same middle [part of] life from the eleventh.[239]

And the middle of the end of life from the seventh, but the beginning of the last [part of] life from the sixth, and the end of that same last [part of] life from the eighth.

You will also look for the middle of the condition of death from the angle of the earth, and for the beginning of the condition of death from the third, but for the end of the condition of death from the fifth.

Whichever one of these were made fortunate, pronounce good in them. And [if] they were impeded, say impediment and evil, and every horrible thing; and aid through the Lords of these houses, and the *mubtazz* over the accidents of these places, if God wills.

The third way for [knowing] the condition is that you should look at the Moon in nativities, to see to how many planets she is being joined in the sign in which she is, because [his] riches [will be] according to the being and number and quantity[240] of those same planets. Which if the Moon were joined to none of the planets, he will be of a condition [which comes] from the Moon in two ways: the first from the sign of the Moon and its place (therefore speak on this [matter] according to the quantity of its weakness [or] strength in the place of the Moon); the second from the Lord of the Moon and its place, and its strength and weakness, and its conjunction with

---

[237] See the excerpt from Serapio in Schmidt 2009, p. 307, and cf. Rhetorius Ch. 46.
[238] Omitting *ex*.
[239] Reading *undecimo* for *undecim*.
[240] Referring perhaps to their angularity, or the natures of the signs they rule.

the planets or the planets' [conjunction] with it, and speak in terms of good and bad according to what you saw.

And I have already explained to you the matter of nourishment from the Ascendant and its Lord, and from the Lords of the triplicity of the Ascendant, and of the Moon and her Lord. And now I will explain what the twelve places signify, if God wills.

[Chapter III.2: Wealth]

If you wished to look in the matter of substance, look at [1] the second from the Ascendant and [2] whatever of the planets is in it, and at [3] the Lord of the second, and at [4] the Lot of Substance and [5] the Lord of the Lot, also at [6] Jupiter and [7] the Lot of Fortune and [8] its Lord. Then look at [9] the *mubtazz* over these places, whether it were one or two. And I have already told you before: because the *mubtazz* [is the one] which was more worthy and authoritative than the rest by a multitude of dignities (that is, which had more portions[241] in the places, in terms of domicile and exaltation, and so on).

After these, look at the soundness of the same, and the *mubtazz*, and its commingling and relationship with the Lord of the Ascendant (from the fourteen ways which signify effecting[242] and knowledge[243] and destruction), and state whether he would have substance or not, according to what you saw.[244] And if you saw there would be substance, know from the condition of the *mubtazz* at which time (in terms of his age) he will acquire substance. For if it were oriental, [he will have substance] in his youth; but if it were occidental, he will gain it in old age.

After these, look at the nature of the second sign: because if it were fit and made fortunate, this will match it (that is, that the *mubtazz* signifies the kind of substance); and if there were an impediment, this kind will impede him.

Likewise, look at the nature of the *mubtazz* over these places: because if it signified bringing [substance] about, his acquisition will be of the nature of the planet.

Then look at all three Lords of the triplicity of the *mubtazz* (namely the first and the second and the third), because they signify in which of his three ages he will be acquiring more, and in which one there will be more good. He will earn good from whatever kind of substance according to the nature of those planets. Which if the first one were stronger, he will earn in the beginning of life; likewise concerning the second and third, by the command of God.

---

[241] *Partes*.
[242] Compare this pairing of effecting and destruction with the Latin *effectus* and *detrimento* (effecting, detriment) and the list of planetary configurations in Sahl's *Introduct.* §5.
[243] Cf. *Introduct.* §§5.8-9.
[244] Omitting an extra *quod*.

[Chapter III.3: Siblings]

If you wished to look in the matter of siblings, look at [1] the third and [2] its Lord, and [3] whatever of the planets were in the third, and at [4] the Lot of Brothers and [5] its Lord, and at [6] Mars (because he signifies brothers), and at [7] the Lords of the triplicity of Mars. You will also look at [8] the planetary *mubtazz* over these places, whether it were one or two.

After these, you will look at the Lord of the Ascendant and the *mubtazz*, to see if there were some one of the fourteen ways between them which signify effecting and destruction.

Or,[245] were the sign of siblings of the signs of many children, or were the *mubtazz* in one, the native will have[246] brothers and sisters.

Look even to see if the significators[247] were in masculine signs and in masculine places (especially the Lot of Brothers): they will be male. But if they were in feminine signs, more of them will be female.

Then[248] look from the concord of the *mubtazz* over the house of brothers with the *mubtazz* over the Ascendant: if there were concord between them, say that there will be esteem and peace between them; and if there were not concord and peace between them, it signifies hatred and enmities.

After[249] this, [look to see] whether the native or the siblings are of greater dignity, from the strength of the *mubtazz* over the Ascendant or that of the *mubtazz* over the house of siblings: because the stronger of them will be in charge.

Then[250] look at the Lords of the triplicity of Mars (namely at the first and the second and third), and see which one of them is stronger and of middling condition, because it signifies the matter of siblings. For the first signifies the older ones of them, and the second one the middle ones, but the third the younger ones, by the command of God.

After[251] this, for knowing which of them will endure, and which of them death will consume, and so on, [and] which things happen to them, look at what there was between the Midheaven and the Ascendant. If there were fortunate planets in that same place, children were already born to his father

---

[245] Cf. *BA* III.3.3 pp. 95-96; *JN* Ch. 12 p. 265.
[246] Omitting *filius*.
[247] Reading *significatores* for *significationes*.
[248] Cf. *JN* Ch. 15 p. 269.
[249] Cf. *JN* Ch. 14 p. 269.
[250] Cf. *JN* Ch. 14 p. 268. Abū 'Ali uses the triplicity Lords of the 3rd, not Mars.
[251] For the next two paragraphs, cf. *BA* III.3.3, *JN* Ch. 13, and *Carmen* I.17.

before him, and they have endured up to now; and if there were bad ones in that same place, it signifies that they are dead. But if there were fortunes and bad ones in common signs, the brothers who have remained or died, were two.

Then, afterwards, look (for those who are born) at what is between the Ascendant and the angle of the earth. If there were planets in it, brothers and sisters are born after him according to the quantity of the stars which you found. Which if you found some one of the planets in common[252] signs, this doubles their number. But if there were bad ones in it, it signifies death; and if they were good, lastingness.

[Also, the Sun and Saturn indicate older brothers, but Jupiter and Mars the middle ones, and Mercury the younger ones; Venus indicates younger sisters and the Moon older ones.][253]

Moreover,[254] the Moon's separation from the planets signifies those who were born before him, and the Moon's conjunction signifies those who are born after him.

Therefore,[255] look at the Lords of the triplicity of the Ascendant[256] (the first, second and third), [and] you will add and take the stronger of them which had greater testimony: which if it were in the Ascendant, it signifies that the native is the first or fourth of the mother's children; which if it were in the Midheaven, it signifies that he is the first or fourth or more; and if it were in the seventh, it signifies that he is the seventh or fourth or first; but if it were in the fourth, it signifies that he is the first or fourth. And likewise all the places signify according to the quantity of the place.

---

[252] Reading *communibus* for *omnibus*.
[253] Replacing the following sentence on parents with the appropriate sentence from *BA* III.3.2, *JN* Ch. 13 p. 267, and *Carmen* I.21.10: "Also, the Sun and Saturn signify the father, Venus and the Moon signify the mother, by the command of God."
[254] Cf. *BA* III.3.4 p. 97, *JN* Ch. 13 pp. 267-68, and *Carmen* I.21.25-28.
[255] Cf. *BA* III.3.3 p. 94, *JN* Ch. 13 p. 266 and *Carmen* I.17.1-3.
[256] Reading with Abū 'Ali and *Carmen* for the Latin text's "mother."

[Chapter III.4: Parents]

[4.1: The father]

If you wished to look for the father, you will look for him from [1] the fourth sign and [2] its Lord, [3] [the Lot of Fathers and {4} its Lord, at {5} Saturn and the Sun],[257] and you will look at [6] the *mubtazz* over these places. You will even look at [7] the planets which were in the fourth, and you will put them as the significators of the father.

After this you will look at [8] the significator,[258] and you should know from it what will enter upon him in terms of the length or shortness of life, according to what I have explained to you [before],[259] if God wills.

After this,[260] for the life of the father you will direct from the Lot of the Father and [from] the Sun, and [from] the degree of the house of fathers (namely from the one which was more worthy to be the *hīlāj*) to the places of the fortunes and the bad ones. And you will speak to his life according to the number of his years which the *mubtazz* signified.

To be sure, for knowing the [greater] condition of fathers in every year of the profection you will direct from the Lot of Fathers to the places of the fortunes and the bad ones.[261] And you will state the safety of the father from the goodness of the Lord of the Year.

But[262] [for] his loftiness and to which rank he arrives, [look] from the *dustūriyyah* of the Sun from the diurnal planets. (And *dustūriyyah* signifies oriental planets which arise in the morning, and in the night from the *dustūriyyah* of Saturn from the Sun in particular.) For if he had a *dustūriyyah*, he will be of a father of great quantity, and he will find honor.

And[263] you will speak [about] the first and second condition of the father from the Lords of the triplicity of the Sun in the day, and from the Lords of the triplicity of Saturn in the night, according to this likeness.

You will speak on the severity of the father's death from the impediment of the *mubtazz* over the matters of fathers: which if it were impeded by

---

[257] Adding based on two separate comments from Abū Bakr II.5.10 and 5.14.
[258] That is, the *mubtazz*.
[259] See above, II.5.
[260] *JN* Chs. 17, 19.
[261] That is, profecting the Lot of the Father in 30° increments as described above in II.5.
[262] *BA* III.4.1, III.4.3; *JN* Ch. 16 p. 272.
[263] Cf. *BA* III.4.3, *JN* Ch. 16.

Mars[264] in the day and by Saturn in the night, from a square aspect or opposition without the aspect of the fortunes, and without reception, this signifies the severity of his death. And if the impeding bad one were [also] the Lord of the Ascendant or the *mubtazz* over the Ascendant,[265] perhaps the native will kill his own father.

And[266] you will speak on the concord of the father and the native from the concord of the *mubtazz* over the house of fathers and the *mubtazz* over the Ascendant, and on their discord. For if they were discordant, it signifies hatred and enmities. And you will say that the native is not legitimate, and that the father has[267] suspicion, if the Sun were impeded in the day by Mars (and in the night by Saturn) by a square aspect or opposition. And you will say that the mother hates the child and does not have confidence in the one born to her[268] if the Moon were impeded in the day by Mars, and in the night by Saturn.

But certain ones of the ancients said that if the Lord of the house of fathers did not aspect the house of children,[269] nor the Sun the Lord of his own domicile, nor the Lord of the Lot of the Father [the Lot], the native will not be the son of his father. But if one of them aspected, he will be legitimate.

[4.2: The mother]

If you wanted to look in the matter of the mother, by the command of God, look at [1] the tenth sign[270] and [2] its Lord, and [3] the Lot of the Mother and[271] [4] its Lord, and [5] Venus [and the Moon],[272] and also [6] the planetary *mubtazz* over these places, because it will be the significator of the mother.

---

[264] Reading *Marte* for *morte*.
[265] Reading *ascendens* for *ascendentis*.
[266] Cf. *BA* III.1.4, 4.5, and 12.7.
[267] Reading with Abū Bakr.
[268] Abū Bakr (II.5.4) says that this condition of the Moon is evidence that the mother is untrustworthy, that the native may be illegitimate.
[269] Abū Bakr reads "its own domicile," which I suspect is correct.
[270] The attribution of the tenth sign to the mother is not standard and seems to come from a misreading of *Tet.* III.6. We should consider this particular sentence (and its subsequent adoption by Bonatti and others) as a main source for this attribution in later Western astrology.
[271] Reading *et* for *secundum*.
[272] Adding based on all the traditional texts: Venus by day, the Moon by night.

After this, look to see what [the *mubtazz*] would signify in terms of years, and who increases or subtracts from it according to what I have indicated to you in terms of years.

Then,[273] for the condition of the mother and the quantity of her dignity, look from the *dustūriyyah* of the nocturnal[274] planets from the Moon in the night,[275] and from the *dustūriyyah* of Venus from the Moon in the day, by the command of God.

And[276] look from the Lot of the Mother and the Moon,[277] namely from those which were [more worthy to be] the *hīlāj* signifying[278] the life of the mother. And you will direct the *hīlāj* to the places of the fortunes and the bad ones, and where it arrived at a bad one, there will be danger in that same place. But[279] if the Moon and the Lot of the Mother [were] in the place of the *hīlāj*, and you wished to know the place which you will direct for the mother, direct from the degree of the Moon: whenever it arrived at bad ones, it will signify danger or the mother's death, if God wills.

After this, look at her concord and esteem towards the child (or her hatred), from the *mubtazz* over the Ascendant and [the *mubtazz*] over the places for mothers which we said before: which if both significators were concordant and esteeming each other (that is, if the *mubtazz* of the mother and the *mubtazz* of the native were in concord), speak according to what you saw.

Concerning this, look likewise for the concord and esteem of the mother toward the father, and speak according to the quantity of the concord of each of the significators (which are the *mubtazz* of the mother and the *mubtazz* of the father).

After this,[280] for the knowledge of the condition of the mother, look from the Lords of the triplicity of the Moon in the night and [of Venus in the][281]

---

[273] Cf. *BA* III.4.1, *JN* Ch. 16 p. 272.
[274] Reading "nocturnal" for "three," to parallel the account of the father above.
[275] Moving "in the night" here instead of at the end of the sentence, to parallel the account of Saturn and the Sun above.
[276] Cf. *BA* III.4.9, *JN* Chs. 18-19.
[277] One would expect 'Umar to mention the Midheaven, but neither he nor Abū Bakr (who copies 'Umar's text) does.
[278] Omitting the redundant *matris* and adding the operative verb, to parallel the account of the father above.
[279] *JN* Ch. 19 p. 275 might have a clearer explanation of this: "And if you *did not find* a *hīlāj*, direct the degree of the Moon…" (emphasis mine).
[280] Cf. *JN* Ch. 16 p. 271.
[281] Adding to match the account for the father above.

day, since the first one signifies the beginning of its matter, and the second one the middle, but the third the third [part], if God wills.

Then ['Umar] speaks concerning the severity of the mother's death (and its ease) from the impediment of the Moon and her Lord, and the Lot of the Mother and its Lord:[282] because if they were impeded by the bad ones, it signifies a bad death.

And speak on the quickness of their death and the quickness of the entrance of each *mubtazz* under the earth, according to what Dorotheus said.[283]

---

[282] Undoubtedly through a square or opposition of Mars (in the day) or Saturn (in the night).

[283] *Carmen* I.15; see also *BA* III.4.7. I have put this paragraph at the end of the chapter instead of the middle, and have deleted a redundant version of it which appeared in this place: "And speak concerning the quickness of the parents' death (that is, which of them will die first), from the quickness of the entrance of some one of their significators under the earth."

[Chapter III.5: Marriage]

It is necessary for you to look concerning marriage after you have delayed[284] looking concerning children. If therefore you wished to look with respect to the marriage-union of the native, look from [1] the 7th and [2] its Lord, and look to see [3] what of the planets is in the 7th, also at [4] the Moon and [5] Venus, and at [6] the Lot of Marriage-Union and [7] its Lord. And you will look, by the command of God, at [8] the *mubtazz* over these places, whether it were one or two.

After this you will look into the fourteen complexions, and into the concord which was between it (that is, the *mubtazz* of marriage-union) and the *mubtazz* over the Ascendant: if there were some complexion of concord between them, the native will marry, by the command of God. But if it were a sign of many children, or there were a commingling (that is, an aspect) of the significators from out of signs of many children, you will say that the native will have many women, by the command of God. And if it were otherwise, to the contrary.

Also, Ptolemy said:[285] [for male natives,] look at the Moon: if she were between the Midheaven and the Ascendant, the native will marry in his youth; likewise if she were between[286] the 7th and the angle of the earth in eastern quarters.[287] But if she were in western quarters, he will postpone his marriage-union, and he will in his old age, by the command of God.

And Dorotheus said:[288] look at the Lords of the triplicity of Venus (the first, second, and third). If all or many of them were oriental, of a good place without impediment, and were not under the rays nor impeded, the native will be made fortunate in women, and he will marry in his youth; and if it were otherwise, he will not be made fortunate in women, and especially if the Lords of the triplicity of Venus were eclipsed under the rays of the Sun, not

---

[284] Translation somewhat stretched (*postquam cessasti*). Really this should read *antequam incepisti*, "before you have begun." 'Umar means that the natural step after the 4th house (parents) would be to look at the 5th (children)—but that we must delay doing this until we have established the native's sexual habits and marriage.
[285] *Tet.* IV.6.
[286] Reading *inter* for *in*.
[287] In *Tet.* IV.6 Ptolemy redefines eastern and western quarters for the purposes of marriage. When looking at the Moon, her 1st and 3rd quarters are eastern, and the 2nd and 4th western. When looking at the Sun in women's nativities, use the normal quarters based on the axial degrees: from the Ascendant to the Midheaven and from the 7th to the IC are eastern; the other two quarters are western.
[288] Cf. *Carmen* II.1.1-5 and *BA* III.7.2. *JN* Ch. 25 pp. 283-84 is closer to 'Umar.

aspecting Venus, and she were impeded by the rays of the Sun. And he said that if they were occidental, he will postpone the marriage-union and he will not marry except at a great age, by the command of God.

If[289] Saturn were exalted over Venus from the tenth [sign from her],[290] or he were with Venus or in her square aspect or the opposition, he will be numbed[291] by women, by the command of God, and there will be no necessity in them. If Venus were exalted over Saturn in the tenth [sign from him], there will be a marriage-union in middle age, namely at the time appropriate for it, and the marriage-union will be in the middle, and likewise children.[292]

If[293] Venus were oriental, exalted, and she were in certain ones of her own dignities, the native's women will be elevated over him.

But if Venus and the Sun and the Lot of Marriage-Union, and many of the native's significators, and the Lord of the house of marriage-union [were in signs indicating foul intercourse],[294] the native will be overflowing in sexual intercourse, by a most foul overflowing.

If[295] Venus were in the square aspect of Mars or in his opposition, or with him in one sign, and it came about that Mars is in his own domicile or in his own exaltation (that is, that of Mars), the native will be most foul in sexual intercourse; [and the more so] if [Venus] were in a feminine sign and the native was male, [for] he will be deluded; but if she were in a masculine sign, he will be a sodomite. And[296] likewise in nativities of women, if [Venus] were in feminine signs, she will be a prostitute; and if [Venus] were in masculine signs, she uses women.

But[297] if Mercury were the *mubtazz* over Venus and the Moon and the house of women, and the Lot of those same women,[298] or over many of them, the native's pleasure [will be in boys], and he will deceive them.[299]

---

[289] Cf. *JN* Ch. 26 p. 285.
[290] That is, "overcoming" her.
[291] I.e., indifferent or frigid (*frigidus*).
[292] I am not sure how children fit here.
[293] Cf. *JN* Ch. 26 p. 286.
[294] Omitting the strange *fide coniunctionis* and substituting in brackets based on *BOA* p. 1290. Bonatti lists the signs as Aries, Leo, Libra and Capricorn; Rhetorius Ch. 5 lists Aries, Taurus, Capricorn, Pisces, and Libra in part.
[295] Cf. *JN* Ch. 26 p. 285; *BA* III.7.8. Material in brackets based on Bonatti p. 1290.
[296] Cf. *Tet.* III.15 p. 66.
[297] Cf. *BA* III.7.13, Rhetorius Ch. 66.

If Venus were in domiciles of Saturn, and Saturn aspected her, the native will be frigid[300] in sexual intercourse. And likewise if Saturn conquered, and he were the *mubtazz* over the house of the marriage-union—provided that the Lord of the seventh did not aspect the seventh, and [the Lord] of the Moon the Moon, also the Lord of the Lot of Marriage-Union that same Lot, and the Lord of Venus Venus—then the native will not taste the taste of women, and he will not marry.

If[301] the *mubtazz* were the victor over the Ascendant and the Moon and the Sun and the Lot of Fortune, [and] also the conjunction and the prevention which was before the native's nativity (according to the condition which he said), and more of the planets were feminine, the native will be effeminate or soft. And if masculine planets conquered in these places in the nativities of women, a girl which was born will be manly, practically male. For if, as we have said, more of the planets in the nativities of males were feminine, the native [will be] loose, soft, practically not having a mouth; and if the planets were masculine in the nativities of women, the female native will be manly, as though male, leaving the boundaries[302] of women. And if all of them were thus, we have seen their life be shortened, and [not] nourished on account of the multitude of moisture in men, and the multitude of dryness in women, by the command of God.

---

[298] Probably the Lot of Marriage-Union. But Bonatti seems to omit *mulierum*, and reads "and the house of wives, of a portion of them or over more of them," which is also rather likely.
[299] Reading with Bonatti p. 1291.
[300] Or, "indifferent."
[301] Cf. *BA* II.15, *Tet.* III.15.
[302] *Definitione*, which here must mean the culturally stereotypical activities and demeanor of women.

[Chapter III.6: Children]

If you wished to look in the matter of children, to see whether children will be granted to him or not, and whether his children will be many or few, look at [1] the fifth sign and [2] its Lord,[303] also [3] Venus and Jupiter and [4] the Lot of (his) Children,[304] and [5] its Lord, and look at [6] the *mubtazz* over these places, whether it were one or two.

Then look to see whether there is some coupling or some coming-together (that is, concord, out of the four[teen] ways) between [the *mubtazz* over children] and the *mubtazz* over the Ascendant or the *mubtazz* over the Moon: which if it were so, the native will have a child, and [they] will be of use to him through the 12th and its Lord.[305] But if there were no complexion between the *mubtazz* over the house of children and the *mubtazz* over the Ascendant, and Jupiter[306] were burned up and Venus impeded, the native will be sterile, lacking children.

After this,[307] look at the sign of children and the sign of the *mubtazz* over the native's matters and at the Ascendant: which if the signs were those of many children, the native will abound in children, if God wills.

Likewise even, if the Ascendant were a movable sign, [and] also were the majority of the significators of children in sterile signs, the native will be sterile, without a child for his whole life, if God wills. The sterile signs, however, are Leo, Taurus, Capricorn, Libra, and Aquarius.[308]

And if the *mubtazz*, or Jupiter, or the Lord of the house of the *mubtazz* over the house of children[309] [were] oriental, a child will be given to the native in his youth. If it were not oriental, [one] will be born to him in old

---

[303] Reading *dominum* for *domum*.

[304] Probably the Jupiter-Saturn Lot: from Jupiter to Saturn by day (and the reverse by night), projected from the Ascendant.

[305] *Et auxiliare cum eo per xii. et dominum eius*. This is an awkward use of the verb in Latin and the 12th does not make sense. I suggest that perhaps the 11th or 2nd is meant: both the 2nd and 11th signify allies and friends, and the 11th is also the 7th from the 5th, indicating partnerships.

[306] For the rest of this sentence, cf. *BA* III.5.3 and *JN* Ch. 20, pp. 275-76.

[307] Cf. *JN* Ch. 20 pp. 275-76.

[308] There is broad disagreement among traditional authorities as to the sterile signs. *Carmen* I.19.3 (and *JN* 12, drawing on it) have Leo, Virgo, Capricorn and Aquarius. *BA* III.3.2 follows Rhetorius Ch. 106: Gemini, Leo, Virgo, Capricorn, Sagittarius. But *Carmen* II.10.12 has Gemini, Leo, Virgo, Capricorn, the beginning of Taurus and the middle of Libra, Aries, and Sagittarius.

[309] That is, the dispositor of the *mubtazz*. Reading with Bonatti p. 1258. Cf. *JN* Ch. 21 p. 277.

age. He speaks likewise concerning the first, second, and third Lords of the triplicity of Jupiter, by the command of God.

Speak also[310] regarding the multitude of children from Jupiter and Venus (if Jupiter or Venus aspected the *mubtazz*, or were the *mubtazz*), and on their scarcity from Saturn and Mars, but on their middling amount from the Sun and Moon. But if Mercury were with these which signify scarcity, he will signify scarcity; and if he were with these which signify a multitude, they signify a multitude, by the command of God.

And Ptolemy thought[311] that one looks for children from the eleventh and its Lord, and the planets which were in it, and one looks for the father from the Midheaven in the day, and from the angle of the earth in the night. One also looks for fathers in the day from the Sun and Saturn and the Midheaven; in the night from Saturn and Jupiter and the angle of the earth.[312]

And look at the planets which were the *mubtazz* over the house of children, whether it were one or two. Which if some one of them, or more, are comporting themselves towards the Lord of the Ascendant and the *mubtazz* over the Ascendant,[313] the children will be good and just children, esteeming [their] father. But if it were to the contrary of this which we have said, [the children] will be impeding him. But if the significator of children were a bad one, impeding the Ascendant and its Lord, the child will be introducing diverse impediments to the father. And if it impeded the Moon, it will force diverse [impediments] on the mother. But if the significators of children were safe, the children will be protected, and they will not perish. And if the significators of children were impeded, the children will rarely be in concord, if God wills.

---

[310] Cf. *Tet.* IV.6 p. 26, *JN* Ch. 20 p. 276.
[311] Cf. *Tet.* IV.6 p. 26. Ptolemy includes planets "present or configured with" the Midheaven or the 11th, and if there are none, then to those in the opposites (4th and 5th). This does not seem quite right to me: no planet could be in aversion or outside of *both* the 10th and 11th, since any planet in aversion to the 10th will be in or configured with the 11th (and *vice versa*).
[312] Perhaps 'Umar means for these to represent the native insofar as he is the father to the children, in order to compare the significators (see immediately below).
[313] Presumably in one of the 14 ways 'Umar keeps mentioning.

[Chapter III.7: Infirmities]

Moreover, a new chapter on infirmities and diseases, and inseparable accidents. Here, look from [1] the 6th house and [2] its Lord, and from [3] the planets which are in it, and from [4] Mercury; also from [5] the Lot of Infirmities and Inseparable Accidents[314] and [6] its Lord, [and] [7] the *mubtazz* over these places.

Which if the *mubtazz* over these places were a bad one, and it were commingled with the Lord of the Ascendant, or it were in the angles [or the succeedents], the Ascendant impeded by them,[315] the native will be infirm [with] many infirmities.

If[316] however Saturn were the lord[317] over these places, his infirmities will be from cold and dryness,[318] and they will be far-reaching,[319] like epilepsy, and it will be caused by dropsy and gout.

And if Mars conquered in these places and he were in angles, and he aspected the Lord of the Ascendant and he impeded him, it signifies that his infirmities will be from red choler[320] and the flowing of blood.

But[321] if a fortune conquered in these places, and the fortune aspected the *mubtazz* over the Ascendant, it will signify the native's prosperity and his soundness, and deliverance in the infirmities and the aforesaid accidents, and his infirmities will be few. And he will be made fortunate in animals and slaves and domestics, if [the fortunes] were, as he said, the *mubtazz* over the aforesaid places,[322] or it agreed with the Lord of the Ascendant.

---

[314] This is the Lot of *Zamin* mentioned below.
[315] That is, by the *mubtazz*(es). Reading with Bonatti for the fragmentary *impeditum ascendens ab eis*. *JN* Ch. 24 p. 282 has something very similar.
[316] For the paragraphs on Saturn and Mars, cf. *JN* Ch. 24 p. 282 and *BA* III.6.3 p. 127.
[317] Reading *dominus* for *infirmus*.
[318] Reading *siccitate* with Bonatti p. 1269 and *JN* Ch. 24 p. 282, for the text's *frugi*.
[319] *Prolixae*.
[320] Reading *cholera rubea* for *clausula rubea*.
[321] Cf. *JN* Ch. 24 p. 282.
[322] Reading *loca* for *fortunam* with Bonatti p. 1268.

And if the Lot of the *Zamin*[323] (that is, an inseparable accident) were with the Moon in the ninth, and[324] Mars [were] in the eighth, and in signs of cut-off limbs in the native's nativity, some limb of his will be cut off by iron. Likewise if the Lot were with the Moon in some quarter, and the Ascendant were impeded by some bad one, accidents will come upon the native in the limb belonging to the sign in which the Moon is, or in the left eye[325] in nativities of the day, and in the right eye in nativities of the night.

If[326] the luminaries were in the conjunction or prevention, and bad ones were in the square aspect of the conjunction or prevention, and a bad one is ascending afterwards,[327] the native will lose the right eye from the Sun, and the left one from the Moon. Moreover,[328] if the luminaries were impeded from the square aspect of the bad ones or their opposition, or [they] were with it in one sign,[329] or it did not ascend[330] (provided the fortunes did not aspect the same place), his eyes [will likewise be harmed].

If[331] the Moon were impeded by the bad ones in some sign, without the projection of the rays of the fortunes to that bound, the limb which pertains to the sign in which the Moon is, will be destroyed.

> And[332] if the Moon were in signs which signify impediment in the eyes (like Cancer, Leo, Scorpio, Sagittarius, Capricorn, and Aquarius),[333] it signifies impediments of the eyes.

> Likewise[334] if the Moon were decreasing[335] [in light] in Sagittarius, whether impeded or not impeded by the bad ones, an impediment will happen to him in the eyes, and blindness will be feared for him.

---

[323] Lat. *Azamena*, from the Ar. "the infirm, chronically ill, invalid." This must be the classical Lot of Infirmity (*BA* III.6.3), taken from Saturn to Mars in the day (and the reverse at night), projected from the Ascendant.
[324] Reading *et* with Bonatti p. 1269.
[325] Reading *oculo* for *coelo*.
[326] Cf. *BA* III.6.2 p. 125, *Carmen* IV.1.88-90 and IV.1.103-04, and Rhetorius Ch. 61 pp. 114, 116.
[327] That is, in the following sign.
[328] This sentence seems to be an amalgamation of several statements. Cf. *BA* III.6.2 pp. 125-126, Rhetorius Ch. 61, and *Carmen* IV.1.90-96.
[329] The rest of this sentence is somewhat speculative: *aut non ascenderit dum non aspexerit fortunae ab idem eius oculi.*
[330] Meaning unclear.
[331] Cf. *Carmen* IV.1.77-78.
[332] For this list, cf. Rhetorius Ch. 61 p. 114.
[333] These are the fixed stars harming sight according to Rhetorius (*ibid.*).

If however she were impeded by Mars in Gemini and its triplicity, it signifies rottenness from leprosy if some fortune did not aspect her.[336]

If the Moon were impeded by Saturn in Cancer or its triplicity, without the aspect of the fortunes, it signifies white leprosy and cancers, and gout, and diseases which are called *acila*[337] (that is, an evil [affliction] of the throat).

If the Moon were in the square aspect of the Sun or with him in one sign, or in his opposition,[338] the native will be burned up by fire.

If[339] Venus were impeded by Saturn and by Mars and Mercury and the Sun, without the aspect of the fortunes, the native's testicles will be cut off. Which if then the Lords of the triplicity were strong and fit, he will acquire dignity and honor with respect to this. And if these said [planets] were the Lords of the triplicity of Venus, in addition to what he suffered the native will arrive at labor and affliction, and to something of servitude which he would not be able to escape. And if [the native] were a woman, her breasts will be cut off, and she will be separated from men, and love will not be in her, nor any comfort of Venus, if God wills.

The Moon,[340] if she were in the first degree of signs, or in their end, and bad ones (and especially Saturn) projected her own rays to that bound, [the native] will esteem with the greatest esteem, and it will be made public, if God wills.

---

[334] Cf. *Carmen* IV.1.97-98. Rhetorius Ch. 61 lists additional stars.

[335] Reading *decrescens* or *descendens* for *ascendens* (increasing/ascending) with *Carmen* IV.1.110 and *BA* III.6.2 pp. 126-27, and Rhetorius Ch. 61 p. 114. Rhetorius says that if the Moon is full at this time, the sight will be dimmed but not lost. *Tet.* III.13 p. 52 has the Moon being in an angle and "by herself," but then includes the New Moon: Hand follows this by putting her on the Ascendant in Sagittarius.

[336] The Latin does not specify the gender, but I take it to mean the Moon.

[337] Undoubtedly based on Ar.

[338] Omitting an extra *in quarto aspectu solis*. This sentence mirrors *JN* Ch. 37 p. 305. But another version in III.13 below plausibly includes Mars.

[339] Cf. *Tet.* III.13 p. 53 and *BA* III.6.6 and *Carmen* IV.1.129-34. 'Umar also addresses this in Book I in the section on the number of malefics.

[340] This paragraph does not make sense and must be based on a misunderstanding of the Arabic. Cf. *Carmen* IV.1.135, *BA* III.6.7, and Abū Bakr II.7.11 on midgets/dwarves.

[Chapter III.8: Travel]

Concerning foreign travel and changing [from place to place], and travel, look from [1] the ninth sign and [2] its Lord, and from [3] the planet which was [in] the ninth; also from [4] Mars and [5] the Lot of Foreign Travel and [6] its Lord.

[Then] look at [7] the *mubtazz* over these places, whether it were one or two, and see whether there would be some complexion or commingling or coming-together (of the fourteen ways which I said before) between one of these and the *mubtazz* over the Ascendant. And if it were so, the native will be engaged in foreign travel. And if there were nothing of these things which I have told you between them, the native will persist in his own place and[341] will be engaged in his studies and seek his livelihood in his own home, if God wills.[342]

And[343] Mars in the angles signifies foreign travel.

If the Moon did not aspect the Lord of her own domicile, it signifies that the native's work[344] and his livelihood is on foreign journeys.

After this, look at the Lords of the triplicity of Mars, and which of them were of a better place and better complexion: [in that time] of his life, the native will be of a better condition [on] his foreign travels.

If the Lord of [the ninth] house were impeded,[345] the native will be of bad faith, of much pretense, seeing commingled things in faith, and his foreign travels will not benefit him, and he will perish on them, and his substance will be gone. And[346] likewise if there were bad ones in the 9th.[347]

---

[341] Reading with *JN* Ch. 27 for 'Umar's *erit natus et ex his*.

[342] The following four paragraphs are found virtually verbatim, and in the same order, in *JN* Ch. 27 pp. 287-88. However, only 'Umar mentions faith.

[343] Cf. *JN* Ch. 27. The more accurate version from *BA* III.9.2 and Byzantine Dorotheus Excerpt XX has the following: if the Moon, on the third day of the nativity, is with Mars in the same sign or in his angles, or in one of his domiciles, and *especially if Mars is angular* in the chart, the native will live abroad.

[344] *Exercitium*.

[345] Reading with Dorotheus Excerpt XXI, line 3 for "its/his house." But line 1 of this same Excerpt does mention the dispositor of Mars, so it might also refer to this as well.

[346] Cf. *BA* III.9.2 and Dorotheus Excerpt XXI line 5, which do not mention matters of faith. See also the first paragraph of *JN* Ch. 28.

[347] A paragraph on the native's faith originally appeared after this paragraph, but I have moved it to the section on faith.

[Chapter III.9: Work and Mastery]

In this chapter there is mention of [the native's] work and kingdom and mastery.[348] If you wished to look concerning this, look at [1] the Midheaven and [2] its Lord, also [3] the Sun and [4] the native's Lot of Work and [5] its Lord; [also] look at [6] the *mubtazz* over these places, whether it were one or two.

And look at the complexion and commingling [of the *mubtazz* of work] with the *mubtazz* over the Ascendant, in terms of the fourteen ways of agreeing. Which if [you saw] some one of those which I have said, the native will have many works, and he will be a prince or king, and will not cease to rule, and he will be rational.

Also,[349] look at the Sun: which if he were in eastern quarters, the native will find honor and loftiness and a kingdom in his youth; and [if in western quarters,] at the end of his life.

But[350] [for his] condition in the kingdom and his work, and at what time he will be of greater dignity and honor, look from the Lords of the triplicity of the Sun: which if all three were strong, he will not cease to rule from the beginning of his youth. Speak likewise [about] his changeable condition ([that] he will suffer detriment and weakness) from the three Lords of the triplicity: because if the first one were impeded, he will be of unstable memory at the beginning of his life. And if the second one were impeded, he will be of unstable memory in the middle of his life. But if the third one were impeded, speak likewise that he will be of unstable memory at the end of his life.

The malefics:[351] if[352] Saturn were in an angle in the night, and Mars in the day, and especially in the Ascendant or[353] the Midheaven, the native will not have a memory, nor an assembly, nor work, nor a kingdom, until the fulfillment of the planet's lesser years; which if it passed over that boundary

---

[348] There is also mention of material not related to that: siblings, parents, quality of life and eminence. I have retained these paragraphs here.
[349] This paragraph pertains more to eminence than profession. Source unknown at this time.
[350] Source unknown at this time, but the use of triplicity Lords does suggest a Dorothean (or Dorotheus-inspired) source, as does the brief reference to them in *Carmen* I.23: see the next paragraph and footnote.
[351] Probably from *Carmen* I.23.3 and 23.5, which suggest that this will be especially so if the malefics are the triplicity Lords of the sect light (see previous paragraph).
[352] Reading *cum* for *causa*.
[353] Reading *aut* for *cum*.

[of years], it will be according to the ascension of the sign in which the planet is.³⁵⁴

If Mars were in the angles, and especially in the Ascendant (but in the Midheaven in the day), the native will be endangered because of his work, and his body will be whipped and bound. Likewise if Saturn were in angles in the night, the native will be strongly constrained, and be conquered and restrained and tortured, if God wills.

Saturn in the Ascendant: the native will be single, that is, alone. And³⁵⁵ if there were brothers or sisters, he will send them before himself in death, and he will be constrained, and distress will permeate him, and he will be a glutton,³⁵⁶ and especially in the night.

And if the Sun were in the opposition of the Moon, his parents will hate the native, and there will be a commingling³⁵⁷ in work or in his kingdom, and neither a kingdom nor a princely position will be arranged³⁵⁸ for him. And the wealthy [will be] contrary to him and look down upon him,³⁵⁹ and his father will precede [his] mother in death.

And our example: if work and a kingdom and a princely position and civil office were signified for the native, look at the *mubtazz* over the Midheaven and [over] the Sun and [over] the Lot of Work.³⁶⁰ After this, we will look at the substance of that same *mubtazz* over these places: which if it were Mercury, the native will be a scribe and astrologer and mathematician; and if it were the Sun, the native will be a prince or king, and he will be very wise in the ordering of the kingdom, and of good discretion.

You will speak likewise from the nature of this *mubtazz* and of those aspecting it, whether [the *mubtazz*] were one or many; and even look at the

---

³⁵⁴ That is, if the native still does not have any work or status after the lesser years have expired, the bad condition will continue until the end of the years of the sign's ascensions.
³⁵⁵ Possibly Rhetorius Ch. 57 pp. 51-52.
³⁵⁶ *Gulosus*, which classically only means someone fond of fine foods; but clearly something more extreme is meant here.
³⁵⁷ That is, his career and jobs will be mixed and varied, without the consistency assumed for a great office or career.
³⁵⁸ *Dirigetur*.
³⁵⁹ *Et eius contrarii et contemptores divites [erunt]*.
³⁶⁰ Reading *operis* for *corporis*. This must be an attempt to overcome the distinctions between the Sun, Midheaven, and the Lot—especially since Rhetorius (Ch. 83 p. 141) and *BA* III.10.7 (drawing on Rhetorius) are not very helpful on how the Lot fits in.

mubtazz, and see which of the planets is aspecting it, and mingle their work with every work of the *mubtazz*. And speak[361] according to this.

Ptolemy[362] even says that the native will then have a mastery if there were a planet pertaining-to-arising in the morning, in the Midheaven, to whom the Moon [applies];[363] or, were the *mubtazz* over the Midheaven oriental (even if it did not aspect [the Midheaven]), there will not be a mastery for the generality of those natives.[364] I, however, say that if the *mubtazz* over the Midheaven were commingled with the *mubtazz* over[365] the Ascendant, or with Mercury,[366] these [people] will not lack a mastery, and better than that if there were a planet here, oriental from the Sun or from the Ascendant or from each.

Now,[367] for the substance of the mastery, they looked generally from the quantity of Mars, Venus, and Mercury to each other, and in their commingling and aspect, if God wills. But the quantities are like if a planet is in the square aspect of another, or in its trine[368] or sextile aspect, or with it in one sign.

But[369] certain ones of the wise wanted [it] that the angle of the Midheaven should fall in the 11th, and they abhor that it should fall in the 9th. For its falling in the 9th decreases the quantity of the distributor's[370] dignity, and its falling in the 11th increases his honor and condition,[371] by the command of God. Likewise all places, if they [were] removed toward the receding and malign places (like the sixth, the second, and the eighth and the twelfth), it will be bad. For the 9th[372] and the 12th is bad, and it is good in the Midheaven, if God wills.

---

[361] The text reads, "he speaks," but the *dic- secundum* formulas at the ends of paragraphs are always in the imperative.
[362] *Tet.* IV.4 p. 9.
[363] This would be an ideal situation in Ptolemy's view, not a standard situation. All three of these are distinct for Ptolemy as well as other traditional authors.
[364] That is, if there is no planet making a morning appearance nor in the Midheaven, then the Lord of the Midheaven takes over, though it does not supply a fixed profession (*Tet.* IV.4 p. 10).
[365] Reading *super* for *propter*.
[366] Reading for *aut a Mercurio eos*.
[367] Rhetorius Ch. 84, *Tet.* IV.4 p. 10, *BA* III.10.2, *JN* Ch. 33 p. 298.
[368] Reading *trino* for *termino* (bound).
[369] Cf. al-Rijāl p. 302 and Bonatti p. 673.
[370] *Divisoris.* That is, the planet responsible for distributing a mastery to the native.
[371] Remember that dignity and honor are usually secular. Why couldn't the Midheaven in the 9th show low secular dignities, but a good spiritual condition and profession?
[372] Reading *ix* for *xi*.

[Chapter III.10: Friends]

For this, you should look at [1] the 11th[373] and [2] its Lord, also at [3] Venus and [4] the Lot of Friends, and [5] the planets which were in the house of friends.

And look at [6] the *mubtazz* over these places (whether it were one or two), and at the *mubtazz* over the Ascendant—namely [to see] whether between them there is one of the fourteen complexions (or some coming-together) which I have told you before. If there were something of these, the native will have many friends; and better than that if the sign and its Lord were of the signs of many children.

After this,[374] look at the *mubtazz* over the house of friends:[375] which if it were Venus, or Venus were joined to the *mubtazz* over the Ascendant, the majority of the native's friends will be from [among] women, and they will benefit him. Likewise if the 11th house belonged to the Sun,[376] the native's friends will be rich and noble men; and likewise all the planets signify according to their own substances.

Which[377] if all the significators (or many of them) were in movable signs, the native's friends will not persevere long in his friendship, and they will quickly hate him.

Likewise[378] if the *mubtazz* over the Ascendant were a bad one, or it impeded the *mubtazz* over the house of friends,[379] evil will come to the friends from the native. And if [it were] to the contrary, say the contrary. But if the significators were brought into harmony[380] with each other, they will have good and reverence and success, if God wills.

If[381] however the Lord of the eleventh did not aspect the eleventh, nor Venus the Lord of her domicile, nor the Lord of the Lot of Friends the Lot of Friends, the native will be of whose who have no commingling with friends, nor will he be social,[382] but solitary.

---

[373] Reading *xi* for *xii*. However, I note that *BA* includes friendship along with enmity and synastry in the treatment of the 12th house.
[374] See *JN* Ch. 35.
[375] Reading *amicorum* for *filiorum*.
[376] Omitting *erit planetae*.
[377] See *JN* Ch. 35, which adds the indications for common and fixed signs.
[378] See *JN* Ch. 35.
[379] Reading with *JN* for 'Umar's *et non erit ei almutaz super domum amicorum*.
[380] Reading *conformati* for *formati*.
[381] See *JN* Ch. 35.
[382] *Associabilis*. Technically this word means "liable to join with [others]."

And[383] if there were fortunes in the house of friends, his friends will be rich and of good bearing. But if there were bad ones in it, his friends will be poor and of a bad condition.

Ptolemy,[384] however, says that friendship and enmities come to be in three ways: either it is necessary that a man esteem his associate on account of the concord of the spirits which he has [with him], or on account of profit, or because joy or sorrow will conjoin them.

> Those who esteem each other on account of a concord of spirits, these are those in whose nativities it comes about that in the nativity of one, the Sun [and Moon] is in the same way as the Sun [and Moon] are in the others,[385] or they are cross-changed: that is, that the Sun [in one nativity] is in that sign in which the Moon was [in the other nativity], and the Moon in that one in which the Sun was [in the other],[386] or in a sextile aspect or trine. For these esteem each other naturally,[387] and especially if the fortunes themselves aspect the luminaries in both nativities, and the bad ones do not aspect them.[388]

> But those whose esteem was on account of joy or sorrow, they are those for whom it happens thus: that their sign of the Ascendant is one [and the same], or the [ascending] signs of each nativity aspect each other by a trine or sextile aspect, and it came about that the fortunes aspect the significator of each nativity,[389] and they[390] were free from the aspect of the bad ones.

> However, those whose esteem was in concord on account of profit, these are those in whose nativities it came about that they had the Lot of Fortune in one sign or the triplicity of the same sign, or in its sextile

---

[383] Cf. *JN* Ch. 35, both pp. 301-02.
[384] This division of friendships derives from Aristotle. See *Tet.* IV.7. *BA* focuses more on Lots.
[385] This is the best I can make of the Latin while being faithful to the plain meaning of the condition: *in quorum nativitatibus evenit sol ut sit id est in illis sint in nativitate unius id quibus erant in nativitate alterius eodem modo.*
[386] Omitting the distracting *a luna in uno signo.*
[387] That is, signs configured by sextile or trine.
[388] Reading *ea* (pl.) for *eum* (sing.).
[389] Reading *significatorem utriusque nativitatis aspiciant fortunae.*
[390] Reading *fuerint* for *fuerit*, suggesting the places being free.

aspect: because then the natives will be in concord, and there will be profit from one matter and [from] their effort in the same; and it will provoke their friendship, or their impediment will be from one matter, and they will be concordant in this on account of sorrow, and they will esteem each other on account of this. For this comes about if, in each nativity, the fortunes aspected these places, and the bad ones were cadent from them.

Ptolemy[391] said that there were even causes of esteem and enmity from the aspects of the planets to one another: which if Saturn in each nativity were comparable to the domicile, exaltation, [or] triplicity,[392] and Saturn aspected from a trine or sextile aspect, each native will be conjoined in esteem through lands and waters, or on account of old age and an ancient matter, and paternity, and household members;[393] and likewise falling, that is, in the square aspect or the opposition, or conjoined in one sign, enmity will fall between the natives, and so on, according to what I have said. He speaks likewise about Jupiter and Mars, Venus, Mercury, also the Moon and the Sun—namely about their aspect and esteem and concord, and on their strength, if God wills.

---

[391] *Tet.* IV.7, pp. 31ff.
[392] I believe this means that Saturn plays a key role vis-à-vis these dignities in each chart: for example, perhaps he rules the house of friends in one chart and the triplicity of the house of friends in the other.
[393] Or perhaps, "domestics" (*domesticos*).

[Chapter III.11: Enemies]

For enemies, look from [1] the 12th and [2] its Lord, and [3] the Lot of Enemies[394] and [4] [its Lord],[395] from [5] Saturn also and [6] the planets which were in[396] the 12th.

You will [also] look at [7] the *mubtazz* over these places, whether it were one or two: that is, look at the fourteen aforesaid complexions and comings-together. If there were some one of these fourteen between the *mubtazz* over the Ascendant and the *mubtazz* over the house of enemies, the native will have many enemies.

> If however the *mubtazz* over the house of enemies aspected the *mubtazz* over the Ascendant,[397] and it impeded it, the native will encounter differences with enemies, and ruin.

And if the Lord of the Ascendant had some power,[398] and the Lord of the 12th impeded it, the native will die at the hands of his enemies, and especially if that planet were Mars: then his death will be at the hands of his enemies in a war with [his] enemies.

And if the *mubtazz* over the house of enemies did not aspect the *mubtazz* over the Ascendant, the native will have few enemies.

And if the native's *mubtazz* were a bad one, and it impeded the *mubtazz* over the house of enemies, the native will have many enemies, but he would avoid them and the enemies would be endangered at his hands, and *they* will perish.

And look at the place in which the Lot of Enemies fell, because the native will hate that sign and that image of the circle.

---

[394] In *BA*, this Lot is left undefined. Abū Ma'shar (*Gr. Intr.* VIII.4.1510-16) gives two: the first is taken by both day and night from Saturn to Mars, and projected from the Ascendant. According to "Hermes," it is taken in both day and night from the Lord of the house of enemies (the 12th) to the degree of the house of enemies, and projected from the Ascendant.
[395] Adding *domino*.
[396] Reading *in* for *ex*.
[397] Reading *ascendentis* for *cadens*.
[398] This might mean, "dignity" (*potestas*).

And[399] if Saturn were in the house of enemies, he will destroy the house of the enemies; or if he impeded the *mubtazz* over the house of enemies, the native will not cease to rejoice regarding his enemies, and he will send them into death before himself, and he will see their ruin. Try it out likewise [for yourself].[400] And he even speaks about the presence of Mars [in the] 12th according to what I have told you, by the command of God.

---

[399] *JN* Ch. 36.
[400] *Similiter experire.*

[Chapter III.12: Faith][401]

For the native's faith, look from [1] the ninth and [2] its Lord, and from [3] the third[402] and [4] its Lord, and from [5] the planets which are in the third and in the ninth; also[403] from [6] the Lot of Faith and [7] its Lord.

You will also look at [8] the *mubtazz* over these places. Which if it were Saturn, and he were safe from the bad ones and from burning up and retrogradation (or if it were Jupiter or Mars or the Sun, or some one of the superior planets, and it were free from bad ones), the native will be of the worshippers of one God, without a diversity of intention. Likewise if the planetary *mubtazz* over the house of faith were free, the native will be saved: that is, he will safeguard his own faith, and it will not be changed to another.[404]

If[405] the Lord of the ninth and the *mubtazz* over it were Mercury, and he agreed[406] with the Lord of the Ascendant, the native will be contending in faith, and a disputer, having teaching in [his] words. But if Mercury were then made fortunate and oriental, he will have discretion in this, and he will acquire substance from this, and its end will be good and praiseworthy. But if [he were] impeded and occidental,[407] evil will come to him, if God wills.

And if there were bad ones in the ninth or in the third, he will have disputations and contentions in faith and because of a difference of teachings.[408]

Moreover,[409] for [his] faith, so that you might even look at a man's sect,[410] [to see] at what age it would be better, you will look at the Lords of the triplicity of the Lot of Faith: whichever one of them was a good one and of a better condition,[411] the native will be of a better faith and religion at that age.

---

[401] This topic's place at the end of the other topics in life is a hint that it was conceptualized during the Sassanian or early Arabic period.
[402] Reading *tertio* for *termino*.
[403] Reading *quoque* for *quo*.
[404] Note that 'Umar makes this a function of the *mubtazz*'s condition, whereas Abū 'Ali makes it (in part) a question of the sign of the 9th.
[405] This paragraph originally appeared at the end of the section on travel. Cf. *JN* Ch. 29.
[406] *Congruerit*.
[407] Reading *occidentalis* for *orientalis*.
[408] Tentatively following Hand in reading *causa disciplinarum distinctione* for *causis disciplinarum a descriptione*. But it could also read "from an indictment of teachings [in] matters," which amounts to much the same thing.
[409] This paragraph originally appeared in the next chapter on death. Cf. *JN* Ch. 29 p. 294.
[410] Reading *sectam* for *secretum* with Hand.
[411] Abū 'Ali adds, "and in the third from the Sun."

[Chapter III.13: Death]

Ptolemy said:[412] look at the planetary *mubtazz* over these places, and if the Moon were impeded [by Mars][413] in a comparable place, he will be impeded.

For if the *mubtazz* (and the Moon) were impeded in places [like] *al-Ḥawwāʾ*[414] (who restrains the serpent, and in Latin it is called Serpentarius),[415] or from the place of the serpent which is called *al-Shujaʿ*[416] (the interpretation of which is "Bold"), or [from the place] which is along the Head of the Dragon[417] in Scorpio, the native will die because of a serpent bite, or from the striking of poisoners,[418] or through the cleverness of some poison.

And if they were impeded in the place of the Vultures[419] or the Crow[420] or the Hawk,[421] his death will be without a burial, and the birds will eat him.

And if they were impeded in the place of Aries or Taurus, and Capricorn, and in the place of the Horse (or the Bull),[422] he will be killed by horses and animals.

And if they were impeded in the place of *Caput Algol* (which is an image which holds a head), and in the place of Perseus (which is a body without a head), it signifies that the native's head will be cut off.

And if the bad ones[423] were participating with the Sun or the Moon or Jupiter in the place of death, [and] after this they were impeded by the

---

[412] *Tet.* IV.9 pp. 39-41.
[413] Adding with Ptolemy.
[414] Lit. "Eve" (Lat. *alhaure*), but which Kunitsch (2006 p. 44) describes as the "Serpent Collector" because of the verb root. The connection between Eve and the Serpent is obvious.
[415] The constellation Ophiuchus.
[416] Lat. *Alsuta*. Hydra, but perhaps also Draco.
[417] Unclear at this time.
[418] *Venenatorum*, but perhaps "hunters" (*venatorum*).
[419] *Vultur cadens* and *vultur volans*, Lyra and Aquila respectively.
[420] The constellation Corvus.
[421] Lat. *Astur*, perhaps a synonym for Corvus.
[422] I.e., Sagittarius. These correspond to the passage on quadrupedal signs in Ptolemy.

bad ones, they signify the worst death. Which if they were opposite these, it will be by the hands of the rich and the king.[424]

Moreover,[425] if the significators of death were impeded and they were above the earth, the generality of their death [will be] appearing high up, like crucifixion and the rest suchlike. If these significators were impeded below the earth, their death will be from the fall of some thing falling from above, or a shipwreck, and the bodies of many of them will not be able to be found, especially if the significator of death were impeded under the earth in the burnt path or under the rays, if God wills.

If the Moon were joined to the Sun in one sign [or] in the square aspect of Mars,[426] or with [Mars] in one sign, the native will be burned up by fire.

And[427] if the significator of death were impeded, and the *mubtazz* over [death] in earthy signs, it signifies that the native's death would be from the falling of some thing which falls upon him, or in the earth or mountains. And if it were impeded in fiery signs, it signifies that his death would be by means of fire and wolves. And if it were impeded in airy signs, it signifies that his death would be from the gibbet, or through the hands of men, or on the backs[428] of animals. For if they were impeded in watery signs, it signifies that his death would be from submersion, or the fierceness of things creeping on the earth,[429] and he will be the food of fishes.

---

[423] Reading *mali* for *nati* with Ptolemy.
[424] See Ptolemy. The opposition makes things worse, it is not related the wealthy or the king.
[425] Cf. *JN* Ch. 37.
[426] Reading *Martis* for *mortis*. Cf. another version of this sentence in III.7 above.
[427] Cf. *JN* Ch. 37 p. 306.
[428] Reading *dorsa* for *densa*, with Abū 'Ali.
[429] I.e., "reptiles."

ON NATIVITIES
Abū Bakr, Son of the Great al-Khasībī:[430]

BOOK I: OVERVIEW, PREGNANCY, LONGEVITY

Chapter I.1.0: What is proper to know for him who wishes to establish the judgments of nativities

The first thing which it is proper to do in a nativity, is that we should take up the degree of the Ascendant and its minute; likewise, the degrees of the other houses[431] signifying the matters of the native (like his life, money, siblings, parents, children, illnesses, marriage-unions, death, travels, kings, friends, and enemies.

It is even proper for you to verify the planets. Therefore you should know their motions: namely their longitude and latitude, orientality and occidentality, stations, retrogradations; likewise their ascending and descending, and which of them are strong or weak, light and heavy, the superiors and inferiors, fortunes and infortunes, and their joys; and even which ones are of good mind or bad,[432] masculine or feminine; likewise their binding[433] and separation, ʾ*iqbāl* and ʾ*idbār*,[434] their changes, turnings-back, receptions and the conjunctions of their lights.

Likewise you should know the aspects of one of them to another, namely a right [aspect] and left one,[435] the trine, sextile, square and opposite, and the projections of rays;[436] the domiciles, exaltations, bounds, faces and triplicities,

---

[430] Lat. *Alchasili*.
[431] A straightforward appeal to quadrant houses.
[432] *Boni animi vel mali*. Meaning uncertain.
[433] That is, an application within orbs. The notion of applications as a kind of binding or even "gluing" can be found in Sahl *Introduct*. §5.3 and goes back to Antiochus (Schmidt 2009 pp. 161-64).
[434] That is, being in an angular/succeedent, or cadent place, respectively. See e.g. Sahl's *Introduct*. §§5.0-5.2.
[435] That is, dexter and sinister aspects.
[436] Possibly a reference to the "hurling of rays." See Rhetorius Ch. 21 and Schmidt 2009, pp. 202ff.

and their *jārbakhtār*;[437] likewise their addition and diminution, friendship [and] enmity, and eclipse, and which is superadding or subtracting in computation,[438] and their complexion.[439]

Moreover you should come to know the stable, movable, and common signs; the ones ascending directly and crookedly, and which ones [are] fiery, airy, watery, or earthy; likewise their colors and their forms, easternness and westernness, and which are southern or northern, spring-like or summery, autumnal or wintry; likewise their tastes and odors, their bright and dark degrees, the empty and smoky ones, and the degrees of the shadow, or shadowy ones, the windy and not windy; even the *zamīn*[440] degrees and the welled ones, which give chronic illnesses.

Afterwards it is right to know the manner, significations, and *biyābānīya*[441] degrees (that is, those of the fixed stars of the first or second magnitude).

You should not even forget the status of the Moon, like her adding and diminution, and the equality or inequality of her journey,[442] likewise her fitness, emptiness,[443] concealment and appearance,[444] and her place in the ends of the signs,[445] and [in] the bounds of both the fortunes and infortunes; likewise her conjunction or aspects to the fortunes or infortunes at the hour of the nativity, and even through the 40 days before or after the nativity;[446] and her conjunction and opposition with the Sun.

---

[437] *Algebutar*. The bound Lord of either the direct *hīlāj* or of the directed Ascendant. See *BA* III.1.10 and IV (throughout), *TBN* II.2ff, and Abū Ma'shar's *On Rev. Nat.* (throughout).

[438] This is a reference to motion in the epicycle and on the deferent circle. See Abū Ma'shar's *Abbreviation* II.

[439] Reading *complexionem* for *complexione* (which would make it seem that there is such a thing as adding or subtracting in complexion).

[440] Lat. *azemena*, from the Ar. "infirm, chronically ill, invalid."

[441] Or, "fixed," an Arabic term formed from Persian.

[442] This probably refers to her speed, whether it is average or not.

[443] That is, being void in course.

[444] That is, relative to the Sun.

[445] See *Carmen* V.5.8 for this clause and the next.

[446] See for example *BA* III.8.1 p. 156, and I.12.5 below. It is an indicator of violent death.

[Chapter I.1.2: The native's body, mind, and topics of life]

You should even know the form of the native, and his kind—and if the nativity is of a man or another animal, or of a flying [type], or fishes, just as[447] the order of the aforesaid 12 domiciles follows.[448]

Look even at the hour of the falling of the sperm into the womb,[449] and the native's stay in the mother's belly, and if the birth will be fast or slow, and whether (should he be born prematurely)[450] he will die in that very hour, or whether he will live a long time, or will have a short life.

Likewise, [know] the manner of the native in his nature and complexion, and his faithfulness and unfaithfulness, knowledge or stupidity, beauty or ugliness, obedience and disobedience; his slowness and quickness in matters; boldness and fear; his hardness and smoothness in speech; gladness, anger and sorrow; his [good] disposition in his heart in terms of those things which are said about him (and his bad disposition [about these things]); lying and truthfulness; strength and weakness; generosity and avarice; humility and pride; modesty and shamelessness, good fortune and bad fortune.

> You would even be able to know, through the stated observations, whether the native will be rich or poor, and by what means he would be able to make or lose money, and of what mastery he will be, and how he will behave in his childhood, and if he who raises[451] him is his father or not.

> You would even be able to know the status of his brothers, both the older ones and the middle and younger ones, and even the status of his sisters, or how many brothers or sisters there will be, and which of them will die before or after him; likewise the status of [their] friendship and enmity, [and] of their profit or loss relative to one another; and if the native's brothers will have his inheritance or he their inheritance, and which one of the brothers will be rich or poor.

---

[447] *Modo*.
[448] This indicates the type of life and behavior the native will have. Abū Bakr is not talking about casting nativities for pets.
[449] *Matricis*.
[450] *Abortivus*. Or perhaps, "miscarried."
[451] *Nutrit*, lit. "nourishes." Below we will see the ambiguity between feeding or nourishing the infant and raising it.

You would even be able to know the kinship of the native's parents, if they are of a small or great lineage, and whether they are of one status or different ones, and which of them (namely the father or mother) is greater than the other, and if the native will be loved by them or not, and if they will raise him or put him in the road; likewise, which of the parents loves him more, and which one of them (namely the father or mother or their brothers) he will be more like; and if his father will be infirm with a curable or incurable infirmity, and likewise the mother; and which will die first; and by what illness their death will be, and if the native will have inheritances or not, and when; likewise what the parents will have from the native in terms of profit or labor, and whether the native will stay with them or be separated from them.

You would even be able to know whether the native is fit to have children or not, and, if fit, whether he will have children,[452] and at what time; likewise how many will be male and female, if they will live or not, if they will advance[453] or not, and which of them will be raised up or pressed down; and if the male ones will be stronger or weaker than the female ones; likewise which of the children will be fortunate or unfortunate, free or slaves; and if they will die before him, or he before them.

You would even be able to know the status of the native's illness, and where his illnesses will be, and at what time; and whether the illness will be in the body or spirit, and in what limb.

You would even be able to know the native's marriage-union, whether he will have a wife or not: which if he is supposed to have a wife, in what way he will take her; and whether the wife will be of greater lineage or a lesser one than he is, if she will be a girl or not, small or great, noble or of the [common] people, free or a slave, and if she will be fortunate or unfortunate with him, or if he will obtain profit or loss with her, or if she will be a fornicator or not, if she will love him or not, if the native will be in the wife's power or the wife in the native's power; if the native will be jealous concerning the wife, or will have

---

[452] Reading *filios* for *filias*.
[453] *Proficient*.

trust concerning her, if he will care much about her or not; if the wife will be healthy or sick; and how many wives he will have, from which one he will have children; likewise if he will die before the wives or not.

You would even be able to know well how the native's death will be: if he will be killed by another or not, if he will die naturally through himself or through a shameful death, [or] if he will die in his own land or in a foreign land.

You would even be able to know his travels, and if he will travel or not, if the travels will be by land or by sea, and if they will profit him or not, and even at what time they will take place; likewise if he will make them openly or in a hidden way, and for what reasons; and if he will turn back from them to his own place or not.

You would even be able to know the native's mastery and his rulership, if he will have it from a king or not, or if he will acquire loss or profit from the king; in what way it will be for him with the king, whether he will be powerful or not, if he will die in the kingdom or outside the kingdom, if he will acquire some kingdom or rulership in his own land or in another, and how he will attain that kingdom or rulership.

You would even be able to know the status of the native's friends: whether they will be powerful or poor, or if he will lack friends, or if his friends will need him, or he them; and if they will love him or not, if men will esteem his friendship or reject it, and if his friends will obtain loss or profit from him, or he from them.

You would even be able to know the status of his enemies, and their multitude or scarcity, strength and weakness, and if he will incur loss from them or not, or if they will be outsiders or those close [to him].

And these things should be said about the 12 houses.

[Chapter I.1.3: Prediction, the *hīlāj*, *kadukhudhāh*, and primary directions]

Through the *hīlāj* and the *kadukhudhāh* and the planets aspecting them, you would even be able to know the status and quantity of the native's life, by the command of God.

Through the Lords of the triplicity you would be able to know the good or bad [which] there will be for the native in the first, second, and third parts of life.

Through the Lord of the bound (which is called the "distributor"), you would be able to come to know the native's fortune and labor.

By the *tasyīr* of the *hīlāj* to the aspects of the fortunes and infortunes, you will know the times at which good or evil will happen to the native, and how, and whether [it will happen] or not.

By the *tasyīr* of the Sun you will know his loftiness or being put down, and the status of the father and the older brothers; likewise that of [his] kingdom and rulership (if he had a kingdom or rulership).

By the *tasyīr* of the Moon you would be able to know the illness which he will have in body or in soul, and his marriage.

By the *tasyīr* of the Lot of Fortune you will know his fortune, height and elevation, and how he will behave in this.

By the *tasyīr* of the degree of the Ascendant you will know the status of his life and his foreign travel, and how he will behave in his own land.

By the *tasyīr* of the 10th house[454] you will know the native's works and masteries, and his honor, what he will have of good or evil, beauty and deformity.

By the *tasyīr* of Saturn you will know the explanation of the native's matters, you will know the travels, friends and matters of

---

[454] That is, the degree of the Midheaven.

grandfathers[455] and fathers and older brothers, and the status of their real estate.[456]

By the *tasyīr* of Jupiter you will know the friendship which the native will have with kings or powerful men, and whatever will be concerning form and beauty and its kind.

By the *tasyīr* of Mars you will know his fornications, nuptials, loves, friendships, loss or profit from women, legal actions,[457] words, and contrarieties.

By the *tasyīr* of Venus you will know love and nuptials, sexual intercourse and happinesses, goodness of soul and [his] joy with women and girls.

With the aforesaid, it is also proper to know the place of the Head of the Dragon and its Tail, and the conjunction of the planets with them.

And once you have diligently scrutinized the things we said, and you put together the figure of heaven well, judge in every nativity according to the judgments handed down in this book, in which I have explained and recollected (as best I could) the sayings of all the sages who were before me. But you should know that a sage, by his wisdom and subtlety, would easily be able to employ the propositions concerning the judgments of nativities declared in this volume, for truth and the true path in knowledge.

Chapter I.2: On the projection of seed into the womb

The earliest sages, who were of sound intellect and were proven in the significations of the stars, said that the projection of seed has a likeness, in the signification and status of the native, above all the significations taken from the Ascendant when the native goes out from the mother's uterus. For the projection of seed into the womb is just like the heat of fire, which exceeds all hotness of baths, and just like the string in a bow, iron in a spear,

---

[455] Or, "forefathers."
[456] Or perhaps, "inheritances."
[457] *Causas.*

a sword in the hand, and just like the weight[458] in a wheel; and it is the root from which the said things are extracted and established. Therefore, if you knew the hour and day of the projection of seed into the womb, and the places of the planets in the months which signify that seed, then you will be secure regarding what judgment of yours you could establish and make firm. Which if you were ignorant of this, perhaps you would be deceived. Therefore, I wish to hand down the status of the falling of the sperm, from the day on which it fell up to the day on which he will go out from the mother's uterus, and the quantity of his stay in the womb, and the order of the planets with him, by the command of God, just as the sages stated and preserved in their books.

You should know that the matter of the woman will be according to the likeness of foods received in the body, and the root of that matter is coldness and moisture. But when natural heat operates in the womb, it renders it hot and moist. But the hotness and moisture appearing in any limb of the body, makes [it so] that matter from every place of the [man's] body[459] descends through the motion of sexual intercourse, and becomes white like the milk existing in [a woman's] breasts—which, transmitted[460] from diverse sperm in the appearance of blood to the breasts, is turned to whiteness through the ripening of natural heat, just like [the man's] seed [is] through agitation and natural heat.

Therefore, first the matter of the seed descends from the brain, which is white, cold, and moist. Secondly, it is principally from the liver, which is hot and moist and the ore-mine of the blood.[461] But thirdly it is next from the other organs until it arrives to the testicles, and the testicles give it to the [male] member, and the member to the womb. And the sages say that the womb has many small sacks[462] or places in which that seed can be distributed. And the woman, according to the quantity of the places in which the matter is distributed, could have more sons or daughters, according to the quantity of the material in the said small sacks, which are seven receptacles. For if the seed only descended to one small sack of the womb, she will have a single son or daughter; if to two, two; and thus up to seven. Therefore when the seed would fall into the womb, the menstrual blood will

---

[458] Or, "equilibrium, balance" (*pondus*).
[459] Omitting a redundant *ab omni loco corporis*.
[460] Reading *transmissa* for *transmissus*.
[461] Blood was anciently thought to be produced by the liver.
[462] *Folliculos*, the root of our "follicle."

nourish it, and it will be the matter of that seed; and therefore that blood is wanting in women until the fetus would go out of the uterus.

When the seed would first fall into the womb, Saturn will dispose it in the first month, because he is higher than the rest of the planets, and his circle [is] superior. Therefore the seed will be cold and congealed[463] in that month according to his own nature,[464] and this according to the quantity of Saturn's coldness and dryness. And since Saturn's nature is more a neighbor of and disposed to death than to life, therefore the man's seed in that month will not be mixed with the woman's seed, but each will be separated like the white of an egg from the yolk, and thus it will remain from the day on which the seed fell into the womb until the first month passes by.[465]

Afterwards, Jupiter (who is a planet of wind and change) will dispose the seed, and the wind of Jupiter will move it, by the command of God, until each [kind of] seed is mixed together [and] made [to be] of one nature: and then the seed will be movable, from which motion in the vessel of the woman, nausea and a change of soul happens to the woman, indeed so that the whole body is changed immoderately by the change of the wind and seed in the womb. Therefore a native who had much of such wind will be wise, since that wind is more subtle than the soul, and it will be mixed with the body, and goes out of him before the soul [does]. And that wind has a seat in the [soul, the soul in the] body, [and it has its place in the heart], and the soul in the brain. For from that wind proceed the native's deliberations, just as from the soul proceed the five senses. Therefore this wind directs natural heat, so that when a man dies, heat of that wind remains in the man's heart, and afterwards goes away; from which receding the whole body gets cold afterwards and dries out. Certain sages said that when, in the second month, each seed (namely that of the man and woman) is mixed together by the virtue of that wind, he will be just like a sleeping person who always sleeps, indeed so that such motion cannot be said to be life or death; but in addition it is quickening with that wind, [and] the wind in the fourth month will mingle the soul with the seed, and it will remain in the body with the soul. But when that wind would have dominion over the soul, it will confer life. But when the soul will have dominion over the wind, it will stream the nature of sleep [into the native], and the seed will have a different change in

---

[463] *Congelatum.* Or, "frozen, curdled."
[464] Reading *suam* for *sui.*
[465] One would thereby think that the first month of pregnancy is the most precarious.

accordance with how one would have dominion over the other. For when one will have dominion over the other, its effect will appear, and the effect of the other will in some sense flow out: just as when the Sun would have dominion over the Moon by the conjunction, the light of the Moon will not have vigor on account of the Sun's light.[466]

Therefore Jupiter's wind will not be moved from the seed until the third month comes, which will then be disposed by Mars, because the circle of Mars follows the circle of Jupiter. And since Mars is a planet of blood, the seed will change into his nature and heat, by the command of God. Therefore the seed will be coagulated into the form of blood, and the wind of Jupiter will conceal itself and rest, [so] that it will be moved from the body through that wind, just like the nausea which the woman was having in the second month.

Therefore the seed will remain in the disposition of Mars until the fourth month comes, and then it will come to be in the disposition of the Sun, who will remove its overflowing moisture with his dryness. And it will revert [to being] as a mixed thing, in which God will give strength and soul, and the mind[467] will be completed in it, and they will appear in it, and he will receive strength and the shape of a man.

Afterwards, the disposition in the fifth month will revert, by the command of God, to Venus, through whom the shape of the limbs[468] is shaped, and their uses will appear. Then hairs will sprout on him, and he will take on sense[-perception].

Then the disposition of the sixth month will revert to Mercury, which is a planet of yelling and sensing. Then, therefore, his tongue will be moved, and his limbs distended, and he will beat in the womb with hands and feet, and his motion will be strengthened, so that he will not desire to remain in such a narrow place, but he will have trouble enough[469] seeking, with all his powers, an exit from the darkness of the uterus to the world.

But in the seventh month his disposition will come to the Moon. And since his shape is complete, and the strength of the limbs, if someone would

---

[466] Perhaps then the lunar phase at the beginning of the second month or after the prenatal lunation could show a predominance of mind (the Sun, a conjunctional birth) or body and lower soul (the Moon, a preventional birth).

[467] *Animus*. Note that the Sun is associated with mind, as he is in Valens I.1 and in many philosophical and religious systems (Platonism, Qabalism, etc.).

[468] Or perhaps "organs" (*membra*).

[469] *Satagit*.

be born in that month he will be complete and suitable for life. Which if he persisted in the uterus up to the eighth month, his disposition will revert for a second time to Saturn, from which he will be made cold according to [Saturn's] nature, and he will be congealed, and the coldness will remain in him throughout that whole month. Wherefore if someone would be born in that month, he will be cold and dry, and fit for a middling life,[470] and frequently many dead [fetuses] are born in that month, or they die suddenly.

Afterwards, in the ninth month his disposition will revert again to Jupiter: therefore those that are born in that month, on account of Jupiter's nature for life, are disposed in common [with his nature].

On account of which, one must know that those who are born in the months attributed to Saturn, Mars, the Sun, and Mercury, die quickly or go out [of the womb] dead, especially if the aforesaid four planets were made unfortunate. Therefore there will be an advance toward a life disposed in the months attributed to Jupiter, Venus, and the Moon.[471]

Chapter I.3: On the native's stay in the mother's womb

Certain people said that [the native's stay] will be according to the quantity of the sign in which the Sun is, toward the ninth sign, according to the space between his domicile and exaltation: because from Leo (which is the domicile of the Sun) up to Aries (in which the Sun is exalted) are nine signs. Therefore, give one month to every sign according to the stated method,[472] and indeed it will seem that the Sun would signify the matters of the native and its hour, likewise the ascending degree, the angles, houses, and his creation. Therefore, through him you will know the status of the native, and his years and times, loss and profit.

Therefore if the seed fell into the woman's womb, and the Sun were in some one of the signs, he will be the significator of it from the hour of the seed's falling into the womb, up to the hour of the native's going out from the mother's uterus. And the Sun will not be moved from that signification in the sign, and [from] its change, until he goes out from the mother's uterus. Therefore the Sun brings him forth from type to type, up to where he would

---

[470] Or perhaps, "for a life of moderate length" (*ad vitam modicam*).
[471] One can imagine this as being one reason for these planets being natural significators of offspring in delineations of children.
[472] See below.

arrive at the fifth sign [from] the place in which he was when he began: because in the said space of signs, the four natures (namely fire, water, air, and earth) are completed.[473] And then the Sun will revert to the nature of the sign in which he began: and this comes to be in the fifth month from the projection of the seed, in which the native's shape is completed, and his limbs are made into flesh, sight is opened, and he begins to be in the shape of his parents.[474] Therefore the fifth sign signifies children on account of the nature by likeness which it has with the Ascendant.[475] For if the Ascendant were earthy, the fifth sign will be earthy; and if it were fiery, it will be fiery; if watery, watery; if airy, airy.

And when the Sun would enter the ninth sign, and would have completed the triplicity of heaven and [completed] his own nature,[476] and he would equate his changes in the signs with his elevation, and descension, addition and diminution, the shape and building [of the native's body] will be completed, and the native will appear and be born, by the command of God, when he was complete in the womb: he will have hands and a face over his knees,[477] and his navel is conjoined to the mother's navel, through which he sucks the food by which he is nourished. Which if [the fetus] were male, his face will be turned toward the mother's kidneys; if female, her face will be turned toward the mother's belly. Therefore, when a male one goes out, he will have his face lifted up into the heaven; but a female one to the ground.[478] Therefore when he goes out from the darkness of the uterus, then on account of the flaying which he suffers, and the pressure of the wind existing in the mother's belly, he sneezes violently and emits painful cries.

And afterwards, if the nativity were diurnal, he raises up his eyes to the light of the Sun; if nocturnal, to the light of a candle or other light, and he is in wonder concerning the status in which he is, and concerning that in which he was before.

God has even put it that he would have a concern or worry in his heart,[479] and we see this by experience. For when we lift up little ones from the

---

[473] Probably because the Sun will have moved through signs of each triplicity by the fifth month.
[474] This is Venus's month, as stated above.
[475] Another explanation of the 5th house's significations (see also above).
[476] That is, having traversed all quadruplicities of the element he began with.
[477] That is, with his body bent in the classical "fetal" position.
[478] Unless Abū Bakr has this reversed, that would only happen if a woman gave birth while facing the ground.
[479] *Curam sui in corde eius metum.*

ground into the air, they always will hold themselves to us, or to our clothes; which if they cannot do this, they emit cries. And this is the first thing which God has put in [the child's] heart, and He has even directed the intellect in the brain, by virtue of which he seeks to nurse with the milk of the mother, and to suck her breasts; moreover to cry on account of one who hurts him, and to grow quiet with him who nourishes [or raises] him.

Therefore may God be glorified, Who makes such wondrous things by His wisdom, which man cannot reach. Blessed be even His name, for He gives life and death when He wills.

Chapter I.4: On knowing the *namūdār*,[480] and the hour of the projection of seed into the womb

If you wished to know the ascending degree and its minute at the hour of the nativity, and the native's stay in the mother's belly, direct the ascending degree and the planets [to the hour at which you believed he had come out of the mother's belly, and establish the angles.]

[4.1: First method] [481]

Afterwards, look at the Moon: which if she were under the earth between the ascending degree and the degree of the west, take the degrees appearing from the degree of the Ascendant [counterclockwise] up to the degree of the Moon, and double that. Then divide the doubled [result] by 24,[482] and what remained after the division will be days, and what appeared in the quotient-number will be hours,[483] which you should add to the 273 days through which the middle stay in the uterus is indicated; and what came out, will be the native's stay in the mother's uterus.

But if you found the Moon above the earth between the ascending degree and the degree of the west, take the degrees which are from the degree of the west [counterclockwise] up to the degree of the Moon, and double them.

---

[480] Ar. "indicator" (Lat. *animodar*). Cf. *BA* III.1.10 p. 67, *TBN* I.2, and *Tet.* III.3.
[481] This is the Trutine of Hermes, based on the position of the Moon at the approximate time of birth, with an assumed 273-day average gestation period. Cf. *BA* III.1.10, Hephaistio II.1, and Appendix C.
[482] This is equivalent to multiplying by 1/12, an approximation of the Moon's average daily motion.
[483] Switching "days" and "hours" in the text to match the paragraph below.

Then divide the doubled [result] by 24, and what came out will be days; but what remained, will be hours—the which days and hours you must add to the lesser stay (which is one of 258 days); and what came out will be the native's stay in the mother's uterus. From which it appears that the middle stay is greater than the lesser stay by 15 days, which, if you added [those days] to the middle stay, the greater stay will result, which contains 288 [days]. If therefore you found the Moon in the degree of the west [under the earth],[484] the stay in the mother's uterus will be 288 days.

[4.2: Second method][485]

Otherwise, direct the Ascendant according to your ability, according to what you wanted. Then take the degrees which are from the degree of the west up to the degree of the Moon. Adjoin these to the degrees of the equation put [down] in the table of the right circle, and divide the sum by 12. And what remained will be the average course of the Sun, to which you must add 258; and what came out after the addition, will be the native's stay in the mother's belly. Then extract from the average course of the Sun: you will have his course of days in the native's stay in the mother's belly to the hour of the exiting from the mother's belly, and what remained will be the average course of the Sun. Afterwards, verify the average course, and where you saw the Sun, look to see how many hours of the day they are. Then multiply those [hours] by the time of the hours. Afterwards you will find the ascending degree, which agrees with the degree of the Moon in the nativity. And then see which degree of the Moon it will be then, and project so much from the degree of that Ascendant, and what came out by the multiplication of the hours returns[486] to equal hours, which you will add with the average course of the Moon, in the hour at which the Sun begins to ascend on that day.

---

[484] Omitting *orientis vel*.
[485] This seems to be the continuation of the Trutine as Kennedy describes it in the work of Kashi (Kennedy 1998 Article XVIII, p. 142), which fine-tunes the time based on the position of the Sun at noon on the potential conception date. However, it could also be related to the method presented only in fragments in *BA* I.5, and referred to in Hephaistio II.1 and *Anth*. VIII.3 (and described by Kennedy on pp. 143-44). In any event I confess I do not really understand the instructions here.
[486] *Rediit*.

Afterwards,[487] direct the place of the Moon in her own sign, and you should know that the native whose stay in the mother's belly was from the middle stay up to the greater one, will have some likeness in his body which will be added in some limb of his body. And the native whose stay was toward the lesser one, will have a diminution or defect in some limb of his body.

4.3: Another way concerning the native's stay in the mother's belly[488]

Direct the Moon at the hour of the nativity, and you should know her place. Then direct her through one full year after the nativity, and through one full year before the nativity. Having done this, consider the aforesaid three places.[489] And if they aspected each other by the trine aspect, the native's stay in the mother's belly was nine months—and then the native will live, by the command of God. If however they did not aspect each other, the native stood fast in the uterus through eight months. But if only two of the aforesaid places aspected each other, the native's stay in the belly was seven months. Therefore, if you had the hour of the seed's falling into the womb, and the native's stay in the uterus, direct[490] the planets and their places, starting the months from the hour in which the seed fell into the womb.

[Chapter I.5: Detailed planetary dispositions of the months]

And so, these things having been explained, let us pass over to the signification of the months according to the order of the planets.[491] And we have already stated that Saturn has the disposition of the first month, from

---

[487] A medieval analysis of birth defects.
[488] This seems to be a way of determining whether the birth was premature or not, to help in judging the date of conception. See Appendix C.
[489] This must mean (1) the place of the natal Moon, her directed place (2) one year after the nativity, and (3) one year before the nativity. However, an unspecified timing mechanism is being used here, because by normal directions these places would only be about 1° apart. Could Abū Bakr simply mean the transiting Moon?
[490] Using transits, as described above and below.
[491] Here we see more clearly that this is the astrological equivalent of genetics, since the native's attitudes and abilities will be signified while already in the womb, and not through teaching or experience after birth. This must be why Abū Bakr reports that these months are considered by some to be more important than the nativity (at least in terms of the native's behavior and character).

the falling of the seed into the womb. Therefore if Saturn were strong in that month, and in his own domicile, exaltation, triplicity, bound or face, the seed will be light, and the pregnant woman will be freed from pain and illness harming her. And the seed will be lifted up to the upper parts of the belly, and her breathing [will be] quiet and her moral qualities will be beautiful.

And if Saturn were in the bound of Jupiter, the pregnant woman will rejoice because of her pregnancy,[492] she will have good thinking and confidence in God that he will free her, and she will be sound in body, and have good breathing, hoping that the end of the pregnancy will be good.

If he were in the bound of Mars, many hot things will invade her, and she will have illnesses and many changes in her body. And she will see menstrual blood in her pregnancy, she will have pains in the lower part of the belly, and her pregnancy will be from the right side.[493]

If he were in the bound of Venus, she will be happy and the seed healthy; she will have strength and healthiness in the pregnancy; and her color will be handsome, and handsomeness will appear in her face.

If in the bound or in the domicile of Mercury, she will be light and rejoicing in the pregnancy, [and] with much change and little rest, and this will last for as long as the pregnancy does; and she will recite the months and days of her pregnancy and birth.[494]

Which if Saturn [were] in his own descension,[495] decreased in number, in his own domicile or bound, the breathing of the pregnant woman will be uneasy, and she will have constriction in the chest, and worry in the pregnancy, and pain with little joy, and her mind will not be at rest, but she will fear much concerning her soul. She will have bad dreams, and she will see fearful things when sleeping and awake, and she will be

---

[492] Here and below the text reads "impregnation," focusing on the fact and status of the seed in the womb, rather than the general condition of pregnancy itself. I will tend to use "pregnancy" because it is more natural in English; but one should keep the distinction in mind.
[493] *A parte dextra*. Meaning unknown at this time.
[494] My sense is that the pregnant woman will be very talkative about what she is experiencing, both during the pregnancy and afterwards.
[495] That is, in the circle of his *awj*, as is stated below.

thinking every day about death, and she will ponder the birth much, and pain will descend to the lower parts of the belly; neither dread nor crying will be removed from her until after the birth.

And if Saturn were appearing in that disposition in the bound of Mars, the pregnant woman will have hot and moist pains, and bleeding ones, but she will be rejoicing and have much movement.

And if Saturn were so disposed in the domicile or bound of Jupiter, the pregnant woman will suffer a windy and hot illness,[496] but the end of her birth will however be healthful [and] strong.

And if Saturn were so disposed in the bound of Venus, the joy of the pregnant woman will be reduced, and she will wish that she was not impregnated, but the end of it will be good, and her birth healthful.

And if Saturn were so disposed in the bound of Mars or with the Tail of the Dragon, fear will invade the pregnancy, so that the fetus would perish in the womb, unless God wished to preserve it.

Jupiter has the disposition of the second month from the falling of the seed into the womb, and he signifies faith, sense, intellect and knowledge. Therefore if he were strong in the second month, and in his own ascension (that is, ascending in his own circle), and adding in number, he will dispose the native's sense and his simplicity, intellect and wisdom; and according to his ascension and elevation he will dispose wisdom and faith in [the native's] statements, and he will give to him knowledge which he did not hear, nor did someone teach it to him. And if in addition he were in his own *awj*, it signifies that he will be a reciter of things which other people do not know; and it will put the basis [for it] in himself, he will speak with foresight and will be reputed to be practically a prophet.

And if he were in his own domicile, it signifies that the native will be wise in the books of faith. And if he were in his exaltation, the native

---

[496] In medieval medicine, the sanguine humor and blood and air and Jupiter were all associated together. All of these have hot qualities.

will stimulate men to faith [and] he will teach them the miraculous things of the saints ([but] especially if he were in Sagittarius).

And if Jupiter were in the domicile or bound of Mars, the native will destroy men, and will stimulate them to killings and wars.

And if he were in the domicile or bound of Venus, the native will be a giver of sermons and a preacher, he will be speaking beautifully and be a singer, indeed so that he will stimulate men to tears by song and his words.

And if he were in the domicile or bound of Mercury, the native will attract men to himself by the charm of [his] words and their keenness.

And if he were in the domicile or bound of Saturn, he will be an experienced man,[497] and he will seek to do miraculous things to men, and to shock them in an amazing way, both by lying and by his art.

And if Jupiter were in his own descension, it signifies the detriment of the native and the poverty of his intellect; neither does he do nor say anything he has heard and seen from others, and this will be according to the quantity of his descension: which if he were in the opposite of the *awj* in that month, the native will have a lazy intellect; and if Jupiter were descending in his own epicycle, decreased in number, the native will be hard-headed,[498] so that he would be able to learn nothing new, and he will be like a beast who doesn't know how to do anything but eat and drink.

Mars has the disposition of the third month from the projection of the seed into the womb, and he is a planet or boldness and strength and hotness. Therefore if Mars were in his own ascension in the third month, it signifies boldness and the fulfillment of matters with boldness, and the native will have a strong anger and be light in body. He will have an appetite for lawsuits, and will provoke them without fear, nor will he feel sorry about any thing which he has done. And if in addition Mars were in his own *awj*, the

---

[497] *Experimentor*, in the sense of testing and trying things by experience rather than through theory.
[498] *Duri ingenii*.

native will be a beginner of wars and battles, and a sower of discord after peace is made—especially if Mars were in his own domicile or his bound, and in Scorpio. Which if the nativity were nocturnal (with Mars so disposed), the native will be a master of wars and death, and besides that bold in all matters, nor would he be able to tolerate with injuries. And if the nativity were diurnal, the native will be wrathful, have a great heart, and be a cruel shedder of blood, of little piety, with a cruel will, high in mind, and exceedingly boastful.

And if Mars were in the domicile or bound of Jupiter, it signifies that the native's boldness and strength will be with sense, and he will do things with deliberation and knowledge, he will seek to avoid wars, betrayals, and matters which are without cause.

And if Mars were in the domicile or bound of Venus, the native will be jealous to such a degree that on the occasion of his jealousy he will arrive at killings and other evil things.

And if he were in the domicile of Mercury, the native will bring in dread to others, with hastening and malice.

And if he were in the domicile of Saturn, the native will be wrathful and have a heavy [or grave] heart, and able to be moved to evil, slow to wars and killings.

Which if Mars were in his own descending, the native will be fearful, have a weak heart, fearing wars and the shedding of blood. And if he were in the opposition of his own *awj*, he will be a hermaphrodite (like women), feeling and tolerating injuries beyond measure. Which if in addition Mars were in his own domicile or his bound with the Tail of the Dragon, the native will be stupid, and will cast stones after men, and he will have a bad and filthy surname,[499] and, thinking about this, he will be quickly provoked to anger, and he will quickly cast stones about it.

---

[499] I take this to be a statement about his family background.

The Sun has the disposition of the fourth month from the projection of the seed into the womb, and he is a planet of height, loftiness, beauty, strength and victory, beyond the rest of the planets. Therefore if the Sun were in his own domicile or exaltation or triplicity or face in the fourth month, or other planets received him, it will signify the completion of the limbs and their perfection, handsomeness, virtue, and the ascent of the body: therefore the native will have a strong body and have all the limbs [strong], indeed so that by virtue of his strength he would be able to conquer wild animals and destroy them, and to break hard stones.

And if the Sun were in the domicile or bound of Mars, the native will have boldness with his strength, and completion in all of his limbs; and he will be magnanimous, on the occasion of which he will wish to be thought rich, and will take his things away from men without cause; and he will have power in his matters.

And if the Sun were in the domicile or bound of Mercury, or he were pushed and received by him, the native will be wise and rejoicing, and his strength will be with art, ingenuity and knowledge, especially if the Sun were in Gemini, because there he will be strengthened on account of his great ascent. Therefore [the Sun] will dispose the native in the shaping of the limbs and in the completion of his body, so that the native will perfect things quickly by the strength of his hands.

And if the Sun were in a sign[500] of Venus, especially in Taurus, the native will be beautiful, complete, stout, strong, astute and sharp, and his strength will be in the neck and shoulders, indeed so that with his powers he would be able to lift and hold up as much weight as three or four men can hold up. But he will be lazy, and weighty, and have a hard-[headed] intellect, just like a donkey.

And if the Sun were in some one of the domiciles of Saturn, especially in Aquarius, the native will be strong, but timid and a lover of rest and emptiness, putting up with injuries, nor seeking revenge from them, on account of the fact that he will be reputed contemptible by many people.

---

[500] Reading with Jag. for "strength" (i.e., a dignity).

And if the Sun were in his own descension, or would be moved less than his own average motion, or he were decreased in number, the native will be weak, with soft [or effeminate] powers, fearful of heart and with a hard-[headed] intellect (like a donkey), especially of the Sun were in a watery sign—and in addition the signification will be worse if the watery sign were movable.[501]

Venus has the disposition of the fifth month from the projection of the seed into the womb, and she is a planet of beauty, shapeliness and happiness. Therefore if Venus were in her own ascension in the fifth month, and in her own domicile (especially in Taurus), from the first hour of the day to the third, the native will be beautiful in face, with complete limbs, with great looks, ruddy, happy, and someone who provokes men to laughter by his words. He will even be filled with piety, a fornicator, having an appetite for beautiful things in order to adorn himself in the manner of women.

And if in addition Venus were in the face of Mars at the hour of the projection, the native, from the fourth hour to the sixth, will have flaxen hair, and varied eyes; he will be beautiful and lofty, without fear, not holding back [his] anger.

And if Venus were in the face of Saturn at the hour of the projection of the seed into the womb, the native, from the seventh hour up to the ninth, will be white, of subtle color, beautiful looks, curly [or wavy] hair on the head, dry in body, lean, having much illness and travels, and besides that retaining injuries done to him in his heart; astute, and insufficiently fearing God; a plunderer of foreigners, and ready for evils to be done.

And if Venus were in the face of the Moon at the hour of the projection of the seed, from the tenth hour up to the twelfth, the native will have a beautiful face and deformed[502] body, but he will have a large body with much flesh,[503] and much moisture and coldness. He will even be stupid and have a crude mind, weighty, asinine, fearful,

---

[501] I.e., Cancer.
[502] Reading *deformum* for *deformae*.
[503] *Carnis*. I am not sure whether this means muscle in particular or mere bulk (including being fat).

with little thinking and knowledge. And divide the hours of the night like [those of] the day according to this, and judge by them.

And if Venus were appearing in the face of Jupiter, in human signs (of which in this case the better ones are Gemini and Libra), the native will be tall and corpulent, with a beautiful body and face, having complete limbs, wise, upright [in character] and easy-going, but rendering evil for evil, serious in his acts, and commended in doing all things.

And if Venus (especially in the night) were in the face of Mercury, the native will have a lean face, a long jaw, round eyes; he will be infirm, with little flesh, a slender body, a liar, with much laughter and many words.

And if Venus [were] appearing in her own descension, and in the domicile and face of Saturn (especially in the dark degrees), the native will have an eclipsed[504] body, ugly in the face, a filthy appearance, weighty, sad, of little laughter, and always hurting.

Which if Venus were with some infortune or the Tail of the Dragon, in the face of Saturn, or burned up, the native will be made unfortunate in all of his matters, nor will someone have a desire to meet with him on account of the small size of his limbs.[505]

Mercury has the disposition of the sixth month from the projection of the seed into the womb, and he is a planet of teaching, eloquence, and knowledge. Therefore if Mercury were in his own ascension in the sixth month, the native will be of good eloquence, and his words will please men, and he will have great powers and be the secretary of powerful people; he will be provoked to laughter quickly and on a middling occasion, and without premeditation—and this will be more strongly so if Mercury were in his own domicile or bound. And if, with Mercury being so disposed, Jupiter aspected him, he will most eloquent, wise in books, and a wonderful giver of sermons, and expressing many words instead of few.

---

[504] *Eclipsati*. Evidently a misread of the Arabic, but the context shows it is not good for the native's body.
[505] I am not sure if this indicates being socially ignored or sexually rejected.

And if Mercury were in the domicile or bound of Jupiter, he will be of good eloquence, wise and subtle of mind.

And if Mercury were in the domicile or bound of Venus, he will be wonderful in speech and language, mild in word, and one who will ask questions frequently.

And if Mercury were in the domicile or bound of Saturn, the native will have an impeded tongue, indeed so that he would not be able to unfold his words well, but he will be of sound thinking and good intellect. Which if Mercury, so disposed, were in his own descension, the native will be practically a mute, especially if he would be placed in the signs lacking a voice.

The Moon has the disposition of the seventh month from the projection of the seed into the womb, and she is the planet completing the native's limbs, and the perfection of him. He therefore who will be born in that month, will be complete in limbs on account of the completion of the significations of the planets. And if the birth would be deferred to the eighth month, the disposition is deferred to Saturn. Therefore those born in that month will come out dead or will die quickly. And if the birth would be deferred to the ninth month, the disposition reverts to Jupiter, and he is a planet of wind and motion. Therefore the wind of Jupiter, by the command of God, moves the boy and leads him out into the world.

Chapter I.6: Whether the birth is legitimate or from adultery

If[506] you wished to know this, look at the Lot of the Father: which if it aspected the Lot of Fortune[507] from reception, from the domicile, exaltation, triplicity and bound, the birth will be legitimate; and if you found nothing of these things, it will be from adultery. And if the Moon were conjoined to the Sun, or under his rays, his birth will be furtive, and from adultery, and the native will be disturbed by an incurable illness. And you should know that

---

[506] Cf. *BA* III.4.2, which claims to be based on Buzurjmihr.
[507] Reading with *BA* III.4.2, for Abū Bakr's "Lot of the Native."

the aforesaid significations will be worse if the Moon were positioned in the Tail of the Dragon at the end of a sign.

Chapter I.7: On the native's progression out of the mother's belly, whether it was quick or slow

If the Moon were in an angle and in a feminine sign, the progression of the native will be hastened, and perhaps on the road or [in] the bath, or in another place outside the home.

If the fortunes found the Moon by aspect or conjunction, or if the Sun or the Moon [were] in a masculine sign of straight ascension in the nativity of a masculine [native] (or in a feminine sign in the nativity of a feminine one), they signify the hastening of the progression with good health and directness.

If the Moon were with Mars or in his good aspect, and Jupiter aspected them by a good aspect, it portends the hastening of the progression with the native's passing through and health. If Mercury were in the Ascendant and in a domicile of Mars, and Mars were made fortunate in a good place, judge the same. If the Moon were in the Ascendant or the Midheaven, having escaped from the rays, you will even judge the same.

If Venus and the Moon were in a feminine sign in the nativity of female natives, they indicate the mother's beauty and the progression of the female native, with hastening.

If Jupiter and the Moon were in a good place in the nativity of a male, they signify the hastening of the progression with health, passing through, and the mother's joy with the native.

If the infortunes were in the 12th house,[508] they signify a slow progression, with the oppression of the mother: for the mother will be taken infirm and suffer pain in the belly, and also she will have evil, sorrow, and labor from that progression.

If the Moon were separated from Saturn, it portends oppression and the difficulty of the progression for the mother, and also sorrow and labor from the pregnancy.

If the Sun, Moon, and the Lord of the Ascendant were in a feminine sign and one of crooked ascension in a masculine nativity, or in a feminine sign in

---

[508] For the 12th as matters just before birth, see Serapio, quoted in Schmidt 2009 p. 307.

a feminine nativity, it signifies oppression, sorrow, prolonging or labor in the progression of the male or female native.

Which if Saturn were stationary in some one of the angles, perhaps the woman will not give birth until [the native] touches death.

If a stationary or retrograde planet were in the Ascendant, it signifies the slowness of the progression, and oppression in the birth.

If the Moon were going to the prevention, and there were less than 12° between her and the point of the prevention, or [if] the Moon were void in course, the mother will delay in the birth, and she will have oppression and labor in it.

If the Sun, Moon, and Venus were in Scorpio, Capricorn or Aquarius, the mother will be burdened in the birth, and she will have evil and labor in it.

If the Moon were in a sign of crooked ascension,[509] and the infortunes aspected her[510] by a bad aspect, the progression [out of the uterus] will be difficult, slow, and laborious, and perhaps she[511] will die.

Chapter I.8: On the types of the native, and of what nature he will be, and whether he will be a man or a brute animal

You should know that the signification of the native in [his] types will be by no [other method] than by the motion of the planets and their changing in the human signs, and the parts of signs, and the angles. For when more planets were in angles (especially the Lord of the triplicity of the Ascendant, the Sun,[512] the Moon, the Lot of Fortune, the degree of the conjunction or opposition preceding the nativity), they signify the type of the native's loftiness, his elements, his nature and human shape. And if all the aforesaid (or the majority of them), were cadent or made unfortunate, and in signs of beasts, it is a sign that the fetus will lack a human shape. Likewise if the Lord of the Ascendant [did not][513] aspect the Moon, and the Lord of the sign of life [did not] even aspect his own sign, it is a sign that the native will be monstrous, or will have the look of the brute animals. And if in addition the

---

[509] Jag. adds: "in the Ascendant."
[510] Reading *ipsam* with Jag. for *ipsum*.
[511] Reading *illa* with Jag.
[512] The Sun himself, not the Lord of the triplicity of the Sun (and so on for the rest of the places listed here).
[513] Adding with Jag.

infortunes aspected the Lord of the sign of life, the nails and hair will be like that of cats and dogs. Which if the said infortunes aspected the Lord of the sign of life from the angles without the aspect of a fortune, the native will be of the kind of beasts hunting men.

Hermes,[514] who was the head of the sages, said that when a male planet would be in the feminine part of the Ascendant, and in a feminine sign, and an infortune likewise aspected him from a feminine part, [then], were the nativity nocturnal, or Saturn and Mars [were] appearing [in a place such that they] aspected the said planet, or Mercury were made unfortunate, or he were with Mars in a bad place, and the Moon [were] burned up in the middle of a sign (that is, not having latitude), and appearing in a quadrupedal sign or one of eight feet,[515] and the Sun bore himself according to this type, and besides that the Lord of the hour [were] made unfortunate or cadent, or occidental or retrograde, or crooked in his ascent, or were in the right part—that nativity will not be of a man, but of some malign spirit.

And you should not say he is of the animals devouring men, unless Jupiter aspected Mars, or Mars offered testimony to Jupiter. Which if Mars were with Saturn, the woman will give birth to a scorpion or serpent, or to some animal of like appearance.

Moreover, look at the twelfth-part of the seven planets, and principally of the Sun and Moon. Look even at the Ascendant and which planet was in it, and which would aspect it, and whether the Ascendant is of human shapes, or that of beasts. Which if the twelfth-part of the planets fell in a sign of beasts, the native will be like beasts or be monstrous, and this more strongly so if the Sun or the Moon would be in the Ascendant, or the Lot of Fortune, or the Lord of its domicile. But if a fortune aspected into it, the native will not be like beasts, but someone who raises beasts devouring men.

Likewise, if the Moon did not aspect the Lord of her domicile, and she were in its opposition, or the Moon were in a bestial sign and in the aspect of an infortune, it is a sign that the native will be like some one of the animals.

And I will show you a certain likeness which I have discovered in the books of the sages:[516]

---

[514] Source unknown at this time.
[515] Jag. reads, "bipedal," which goes against the idea of him being like a lower animal.
[516] The following two charts were devised by Dykes. Neither 1540 nor Jag. have diagrams.

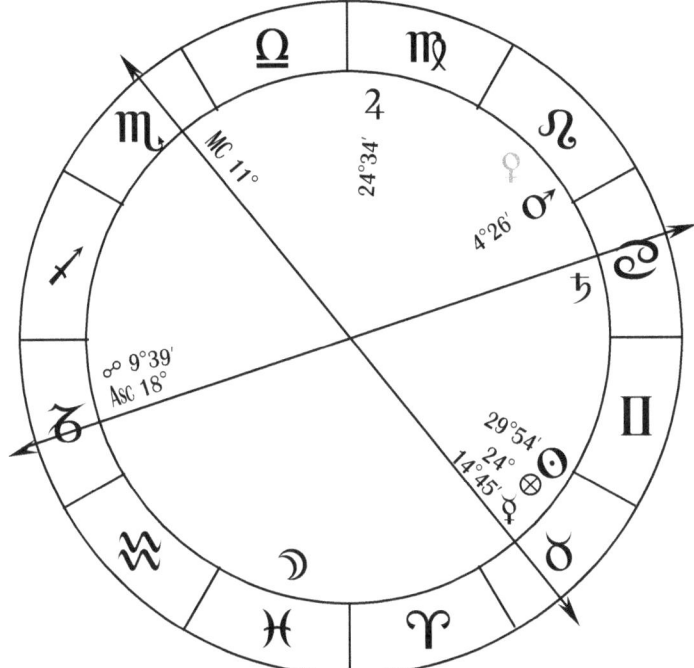

Figure 6: Monstrous birth #1

There was a certain nativity whose Ascendant was 18° of Capricorn, the Midheaven 11° of Scorpio, and the opposition in 9° Capricorn and 39', the Lot of Fortune 24° of Taurus, the Sun 29° 54' of Taurus, Jupiter 24° 34' of Virgo, Mars 4° 26' of Leo, and Mercury 14° 45' of Taurus.[517] Since therefore Jupiter, the Moon, and Mercury are cadent from the angles, and Saturn (the Lord of the Ascendant) [is] in the opposite of his domicile, and likewise Jupiter, and even though the Sun is in an angle, he is still cadent.[518] And Saturn, who is the Lord of the domicile of the completed[519] opposition, is in the opposite of the said opposition, and even of the Ascendant: it is a sign that the woman will not give birth to a man, but to a brute animal. And since the Lot of Fortune fell in a quadrupedal sign of the triplicity of the Moon,

---

[517] Based on the Ascendant and Midheaven, we can assume a latitude of about 39° N, a line running through the middle of modern Turkey. However, as it stands the chart is impossible and I have been unable to date it. The relationship between the Moon, Sun, and Lot of Fortune is impossible, as is the relation between the Sun and the pre-natal opposition. Nor can Venus be that far away from the Sun.

[518] A signal that being angular and cadent had explicitly blurred meanings.

[519] *Transactae.*

which signifies food or nourishment,[520] and even the Lord of the third and the Lord of the domicile of the Moon, [and of the Ascendant],[521] and of the twelfth-part of the Moon, [is] in a quadrupedal sign, and likewise the Ascendant [is] a quadrupedal sign: all of this signifies that the brute animal would be a dog. And since the place of the Moon (who is the Lady of the night) was aspecting Jupiter and the Lord of her domicile, and Venus (who is the Lady of the Lot of Fortune) was aspecting the Lot of Fortune from the square, and the Moon [was] in the 11th from the Lot of Fortune, it is a sign that his nurturing would be in a good place.

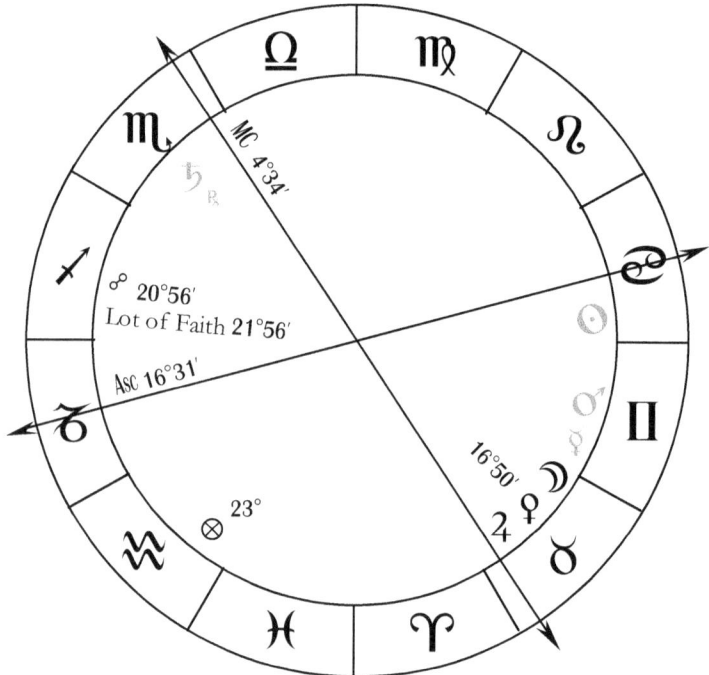

Figure 7: Monstrous birth #2

Likewise[522] there was a certain nativity whose Ascendant was 16° 31' of Capricorn, the Midheaven 4° 34' of Scorpio. The opposition preceding this

---

[520] Omitting redundant *in signo quadrupede*.
[521] Adding with Jag.
[522] This chart would have been cast for a latitude of approximately 31°, and it is reasonable to assume it is Alexandria (31° N 12').The date is June 19, 719 AD JC at 8:08 PM LMT. The positions are not all right, but I have used the values reported in the 1540 edition (with additions from Jag.), and added the remaining planets in gray.

nativity was in 20° 56' of Sagittarius, [the Lot of Fortune in 23° Aquarius, the Lot of Faith in 21° 56' Sagittarius], Venus in 16° 50' of Taurus, Jupiter and the Moon in Taurus. Look therefore at the Lord of the degree of the opposition preceding the said nativity, how the said degree is separated from him.[523] Therefore look at the Lord of the triplicity of the Moon (which is the Lord of the said degree),[524] how they are diverse, and one does not aspect the other, and how they are separated from the Ascendant and from the Lord of its domicile. Likewise look at Saturn, who is the Lord of the Lot of Fortune and of the Ascendant, how he falls from the second and third from the angles.[525] Then look at the twelfth-part of the Sun and Moon, and how it is positioned in a quadrupedal sign,[526] and how all the planets are cadent from the angles and separated (apart from the Moon and Jupiter [and Venus], who are in the house of the end of the matter below the earth).[527] All of this signified that the woman would give birth to a donkey.[528] And since the Moon is in the triplicity of the Ascendant with Jupiter, and in her own exaltation, it is a sign that the donkey would have beautiful nourishment and manner.

Chapter I.9: On the native's face

You should know that the ancient sages inquired into many things concerning the type[529] of men's faces, and their colors, in accordance with the disposition of the firmament and its signification; but some of them said that it is nothing. But the philosophers affirmed and verified it. But those who feel the contrary, argue thus: "Do you not see that someone is born in the land of the blacks, and you already know the type of his parents, and the blackness of the city in which he was born, and still you have found the Ascendant and its Lord, and besides that the Lord of the face of the Ascendant, and other planets contrary in the signification of his color, and

---

[523] The sign of the prenatal lunation (Sagittarius) is in aversion to Jupiter.
[524] Obviously something is wrong: the primary triplicity Lord of the Moon here is the Moon herself, not Jupiter; nor is the Moon or Jupiter in aversion from the Ascendant.
[525] This must be some kind of mistake.
[526] The Sun's twelfth-part is not in a quadrupedal sign.
[527] Note how Abū Bakr identifies the region beyond the IC as the house, rather than the fourth sign.
[528] There are perhaps many women who would agree that their sons are jackasses.
[529] Reading *modo* for *domo*.

that he ought to be white or red, or having white eyes[530] in the manner of the Italians or French?"

Therefore, let those who spoke in this way of believing know (and it pertains to the men who have prevailed [in this argument], lest they come into error, that if the nativity of a Moor (that is, of some Ethiopian) signified whiteness, we should not judge on account of this that he will be white or red, but that he will be less black than his parents. And likewise about some Italian or Frenchman: we should not judge by the signification of a strong signification of the blackness of Saturn, that he will be black like a Moor, but that he will not be so white as the parents. For those who [say] the contrary fall into error in front of those testing them, who seek to make them foolish, and they defame them, and condemn knowledge on the occasion of them.

And we have found in the books of the sages, that the nativities of children are overturned from the nativities of fathers, and the colors are changed according to the position of the lands; that whiteness and blackness will be according to the disposition of the Sun in his coming closer to, or elongation from, the regions—with the exception that some planets add or subtract in the colors of those being born. For we have found certain people black and certain ones blacker, but certain ones white and certain ones whiter, and so on concerning the other colors, according to the diversity of the Ascendant and the signification of the planets toward the color of the citizens of some city or region, and the root of kinship.

Al-Andarzaghar[531] said that the diversity of the color of men is hard to explain, and we have not found someone who might have explained it. And Ptolemy said,[532] in the great book of the planets, that in every [day] ascend 24,000 [degrees of right ascension],[533] and every [degree of right ascension]

---

[530] This probably refers to blue eyes, indicating that blueness and clarity were seen as similar.

[531] Lat. *Andoroar* (1540), *Amdasoar* (Jag.).

[532] Abū Bakr may very well be getting this from *BA* I.1 pp. 10-11. Following is an adaptation of my footnote there: "This is a reference not to Ptolemy but to a doctrine of assigning predictions to every minute of every degree (*myriagenesis*, see e.g. Firmicus Maternus V.1.36). The celestial equator turns once or 360° of RA every 24 hours: therefore every individual hour equals 15° of RA (360°/24 = 15°). But each hour or 15° of RA is therefore equivalent to 900' of RA (15° x 60'), which Abū Bakr or his source has implicitly rounded up to 1000'. So every hour has 900' (or 1000') of RA. That would mean a complete day of 24 hours would have 21,600' (or the rounded-up value of 24,000'), obviously making that many possible individual predictions.

[533] Lat. *Roboat*, for the Ar.

contains 1,000[534] moments, and every moment its own color, taste, and nature. And this is so precise that human sense could not examine it thoroughly, nor would a man know it, except God alone.

If therefore you wished to know the type and color of the native, look at what is ascending; and if you found its Lord or the Lord of its exaltation, triplicity, or bound there, judge by that [Lord]. Which if there were many planets in the Ascendant, look at the one who belongs to the face of the Ascendant, and judge according to its signification, but by mixing with its signification[535] that of the planet to whom the Lord of the face commits its own strength. And if there were no planet in the Ascendant, take firstly the Lord of the face of the Ascendant, provided however that it aspects the Ascendant;[536] which if it were cadent from the Ascendant, look at the planet nearer to the Ascendant or who aspects the Ascendant by a better aspect (like from the domicile, exaltation, triplicity or bound),[537] and mix the colors of the planets with the colors of the signs and bounds in which the planets were, and say the color or shape of the face [is] according to the color and shape of the planet, or [that] the color or shape of the body [is] according to the color of the sign.

Therefore you should know that beauty is attributed to Jupiter and Venus; but refinement and clarity to the Sun and Moon; but ugliness to Mars and Saturn. Mercury, however, appearing with a shapely planet, confers beauty—but with an ugly one, ugliness. Likewise the domiciles of the fortunes are said to be beautiful, and those of the infortunes, ugly. Even days and the bright stars assist in beautify and refinement; but nights, with their darkness, offer aid to ugliness.

Chapter I.10.1: On the colors of the planets

Saturn, from his own nature, makes the native gray-green[538] or dark-skinned, having coarse color and coarse [or thick] eyes, of which one will be

---

[534] Reading for *10 milia*.
[535] Omitting a redundant repetition of the previous phrase.
[536] Probably by a whole-sign configuration.
[537] This probably means that the "better" aspect will be from a planet in *its own* domicile, exaltation, *etc*. But one would think that an aspect by a Lord of the rising sign itself would be a good thing, too.
[538] *Pallidum*.

a little bit dark[539] or bigger than the other; having black hair on the head and a large face, and especially big jaws; the gaze of whom will be fixed on the ground. And in addition that native will be sad in mind, ugly in the face, having a bad look, jumbled teeth, and shaggy hair on the body.

Jupiter, from his own nature, makes [him] white, declining a little bit to blackness; large and prominent eyes, the pupils of which will be small; the hair on his head will not be perfectly curly, nor perfectly straight, but in the middle.[540] His beard will be curly, his type will be shapely, he will have the head (with the jaw) lifted up a little bit; a large and even nose. In his flesh and stature he will be even, and his face lively [or cheerful].

Mars, from his own nature, makes the native red, having red or inflamed eyes, and a round face; and perhaps he will have a red mark or scar on his face, or he will have a big nose. He will even have a sharp and subtle intellect; full of anger, handsome in his righteousness; his face a little bit haughty, jealous, sad, and speaking evil, and thinking evilly. His fingers [will be] long and with little flesh, his chest narrow, long in his stride, and remarkable[541] in his heart.

The Sun, from his own nature, makes the native large, the whiteness of whose eyes will be small, a found face, large head, his color bright, the forehead [or brow] wide, prominent eyes, silent in voice, even in stature, one who triumphs, and who speaks in derision about others without shame; his appearance suggests[542] rulership; in youth he will have yellow [or reddish-yellow] hair on his head, but afterwards he will be made bald.

Venus, from her own nature, makes the native have a shining color, and white mixed with red; beautiful eyes, the look of whom will be graceful and sweet like the gleaming dawn; the eyebrows small, his head round, the blackness of the eyes will be greater than the whiteness, his mouth fine and small, fleshy jaws, a shapely neck, narrow chest, short fingers, large legs; and perhaps that the whiteness of the native's eyes tends to blackness.

Mercury, from his own nature, makes the native to have white color tending to greenness; his face will be narrow, appropriate jaws, joined eyebrows, beautiful nostrils, a wide mouth, his eyes movable, small teeth, sparse beard, a beautiful face but he will be skinny; his stature even, his pace

---

[539] Reading *fuscus* for *luscus* ("one-eyed").
[540] I.e., "wavy."
[541] *Mirabilis*.
[542] Lit. "brings in" (*importat*).

short, fine limbs, having much sense and intellect, and expressing many good words.

The Moon, from her own nature, makes the native have white color, the face of whom will be round, the appearance graceful, a weak[543] beard but with a beautiful and clear color; a sound body and complete in limbs.

Therefore you should know the said types and colors of the planets, and mix them with the types and colors of the signs.

Chapter I.10.2: On the colors of the signs

Aries, from its own nature, makes the native to be of a color tending to whiteness; the hair on his head will be curly, his vision not straight, a long face, large eyes, small ears, and a large neck.

Taurus, from its own nature, makes the native to be of a reddish[544] color, a wide forehead, long nose, and flared[545] nostrils, and large eyes, the hair on whose head will be curly, erect and black; and his limbs diverse; the upper part of the neck thick and strong, his stride beautiful, but his sense will be weak.

Gemini, from its own nature, makes the native to be of a mixed color, an even stature, a wide chest; he will be faithful, and his masteries will revolve around writing or computation.

Cancer, from its own nature, makes the native to be of a pallid[546] color, thick limbs, and a shaggy neck; and the lower parts of his body will be greater than the upper ones; a big forehead and twisted teeth; he will have curly hair and [a curly] beard; he will be short of stature, and [with] small eyes and wide shoulders.

Leo, from its own nature, makes the native to be of a yellow [or reddish-yellow] color, and yellow [or reddish-yellow] hair on the head, and a beautiful stature, the upper parts of whom will be bigger than the lower ones, a broad chest, sharp vision, a serious face, thin legs; and he will be famous, but hostile in encounters.[547]

---

[543] Or simply "soft" (*mollis*, with Jag.).
[544] *Ruffi* (*rufi*).
[545] *Patentium*, "stretched out, layed open," as a bull's nostrils are flared and large.
[546] *Pallidi*, or "grey-green" as above.
[547] *Malae obviationis*.

Virgo, from its own nature, makes the native to be of black color, beautiful and even stature, and shapely limbs.

Libra, from its own nature, makes the native to have two colors, of shapely stature; he will be even [or balanced] in flesh, stature and type.

Scorpio, from its own nature, makes the native to be of an ashen color, reddish, white and small eyes tending to blackness, much hair on the head, a small face, long legs, big feet, light body, and one who will sow discord between others and will be bad.

Sagittarius, from its own nature, makes the native to be of white color, or yellow [or reddish-yellow]; white or yellow [or reddish-yellow] and fine hair on the head; with a long face and beard, large belly, the hind part of whom will be more shapely for looking at than the front part.

Capricorn, from its own nature, makes the native to be of a black color, shaggy, a dry body, long face, narrow beard, and fine ears.

Aquarius, from its own nature, makes the native to be of a green-black color, short stature, great mind, great goodness with men, liberal, [generating] great expense; and he will be wasteful; he will have one leg bigger than the other, his blood and color appearing.[548]

Pisces, from its own nature, makes the native to be of white color, a small head, suitable beard, wide jaws, big chest, and his limbs will be badly arranged, or he will be made lame or hunchbacked.

And you will know that the signs ascending directly make natives big in body, by their own nature; but those ascending crookedly [make] small ones.

Chapter I.11: On the one to whom the boy will be likened: namely to the father or mother, paternal uncle or maternal uncle

If you wished to know to whom the native will be likened, look at the face of the Ascendant, to which planet it belongs. Because if the Sun were the Lord of the said face, the native will be like the father; and if the Moon were its Lady, he will be like the mother. Likewise if the Lord of the face of the Ascendant were the Lord of the 4th house, and the native were a son, he will be like the father; if [the native] were a daughter, she will be like the mother. And if the Lord of the face of the Ascendant were the Lord of the place of

---

[548] I think this means that he will display changes in color easily.

the Sun, the native will be like the paternal uncle; and if it were the Lord of the place of the Moon, he will be like the maternal uncle.

Operate therefore in the remaining things according to this method. And, these things having been stated, we come down to the nourishing of boys.

Chapter I.12: On the nourishing of boys[549]

You should know that there are ways of being born. The first is, that someone would be born dead. The second, that he would be born alive, but will not live nor be nourished. The third, that he would be born alive, and will be nourished and live, but he will not reach old age. The fourth, that he would be born alive, and will live and be nourished, and will even reach a good old age.

In order to know these four types, it is necessary that you should know the eight divisions which follow, and they are: [1] the Ascendant and [2] its Lord, [3] the Lot of Fortune and [4] its Lord, [5] the Sun and [6] the Moon, [7] the conjunction [preceding the nativity] and [8] the opposition [preceding it].

[1-2] The Ascendant of [the native] signifies the native's likeness, type and his appearance, and [his] ascension[550] after being shrouded in darkness.

[3-4] The Lot of Fortune is said to be "the Ascendant of the Moon," just as the Ascendant of the nativity is said to be "the Ascendant of the Sun."[551]

[5] The Sun is the light of heaven and its candle, the king of the stars and their dispositor, the supporter of times and the director of the life of beasts, trees, herbs and bodies.

[6] The Moon, [because of] the circuit of her orb and its closeness to the world, [is] more like man than the rest in her beginning and

---

[549] Cf. *TBN* I.3, *Nativities*, and *JN* Ch. 1. *Nutrimentum* can mean either nourishment (i.e., food), or rearing—since presumably those who rear us also feed us.
[550] Reading *ascensionem* for *descensionem*. Cf. Sahl's *Introduct.* §3 p. 4 on the Ascendant.
[551] *Tet.* III.11 p. 35, and *TBN* I.4.1.

completion, and even in her diminution, destruction, and annihilation, and she is a partner in the signification of the stars and planets; and she has ascension and diminution with respect to the likeness of the native in his nativity.

[7] The conjunction is said to be the likeness of the parents, who behave toward the native in the manner of the conjunction and separation, and of the light which proceeds from them.

[8] The prevention or Moon's opposition is said to be the likeness of the native when he is in his strength, and in the middle of his life—which, so long as he passed it, he will begin to decrease every day until he reaches the end of his life.

And these things cannot be known except by means of the Lords of the triplicity (namely in their strength and weakness), and also the ʾ*iqbāl* and ʾ*idbār*,[552] in their firmness and fall: because the Lords of the triplicity signify the ordering of the day and night, and the change of the native will be with the succession of the night to day, and of the day to night.

[12.1: Type 1][553]

Therefore the native who will be born dead will be the one who will have three significators and the Lords of the triplicity cadent from the angles in his nativity—especially if some one of the infortunes, strong, had dominion for evil in the Ascendant: for then it will signify the native's destruction and fall.

If the Moon were in the west without the aspect of some fortune, and [in] one of the angles was an [in]fortune aspecting her, he who will be born will not live one hour.

Likewise if the Moon were in the 4th house, if one of the infortunes aspected the Moon from the opposition,[554] the native will go out dead.

---

[552] Lat. *Alicbel & Alicher*. See Sahl's *Introduct.* §§5.0-5.2. √*Iqbl* / means being angular, and √*idbl* r means being cadent, as is intimated in the rest of the sentence. Being angular is akin to being firm and established, being cadent or "falling" from an angle is akin to falling down and passing away.

[553] Cf. *TBN* I.3.1.

[554] *Carmen* I.7.13. Dorotheus also adds that the infortune might be with the Moon in the 4th.

When the sign in which the conjunction or prevention preceding the nativity, the *kadukhudhāh*, and the Lord of the bound of the Sun, and besides that the Moon and the Ascendant, and the Lord of the triplicity of the Sun by day (and of the Moon by night), and the Lot of Fortune, were [all] made unfortunate, the native will go out dead.

Look at the Lord of the [triplicities of the] luminaries in the day and night, lest some one of the planets be conjoined to it; also [look at] the place of the Lot of Fortune and of the Lot of the Hidden,[555] whether they are in fixed places or cadent ones, and who their Lords are. For if they were under the rays, and they would be aspected by the infortunes, [and] they would be joined to them or they were joined between them, the native will not taste life. And this signification will be worse if the infortunes aspected the Sun and Moon, or were bound with[556] them: for if it were so, the native will not live for one moment.

If all the planets, or the majority of them, were in the 6th, 8th, or 12th house, and the Lord of the Ascendant did not aspect them, the native will not taste life.

If the Moon were made unfortunate by an infortune not receiving her and in an angle of the Ascendant, or appearing in the 10th,[557] and the fortunes cadent, the native will not taste life—especially if the Moon were with an infortune in some one of the angles, or the Lord of the Ascendant or the ascending degree were in the square or opposite aspect of an infortune (unless the fortunes, free from every impediment, aspected the degree of the Ascendant or the Moon from some one of the angles: for in this case the native will have life, by the command of God).

The Moon in the Midheaven, in the aspect of[558] Mars, signifies that the native will go out dead, in vain.[559]

If the Moon and Mars were in the Ascendant, and Saturn in the west, the native will go out dead, particularly if a fortune did not aspect the Moon.

And if the Moon were in the west with Mars, and Saturn in the Ascendant, the native will not live one full day.

---

[555] The Lot of Spirit.
[556] The translator of Abū Bakr uses this verb (*alligo*) to indicate applications.
[557] That is, with the infortune being in the 10th.
[558] Omitting "of a fortune with," following Jag.
[559] *Per frustra*, which can also mean "in pieces" (which sounds like an abortion).

[12.2: Type 2][560]

A native who will be born and will see the world but not be nourished, will be if some one of the significators and the Lords of the triplicity were in the angles, and the majority of the others cadent from the angles and made unfortunate.

Hermes said[561] that if the luminaries did not aspect the Ascendant, or the Moon were under the rays of the Sun, the native will live a little bit.

The Moon joined to Saturn in his triplicity,[562] or in his square or opposite aspect, signifies that the native will live, but he will have bad nourishment.

If the Moon were with Saturn and the Sun, the native will not be nourished. And if the Moon were with the Sun and Mars, or besieged between Mars and the Sun, the native will have a short life.

If the Moon were in her own descension and in the west, the native will not live nor even be nourished, particularly if the Moon, appearing in front of the angles, were made unfortunate by Saturn.

If[563] the Moon were between two [in]fortunes,[564] and a fortune did not aspect[565] her, the native will live a little bit.

If Mars and Saturn were in the Ascendant, and the fortunes cadent from the Ascendant or from the sign of the conjunction or prevention, and the infortunes aspect the said two places, the native will not be nourished, particularly if the fortunes did not aspect the Moon and Sun.

If the Moon were in the same degree with the Sun, and Saturn aspected them by a square or opposite aspect, the native will not be nourished.

If the Moon were in Aries and in the opposition of Mars, and a fortune did not aspect her, the native will be of weak nourishment and a short life.

If the Ascendant and the Lord of the Sun's place, and of the Moon and of the Lot of Fortune, were under the rays of the Sun, the native will be of scarce life.

If the Moon were in Capricorn, and both infortunes in the 4th house from the Ascendant, the native will not be nourished.

---

[560] Cf. *TBN* I.3.2.
[561] Source unknown at this time.
[562] That is, in a trine (probably by whole signs alone, but more so if by degree).
[563] Cf. *BA* III.1.2, item [1].
[564] Reading *infortunas* for *fortunas*.
[565] Reading *aspexerit* for *aspexerint*.

If[566] the Moon, decreased in light, were besieged between the two infortunes, the native will live a little.

If the fortunes aspected each other by an opposite aspect, so that one is in the Ascendant and the other is in the west, and the Moon aspected them from the Midheaven or from the 4th house, the native will not be nourished.

If some one of the infortunes were in the 7th house, and the Sun and Moon (appearing peregrine) aspected it, the native will not be nourished.

If the Moon were in an angle, in the bound and aspect of an infortune, with a fortune not aspecting her, the native will not be nourished.

If Saturn were in the Ascendant, and Mars in the 7th house, the native will live a little bit; and for as long as he did live, he will have evil. Likewise if Saturn were in the Ascendant, and a peregrine Moon [were] appearing in the west, the native will live a little, and he will be ugly.[567]

If Venus, appearing in her own fall, were in the west, and Saturn in the east, the native will not be nourished.

And certain people said[568] that if some one of the infortunes projected its own rays upon the ascending degree, the native will not escape that hour, unless the fortunes assisted the rays of the prominent infortunes in that same place, even if the Moon and the Lord of the Ascendant and of the triplicity were free of the infortunes.

If the Moon were in the 7th or 4th house with an infortune, the nourishing will be bad, particularly if the said infortune projected its own rays upon the degree of the Ascendant, and that the Lord of the triplicity is falling[569] in the 7th house.

If[570] the Moon were impeded by the infortunes, and in her fall, and you wished to know if the native will be nourished, consider if the circuit of the Moon, being made through the places of the infortunes, and [having] returned to the Ascendant, and applying to the infortunes, and afterwards crossed over to the fortunes: if the native were not dead then, he will live until 12 revolutions are completed.

---

[566] Cf. *BA* III.1.2, item [1].
[567] *Turpis*.
[568] Cf. *Nativities* p. 395 and *TBN* I.3.2.
[569] *Cadens*. This might also mean that it is in the seventh domicile, but falling away from the Descendant by degree.
[570] Cf. *TBN* I.3.3, *Nativities* §1 p. 395, *JN* Ch. 1 p. 230.

[12.3: Type 3][571]

An infant who will be nourished and live, but will not reach old age, is one who has the eight significations and the Lords of the triplicity unequal: that is, some of which will be made fortunate, and some unfortunate, or some strong and others cadent, and especially the two Lords of the triplicity of the Ascendant (namely the first and second ones). For if some one of these were in a good place, and had more testimonies (like if the Sun is the Lord of the triplicity of the Ascendant, and [is also] the Lord of the Lot of Fortune), and free of the infortunes and fall, you will judge life and nourishment for the native, but he will not reach old age.

Dorotheus said[572] that if the distributor of life were in a good place, it signifies the native's staying in the world, and good nourishing.

If Jupiter were in the Ascendant, or aspected with a trine aspect, the native will be well nourished. Likewise, if Jupiter were in one of the angles or the succeedents, and Venus (being free from the infortunes, retrogradation, and burning up) did not aspect him, the native will be nourished and live, but he will not reach old age.

And if in a diurnal nativity Saturn were in the angles or [in] the triplicity of the Ascendant, the native will live and be nourished.

If the Moon and Mercury were in the 7th house and Jupiter in the 4th, the native will live.

If the Moon were free from the infortunes, descension and peregrination, and the Lords of the triplicity of the Ascendant [were] in their own domiciles or exaltations, or in the bright degrees, not retrograde or burned up, nor even made unfortunate, the native will be nourished and live, especially if the Sun were in his own exaltation and the Moon were adding in light and motion, with a fortune and free from Mars (because Mars destroys nourishing, especially in diurnal nativities, and especially if he were above the earth).[573]

If Saturn and Mars were in the Ascendant or another strong and fortunate place,[574] and appearing from under the rays of the Sun, they signify sound nourishing, and the native's staying in the world. And the diurnal planets in

---

[571] Cf. *TBN* I.3.3.
[572] Exact source uncertain.
[573] This is because Mars would be the malefic contrary to the sect, and would be on the side of the horizon he disprefers during the day. Likewise Saturn had good indications above in a diurnal nativity, because while the malefic, he would be the malefic of the sect.
[574] Omitting *tantum*, which emphasizes that this condition only holds while they are both in such places.

diurnal signs signify this same thing (and the nocturnal ones in nocturnal ones), and in the angle of the Ascendant or appearing in the Midheaven.

If it[575] transited the middle of the sign in which it is, and were that sign the Ascendant or the tenth, the native will live and be nourished, but he will not reach old age.

If the Lord of the triplicity of the Ascendant were strong and in the Midheaven, or in some strength, or in the 4th house, it signifies the beauty of the nourishment, by the command of God.

[12.4: Type 4][576]

An infant who will live and be nourished, and will reach old age, is one who has the aforenamed significators fixed[577] and strong in angles, and free, and not cadent from the angles. And likewise if the *kadukḥudhāh* of the native were strong and stable and [there were] a planet which pushes to it from places in which it would have some dignity, strong, and safe from retrogradation and misfortune. For then the *kadukḥudhāh* will give him its own greater years.

If the Sun and the Moon were made fortunate in succeedents, the native will enter into years, and will have it well, and will be the master of his own nature.

If the Moon were in the Midheaven and in the aspect of a fortune, and the infortunes [were] cadent from her, the native will have a long stay in the world.

If the fortunes were in the 4th house, the native will reach old age, and his death will be in a [condition of] great social standing.

If Jupiter were in his domicile and bound, it signifies the long length of life, so that the native will see his sons, and the sons of his sons. If the Sun were in the bound of Saturn, and in his own domicile or exaltation, the native will make a long stay in the world, and will have greatness at [his] death. If the Sun [were] appearing in his own domicile or dignity, so that the infortunes do not aspect him, the native will live a long time, and he will be the master of his own nature.

---

[575] I am not sure which planet this means. It is probably a variation on one of the "15°" rules" in *Carmen*.

[576] Cf. *TBN* I.3.4.

[577] This probably does not mean "in a fixed sign," but that they are well-placed in the angles (e.g., not separated from the axial degree by more than a few degrees).

If the Sun were free from the infortunes in the Midheaven, the native will have a long life with prominence. If Venus [were] in the Ascendant and the infortunes cadent from her, and Jupiter aspected her, the native will have a long stay, and a beautiful life in this world. If the Moon were in the Ascendant without the aspect of an infortune, the native will have a long life.

If Mercury, Venus, and the Sun aspected the Moon by a good aspect, the native will have a long life, and be even and sound in his nature.

If the Moon and Mercury were in the same sign, and besides that in the west or 4th house, the native will have a long life.

If the Lot of Fortune or its Lord were oriental, and outside the rays without the aspect of a fortune, in the Ascendant, the native will have a long life.

[12.5: Days of the Moon][578]

In the matter of nourishing, certain sages look at the following three conditions of the Moon: namely on the third day from the nativity, [and] on the seventh and fortieth days. For the Moon in these periods will cross over the nature of all the planets and signs, and she will fall from the one who was aspecting her, and she will aspect the one who was falling from her.[579]

> And therefore when three days are completed, the native begins to suckle milk, and gets to know the mother, and begins to perceive a taste in the sweetness of milk; after three years, he will begin to go on his own feet and speak, and his intellect will be made greater.

> In the other seven days the Moon will complete another part of the circle, and it will change her complexion, and she will have the nature of the signs,[580] and it will signify the multitude or scarcity of the milk, and the weakness or strength of the lactation. When the native will have crossed seven days, and were [the days] good, he will have trust in

---

[578] Cf. *Anth.* I.14, *BA* III.8.1, *Carmen* I.12.
[579] On the 40th day after birth, the Moon will be in roughly the sixth sign from her position at birth, and thereby configured by whole-signs with houses to which she was in aversion at birth, and vice-versa. For example, if she were in Aries at birth, she would be in aversion or unconnected to anything in Pisces, Taurus, Virgo or Scorpio. But on the 40th day, she will be in Virgo, which aspects all of these but is in aversion to some to which she was connected at birth.
[580] That is, she will have passed through signs of each triplicity. See above, I.3.

good nourishing, and of a long stay in this world, and he will be free from bad illnesses; then if he were the son of a Jew or Moor he will be circumcised, and if the son of a Christian he will be baptized or be taught the elements of [his] religion. And when the native will have reached seven years, then he will discern and go eagerly for[581] doctrine, sense, and life according to the matters of faith.

In[582] forty years he will complete the years of strength and nature, after which he will begin to decline everyday until the life which God gave is completed.

You[583] should know that if the Moon were cadent from the angles on the third day, unless she applied to a fortune by conjunction or aspect, it signifies the scarcity of milk and the difficulty of nourishing. If the significator of nutrition were an infortune (and especially Saturn), and were peregrine, it signifies the native's destruction, and that he will live in a disorderly way. The Sun appearing in the bound of Saturn in a diurnal nativity, signifies that in the nourishing of the native there will be labor and shamefulness [or filthiness]. If Saturn and Mars projected their own rays upon the bound of the Ascendant, they signify misfortune in nourishing. If the Lot of Fortune were made unfortunate in the 4th house, it signifies bad nourishing. If the Lord of the Ascendant and the Lord of the nourishing were bound up with the Lot of Fortune, and one of them strong in its own place, they signify the condemnation of the nourishing. If the Lot of Fortune were in the 11th house,[584] and its Lord without reception, the native will be bad for nourishing, and evil will be added to evil. When the Moon would be separating from an infortune, it signifies many illnesses for the native at the time of nourishing, labor in nourishment, and the native will have welts on his body and pains in his blood.

---

[581] Reading *arripiet* for *eripiet*.
[582] Cf. *BA* III.8.1 p. 156 and Rhetorius Ch. 77.
[583] Cf. *Carmen* I.12.
[584] Jag. reads "5th."

12.6: On the signification of the faces of the signs with respect to nourishing[585]

The first face of Aries signifies illnesses in nourishing and the pain of stones, and that rottenness will go out from his flesh. The second face of Aries will multiply illnesses, but he will directed [away] from them and be healed. He who will be born in the third face of Aries will be made infirm after five months from the nativity.

He who will be born in the first face of Taurus, pains and illnesses will invade him when he is one-and-a-half years old, namely ones persisting until he reaches around the end of life. And when he has thirty months, he will have hot pains. And when he is six years old he will have disorderly illnesses, and things weighing him down. He who will be born in the second face of Taurus will be sound until seven years have passed from the nativity, and then illnesses will invade him; but he will be freed from them by the command of God.[586]

He who will be born in the first face of Gemini, will be made infirm with a great illness by five months from the nativity. And when he is one-and-a-half years old, he will fall from one illness into another, until three-and-a-half years, and then eczema will invade him. He who will be born in the second face of Gemini, illnesses will not be removed from him from the second month of his age until he reaches one and-a-half years. And when he is four years old he will be made infirm by a serious illness, so that it will be feared concerning his death.[587]

He who will be born in the first face of Leo will be made ill after six months from the nativity, and wounds and the pain of stones will appear in his flesh, nor will it be removed from him until he reaches the seventh year of his age. He who will be born in the second and even the third face of Leo will be made infirm every day through seven years computed from the hour of the nativity.[588]

He who will be born in the first face of Libra, will be nourished with the milk of two women. And when he is three months in age, pains will find him. But when he passes nine months, he will have a flowing of blood from

---

[585] In both 1540 and Jag. some of the faces are missing, but they are mismatched. For example, Jag.'s first face of Cancer is 1540's first face of Taurus. More manuscripts are needed to make sense of them. Above is the version from 1540.
[586] The text omits the third face.
[587] Third face of Gemini and all of Cancer missing.
[588] All of Virgo missing.

his nostrils. When he reached the age of one and-a-half, he will be made infirm by a serious illness, from which, while he is healed, pains will invade him in the head through two years, six months, twenty days.[589]

He who will be born in the first face of Scorpio, pains will invade him after five years from the nativity.[590]

He who will be born in the first face of Sagittarius will have great illnesses after twenty-five months from his nativity, so that it will be feared concerning his death; and he will become ill in the head at ten months, but he will be freed by a flowing of the belly. When he even enters the tenth year, he will be made infirm by a serious illness, from which, if he gets better, he will live long. He who will be born in the second face of Sagittarius, when he reaches four months of his nativity, illnesses will invade him. And when he reached the second year, he will become ill with a serious infirmity, from which, if he gets better, he will have a long life. He who will be born in the third face of Sagittarius, pains and illnesses will invade him until he passes four months of his age. And if he gets better, he will live much.

He who will be born in the first face of Capricorn, it will be feared concerning his death, until two years from his nativity have passed.[591] He who will be born in the third face of Capricorn will become ill with a serious illness, and will have many windy [ailments], and his parents will die, and an alien[592] woman will nourish him.

He who will be born in the first face of Aquarius, will be made infirm after ten months from the nativity, and he will live after this, and he will have decent nourishment. He who will be born in the second face of Aquarius will be made infirm with a serious illness after six months from the nativity. He who will be born in the third face of Aquarius, an illness will not be removed from him until seven years from his nativity have passed; afterwards he will be healed, and his life will be prolonged.[593]

---

[589] Second and third faces of Libra missing.
[590] Second and third faces of Scorpio missing.
[591] Second face of Capricorn missing.
[592] Or, "foreign."
[593] All of Pisces missing.

Chapter I.13: On the abandonment of the native

Look[594] at the Moon: which if she were with a fortune in some one of the angles or succeedents, and an infortune will aspect her,[595] the native will be nourished, but his own mother will abandon him. Which if the Moon were in the bound of an infortune, both parents will abandon him. If Mars were in the fourth sign after the Sun in a diurnal nativity, and the Moon (appearing peregrine) aspected him from the 7th house, the native will be abandoned. And you will judge in the same way by Saturn in a nocturnal nativity.

Chapter I.14: On the beauty of the native's nourishment

One must know that the separation of the Moon[596] from an infortune signifies the beauty of the nourishment, and that the native will be fortunate amongst his siblings, and he will direct the works of the siblings.

If the Lot of Fortune were with the Moon, so that Jupiter aspected it in a diurnal nativity (and Venus [did so] in a nocturnal nativity), it signifies the beauty of the nourishment, especially if the said Lot and planet [were] appearing oriental in a masculine sign in a diurnal nativity:[597] his strength will be firm and sound in the matter of nourishment. And speak thusly about a planet [which is] occidental and appearing in a feminine sign in a nocturnal nativity.

And[598] in whatever way we judge concerning the beauty of the nourishment by the Lot of Fortune, so we would be able to judge by the Lot of Absence.[599] The Lot of Absence is taken in the day from the Moon to the Sun, and in the night the reverse, and it is projected from the Ascendant; and where the boundary ended, there will be the said Lot. Which if it were with the Moon or some one of the fortunes, or it aspected the Moon,[600] the native will be of beautiful stature and nourishing, and his teeth will erupt without pain.

---

[594] For this paragraph, cf. *Carmen* I.7, *ll.* 10, 19, 21, 24; also *BA* III.1.4.
[595] Reading *eam* for *eum*.
[596] Adding "of the Moon" with Jag.
[597] Jag. has them in "good places."
[598] For this paragraph, cf. *BA* III.1.4.
[599] The Lot of Spirit.
[600] Technically Lots cannot cast aspects. It must mean that it has a whole-sign relation to the Moon, or that the Moon aspects it closely by degree (probably the former).

Chapter I.15: On the knowledge of the *hīlāj* and the *kadukhudhāh*[601]

Now the *hīlāj* signifies the native's life and death, and by its *tasyīr* to the aspect of the fortunes or infortunes you will know the native's life and death, by the command of God. And you should know that the sages extracted *hīlāj*es by means of five places: firstly, from the Sun; secondly, from the Moon; thirdly from the degree of the Ascendant; fourthly, from the Lot of Fortune; and fifthly, from the degree of the conjunction or prevention preceding the nativity.

If therefore the nativity were diurnal, we would begin firstly from the Sun, who dominates the planets and times, and is the luminary of the day. Which if the nativity were nocturnal, we would begin firstly from the Moon, who is the luminary of the night, and who possesses the orderly arrangement of the night.

If therefore the Sun, in a diurnal nativity, is in the Ascendant or the 10th or 11th house (which is the house of trust and fortune), whether the sign be masculine or feminine, he will be fit to be the *hīlāj*—provided however that the Lord of the domicile, exaltation, triplicity or bound aspected him. If however some one of these Lords did not aspect him, the Sun would not be able to be the *hīlāj*. And if the Sun were not in these places, but in the 7th or 8th house, or the 9th, in a masculine sign, he will be fit to be the *hīlāj*, provided however that some one of the aforesaid Lords aspected him.

But Ptolemy[602] did not want that the Sun should be the *hīlāj* [when] appearing in the 8th house; but with him appearing in the 4th house and in a masculine sign, he is fit (according to the same [author]) to be the *hīlāj*,[603] provided however that some one of the aforesaid Lords aspected him. In the same way, Ptolemy denied that the Moon in the 8th house could be the *hīlāj*, but [could] well be in the above-stated places, provided that she were in a feminine sign, and some one of the aforesaid Lords aspected her.

If therefore the Sun were the *hīlāj*, the planet aspecting him will be the *kadukhudhāh*. But in nocturnal nativities we begin firstly from the Moon, just

---

[601] For this whole chapter, cf. *Carmen* III.1.1-26 and 2.1-18, *Anth.* III.1-3, *Tet.* III.11, *BA* III.1.5-1.9, *JN* Chs. 2-4, and *TBN* I.4.
[602] *Tet.* III.11 pp. 32-33.
[603] Abū Bakr is plainly copying 'Umar, who likewise attributes this view to "the same" Ptolemy. But Ptolemy did not allow the *hīlāj* to be below the earth. Since 'Umar is among the earliest Arabic writers in astrology, this attribution probably comes from earlier Persian commentaries.

as was said: which if she were in [the angles or] the 3rd, 4th, 5th or 9th[604] house, and in a feminine sign, she will be fit to be the *hīlāj*, provided however that some one of the aforesaid Lords aspected her; and the one which aspected her is called the *kadukhudhāh*. Afterwards, seek the *tasyīr* of the *hīlāj*, and its aspect to the fortunes or infortunes, and [to] their rays.

Which if the Sun and Moon were not fit to be the *hīlāj*, see whether the degree of the Ascendant were free from the infortunes, and its Lord strong and free, and appearing in the angles or succeedents, not retrograde, nor cadent or burned up: then it[605] will be fit to be the *hīlāj*, and take the *tasyīr* from that.

Which if the degree of the Ascendant could not be the *hīlāj*, look at the Lot of Fortune: which if it [were in] the angles or succeedents, and free from the infortunes, and also some one of the aforesaid Lords aspected it, it will be fit to be the *hīlāj*, and the one aspecting it [is] the *kadukhudhāh*—then take the *tasyīr* from [the Lot], and the times by it.

Which if the Lot of Fortune is not fit to be the *hīlāj*, look at the conjunction or prevention which preceded the nativity of the native. And if it were free from the impediments which we stated, and some one of its Lords aspected it, it will be fit to be the *hīlāj*. Look therefore at the degree in which the conjunction or prevention was, [and] take the *tasyīr* from it just as we said regarding the degree of the Ascendant, by giving a year to every degree. And if the *tasyīr* reached an infortune, with a fortune not aspecting that same place, the native will die in that year.

Certain sages said that if, in a diurnal nativity, the Sun would not be able to be the *hīlāj*, we ought to look at the Moon: which if she were in the Ascendant or in the angles, or in a planet where she has some dignity, and in a feminine sign, she will be fit to be the *hīlāj*. And likewise in a nocturnal nativity, when the Moon cannot be the *hīlāj*, look at the Sun: which if he were in the angle of the earth, the 3rd, or 5th house, he will be a fit *hīlāj*, and look at the *kadukhudhāh*.

Dorotheus said:[606] when some one of the five above-stated [places] could not be the *hīlāj*, and the Lot of Fortune were in the Ascendant, and its Lord made fortunate, but [the Lot is] in the Ascendant after 25° of the angle,[607] [the Lot] will be fit to be the *hīlāj*. If the Sun and Moon were in the 9th

---

[604] Reading with Jag. for "8th."
[605] I.e., the degree of the Ascendant.
[606] Cf. *Carmen* III.2.2 and 2.8-13.
[607] Here Abū Bakr is equating the "angle" with the axial degree.

house, not made unfortunate, they will be fit to be the *hīlāj*, provided however that in a diurnal nativity the Sun is in a masculine sign, and the Moon in a feminine one, and in their own domiciles or places, where they would have some dignity: like if Leo will be ascending, and the Sun in Aries; or Cancer ascending, and the Moon in Taurus.[608] For if planets were in their own domicile or exaltation, and triplicity or bound, they will have strength. But for a *hīlāj* which is taken from the degree of the Ascendant or the Lot of Fortune, or that of the conjunction or opposition preceding the nativity, we should not look to see whether it is a masculine or feminine sign, or whether the nativity is diurnal or nocturnal, but [rather] whether their Lords aspect the *hīlāj* itself.

If therefore you had the *hīlāj*, you would make its *tasyīr* to the places of the infortunes, because whenever it reached the square or opposite aspect of an infortune, and the fortunes did not project their own rays to that same place, one must fear concerning the native's death. Which if the fortunes did project their own rays to that place (namely that of an infortune), the native will suffer a great impediment or illness, but in the end he will be freed, by the command of God.

Certain others said that if the Sun could not be the *hīlāj* in a diurnal nativity, nor the Moon in a nocturnal one, and the nativity were conjunctional, then we should take the degree of the Ascendant; and if it were preventional, take the Lot of Fortune, and operate with the *tasyīr* of the Moon, just as Ptolemy said. Because even if the Moon is not the *hīlāj*, still it is necessary that she have a *tasyīr* to the fortunes or infortunes. For if she arrived to an infortune, it will make one thing from two, or will introduce an evil like death, or an effect of the infortunes, [or] it will assist death (if they would signify death).

If the Moon were the *hīlāj*, and the degree of the Ascendant made unfortunate in the root of the nativity, and it arrived with the Moon or with the Sun, or the conjunction of an infortune, at an unfortunate time [in] the nativity, the native will be in danger of death. Likewise if the degree of the Ascendant were the *hīlāj*, and made unfortunate in the root of the nativity, or it bound itself with an unfortunate Lord of the Ascendant or of the conjunction, the native will have a great illness, so that it will have to be feared concerning his death.

---

[608] Reading *Tauro* for *Piscibus*. Cf. *JN* Ch. 3 p. 233.

If you made the *tasyīr* by the degrees of the conjunction or prevention to the aspect of the fortunes and infortunes, and the *tasyīr* bound itself with one of the infortunes, one must fear concerning the native's death. And if the *tasyīr* would bind itself to the bound of an infortune, he will kill someone, or it will introduce an evil like killing, unless a strong fortune aspected that bound, or the Sun (appearing strong in the nativity), would arrive to the one with whom the infortune is bound with: for it will signify liberation,[609] by the command of God.

If you found the *hīlāj*, and one of the Lords having dignity in the [place of the] *hīlāj* aspected, make [that Lord] the *kadukhudhāh*, and it will give him years according to the strength of its own place, and even [according to] the planet to which it gave its own power by conjunction or aspect. Which if some one of the aforesaid Lords did not aspect the *hīlāj*, the native will not have a *kadukhudhāh*: therefore make the *tasyīr* for him with the degree of the Ascendant, from the place of the infortunes. And when it arrived at an infortune signifying the native's death, it will be the boundary of the native's life. And certain people did with the *hīlāj* just as they did with the *kadukhudhāh*, according to the addition or diminution of the years of the planet aspecting the *hīlāj*.

And you should know that if the Lord of the domicile of the *hīlāj* aspected it, it is to be preferred as the *kadukhudhāh* over the Lord of the exaltation; and the Lord of the triplicity to the Lord of the bound, and the Lord of the bound to the Lord of the face. Therefore the planet which had more dignities in the place of the *hīlāj* is more fit to be the *kadukhudhāh* than another which had fewer dignities.

> Therefore you should know that if the *kadukhudhāh* were in the 10th or 1st, strong, and free from the infortunes, and also in its own domicile, exaltation, triplicity or bound, it will give its own greater years to the native. And if it were peregrine in the said places, it will give its own middle years. And if it were retrograde or burned up or made unfortunate, it will give its own lesser years.

> But if it were in the 4th, 5th, or the 11th house, and in its own domicile, exaltation, triplicity or bound, it will give its own lesser years to the

---

[609] This is very much like the doctrine that the Sun's rays can shatter the besiegement of planets. Cf. *BA* II.6 and II.16 p. 33.

native. But if it were [in those places and] retrograde or burned up or in its fall, or made unfortunate, it will give months for its lesser years.

And if it were in the 6th or in the 12th house, or in the 9th, but strong and received, free from infortunes, it will even give months to the native for its lesser years. But if it were in the said places, retrograde or burned up or made unfortunate, it will give days or hours for its own lesser years.

Which if planets aspecting the *kadukhudhāh* were in the Ascendant, the 10th or 7th house, they will give their own lesser years. If they were in the 5th, in the 10th or 4th, and in their own domiciles, exaltations, triplicities or bounds, they will confer their own lesser years. But if they were retrograde, burned up or unfortunate, they will give months for their own lesser years. And if they were in angles or succeedents, and also retrograde, burned up or impeded, or in their own fall, as was said, they will give days or hours for the lesser years.

Therefore operate according to this method by adding with the fortunes and diminishing with the infortunes. And the fortunes add to the native's years by conjunction or the sextile or trine aspect, but the infortunes subtract by their conjunction or square aspect or the opposition.

[Abū Bakr] al-Hasan[610] said: if you saw the *kadukhudhāh* pushing to some planet, and that planet were strong, set the *kadukhudhāh* aside and take that planet as the *kadukhudhāh*, especially if it received [it], nor did it return its own light and its orderly arrangement.[611] For a pusher is like one who means to give something to another, [and] reception is just like one who receives a gift. And he who returns [the light] is [like] one who cannot take care of the received gift.[612] Therefore if the *kadukhudhāh* pushed to a planet having a power in the Ascendant or in the *hīlāj*, the signification will pertain to it.[613]

Certain sages said that if a planet were in its own dignity, and were in the angles and occidental, it will give its own middle years. Which if it were

---

[610] Lat. *Abucussan*.
[611] *Ordinationem*.
[612] See Sahl's *Introduct.* §5.11.
[613] Reading with Jag. for "Therefore if the *kadukhudhāh* of a planet, in the Ascendant, or in the *hīlāj*, pushed to one having a dignity, [you will] hand over the signification to that same planet—provided however that that planet does not confer its own power to another planet, but returns its own power [to] the *kadukhudhāh* itself."

retrograde or made unfortunate or under the rays, it will give its own lesser years, unless it were separated from the Sun. And if it were in the Ascendant, or the Midheaven, it will give its own lesser years; but if it did not have any dignity in that same place, and if it were in the 4th or 7th house, and it had some power in that same place, or even were it oriental, it will even give its own lesser years. Which if it did not have any dignity in that same place, it will confer its own middle years.

If the *kadukhudhāh* were oriental, appearing in the 5th or 11th house, it will give its own middle years; which if it were weak, it will confer its own lesser years. If the *kadukhudhāh*, appearing in the 9th house and having dignity in it, were oriental, it will give its own middle years. But if it were peregrine in that same place, it will confer its own lesser years; and speak thus if it were in the 3rd house, except for the fact that the 3rd house is less strong than the 9th. And if the *kadukhudhāh* were in the 6th or 12th house, and at the end of its own strength or dignity, it will give its own lesser years. Which if it were weakened in the said houses, it will confer months; if retrograde or peregrine, days; if burned up, hours.

If an infortune aspected the significator of life from the square or opposite aspect, it will subtract from it its own years from the given years. And if the said infortune aspected the said significator by a trine or sextile aspect, and from a good place, it will add its own lesser years with the given years. And if a fortune aspected it by any aspect, it will subtract nothing from the given years, but it will always add. If the Head of the Dragon were with the *kadukhudhāh*, it will subtract one-fourth of the years.

You should know that retrograde planets, because of the weakness of their significations, do not make good nor evil. If fortunes were in the opposite of their own domiciles, or in the opposite of the infortunes, they do not confer any good, but rather evil. And you should know that the infortunes are said to be worse if one aspected the other by the opposite aspect.

If the *kadukhudhāh* gave some years to a native,[614] and it were verified, an infortune cannot destroy those years. But if the *kadukhudhāh* were retrograde or made unfortunate, that malefic will [destroy those years, and he will have what is contrary to him].[615]

---

[614] Reading *nato* for *natos*.
[615] Reading with Jag. for "the malefic will have those years of the native, which will be contrary to him."

If the infortunes reached the dominion of the *kadukhudhāh* from the angles, and between them there were a space greater than its own body, they will not subtract their years, but rather they will add; but they will unite the native to innumerable dangers. A fortune will not add to the years of the *kadukhudhāh* from the angles, unless [the fortune] would receive [the *kadukhudhāh*] and [the *kadukhudhāh*] [the fortune]; but there will not be an addition or subtraction, except with binding.

If the Sun and Moon were made unfortunate, they destroy, and they add to the infortunes[616] in evil and destruction. Which if it were in their dignity or with fortunes, they will remove evil from the infortunes. But this is not to be said about Mercury: for if he were with an infortune, he will increase the evil and misfortune. If the infortunes were surrounded by the luminaries in some nativity, they will not have strength to harm (by the command of God), or at least they will harm [only] a little. Likewise if [there were] cadent infortunes in the nativity [which is not in the angles of the Ascendant or in the angles of the][617] *hīlāj*, they will not harm (unless it is only a little) in a revolution of years. If the Lord of the *kadukhudhāh*[618] were joined to the Sun in a nativity, he will add his own small years.

And the Head fortifies the *kadukhudhāh*, and the Tail weakens and introduces the native's illnesses.[619] Thābit [bin Qurra] said:[620] if the *kadukhudhāh* were in the same degree with the Head of the Dragon, it will add one-fourth of its own years to the *kadukhudhāh*; but if it were with the Tail, it subtracts its one-fourth from the *kadukhudhāh*.

And[621] if someone is born, the native's Ascendant signifies his life and strength. And if the planet which is the significator in the nativity is directed and it reached what is better, it will push the native from weakness to

---

[616] Reading *infortunis* for *infortunas*.
[617] Reading with Jag.
[618] I believe this actually refers to the *kadukhudhāh* itself.
[619] Reading with Jag. for "Even the Head of the Dragon does not add, nor even does it subtract. But the Head of the Dragon strengthens the *kadukhudhāh*. But the Tail weakens, and brings in illnesses to the native."
[620] Jag. seems to read *Dalbarih*, which suggests ['Umar] al-Tabarī, *TBN* I.4.4. It seems implausible that Abū Bakr would be quoting Thabit bin Qurra on this, since ibn Qurra was only born in 826 AD.
[621] Reading this paragraph with Jag. for "And if a planet in the nativity, appearing stronger, arrived at what is better than what then was, it will direct and impel the native from weakness to strength and loftiness. But if it arrived at what is worse, it will do the contrary."

strength and loftiness. And if it arrived [by direction] to what is worse, it decreases his strength.

If, in the nativity of some son of a king or prince, the disposition of heaven were bad, he will be unfortunate in his kingdom or sovereignty; and this signification will be stronger if the planets from which the misfortune arrived were in their ascension, especially should they be inimical (namely the one causing the misfortune and the one made unfortunate). For in that case the enmities of those living there and in that place will happen to the native. Which if in addition the infortune were strong, and the one which is being made unfortunate [were] in a weak place, and that the Lord of its domicile would aspect him, nor [would] a fortune [aspect] him, nor would the fortunes even apply by conjunction or aspect, [then] look, in the nativity of one whose life is short, at the descension of the planets, and at their misfortune, and besides that at the Sun, Moon, Ascendant, Lot of Fortune, and the degrees of the conjunction or prevention preceding the nativity, and [see] which ones of these significations are binding with an infortune: for then the native will die and his years will be ended. Nor will you look in this to the weakness of the infortune, since, in whatever way it was (whether cadent, retrograde, or burned up), and were one of the aforesaid significations to bind with it, it will kill the native—especially if his planets were unfortunate, and the infortunes in angles.

If the Moon were in the opposite of her own place, it will kill the native. If the Sun were in a cadent house at the time of the nativity, and an infortune appearing in an angle aspected him, the native will die in that hour in which the Sun reached the said infortune.

If the *kadukhudhāh* were made unfortunate at the time of the nativity, or in a weak place, [and] [its] aspect reached the square [or] opposite of its [natal] place, it will kill the native.

If[622] the native did not have a *kadukhudhāh*, look at the Lot of Fortune, and its Lord, to see in what sign they fell, and take the degree of the ascension of that sign in which the Lot of Fortune is (for the clime or latitude of that city in which he was born), and add on top of this the circuit or revolution of the Lord of the Lot of Fortune, and say that the native will live so many months, days, or years according to what the number of those degrees will be, or in accordance with what you will find in the years of the

---

[622] This is a Lot of Fortune method from *Anth*. III.11, mentioned briefly in *BA* III.1.7 pp. 59-60.

planets; for when the nativity is made unfortunate and the planets made unfortunate, and the Lord of the Lot of Fortune made unfortunate, say that the native will live for so many hours according to the aforesaid number. Which if the said planets were in the 10th house, [it indicates months and days, and] the native will not complete a full year, unless God wills.

You[623] should know that if the ascending sign were 29°, the *tasyīr* is of that 29°, and the better thing for this is that there is a fortune in the second sign, because the Lord of the second will be a partner with the Lord of the Ascendant in that year, and in the following year he alone will be [the significator], without the partnership of the first.

Chapter I.16: On the years of the planets which the sages used in the distribution of the nativity

And[624] these are the years, from the bounds of the planets which the sages used in the operation of the nativity. And they looked at the revolutions or bounds of the five planets —namely that of Saturn, Jupiter, Mars, Venus, and Mercury, according to their bounds through the twelve signs; and they made the greater years of the planets according to their quantity.

But for the Sun and Moon they took up their *firdāriyyāt*. And because the years of the Sun's *firdāriyyah* are 10, they multiplied them by 12 and 120 years resulted, which they called the greater years of the Sun. Likewise the years of the Moon's *firdāriyyah* are 9, which, multiplied by 12, will come out [as] 108 years: therefore the Moon's greater years are 108. But they took up the middle years of the Sun and Moon by the halving of their greater years and the addition of their lesser years, and the halving of all of them assembled together. For the greater years are 120 (as was said), which, when halved, come out to 60; on top of which, if we added the lesser years of the Sun (which are 19), 79 years come out; which, if we halved them, the middle years of the Sun come out, which are 39 ½.[625]

---

[623] This may be related to *Carmen* I.7.6-7. But it is definitely reflected in early modern astrology such as that of J.B. Morin, who allowed planets in the sign following a late cusp to participate in the matter of that house.
[624] Reading this paragraph largely with Jag. for clarity.
[625] Currently I do not know where Abū Bakr is getting this idea. The middle years of the Sun are traditionally 69 ½, which is simply the average of his greater years (120) and lesser years (19).

But the reason why the lesser years of the Sun are 19 is because there are 19° between the beginning of Aries up to the degree in which he is exalted. Therefore the ancient sages made his minor years [to be] according to the quantity of these degrees.

And since there are 25 days from the Moon's appearance after her conjunction with the Sun until [her sinking under the rays], they said that the Moon's lesser years are 25.[626]

But the [lesser] years of Mercury are 20 because there are 20 days from the beginning of his concealment under the rays of the Sun until his appearance.[627]

But the lesser years of Saturn are 30, and therefore he perfects the circuit of his circle in 30 years.

Likewise the lesser years of Jupiter are 12 because he perfects the circuit of his own circle in 12 years.

But the lesser years of Mars are 15, because he makes the circle from the house of his diurnal sign (which is Aries) up to his nocturnal sign[628] (which is Scorpio), in so many months.[629]

But the lesser years of Venus are eight, because she completes her own circle in eight months.[630]

But the middle [years] of the five aforesaid planets (namely Saturn, Jupiter, Venus and Mercury) are had thus: look at their lesser or small years, and add [them] with their greater ones, and then subtract a half, and what you arrived at after the subtraction will be the middle years.

---

[626] Reading with Jag. The Moon comes out of the Sun's rays at about 12°. After 25 days, the Moon will be about 12° on the other side of the Sun's *original position*, but not sinking under the rays in the place he would actually be at that time.
[627] This is roughly true if he begins retrograding under the rays from about 15° away from the Sun.
[628] Reading *signi* for signum, to parallel the previous clause.
[629] This is only occasionally true. In some cases he will only reach Libra; in others as far as Capricorn.
[630] This is not true, unless there is a special understanding of her circle at work here.

Chapter I.17: On the knowledge of the distributors or distribution of the native's years[631]

If you wished to have the distributor of years in the nativity, see to which planet the bound of the degree of the Ascendant belongs to, because that planet will be the distributor, giving one year to every degree.[632] And if the bound of the degree of the Ascendant passed by,[633] look at the following bound, for the Lord of the said following bound will be the distributor. And do thus from bound to bound, until the native's life[634] is complete.

Therefore look to the planets aspecting the Lord of the bound, and mix their significations with the significations of the Lord of the bound. Which if the Lord of the bound and the planets aspecting him were fortunes, their significations will be for the good; if infortunes, for evil. And if the Lord of the bound were an infortune, and a fortune aspected that Lord, mix their significations together, and judge according to this.

An example of this: if Mercury were the Lord of the bound of the degree of the Ascendant in some nativity, and Jupiter aspected him by a square aspect, and Venus [aspected] in a trine, but Saturn and Mars from the opposite, [then] because Mercury is the Lord of the bound, he will give knowledge and a good intellect to the native. But the aspect of Jupiter confers ornamentation[635] to him, and a great standing among high men, and the native will have the friendship of sages, and of Church prelates, not to mention profit from them. Likewise the aspect of Venus to Mercury will give beauty to the native, and a good friendship with men, and happiness with the wife and children. But the aspect of Saturn, who is a planet of pain, crying and sorrow, signifies that some one of his children will die, or that pains and sorrows will invade on account of the wife, money,[636] or melancholy. But the aspect of Mars to Mercury signifies hot illnesses, and evil by fire or the pouring out of blood, or the fear of death, and perhaps that he will be exiled from an honor, and will be forsaken in his social standing.

And if none of the planets aspected the Lord of the bound, the Lord of the bound itself will be the sole dispositor and distributor. However, we must

---

[631] For this chapter, cf. *Carmen* III.1.27-65 and II.19.44, *BA* IV, *TBN* II.2 and II.6, and *On Rev. Nat.* Chs. 24ff.
[632] In oblique ascensions, that is.
[633] That is, once the native has lived as many years as are left in that bound.
[634] Reading *vita* for *vitam*.
[635] *Ornamentum*.
[636] *Pecuniam lucri*.

consider the type of the native and his age, and in what time of life the Lord of the bound disposes him, and according to the quantity and likeness of the planets in the hour of the native, in order to judge as the sages said. For the sages said that if Mercury were the Lord of the bound of the degree of the Ascendant, he disposes knowledge, writing, [and] commerce in the years attributed to his disposition; and his disposition will be from the hour of the nativity up to the years corresponding to the degrees which had passed by the bound of the world.[637]

If for example there are so far three degrees of Mercury's bound to be crossed, we must not judge on account of this that the native will abound in knowledge in these three years, or that he will get himself involved with knowledge or commerce, or that he will have familiarity with princes, since it is not possible for him on account of his age. But we will say concerning the native, that in that short time he will speak and will be moved easily, and that he will be intelligent, of good looks and subtle. We will speak in the same way about the disposition of Venus: [not] that he will take woman as wives, or will expect to lie down with them (since his age is inconsistent with this), but we will say that he will be beautiful and well nourished, pious and with a sweet look—and so on regarding the dispositions of the other planets.

Moreover, we must look at the projection of the planets' rays to the bound: for if the infortunes projected their rays upon the first degree or following one (and so with the others), say that illnesses will invade him in the first or second year; and so on with the others according to the projection of the rays of the infortunes to the degree of the bound.

And I will give you a likeness or example in the disposition of the bounds, and the projection of the rays to the bounds: therefore let the Ascendant be the second degree of Gemini, and that 5° remains of the bound:[638] therefore, direct these degrees according to the tables of the equation of the ascension of the signs in your clime, and let us put it that there remains for Mercury 4° 40'.[639] We will say that the native will speak quickly, and be moved, and he

---

[637] It is by the symbolic revolution of the world that the degrees of the bounds pass across the horizon.
[638] According to the Egyptian bounds, the bound of Mercury covers 0°—5° 59' of Gemini. So the Ascendant is at 1° Gemini, with 5° left.
[639] The text reads as though it is "four minutes." But that would make the nativity around 57°-58° N, an unlikely latitude. Also, 4' only makes a little over 3 weeks of time, not eight months. But if we work back, 40' yields eight months. Finally, if 5° of the bound is equivalent to 4° 40', then each degree of Gemini is equivalent to 0° 56' of ascensional

will have a good tongue and intellect, and it will be so for four years and eight months.

And if Mars projected his own rays upon the second degree of the bound, say that the native will have hot illnesses in the beginning of the second year[640] from the nativity, or evil by iron or fire, or the shedding of blood; and you will judge according to the quality of the signification of Mars, and his ascent or descent, or according to the nature of the sign in which[641] Mars is. And you will do the same for all planets projecting their rays upon the degree of the bound, according to their natures, and those of the signs in which they are.

And when the bound of Mercury is completed, the disposition or distribution arrives to the bound of Jupiter: and you will judge thus regarding the other bounds and [planets which rule them and aspect them].[642] For if Jupiter disposed the native through his dominion in the bound, the native will be well fortunate, and have good encounters, and a good life, and be esteemed by his relatives. And if Saturn projected his rays upon some degree of the said bound, in the first and second year the native will incur cold pains, or will have some impediment from a fall or crash (and thus with the others according to the number of that degree), or will suffer crying and difficulties on account of friends or neighbors.

And when the disposition reached Mars, the native will take up travels and many labors, and foreign ones, he will have friendship with kings, he will lay waste to strangers' places, and will have many illnesses because of which he will incur the fear of death.

And when the disposition reached Saturn, the native will have evil labor and illness, and fevers and cold will invade him, and his body will be made infirm, nor will things begun by him be perfected, and he will be very lonely. Which if he had a wife or offspring, he will incur pain and sorrow on account of them.

Therefore when the bounds of the sign of Gemini were complete, cross over to the following sign, by doing with the bounds of it just as you did with

---

time, or 28° for all of Gemini. This places the example nativity at 45° N. Thus it seems Abū Bakr simply chose the value in the middle of his table, between 0° N and 90° N.

[640] There is a mix-up between the cardinal and ordinal numbers. Abū Bakr means to say that the Ascendant is at 1° Gemini, and the aspect of Mars falls at 2° Gemini, officially taking effect after roughly one year.

[641] Reading *quo* for *quibus*.

[642] Reading for *terminorum et planetarum qui eis dominantur*.

the bounds of the sign of Gemini. And thus it must be done from sign to sign, from bound to bound, up to the end of the native's life.

BOOK II: TOPICS

Chapter II.1.0: On the native's morals and his nature

You should know that the nature and morals of the native are distinguished according to the significations and natures of the seven planets in [their] shapes and morals:

For Saturn, from his own nature, signifies laziness, stupidity, foulness, fear, servitude, injury, lying, sorrow, and a bad will in the heart.

Jupiter, from his own nature, signifies law, faith, knowledge, humbleness, modesty, faithfulness, liberality, patience, sense, sobriety, and a clear face.

Mars, from his own nature, signifies wrath, disgust, violence, wastefulness, cunning, thieving, immodesty, attacks.[643]

The Sun, from his own nature, signifies strength, loftiness, honesty, and great power.

Venus, from her own nature, signifies humbleness, piety, a good will, the esteem of the heart, happiness, and good morals, except that the native will be reputed to be impertinent and effeminate.

Mercury, from his own nature, signifies commerce, speech, the recitation of histories, intellect, quickness of discourse, grammar, logic, rhetoric, arithmetic, and astrology.

The Moon, from her own nature, signifies a heavy tread, weakness, misery, travels, whisperings, and the introduction of evil [into things].

And these significations of the planets will be strong or weak according to the strength or weakness of the planets in themselves, and in their places. Therefore if some one of the planets were in the Ascendant or the Midheaven, it will give morals and a shape to the native according to its

---

[643] Reading *laesionem* for *laetitiam*.

strength; which if a planet inimical to it aspected it, it will alter the morals given, according to the strength or weakness of the aspecting planet. But if the said planets would not be inimical, neither amongst themselves nor by aspect, then the morals given by the first planet will be strengthened, so that if the first planet gave modesty to the native, he himself will be truly modest, so that he will hardly hear to speak;[644] and it must be judged thus for the other significations of morals by means of the significating[645] planets. But if the said planets are inimical to each other by aspect or naturally, one will render its own signification upon the other, and one changes the morals and peculiar qualities of the other, just as you could see here: for in the nativity of one who is without fear, or bold, you will find Mars in the Ascendant or in another strong place.

> And if the Moon or the Lord of the Ascendant aspected him, and he were in a strong place (so that he would have some dignity there),[646] the native will be a lord and master of soldiers, and have much boldness, and great powers, [and] the boldness will appear from out of the source in his heart; he will strive to kill by hand, he will love slaughter, violence and insanity, he will be a traitor, of a hard and ferocious heart, a thick liver and long anger.

> And if Saturn aspected [Mars], he will give him the deliberation of a bad heart, fear, laziness, misery, heaviness, a thickness of heart, and sorrow in his matters.

> And if Jupiter aspected Mars, he will break his anger, and decrease his furor, and will make him come down; he will restrain his frivolity, and will make him gain wealth more quietly than by war; he will restrain his furor, so that he will not kill someone with his own hand, and besides that he will make him turn back from places where he would be captured or killed.

---

[644] This is obviously an idiom, and its meaning seems to be the opposite, just as when we tease quiet people by telling them to stop speaking so much.

[645] Reading *significantes* for *significatis*.

[646] This is an important point not mentioned before: Mars (or any other planet) should be joined to the Moon or the Lord of the Ascendant.

And if the Sun aspected Mars, he will give him strength, dominion, and mastery over men and soldiers, not to mention beauty of form, military discipline, and intellect.

And if Venus aspected Mars, the native will be a great lover of women, and he will have womanly moral qualities, and he will expose himself and his soul to evil and death on account of women and jealousy of them, for he will be jealous beyond measure.

And if Mercury aspected Mars, the native will be fearful, solitary, and someone who will in no way please others, nor even will others please him; he will be stupid in his approach,[647] and lying much, he says what he doesn't know, and wants to do what he cannot.

The *biyābānīya*[648] stars even confer their own significations and peculiar qualities to the native: which, were they with the Sun and the rest of the planets, they confer great and sudden fortune from their own nature. When the *biyābānīya* star which is in the second degree of Taurus (having southern latitude, and second magnitude, not to mention being of the nature of Mars)[649] were in the Ascendant or the Midheaven in a nocturnal nativity, the native will be a soldier, and a master and organizer[650] of wars, and an eyewitness of nearby slaughter, having high greatness, and someone who will be scorned under some condition. But if the nativity were a diurnal one, the native will have a hard intellect, bad profit, and someone who will obtain disgrace. And if instead of the said *biyābānīya* star there were some star of the nature of Jupiter and Mars,[651] the native will be a master of soldiers, and he will go with many banners, and he will be elevated in dominion, and high in his own place, [having] great fame, powerful in matters, fortunate and wise in war, he will have power in faraway lands, he will be strong in cities and lands, he will esteem truth, and will be praised by many.

---

[647] *Incessu*. Normally this refers to one's style of walking, or else advancing in attack.
[648] That is, "fixed." In *BA* III.2.1 these are associated with eminence and prosperity (as they are below in II.2), but here Abū Bakr wants to associate this star at least with character.
[649] *BA* III.2.1 p. 79, Rhetorius Ch. 58 p. 104. This must be Pollux (β Gemini).
[650] Or, an "ordainer of wars," in the sense that he starts wars.
[651] See *BA* III.2.1, p. 78 and Rhetorius Ch. 58 p. 102. These are: Regulus (α Leo), Antares (α Scorpio), Sirius (α Canis Major), Menkalinan (β Auriga), and Altair (α Aquila).

Mars in a nocturnal nativity, appearing in his own domicile, signifies that the native will be one master, and he will have others under himself, and he will be a good soldier, and fortunate in slaughter and in wars, and always conquering, and wise in wars. And if he were in his own domicile in a diurnal nativity, the native will be lazy in those things in which he ought to make money; infirm, greedy, an evil plunderer of strangers, a fornicator, esteeming murders and evils, violent and unsound.[652] And if Mars were in a domicile of Saturn, the native will have a fatty liver, he will be quick in his acts, he will put the evil which is inflicted upon him into his own heart, and will retain it for a long time; and he will express his words hastily. And it was already stated that if Mars would appear in the Midheaven, and he would rejoice in his own place, the native will be fortunate in war and slaughter, and a beautiful organizer of wars, and wise in them. And if a fortune aspected a Mars so disposed, the native will acquire advantage and great fame from his wars.

The Moon, appearing in the aspect of Jupiter and Venus, in some one of the angles or the succeedents, and in some one of her own dignities, signifies that the native will be strong, a master of wars, rejoicing, and having a great heart, and an endurer of all things which happen to him.

When a masculine planet will be in a masculine sign and quarters, the native will be strong, and complete in strength, having good sense, good memory, wise in slaughter but keeping death away, a master of horses, and apt in riding and arms.

If the Lot of Boldness[653] happened to be in the domicile of Mars or his bound, and were in one of the angles (especially in the Midheaven), and besides that in the aspect of Jupiter and Mars from a strong place, the native will be strong and renowned among men; he will be feared by others, he will be fortunate in war, a soldier of the battlefield, and always a victor over his enemies.

---

[652] *Insanus*, the root of our "insane." Nowadays this word has clinical overtones that are not present in the Latin, though Latins would have seen it as roughly equivalent to "crazy," which is a much looser notion.

[653] This is undoubtedly the Hermetic Lot of Mars, as *Pars Audaciae* is also the name used by John of Spain when describing this Lot as given in Abū Ma'shar's *Gr. Intr.* See *JN* Ch. 34.

Chapter II.1.1: On him who has anxiety

If Mars were cadent in someone's nativity, weak and made unfortunate, not aspecting the Ascendant, and Saturn aspected him, the native will be weak of heart, and timid, and besides that abhorring a place of killing.

Likewise, if Venus were in a human sign the native will be weak of heart and timid.

If Saturn were in the Midheaven in a nocturnal nativity, the native will be very fearful, and have a most wretched heart.

If the Lot of Lawsuits or Wars[654] were under the rays of the Sun, and were cadent from the angle, and its Lord were with Saturn, the native will be timid, having a weak heart, and lazy or low-class in war and slaughter.

Chapter II.1.2: On the native's quickness to wars and rage[655]

Mars appearing in the Ascendant renders the native keen for discord and lawsuits, a killer, and having a powerful unsoundness.[656]

If Mercury were in the fourth and appearing from under the rays of the Sun, and besides that in the aspect of Mars and Saturn, the native will have a sharp and quick change, always unsound, and busy.

Mars appearing in the 8th house and a peregrine sign, whether in a diurnal nativity or a nocturnal one, signifies that the native will be unsound, and of lasting unsoundness, and a stupid killer.

If Mercury were in his own domicile, the native will be fearful and unsound.[657]

If the Moon were in a domicile of Mars [and] increased in light, the native will be keen, liable to anger, having a large liver, an appetite for wars and openly expressing abuse toward men.

If the Moon applied to Mars in a nocturnal nativity, and she were increased in light, the native will have a great motion to anger, having an appetite for lawsuits and discords without reason.

---

[654] Jag. simply reads "Lawsuit." Cf. *JN* 34 p. 300 for a Lot of the Military and its possible source in *Gr. Intr.*: from Mars to Saturn (reversed at night), projected from the Ascendant.
[655] Cf. *JN* Ch. 34.
[656] Both here and below, *insania*. This can also mean "frenzy," "mania."
[657] Surely this must be in combination with other conditions, such as the ones above.

If the Lot of Fortune or its Lord, or the Lord of the domicile of life, were in a domicile of Mars, the native will be frenzied, always sad, and have great fury, turning back slowly [from it].

Chapter II.1.3: On the native's humbleness

If Mercury were under the rays of the Sun, and in a watery sign (because they lack a voice), and Mars aspected him, the native will be humble and calm, and serious in his acts.

If Saturn and Mars aspected[658] the Moon and the Sun (or one of them) from the Midheaven or the Ascendant, or from the 7th or the 4th house, the native will be humble and intelligent, particularly if they aspected the Sun in a diurnal nativity and the Moon in a nocturnal nativity, and that the Sun or the Moon were in the bound of a fortune.

If one of the *biyābānīya* stars of the nature of Mars, Jupiter, and Saturn,[659] and of the first magnitude, appeared in the Ascendant or the Midheaven, the native will be humble, of subtle character, and good encounters.

Chapter II.1.4: On the shamelessness of the native

You should know that if Mars aspected Mercury from the opposite aspect, the native will be without shame. But if the Moon aspected Mars from the opposite aspect, she will decrease his shamelessness, and will change his disputes. And if the Moon were decreased in light, and appearing in a bad place with Mars, the native will be without shame. If Venus and Mercury were in the Ascendant, and in the opposite aspect of Mars, the native will have little shame.

---

[658] Reading *aspexerint* (pl.) for *aspexerit* to match the following clause. But I doubt that both malefics must be doing this simultaneously, especially since the passage goes on to say it will be worse if the luminary is also the sect light. Probably any malefic aspecting either would show humility; if it aspected the sect light, more humility; and if Mars aspected the Sun in a diurnal nativity, and Saturn the Moon in a nocturnal one, more humility yet. But could this notion clash with the Sun-Mars combinations above, which showed boldness?

[659] Cf. *BA* III.2.1, p. 78; Rhetorius Ch. 58 p. 103. The first magnitude stars of the nature of Jupiter-Saturn in this list are: Rigel (β Orion) and Capella (α Auriga). I do not see a star of the nature of Mars or Jupiter-Mars which would fit this description.

Chapter II.1.5: On the native's shame

Jupiter, appearing in the Ascendant of some nativity without the aspect of Mars, signifies that the native will be modest. If the Moon were in the Ascendant, and in the bound of Saturn, and in his face, but Mars in the west, and Jupiter aspected the Moon, the native will be modest.

Chapter II.1.6: On the beauty of the native's morals

If the Moon, appearing in the Midheaven, aspected Saturn[660] by a square aspect, with Saturn appearing in the 2nd house,[661] it is a sign that the native will have beautiful morals. The Sun appearing in a domicile of Saturn signifies that the native will have a good mind. Which if a fortune aspected the Sun, the native will have good, and good morals, and happiness.

If Mercury were in the domicile of the Sun in a diurnal nativity, the native will have good morals, especially if he were safe from the aspect of an infortune. If Mercury were in the domicile of the Moon, made fortunate, without the aspect of an infortune, the native will have good morals and a beautiful face.

If the Sun were in the exaltation of Venus without the aspect of an infortune, the native will have beautiful morals, be of subtle character, and a cheerful face, and esteemed by men.

Chapter II.1.7: On the native's lies

If Mars were with Mercury in his[662] domicile, the native will be a liar, and he will express lying words without reason or basis; and his will[663] will adorn his tongue with lies.

If Mars were the Lord of the angle of the earth [and] were in the 6th, the native will be a liar.

If the Sun and Venus were in the 7th house, the native will be full of lies.

---

[660] This should probably read "Jupiter" here and in the next clause.
[661] This should probably read "11th."
[662] Missing in Jag. I am unsure whose domicile is meant.
[663] *Velle*, in the sense of one's personal sense of will or wishing.

If Mars were in the 9th house, the native will bring forward lies, and affirm them with oaths.

If one of the *biyābānīya* [stars] of the nature of Mars and Mercury[664] were in the Ascendant or the Midheaven, the native will be a liar, and will firm up his lies with oaths; and he will write false letters, and he will impart things to other men which are not true.[665]

If the Moon, separated from Mars, applied to Mercury, and both were oriental, the native will be a liar, not to mention a master of fraud and betrayal.

If Mars and Mercury, appearing in the same degree, were in one of the angles without the aspect of some [planet], the native will be a liar, and boastful about things which he did not do, and he will bring forward deceptive words with his statements.

Chapter II.1.8: On the native's truth

If the Moon and Venus were in the Midheaven, the native will be a truth-teller, and fulfilling [his] promises.

He who was born with Sagittarius ascending, and the Moon in it, and in the trine or sextile aspect of Jupiter—it is a sign that the native will be truthful and fulfilling those things which he will promise.

If Jupiter were in the Ascendant, and Mercury in the 7th house under the rays, the native will be a truth-teller.

Mercury appearing in the Ascendant or Midheaven with Venus signifies that the native will be an orator, a truth-teller, fulfilling promises, and expressing the truth, [whether] in his own favor or against himself.

Chapter II.1.9: On the native's religion[666]

Jupiter appearing in the 9th house and in a diurnal nativity signifies that the native will be a cultivator of God, and trusting God, and contemplative,

---

[664] *BA* III.2.1 p. 79 and Rhetorius Ch. 58 p. 105: Bellatrix (γ Orion), Procyon (α Canis Minor), Betelgeuse (α Orion), and Alpheratz (α Andromeda).
[665] Reading with Jag. 1540 adds that he will be a braggart.
[666] Chapter missing in Jag.

so that on account of the decorated glory which he will have in his law, he will be honored by kings and powerful men.

If Saturn were in its[667] triplicity, the native will be fearing and praying to God, and his words [will be] holy, and practically angelic; and he will frequently accept punishment for his offenses, lamenting his sins; and this will be stronger if Jupiter aspected Saturn with reception by a good aspect.

If the Moon were in the Ascendant, and in her exaltation, and besides that in the trine or sextile aspect of Jupiter, the native will be a contemplative, an orator, and a master of churches or a distributor [of goods] to the poor.

If the Sun were in the 3rd house or in a masculine sign, and besides that in a good aspect of Jupiter, it is a sign that the native will be an orator, obedient to God, and leaving behind all worldly matters in the fear and love of God.

If Venus were in the 3rd house and her exaltation, with the nativity being nocturnal, it is a sign that the native will be in the esteem of God, and his obedience sure and firm.

If Mercury, the Sun and Venus were joined in the 9th house without the aspect of an infortune, the native will always have God before his eyes, and [before himself] in dreams; [and] he will extend good to one to whom he wished to do good.

If Venus were in the 9th house, and in her own domicile or exaltation, the native will be a famous hermit,[668] and this most strongly if Jupiter aspected her by a good aspect.

If Mercury were made fortunate and oriental in the 9th house, without the aspect of an infortune, the native will be good and fortunate in his own law.

If the Moon were in the 9th house, and in a feminine sign, and besides that in a good aspect of Jupiter, the nativity being nocturnal, the native will be an orator and hermit.

---

[667] *Eius*. It is impossible to say whether this is Jupiter's triplicity, or Saturn's own triplicity, or perhaps even in the triplicity of the 9th itself.
[668] Perhaps because Venus anciently signified ritual purifications. My sense is that there were more extensive texts on spirituality among the Persians which are missing in the surviving Greek literature.

Chapter II.1.10: On the native's pretended sanctity[669]

If Jupiter in a nocturnal nativity were in the 3rd house with Mars, and in a masculine sign, the native will be a hypocrite.

If Venus appeared peregrine in the 9th house and in a feminine sign, the native will seek what would be said about him—[namely] that he is good—but he will be a hypocrite, seeking novelties[670] in order to create [his] trick.

If the Lot of Absence[671] were in some one of the angles, and its Lord aspected a fortune without reception, and [the Lord] were safe from the infortunes, the native wants that men should speak well of him, and he will pretend to do good, [but] he will do evil.

> But if the said Lot and its Lord were strong, and they were made fortunate and free from the infortunes, the native will have good words, and a secret will.[672]

> And if the said Lot were made unfortunate, and its Lord [were] free from the infortunes, the native will be better from the inside than the outside.

> And if both were in angles, and free from infortunes, the native will be firm and of little pretended sanctity in his appearance.

> Likewise, if the Lord of the said Lot were received, and he aspected his own place, the native will be sure, good and fortunate. But if he were retrograde, the native will doubt in his own faith, and he will change to another faith.

> And if the Lord of the said Lot of Absence were the Lord in[673] the 9th house, it signifies the goodness of faith in the native, particularly if it were received. For if it did not have reception in the said place, it portends contrariety on account of faith, and the division of the world.

---

[669] Chapter missing in Jag.
[670] Reading *novitates* for *novaculas* ("razors"), suggesting the practice of employing novel distractions to keep the public from noticing his true character.
[671] The Lot of Spirit. In this chapter, it seems that the Lot signifies outward character, and the Lord signifies the native's inward character.
[672] That is, his faculty of the will, will be secret.
[673] This should probably read "of."

Which if in addition it were made unfortunate, it signifies doubt in faith, and harm on account of this. And judge the same say if it were in the 3rd house. But if it were so in the 2nd house it signifies constancy in faith, and that he will withdraw from secular matters; and by how much more he would serve, by that much more will he flee worldly things.[674]

The Lord of the Lot of Absence free from the infortunes, and in addition aspecting its own place, will hinder the native from pretended sanctity, and will add goodness to him. Which if it were received, the said goodness will be with truth and rectitude. But if it were made unfortunate, it will destroy the native's goodness on the inside.

If the Lot of Absence were in cadent places, the goodness which the native will have in appearance will be destroyed in the end. Which if the Lord of the said Lot were made unfortunate, the native's goodness will be reputed as being nothing, both in appearance and from inside.

If Jupiter in a diurnal nativity were in the 3rd house, the native will be a hypocrite and will show the people that he is something which he wholly is not. The Sun appearing in the 3rd house and in one of his own dignities, signifies [he will] totally lack faith.[675] And if the Moon were in the 3rd house (it being a nocturnal nativity), the native will be just in his appearance, but more so than this he will show from the outside what he will have in his heart.

Chapter II.1.11: On the native's idolatry[676]

If Jupiter were in the Ascendant and the Moon in the west, and Mars aspected Jupiter, the native will worship the stars and planets.
If Venus were appearing from under the rays in the 2nd house, the native will be an idolater.

---

[674] This is probably because the 2nd also has connotations of *victus*, one's means of support in life: thus spirituality will support or undergird the native's way of life.
[675] Presumably because he is in the opposite of his joy? But why could this not show a solar type of personal faith?
[676] Chapter missing in Jag.

Likewise, Saturn appearing in the 3rd house with the Moon signifies the native is going to be an idolater and contrary to God.

If the Moon were in the 9th house and in a feminine sign, it being a diurnal nativity, the native will be a scorner of God and contrary to Him.[677]

If Venus were besieged by Saturn and Mars in one sign, and the infortunes aspected the Moon and Mercury by a square or opposite aspect, the native will be a cultivator of many idols.

Mars appearing in the Ascendant and in the opposition of Jupiter portends the native [will be] an idolater. Which if Mercury were with Mars in a domicile of Jupiter, the native will be practically like a hermit [worshiping] idols.

If Saturn were the Lord of the Ascendant, or the Lord of the domicile of the Sun or of the Lot of Fortune, or of the opposition or the prevention, and in the 9th house, and Jupiter aspected him, the native will be an abbot or pontifex [worshiping] idols.

And if Mercury were in a domicile of Mars, and Mars [were] with him or aspected him by the opposite aspect, the native will be a heretic; and likewise if the Sun, Moon, and Mercury were in signs of two bodies—more strongly so if Mars sent rays to that same place by the square or opposite aspect.

Chapter II.1.12: On the native's knowledge[678]

If Saturn aspected Jupiter by a trine aspect, the native will be wise, of good counsel and wits, sound thinking, and experienced in all the secrets of nature, so that it will be said about him that he is a philosopher, and he will be a narrator of great deeds, and he will predict [or preach] serious matters just like the haruspices.

If Mercury were in his own domicile or exaltation, and in a good place of the figure, and Mars aspected him by a good aspect, the native will be very wise in the course of the stars, and serious in his own matters, and of deep thinking; he will compose books, and will adjoin many things to himself, and he will say wondrous things.

---

[677] Note the close parallel between this and the Sun in the 3rd in the previous chapter.
[678] Chapter missing in Jag.

If Mercury were with the Sun in his own domicile, the Sun appearing his own proper face,[679] the native will be wise, a natural philosopher,[680] and a composer of verses.

If Mercury were direct in the Midheaven, and appearing in one of his own dignities, [and] aspected the Moon by the square or opposite aspect, and the Moon were in her own domicile or exaltation, the native will be wise, sensible, and an examiner of the stars.

If Mercury were made fortunate in his own proper house, the native will be a lover of books and of the knowledge of the stars, and a commentator on difficult matters [pertaining to] them.

If Mercury appeared in his own domicile or exaltation in the Ascendant, but Saturn in the west, the native will investigate serious and difficult sciences, and on account of this he will have dominion and loftiness.

If Mars aspected Mercury ([who was] appearing in some one of his own dignities) by a trine aspect, and Mars were made fortunate, the native will be wise and an experienced philosopher.

If the Moon were in her own domicile or exaltation, or in the bound of Mercury, the native will be involved with secret and obscure matters, or wise in things below the surface.

If Mercury were in the 3rd house with the Moon, and in her[681] face, and in addition he was the Lord of the Ascendant and of the Lot of Fortune, the native will be a haruspex, and wise in secret matters.

If Mercury were appearing from out of the Sun's rays, and in the said 3rd house, and in a masculine sign, the native will be an augur, and will live from augury, and he will have wealth from thence. Which if Mars, appearing oriental, aspected a Mercury so disposed, the native will have the acquaintance of books, and will be wise in them.

If Mercury were in the 9th house without the aspect of Mars, the native will be an explainer of dreams; and more strongly so if Saturn were in his own domicile or exaltation. Which if Venus were so disposed in the way we spoke about Saturn, the native will likewise be an explainer of dreams.

If Mercury and the Sun were in the 9th house, and in some of their own dignities, the native will be wise, and an expounder of dreams, and practically like a haruspex.

---

[679] I think this simply means in his own decan, not the Ptolemaic condition of "proper face."
[680] *Physicus*, nowadays roughly equivalent to a natural scientist.
[681] *Eius*, assuming it is in parallel with the statement about the Sun above.

If Mercury were oriental in the 9th house, and made fortunate, the native will be an augur.

If the Lot of Fortune and the Lot of Faith [were] in the 9th house or the 3rd house without the aspect of a fortune, and the infortunes aspected them from the opposite of their domicile, the native will be haruspex, and will uncover the secrets of obscure things.

If Saturn and Mercury were in the 3rd house, appearing in their own domicile or exaltation, the native will be wise in the stars, and thence will have profit. And speak thusly if Mercury were appearing [from] under the rays in the 3rd house.

And if Venus were peregrine in the 3rd house, and Saturn aspected from his own domicile or exaltation by a good aspect, the native will be a black magician, or he will do wondrous things by means of an art. And he will seem to be like a prophet, and he will introduce wondrous things, particularly if Venus were in a feminine sign.

If Mercury and Saturn were in the Ascendant or the Midheaven, made fortunate, and free, the native will be a black magician.

If Mercury were in his own domicile or exaltation, and Saturn (being made unfortunate) aspected him by the square or opposite aspect, the native will be a philosopher, but his knowledge will not[682] bring success, and he will be miserable and poor.

If Mercury were made fortunate in a domicile of Saturn, the native will be wise, understanding secrets and the obscurities of matters, talkative, a rhetorician, augur, and expounder of dreams. If Sagittarius or Pisces were the sign of the 3rd house, and Saturn in [that sign], the native will be wise in matters of this kind.

If Mercury were with Venus in the 4th house, the native will be a disputer, lawyer, and an inventor of words, and more strongly so if it were in a peregrine sign.[683]

If the Sun were in the 9th house, the native will be a lawyer, a disputer in faith, and a praiser of God.

If Jupiter were the Lord of the 3rd house in a diurnal nativity, and the sign of the said house [were] masculine, the native will be wise. And if the nativity were nocturnal, the native will be believed to be wise, but he will not be so.

---

[682] Adding *non*.
[683] The reasoning here seems to be that peregrination makes someone who takes a frivolous view of these matters, and is willing to debate for the pleasure of it but without sincerity.

If the Moon, separated from the Sun, will bind to a Mercury appearing in the 3rd house, the native will be a writer, and wise in computation.

If the Sun, Mercury, or Jupiter were in the 9th or 2nd house,[684] and in Leo, the native will be of clear intellect and an organizer of matters.

If Mercury were made fortunate in the Midheaven, the native will be of a subtle and quick wit, and likewise if Mercury were in a domicile of Mars.

If the Moon were with Saturn in his[685] orientality, the native will be understanding, but lazy and soft.

If the Moon, separated from Venus, were joined to Mercury, and both [were] occidental, the native will be subtle and sharp.

If Jupiter received Mars or aspected him by a square aspect, the native will be of good counsel and intellect.

If the Sun were in a domicile of Jupiter or in his trine or sextile aspect, the native will be of good counsel and intellect, and deep knowledge. Which if Mercury were with him, the native will be a lawyer[686] and wise in judgments.

If Mercury were made fortunate in the domicile of the Sun in a diurnal nativity, the native will be sharp and subtle.

Chapter II.1.13: On the native's memory[687]

If the Sun were in a domicile of Mars, and Jupiter aspected with a good aspect, the native will have a good memory.

If Venus and Mars were made well fortunate with the Moon, the native will be mindful, and a deceiver in character.

If Mercury and Mars, made fortunate, aspected the Moon, the native will disclose beautifully what he knows.

If Mercury were in the domicile of the Sun and Jupiter aspected him by a good aspect, the native will be intelligent and mindful, and have a quick intellect. If Jupiter were joined with him, the native will be a judge of clerics or among clerics.

---

[684] This should probably read, "3rd."
[685] Reading as though this is Saturn's orientality, not the Moon's.
[686] *Legisperitus*, which suggests someone who has the "spirit of the law" in mind—not like the earlier lawyer (*causidicus*), whose title refers to a mere spokesman for his client.
[687] Chapter missing in Jag.

Chapter II.1.14: On the native's bad intellect[688]

If Mercury were in the 2nd house and under the rays of the Sun, and the Moon, diminished in light, were made unfortunate, the native will have a bad intellect, weak sense, not receiving teaching [or doctrine].

If Mercury were in the 4th house and he were the Lord of the Lot of Absence, the native will have a bad intellect, ponderous speech, little knowledge and sense.

If the Sun were in the domicile of the Moon, with her made unfortunate below the earth, and diminished in light, the native will have a hard and bad intellect, like a jackass, having much error, weak counsel, and a thick brain.

If Mercury and Saturn were made unfortunate in the Ascendant, and a retrograde and peregrine Jupiter aspected them by the opposite aspect, the native will have a hard and bad intellect, knowing and understanding few things.

Chapter II.1.15: On the native's good and quick intellect[689]

If Jupiter aspected a fortunate Mercury by a trine aspect, the native will be sensible, of good speech, and a quick intellect.

If Mercury were in his own domicile and a fortunate Jupiter aspected [the domicile][690] by a square aspect, the native will be well sensible, of sound counsel and complete intellect, provided however that Jupiter were not in the Midheaven.

If Mercury, made fortunate in the Midheaven, aspected Venus by a square aspect,[691] the native will be sensible and intelligent.

If Mercury were with Saturn in a domicile of Saturn, and in a good aspect to the Moon, with [her] increasing in number and light, the native will be well sensible, of beautiful faith and an organizer of matters.

If Mercury, Venus and the Sun aspected the Moon by a good aspect, the native will be well sensible and serious in his actions.

---

[688] Chapter missing in Jag.
[689] Chapter missing in Jag.
[690] *Ipsam*, indicating the whole sign. But it perhaps could be *ipsum*, Mercury himself.
[691] This could only be by a whole-sign configuration.

If Mars and Mercury were made fortunate, and free from retrogradation and burning up, and aspected a Moon increased in number and light, the native will have a good intellect.

If Mars and Venus [were] made fortunate, and one of them aspected the Sun, the native will be serious in his actions, of good intellect and counsel.

If Jupiter were in the Ascendant and Venus in the west, the native will be of subtle intellect and complete in sense.

If Saturn were in some one of his own dignities, in the west or the Midheaven, with Mercury, the native will have a good intellect, and be powerful in mind, like a philosopher and sage.

Chapter II.1.16: On the native's stupidity

If the Moon [were] diminished in light and number, [and] also were she separated from Mars, and wild,[692] the native will be stupid.

If the Moon were in the opposition of the Sun, separated, in the 7th house, and Mars aspected her with an unfortunate aspect, the native will be stupid.

If the Lot of Fortune or of Faith were in the 9th or 3rd house, and the infortunes aspected them, the native will be stupid.

If Venus were with Saturn, and Mars and Mercury in the place of the Moon, the native will be stupid, and because of his stupidity he will call himself a philosopher, [and] men will deride [him] because of that.

If Saturn and Mercury were peregrine in the Ascendant, and Jupiter in their opposition, the native will be stupid, and have a foul stupidity.

Chapter II.1.17: On those born actors

If Mercury were in his own domicile with Mars, the native will be an actor.

If Mars and Mercury were in a royal sign, and the Sun aspected that sign with a good aspect, the native will be an actor for kings and lords, and they will rejoice over him and his words.

---

[692] I.e., feral (*feralis*). According to al-Qabīsī III.13, when a planet is alone in a sign and no other planet aspects that sign; Sahl (*Introduct.* §5.16) leans more towards being unaspected by orbs.

If Mars and Mercury were in a domicile of Saturn, and cadent from the angles, and besides that the Moon (made fortunate and increasing in light) aspected them, the native will be a public actor, and the people will amuse themselves with him, and he will deceive.[693]

If Venus aspected Mercury, or were joined with him, the native will be a subtle actor, such that men will marvel at his wondrous deeds.

If Mars, Mercury, and the Moon were joined at the same time in a domicile of Venus, the native will be an actor with much and beautiful speech.

Chapter II.1.18: On the native's faithfulness

If Venus were in the Midheaven without the bad aspect of Mercury,[694] the native will be faithful and will faithfully watch over things committed [to him], particularly if the nativity were nocturnal.

If Mercury were with Jupiter, the native will be faithful, and high and lofty men will confide in him.

If Jupiter aspected Saturn and Mars by a good aspect, the native will be good and faithful, and watching over things committed to him.

If Venus were in the Ascendant and in [her own] exaltation, the native will be a faithful preserver of things committed to him.

If Jupiter were in the 3rd house, foreigners will offer their monies to the native in order to watch over them, and men will confide in him.

If Mercury were in the 5th house and in his own face, the native will be a faithful writer, and he will have honor because of his faithfulness.

If Mercury were oriental and in the 2nd house,[695] the native will be faithful to foreigners.

---

[693] *Trufabit.*
[694] That is, the whole-sign square.
[695] This should probably read, "11th."

Chapter II.1.19: On those born wicked,[696] and their unfaithfulness

If an unfortunate Mercury aspected Mars from out of the Midheaven, and the Moon were in the 4th house, the native will be wicked and unfaithful, and denying to men the things committed to him.

If Mars were peregrine and retrograde, and the Moon with him in the 3rd house, the native will be wicked and unfaithful, a plunderer of strangers, and holding onto[697] the things committed to him.

If Mercury were in the bound of Mars, and in the 3rd house with the Moon, with him being peregrine and retrograde, the native will have little faithfulness, especially if Mercury were the Lord of the Ascendant.

Chapter II.1.20: On those born robbers

If Mars, Mercury, and the Moon were made unfortunate in some one of the angles, without the aspect of a fortune, the native will be a robber.

If Saturn were peregrine and wild in the 7th house, and also retrograde, and in the aspect of Mars, Mercury and the Moon ([all] made unfortunate), the native will be a hidden robber, and his end [will be] a hanging.

If Mars were retrograde, peregrine, and weak, in one of the angles without the aspect of some fortune, the native will be a robber, particularly if Saturn aspected him by a bad aspect.

If Saturn, Mars, and Mercury were retrograde and uncivilized[698] in the west, and the Moon (diminished in light and number, and without some dignity) aspected them by the square aspect or the opposition, the native will be a robber, and because of his robbery he will end his days with a bad death.

If Mars and Mercury were joined in one of the angles, and they stood wild or without some dignity, and Saturn aspected them by a bad aspect, the native will steal the handkerchiefs and clothes of the dead.[699]

---

[696] *Sceleratis.* This word also has criminal connotations.
[697] *Retinens.* I take this to mean he will not give them back, or will not give up control.
[698] *Agrestes.* This must be the same as being wild or feral, above (*feralis*).
[699] This must either mean that the native will want to steal everything, *even* such objects, or else that he will be in such a low station that he *must* steal such objects.

Chapter II.1.21: On natives' liberality[700]

If the Sun and Venus aspected the Moon (with her appearing in the Midheaven), the native will be generous, liberal, and easily spending or giving away his goods.

If Mars aspected the Sun by a square aspect, the native will be liberal to such a degree that little or nothing of his substance will remain.

If Mars were the Lord of the Lot of Fortune, and the Lord of the Ascendant, in the 2nd house, the native will be wasteful, and consuming his goods without advantage.

If Saturn were retrograde or burned up, and appearing in one of his own dignities in the Midheaven, the native will hand over so much of his goods to others that he will come down to poverty, especially if Venus aspected by a bad aspect.

If the Lord of the 3rd house aspected the Lord of the 2nd house with a bad aspect, the native will be wasteful, and he will acquire enmities and hatred on the occasion of his riches.

Chapter II.1.22: On the native's greed

If the Head of the Dragon were with the Sun, with Venus and Mercury in the Ascendant, the native will be greedy.

If Mercury were made fortunate, oriental, and in the 2nd house in a diurnal nativity, the native will be stingy, and loving his own money beyond measure.

[And if the Lord {of the 2nd?}, Saturn, were in the Ascendant by day, the native will be greedy.][701]

[And if the Lord of the Ascendant aspected the Lord of the second from the trine aspect (a friendly one), the native will be thrifty, loving his money.]

---

[700] Classically, this connotes honorability, courtesy, generosity.
[701] Adding this and the next sentence with Jag.

Chapter II.1.23: On the native's envy

If Mercury, quick in course, appeared occidental from under the Sun's rays[702] in a nocturnal nativity, and in the 2nd, and he were [in] a bound of Mars, the native will be envious.

If the Moon, separated from Saturn, applied to Mercury, the native will be envious.

If Mercury were binding to Mars in the Ascendant, and Jupiter did not aspect, the native will be envious.

Chapter II.1.24: On the conceit and magnanimity[703] of the native

If Venus and Saturn were with the Moon, or they aspected her, the native will be proud, a braggart, and have a conceited mind.

If Mercury, Jupiter and Mars were aspecting the Moon at once, the native will have a great mind and say great things.[704]

If the Moon, separated from Saturn, were bound to Mercury, the native will be magnanimous and without modesty.

If the Moon[705] were in its own domicile and in the bound of Mars, and bound up with an opposition to the Sun from out of the 7th house, the native will have a conceited mind, and will seek to appear great: on account of this he will cover himself well.[706]

Chapter II.1.25: On the cheerfulness of the native's face

If Venus were in her own domicile or exaltation and in the 7th house,[707] and Mars aspected her with a good aspect, the native will have a cheerful face, and a good [manner of] response, but he will be a flatterer, and practically a fool.

---

[702] Jag. omits this part about the relation to the Sun.
[703] Normally this word refers to bravery and someone high-minded and even generous and noble; but here it is used in the sense of someone with an exaggerated sense of himself.
[704] This might also be taken in the sense of telling stories that are too good or amazing to be true: in English idioms, he has a "big head" or "tells fish stories."
[705] Adding with Jag.
[706] That is, his stories will provide effective cover for the less-impressive truth about him.
[707] Here and in the next few sentences, Jag. has Venus in the Ascendant, not the 7th.

If Venus were in the Midheaven or the 7th house, and Mercury aspected her by a good aspect, the native will have a cheerful face, but be a flatterer, and of good speech.

If Venus were in the 7th house and in her own face, and Mars aspected her from his own domicile by a bad aspect, the native will be without modesty, and a flatterer.

If the Moon were in the Ascendant, and Venus aspected her by a trine aspect, the native will have a cheerful face and good encounters.

Chapter II.1.26: On the native's joyfulness

If the Moon were diminished in light in her own domicile, and in a good place, with Venus, the native will be joyful, and he will go around joyful places without laziness, because of that joyfulness.

If the Moon and the Lord of the Ascendant were made fortunate [and] oriental, and they were free from the aspect of the infortunes, the native will be joyful.

If Mercury were direct, in the domicile or exaltation of the Moon, and outside of the Sun's rays, and Venus aspected him by a good aspect, and he [did the same to] the Moon, the native will be joyful, but movable and [a man] of much change.

If Mercury were in the Ascendant, the 10th, 11th, or 5th house, and the Moon aspected from the exaltation of Mars, or the Lord of the domicile of the Moon did so,[708] or Mercury [aspected] him, the native will be joyful and movable in all of his matters.

Chapter II.1.27: On the native's sorrow and weakness

You[709] should know that Saturn has much power in nativities. And if he will be in the face of the Ascendant, the native will be sad, of bad speech, and unsound.

---

[708] My sense is that the Lord of the Ascendant does not need to be in Capricorn, but it is possible.

[709] Reading with Jag. 1540 has mistaken the general statement about Saturn's power and turned him into the *mubtazz* of the whole nativity.

If Mars were the Lord of the face of the Ascendant, and Saturn aspected him by a good aspect, and Venus from the opposite, the native will be sad.

If Venus were made unfortunate, and she did not aspect the 7th house, but Mars and Saturn aspected the Moon, the native will sad, and have many worries, but proud and with a hard heart.

If Mercury were in the Midheaven with Saturn, the native will be weak, lazy, and without joyfulness; and likewise if the Moon were in a domicile of Saturn.

If the Moon were void in course, and the infortunes aspected her,[710] the native will be without joyfulness, lazy and weak.

If the Moon and Saturn were oriental, and joined together, the native will be without joyfulness.

If the Moon, being separated from Venus, applied by conjunction to a Mars [who was] in a domicile of Saturn and appearing in the hidden places, the native will be without joyfulness, diminished in matters and action.

If the Moon, separated from Mars, were joined to Mercury in a domicile of Saturn, and both [were] oriental, the native will be without joyfulness, lazy, and just like a miserable man.

Chapter II.1.28: On the native's eagerness when eating

If Mars were made fortunate in the 4th house in a diurnal nativity, the native will be an eager glutton,[711] and then he will incur an illness. If he were ascending, and the Sun aspected him by a good aspect,[712] the native will be an eager feaster.

If Mars were the Lord of the Ascendant and in the 2nd house and in a fiery sign, the native will feast eagerly. If Venus were in the first face of Leo and in a bad place, and the Sun aspected her with a good aspect, the native will be a great feaster.

---

[710] This must be a reference to whole-sign aspects.
[711] *Manducabit avide.* Medievally, *manduco* means "eat," but a *manducus* was a theater mask representing a glutton.
[712] Jag. omits this reference to the Sun.

Chapter II.1.29: On natives sowing discord among men

If Mars were in the 9th house, cadent from Jupiter and Venus, the native will be a sower of discord and war.

If the Moon, being separated from a planet in the Ascendant, were bound to a planet arranged in the 7th house, the native will sow discord among men.

If Scorpio were ascending, and Mars aspected it[713] by a bad aspect, the native will be a sower of discord.

Chapter II.1.30: On the native's bad thinking

If Mars and the Sun were in the same place at once, the native will have bad thinking.

If Mercury were in the 6th or 12th house, and the 1st house is one of the domiciles of Mars, the native will always think about what is bad, and will speak wickedly about others.

Chapter II.1.31: On the native's beauty

If Venus aspected the Moon by a trine aspect,[714] the native will be lively, and adorned like a woman.

If Venus aspected Jupiter by a square aspect, the native will have a beautiful stature, and a good condition.

If the Moon aspected Venus by a square aspect,[715] the native will have an appetite for vestments of silk, and he will be [a man] of much vice and rest.

Chapter II.1.32: On the dignified or serious and calm [nature] of natives

If the Lot of Fortune[716] fell in Capricorn, the native will be calm and act with deliberation.

---

[713] *Ipsum*, by a whole-sign aspect.
[714] Jag. seems to add, "from the fourth."
[715] Jag. adds, "from the fourth."
[716] Jag. reads, "if the fortunes fell…".

If the Moon were with Saturn in the Ascendant or the Midheaven, and Jupiter aspected her, the native will be calm.

If Jupiter [were] appearing in the Ascendant [and] Saturn aspected him, and Mars and his Lord were cadent from the Ascendant, the native will be dignified[717] and calm.

If the Moon were with Jupiter in a fixed sign, without the aspect of Mars, the native will be dignified and calm, and this more strongly so if she were with Jupiter in one of the angles.

Chapter II.1.33: On the native's hastiness

If Mars were in the Ascendant without the aspect of Jupiter, the native will act on his matters quickly and without deliberation, and therefore he will be reputed to be stupid.

If the Moon were in the Ascendant, and the Ascendant [were] a fiery sign, and Jupiter aspected it[718] from out of the 7th house, the native will be exceedingly quick in things to be done, and [will be] like a fool because of excessive speed.

If Mars were in the 7th house without the aspect of some fortune, the native will be clever[719] in his matters, not looking at the end of a matter.

If Mars were in the 4th house without the aspect of the Moon, the native will look too little at the end of his matters.

If the Moon and the Lord of the Ascendant were in the Midheaven, and Mars aspected them without the aspect of Jupiter, the native will be treacherous and without any prudence, and someone who will get lawsuits and discords for himself.

---

[717] *Ponderosus*, which also means "heavy, weighty."
[718] The whole sign.
[719] Or, "crafty" (*callidus*).

Chapter II.2.0: Prosperity and Eminence

On account of this,[720] one must know that men's fortunes are diverse:[721]

[1] For the fortune of some is complete (so that they will have riches, honors and dignities through the whole of their life).

[2] But others will be middling in their fortune, to the end of their life.

[3] Certain ones will even be miserable through their whole life, or will be those having nothing or little.

[4] On top of this there are some who will be wealthy or miserable in the beginning, middle or end [of life]; and some will go down from many riches to misery and beggary.

[5] And on the other hand, there are certain people who will be lifted up from out of miseries and beggary to dignities, riches, and honors.

[6] Of men,[722] there are even certain ones who have their fortune from faith and religion, others from the king, others from their knowledge, others from mercantile activity, others from [their own] wit, cunning, or mastery, others from endurance,[723] others from violence and boldness, others by accident.[724]

[7] There are even some who were always miserable, and are made fortunate at the hour of death.[725]

Therefore the ancient sages gathered the native's fortune from many places: namely from [*a*] the Lords of the triplicity of the Sun by day (and of

---

[720] Possibly a reference to II.12.2ff, which now appears in the material for the 10th house.
[721] The first four groups are roughly equivalent to categories in *BA* III.2.0 and *JN* Ch. 7 and *TBN* III.1. In the original text, Abū Bakr first deals with people in specific careers (the last item on the list) and then with the levels and changes in prosperity and wealth in the section on wealth below.
[722] This category refers to regular trades, addressed below throughout Ch. II.12.
[723] *Patientia*.
[724] *Eventu*.
[725] This category seems equivalent to [3] above.

the Moon by night); from [*b*] the Lot of Fortune and [*c*] its Lord, not to mention from [*d*] the Lords of its triplicity; from [*e*] the Midheaven and [*f*] its Lord; from [*g*] the Ascendant and [*h*] its Lord; from [*i*] the 11th house from the Ascendant and [*j*] its Lord; and even from [*k*] the 11th house from the Lot of Fortune and [*l*] its Lord. If therefore the aforesaid places were made fortunate, and the Lords of the triplicity strong and stable, not to mention [if] the fortunes aspected the luminaries, and the Lot of Fortune were in the Ascendant or its sky,[726] the native's fortune will be good, and able to last up to the end of his life. And if there were any of [*m*] the *biyābānīya* stars[727] in the Ascendant or the Midheaven, they signify the native's fortune and his loftiness. And it must be known that planets in their own dignities, and appearing in angles, give greater fortune than elsewhere.

Chapter II.2.1: On natives who are kings, and their fortune[728]

[1] If the Sun were in the degree of the Ascendant, and in his own domicile, exaltation or face, and Jupiter aspected him from a fortunate place, the native will be a famous king, fortunate, a victor in all things, and defended by God, not to mention a man of upright faith and fearing God, and perhaps he will be the head of others.

If Venus were the Lady of the Ascendant and of the Lot of Fortune, appearing in the 5th house and in her exaltation, and [coming out] from under the rays of the Sun, direct and occidental,[729] the native will be a great king, liberal, frank, pleasant, humble, gentle, peace-making, and who is eager to direct his own mind and do good to his subordinates.

If Saturn were in the 5th house, arranged just as we said about Venus, the native will be sad, not caring about evil in the various injuries done to him; he will be of a thick soul, much malice, little piety, and unfortunate in his kingdom.

If Jupiter were in the Midheaven, direct, and increasing in number, received by the Sun, and the infortunes cadent from him, the native will be a great king, and will have dominion over the cities of his kingdom; and his exaltation will be beautiful.

---

[726] That is, the Midheaven (*firmamento*).
[727] These stars are all described in *BA* III.2.1, and Rhetorius Ch. 58.
[728] Cf. *JN* Ch. 6.
[729] This undoubtedly means setting visibly after the Sun.

If the Sun and Moon [were] in the Midheaven, and made fortunate in their own dignities, and the fortunes aspected them by a good aspect without[730] the rays of the unfortunate ones, the native will be a king or the master of cities in which he will be like a duke; and whatever he commanded will be fulfilled; and he will be a sensible man, and of good memory, and fortunate in business dealings.

If the Sun and Venus were joined with Jupiter and the Moon, or they aspected them from a domicile without the aspect of the infortunes, the native will be a great king, ruling in cities and climes, and he will live as an honored man, and he will inherit his kingdom, and will leave it for his own children; indeed they will inherit it after him.

If the Moon aspected the Sun by a good aspect, [and] likewise Saturn aspected Mars from the Midheaven by a good aspect, the native will be a rich king, strong in his kingdom, and fortunate and powerful in his acts, a victor [over] his enemies.

If the Lot of Fortune were appearing in a good place and with its own light,[731] and with fortunes [who are] appearing and strong, and the infortunes did not aspect [the Lot], the native will be a great king or strong duke.

If the Sun were in the Ascendant and in his domicile or exaltation, and the Moon in the west, and both were free from the infortunes, the native will be a great king, decorated and strong, and powerful in his matters and kingdom.

If the Moon were in the Midheaven or her own exaltation, and Jupiter, Mars, Venus and Mercury (appearing direct) aspected her by a good aspect, with Saturn not aspecting her, the native will be a great king and master of peoples and cities, and one who will fulfill his words and deeds in all things.

If Venus were with Jupiter and Saturn, and Venus aspected the Moon from out of the Midheaven, the native will be a great and fortunate king, and loved by his subordinates, and defended by God, not to mention a true and upright man, and obedient to God.

If the Sun were in the Midheaven, and in his own domicile or exaltation, the native will be a king and born of a family of kings, and one who will organize his business dealings with rectitude and goodness; and he will be defended by God, and safe from [his] enemies.

---

[730] Reading *sine* for *sicut*.
[731] Normally this term only refers to planets. It probably means that is outside of the Sun's rays.

And if some one of the *biyābānīya* stars of the nature of Jupiter and Mercury[732] [were] in the Ascendant or the Midheaven, or the Sun and Moon were with it, the native will be an elevated and decorated king, and praised because of his sense and counsel, under whose command his subordinates will be successful; and he will be of good association and good responsiveness (and bad, if it were necessary, provided there were time);[733] he will be agreeable in his words and quick in his business dealings, and his strength apparent; he will fear God, he will do good to his subordinates; his liberality ample, of great piety, and fortunate and supportive in all of his acts.

Chapter II.2.2: On the dominions of natives, and their fortune in them

[1] If Jupiter aspected the Sun from the opposition without the bad aspect of an infortune, the native will be a master or governor of some kingdom, of great reputation, name and dominion, and one who will have the power of commanding and prohibiting.

If the Sun, appearing in his own domicile or exaltation, were in the Midheaven, the native will be great in his own place, and high in rank, and because of this he will obtain rule and dominion in the city.

If the Moon were increasing in number and light, in the 12th house, with the Head of the Dragon,[734] without the aspect of Saturn or Mars, and a fortune [were] in the 11th house, the native will be great and renowned in his province and cities, faithful in the monies and matters of the king.

If the first Lord of the Sun's triplicity by day (or the first Lord of the Moon's triplicity by night) were from the beginning of the sign in which it is, up to the middle of that same sign, and in some one of the angles,[735] the native will have great fame, and be esteemed and elevated by great lords, and he will have the power of commanding [and] prohibiting, not to mention allies, scribes, and followers below him, indeed so that flags or swords will be lowered before him, and his commands will be fulfilled by the people.

---

[732] See *BA* III.2.1 p. 77; Rhetorius Ch. 58 p. 104. These are: Alphecca (α Corona Borealis), Zuben Eschamali (β Libra), and Castor (α Gemini).
[733] Reading *adfuerit* for *affuerit*. That is, he knows how to use delays to his advantage. Jag.'s text is hard to read here and is worded differently.
[734] *Jawzahirr* (Pahlavi).
[735] Cf. *BA* III.2.1 p. 82, *JN* Ch. 7, and *Carmen* I.26.2-4.

If the Sun were in the western angle and in his own domicile or exaltation, and the fortunes aspected him without the rays of the infortunes, the native will have a great dominion, and be praised in it, and he will have a good appointment.[736]

If Venus were with Jupiter, Saturn and Mars, and she aspected the Moon from out of the Midheaven with a good aspect, the native will have command and dominion over other cities, and his command will be fulfilled by the citizens.

If the Moon, appearing in Cancer with Jupiter, were in the Ascendant or the Midheaven, the native will be of good fortune and good memory, and will have dominion from the king of his clime, and the king will trust in him.

If the Sun and the Moon were in the Ascendant and in a domicile of Mars, and the fortunes aspected them, the native will be a lord of many places, and a victor over his enemies, of good decoration, and able to cause evil to his enemies, and quick to kill.

If Jupiter aspected the Sun by a trine aspect, the native will be an elevated and fortunate lord.

If Jupiter were in the Midheaven, and appearing in some one of his own dignities, and free from the infortunes and their aspects, the native will be great and have a high name, and be commanding others.

If Saturn were appearing direct and in the Midheaven, not to mention in his own domicile or exaltation, and it [was] a diurnal nativity, the native will be fortunate and have a great appointment, and be the lord of a place or governor of a kingdom, and have a high command.

If Mercury were in the Midheaven, and in his own domicile or exaltation, and Jupiter and the Moon aspected him by a good aspect, the native will be a judge or a master over litigants, and someone who will govern the people committed to him with piety and rectitude.

Chapter II.2.3: On the native's middling fortune[737]

[2] If the Lot of Fortune were made unfortunate, and a fortune (appearing oriental and strong) aspected it by a good aspect and from a strong [place],

---

[736] *Ordinationis*.
[737] Cf. *BA* III.2.0 and III.2.3; *JN* Ch. 7 p. 255. *TBN* lacks this category.

the native will be fortunate in a middling way, and he will spend according to what he earned.[738]

If the Lord of the triplicity of the luminaries,[739] appearing in the last degree of a sign (which is the bound of the infortunes), were in some one of the angles or succeedents, the native will have a good standing and life, and moderately content, so that he will seek nothing from anyone.

If the infortunes aspected the Lot of Fortune, and the Lord of the Lot of Fortune were strong and fortunate, appearing in a good place, the native's life will be middling, so that the native will not be elevated much nor even be pressed down.

If the three significators (namely the Lord of the Ascendant, the Lord of the Midheaven, and the Lord of the 11th house) were made fortunate, or one of them [were] fortunate and another unfortunate, the native will be fortunate in a middling way, so that he will not be rich nor even poor.

If the Lord of the Lot of Fortune were made unfortunate, and in a bad place, and the fortunes [were] oriental and strong, and appearing in some of their own dignities, [and] they aspected the Moon and the Lot of Fortune, the native's life will be middling, and it will be enough for him.

If the infortunes aspected the Lot of Fortune, and the fortunes fell away from [the Lot], and the Lord of the house of substance were made fortunate, and the Lord of the Ascendant were made fortunate in the 2nd house, he will be neither rich nor poor.

If the diurnal planets in a diurnal nativity (and the nocturnal ones in a nocturnal nativity) aspected each other by a good aspect, and one were made fortunate and another unfortunate, the native will be at one time rich [and] at another time poor.

If the Lot of Fortune were in the bound of a fortune and in a good place, and likewise a planetary fortune (appearing peregrine and retrograde in the 6th house) aspected [the Lot], the native will middling between poverty and riches.

If the Lord of the Ascendant, being a fortune and safe from retrogradation and from burning up, not to mention were it in the 2nd house and in some one of its own dignities, the native's substance is not insufficient for him, but he will acquire it with labor.

---

[738] That is, neither falling behind nor getting ahead.
[739] That is, of the sect light for the particular chart.

Chapter II.2.4: On the native's misery and labor[740]

[3] If the Lord of the 2nd house were retrograde or burned up or peregrine, and the infortunes aspected him by a bad aspect and from a bad place, the native will be in labor and in misery, not to mention living in sorrow and poverty, and his hope will always be destroyed on account of some reason.

If the Lot of Fortune [were] appearing in a square or opposite aspect of the infortunes, and its Lord made unfortunate, not to mention Jupiter and Venus peregrine in bad places, the native will be full of labor and placed in misery.

If the 2nd house were impeded by infortunes, and Jupiter made unfortunate in a bad place, the native will always be poor.

If the Lord of the Ascendant gave its own power to the Lord of the 2nd house, or were bound to it, the native's governance and substance will come with great labor.

If the Lord of the 2nd house were made unfortunate, and [were] an infortune, especially with Saturn appearing as the Lord of the said house, and the Lord of the Ascendant [were] seeking its binding, nor would there be a reception or rendering of light between them, the native will be of so much misery that he will desire death more than he does life.

If the Lord of the triplicity of the Moon were in a good place, and the Lord of the triplicity of the Sun in a bad place and in its detriment[741] or descent, and the infortunes aspected it by a bad aspect, the native will be full of labor and living in poverty.

If the Lot of Possession[742] were in the 2nd house and the Lord of the 2nd house had strength and power in signification, and both infortunes aspected the Lot of Possession by a bad aspect, the native will be full of labor, and will lead his life in labor and misery.

If the Lord of the 2nd house, [being] unfortunate and appearing in a bad place (and were it peregrine in a 2nd house that is made unfortunate),[743] and

---

[740] Cf. *BA* III.2.5, *JN* Ch. 7 p. 242, and *TBN* III.1.
[741] This is a rare mention in medieval literature of the word "detriment" as the seventh sign from a domicile and explicitly distinguished from descension (fall).
[742] Probably the Lot of Money/Substance.
[743] This must be added later by an editor. Jag. lacks references to peregrination and the Sun's wildness, and this condition could only subsist in a quadrant house system, which is not indicated here by Jag.

the Sun, appearing wild, aspected [the Lord][744] by a bad aspect, the native will be full of labor, and miserable in his own life.

If Saturn were uncivilized[745] [and] retrograde in the Ascendant without the aspect of a fortune, and the fortunes [were] cadent from the angles, the native will be miserable and living in poverty.

Chapter II.2.5: On natives returned to servitude

[3] If Saturn were under the rays of the Sun, in his own domicile or exaltation, and in addition in some one of the angles, the native will do something on account of which he will be returned to servitude.

If the Moon were in some one of the angles or the succeedents, particularly in the 2nd house or her own exaltation,[746] joined with some infortune, the native will go down by means of a crime or stain, or perhaps he will be captured and made into a slave. But if Jupiter and Venus aspected the Moon, the native will escape from that dangerous crime or servitude.

If Saturn were eclipsed with the Sun in the angle of the earth, the native will be captured in his childhood and made into a slave.

If[747] the Lot of Slaves, made unfortunate in the angle of the earth, aspected the Ascendant and not its Lord, the native will do something on account of which he will become a slave.

If the Moon were in the 3rd house (it being a diurnal nativity), the native will be a slave [and] he will perform the deeds of a slave, especially if an infortune were joined [to her] or aspected her: for then the native will serve others in order to have his livelihood.

If the Lord of the Ascendant were in the 12th house and in the aspect of an infortune (especially that of Saturn), the native will be transported from his own land, and will be made into a slave.

If the Moon were peregrine in the 6th or 12th house, and the Lord of the triplicity of the sign in which she is made unfortunate and in a bad place, the native will be a slave. But if she were in some one of the angles or

---

[744] Reading with Jag. for "fortune."
[745] *Agrestis*.
[746] Jag. reads, "joy."
[747] This paragraph and the next form one long sentence in Jag., which does not mention the Moon and is ambiguous as to who is doing what to whom, and where.

succeedents with an infortune, and an infortune aspected her, the native will even be made into a slave.

If[748] Mars [were] appearing unfortunate in one of the angles (it being a diurnal nativity),[749] and he were in the sign after the Sun, and he aspected the Moon from a sign in which he has no dignity, the native will become a slave. If Saturn bore himself in that way (just as we said about Mars) in a nocturnal nativity, the mother will expose the native in the streets, and he will be made into a slave.

If Jupiter and Venus were made unfortunate in the 12th house, and Mars and Saturn (being retrograde) aspected them by a bad aspect, the native's life will be spent in servitude and misery.

Chapter II.2.6: On natives who will be incarcerated

[3] If Mars were made unfortunate in the Ascendant, and he aspected the Moon by a bad aspect, the native will be incarcerated.

If the Moon and Jupiter, appearing unfortunate, were joined together, and the Moon were bound to Mars from out of a bad place, and Mars were the Lord of the 12th house [and] peregrine in the 6th house and retrograde, the native will suffer serious evils and prison.

If Saturn, Mars, [and] the Moon were wild in the 4th house, or, being wild, one aspected the other by a bad aspect, fear or sorrow will touch the native because of plagues and prison.

If Jupiter, Saturn, Mars and the Moon were in one sign, and made unfortunate in the 12th house, the native will incur serious evils, and in addition prisons and harms.

If the Moon (being in a diurnal nativity) were in a domicile of Mars, made unfortunate without the aspect of a fortune, and Saturn [were] the Lord of the 12th house, and appearing burned up, [and] he aspected the Moon by a bad aspect, the native will have serious evils, and will stay for a long time in prison.

If Mars and Mercury were made unfortunate, appearing in the west or the angle of the earth, and Mars appeared as the Lord of the 12th house, and

---

[748] This paragraph originally was part of determining nourishishment and rearing, and referred to infant exposure and rejection by parents. Cf. *BA* II.1.4 and *Carmen* I.7.23-24.
[749] Adding with Jag.

Jupiter [were] with them in the same place and in his own bound, the native will sustain need, misery, and prisons—but afterwards he will escape and will have good fortune.

If the one ruling[750] the native were under the rays of the Sun, with the Sun not being in Aries or Leo, but in the 10th house, kings will harm the native and they will crush his feet in foot-shackles. And if some one of the infortunes aspected [the one ruling], kings will kill the native.

If the [Lord of the][751] Ascendant or Mercury (made unfortunate) gave its own power to Saturn (he appearing in the 4th house), the native will spend time in prison and captivity for many years.

If the Lord of the 9th house were burned up in some one of the angles, the native will be captured on a journey, [and] will enter into captivity and into prison.

If the one ruling the native were in the 6th or 12th house, the native will be captured by his enemies.

If Venus, appearing as the Lady of the 6th house, were in the 12th house, and she were joined with a retrograde Mars, evils will come to the native, and he will be incarcerated on the occasion of women.

If Saturn, Mars, and Mercury were burned up in the west, and the Lord of the 12th house, appearing unfortunate, aspected them by a bad aspect, the native will incur evils and sorrow on the occasion of a wife and children, and he will be incarcerated on account of them.

If the Moon were diminished in light and number in the 8th house, and the Lord of the 12th house, peregrine, appearing wild and [being] an infortune, aspected her by a bad aspect, the native will incur pains, blows, and wounds.

Chapter II.2.7: On natives who are beggars[752]

[3] If the infortunes were made unfortunate in the angles, and the fortunes occidental and receding from them, the native will be a beggar. And judge likewise if the Lot of Fortune and the Moon were made unfortunate.

---

[750] *Principans.* Perhaps the *kadukhudhāh.* This and several other statements in this chapter do not appear in Jag.
[751] Adding tentatively, since the Ascendant cannot give power like a planet can. Not in Jag.
[752] Cf. *BA* III.2.2 and 2.5; *JN* Ch. 7 p. 255.

If Saturn and Mars were retrograde [and] with the Moon in the Midheaven, and a fortune did not aspect them, the native will be needy and a beggar.

If Mars, appearing unfortunate, aspected the Moon by a square or opposite ([with the Moon being] without the good aspect of some [fortune]), the native will be poor, and his fortune [will be] with labor and misery.

If the Ascendant, the Sun, the Moon, and the Lot of Fortune were not aspected by the Lords of their domiciles by a good aspect, the native will live in poverty and trouble.

If the Lord of the western angle and the Lord of the 2nd house and the Lord of the angle of the earth did not aspect the Sun in a diurnal nativity (or the Moon in a nocturnal nativity), but they were cadent from the angles and made unfortunate, the native will be poor and miserable.

If the Lot of Fortune were[753] in an unfortunate place, and in the square or opposite aspect of an infortune, and neither the Lord of the said Lot nor the fortunes aspected it, nor did even the said Lord aspect the Sun, the native will be a beggar.

If the Sun [were] appearing unfortunate in a diurnal nativity, and in addition cadent from the angles, and the Lord of the 2nd house were burned up, the native will be poor and needy.

If Mars were in the 2nd house, made unfortunate, and in addition retrograde and without the aspect of the fortunes, and the fortunes appeared cadent and uncivilized with the Lord of the 2nd house, the native will always be in need.

If a peregrine Saturn were with the Moon in some one of the angles, and Mars aspected them by a bad aspect, the native will be in need and living a filthy life.

If the Lord of the conjunction or the prevention of the nativity were an infortune and were made unfortunate, and in addition cadent from an angle (especially in the 6th house), the native will be poor.

If[754] the Lot of Fortune [were] appearing in the 12th house, and [neither] the Moon nor the infortunes aspected it, and the infortunes were made unfortunate in angles or succeedents, the native will be poor and in need.

If the Moon were with a peregrine infortune, and in the bad aspect of an infortune, and the fortunes cadent, the native will be poor.

---

[753] Reading *fuerit* for *fuerint*.
[754] Cf. *BA* III.2.5, item 5.2.

If[755] the *hīlāj* were cadent, and the infortunes made it firm,[756] they signify a fall [in status] and being in need.

If the Lords of the angles and succeedents were cadent, the native will be in need.

If the Moon, separated from a fortune, were bound to Saturn (he being in a bad place), and the Lord of the 2nd house[757] were made unfortunate and in their aspect, and the fortunes cadent, the native will be poor and full of labor.

If the Moon, diminished in number and light, and in addition appearing peregrine, were separated from Mars, and she applied by conjunction to Saturn[758] in a bad place, the native will be in need.

If some one of the infortunes were peregrine in the house of substance, and the Lord of the house of substance [were] impeded in a bad place, and, appearing unfortunate, were made firm[759] by the infortunes, and the fortunes fell away from it, the native will be a beggar.

If[760] the Lot of Money and its Lord were cadent and occidental or made unfortunate, and the fortunes [were] wild and cadent, the native will be full of labor, miserable, and needy.

If the Lords of the bounds[761] of the Sun and Moon were cadent and burned up, and without the aspect of a fortune, and the fortunes and the Lord of the house of substance [were] made unfortunate in bad places, the native will suffer poverty, need, and trouble.

Chapter II.2.8: On natives who come down from riches to poverty[762]

[4] If[763] the Lords of the triplicity of the Sun in a diurnal nativity (and of the Moon in a nocturnal one) were in good places, and the infortunes made

---

[755] Cf. *BA* III.2.2, item 2.12. *JN* Ch. 7 p. 255, except that Abū 'Alī and Māshā'allāh use the *kadukhudhāh*.
[756] In the context of *BA* III.2.2, this seems to mean "if the infortunes *confirmed* its bad status by an aspect from them."
[757] This is omitted in Jag.
[758] Omitted in Jag.
[759] Reading *firmatus fuerit* for *firmaverit*. Again, this suggests that the infortunes are confirming his bad condition through an aspect.
[760] Cf. *BA* III.2.5, item 5.5. Reading "fortunes" for "infortunes."
[761] Reading *domini terminorum* (pl.) for *dominus termini*.
[762] This corresponds to topic [4] above. Cf. *BA* III.2.2 and *JN* Ch. 7 p. 255.
[763] Cf. *BA* III.2.2, item 2.1.

them unfortunate without reception, the native will come down from riches to poverty.

If the Lord of the Ascendant were made unfortunate, and in the 2nd house, and in some one of his own dignities, and the fortunes did not aspect [the Lord] by a good aspect with reception, the native will squander [his] substance by his own will. And if the said fortune were not in some one of his dignities, the native's substance will be secretly stolen, or robbers attacking him will openly snatch it away.

If[764] both infortunes were in the 2nd house without the aspect of the fortunes, the native will descend from riches to neediness.

If[765] the Moon were joined to Saturn in some one of the angles, the native will come to neediness. And if the native were a king or prince, his command will [not][766] be perfected, and his peoples will forsake him.

If[767] the Lot of Fortune and its Lord were cadent from the Sun, the native will be made unfortunate after [having] fortune. If[768] the Lot of Fortune and its Lord were strong and unfortunate in good places, and the infortunes made them unfortunate, the native will descend from riches to misfortune.

If[769] the Lord of the conjunction or prevention of the nativity, and the Lord of its domicile, were in bad places and in their own dignities, the beginning of life will be better than the end.

If an infortune were in the 2nd house, and it aspected the Lord of the 2nd house by a bad aspect, or it were joined with it in a bad place, it portends loss, a fall, and misfortune for the native according to the quality of its sign.[770] For[771] if the sign were of the nature of Saturn, his loss will proceed on the occasion of slaves and miserable people. If [it were] of the nature of Jupiter, on the occasion of great men or churchmen. If of the nature of Mars, on the occasion of soldiers, robbers or wars. If of the nature of the Sun, on the occasion of parents, grandfathers, or real estate. If of the nature of Venus, on the occasion of noble women. If of the nature of Mercury, on the occasion of the wise, or scribes or commerce. If of the nature of the Moon, on the occasion of infirm women, heralds, or messengers.

---

[764] Cf. *BA* III.2.2, item 2.4.
[765] Cf. *BA* III.2.2, item 2.7.
[766] Adding with *BA*.
[767] Cf. *BA* III.2.2, item 2.8.
[768] Cf. *BA* III.2.2, item 2.2.
[769] Cf. *BA* III.2.2, item 2.9.
[770] This probably refers to whatever sign the malefic is in.
[771] *Carmen* I.27.6-12.

If you found one of the infortunes in the Midheaven without dignity, and the other at the end of a sign in which it had no dignity or strength, and in addition it would be in a bad place, and the Lord of the house of substance were burned up,[772] and if Jupiter and Venus [were] made unfortunate in a bad place, you will not fear to judge evil for the native, and also the loss of his things and the removal of fortune—unless God preserved him.

Chapter II.2.9: On natives who are raised up from out of poverty to riches[773]

[5] If[774] the two infortunes were in angles, and the fortunes made fortunate in the succeedents, the native will be miserable at the beginning of his life, but rich at the end.

If[775] the Lords of the triplicity [of the Sun by day or the Moon by night] were direct, in each other's domicile, and safe from burning up, the native will be elevated from evil to good at the end of life.

If[776] the Lot of Fortune and its Lord were made unfortunate in good places, and other planets aspected them from bad places, the native will be needy at the beginning of his life, but fortunate at the end. And[777] you should know that the Lot of Fortune signifies the beginning of life, and its Lord the end.

If the sign of the conjunction or prevention of the nativity were made unfortunate, and [its] Lord made fortunate in a good place, the native will have labor at the beginning of life, and riches at the end.

And judge the same if the sign in which the Moon was on the third day from the nativity were made unfortunate, and its Lord made fortunate and strong.

---

[772] 1540 ends the sentence here, but the end of the next sentence reflects Jag., so I have let it continue.
[773] Cf. *BA* III.2.4, *JN* Ch. 7 pp. 242 and 246; also *TBN* III.1.
[774] Cf. *BA* III.2.4, item 4.1; *JN* Ch. 7, p. 256.
[775] Cf. *BA* III.2.4, item 4.4. Reading with *BA* and Jag. for "the Lords of the four triplicities."
[776] Cf. *BA* III.2.4, item 4.5.
[777] Cf. *BA* III.2.4, item 4.6.

If the place of the conjunction or prevention of the nativity were made unfortunate, and its Lord in a good place, and the fortunes aspected it,[778] the native will be raised up to fortune and riches after need and labor.

If the Moon were made unfortunate, and [there were] 15° between her and the Sun in the east (that is, in the beginning of her hiddenness), and her Lord made fortunate and in a strong place, the native will be raised up out of misfortune to fortune.

[And if one of the infortunes is in the Ascendant and the other in the west, the native will be poor at the beginning of life, and he will return to fortune at the end of life.]

If Jupiter, appearing in the angle of the earth, made unfortunate, were in some one of his own dignities, and [there were] a peregrine infortune in the Ascendant,[779] and in the aspect of a fortune, the native will be raised up out of misfortune to fortune.

If Saturn (appearing in his own bound) and Venus ([being] in her own domicile) aspected the Moon by a good aspect, the native will be raised up out of misfortune to fortune on the occasion of women.

[And likewise if Saturn and the Sun aspected the Moon, the native will have adversity at the beginning of his life, and {at the end} he will be returned to high and greater goods, and honor and dominion.]

If the first Lord of the triplicity of the Sun in a diurnal nativity (and of the Moon in a nocturnal one) were made unfortunate in good places, and the fortunes aspected [the Lord] by a good aspect with reception, the native will be raised up out of neediness to fortune.

[If Saturn will be in the Ascendant, the native will have 30 years of evil and impediment, and after that he will be returned to the good.]

If[780] Jupiter [were] appearing in the Ascendant, 10th, or 11th house, neither retrograde nor under the rays of the Sun, the native will have fortune before the middle of his days. And if he were in angles or the cadents, the native will be made fortunate after one-half of his years. And if he were oriental from the Sun (that is, in his first station or after the opposition of the Sun in the second station),[781] he will have honor and riches before one-half of his years.

---

[778] I believe this refers to the Lord, not the sign of the prenatal lunation.
[779] Jag. reads, "the seventh."
[780] The following two paragraphs do not appear in Jag. and must derive from some other source.
[781] Jupiter probably does not need to be in the station—it must mean that Jupiter is outside of the beams and direct.

But you will know the quantity of the riches according to the strength of Jupiter, and this will be more strongly so if Jupiter were the one ruling the native, or the Lord of the hour, or the Lord of the place of the Sun (in a diurnal nativity) or of the place of the Moon (in a nocturnal nativity). Which if Jupiter were the one ruling over the aforesaid places, the native[782] will have few riches.

Chapter II.2.10: On natives who are greater than their own parents

If Saturn aspected Jupiter from his own domicile by a trine aspect, the native will be greater than his own parents and everyone from his house.

If Jupiter were in his own domicile, and he aspected the Moon in a trine aspect from the Midheaven, the native will be greater than his kin,[783] and more noble than all of his ancestors.

If Saturn and the Sun were with Jupiter in their own domicile or exaltation, and they aspected the Moon and Venus from the Ascendant or the Midheaven by a good aspect, the native will have height and dominion and great fortune, and he will be made more noble than his kin.

If the Sun, appearing in some one of his own dignities, were in the Ascendant without the aspect of an infortune, and a fortune aspected him from out of the Midheaven, the native will have dominion from the king, and will be esteemed by him, and he will be wealthy and more noble than all of his kin.

If the Sun were made fortunate in the Midheaven, and the infortunes were cadent from him, the native will be more noble than all of his kin.

If Mercury were made fortunate in the Ascendant without the aspect of an infortune, and the Moon aspected him a good aspect, the native will have good sense and depth of knowledge, and because of this he will acquire a dominion, and he will be made more noble than his parents.

If the Sun and the Moon, were made fortunate in the angles and in a diurnal nativity, the native will be more noble than his own parents.

If Jupiter were made fortunate [and] in some one of his dignities, and he aspected Venus by a square aspect, the native will be more noble than his kin.

---

[782] Reading *natus* for *natos*.
[783] *Parentela*, here and below.

While Jupiter is made fortunate in his own domicile, and were free from the infortunes, and Mercury aspected him from out of some one of the angles, the native will be wealthy and fortunate, and of a higher status than his kin.

[Chapter II.3.0: Wealth]

[Chapter II.3.1: Indications of great wealth]

If Saturn, appearing in his own domicile, aspected the Sun[784] by a trine aspect with reception, and Jupiter likewise aspected Saturn by a good aspect and with reception, from out of an angle, the native will be wealthy, with much money and a good reputation.

If Venus were in Taurus, and Saturn [were] in Libra (it being a diurnal nativity), the native will be wealthy, praised, with much money, and with an appetite for women and children.

If the Lord of the Lot of Fortune were made fortunate and in a good place (like in the 9th or 11th house), and it aspected the Lot of Fortune with a good aspect, the native will be wealthy and of ample substance, and pleasant.

If the Lot of Fortune or its Lord were in the Ascendant, oriental and outside the rays [of the Sun], and without the aspect of the infortunes, and a fortunate Jupiter aspected [the Lot] from out of the angle of the earth, the native will be wealthy and have much money, but he will hide it; and judge the same (namely, that he will be wealthy) with it being posited that Jupiter aspected [the Lot] and its Lord.[785]

If the Lord of the house of substance were made fortunate in the Ascendant, the native will be wealthy and have a good life.

If the Lot of Fortune aspected the Sun, or were with him, appearing from under the rays without the aspect of an [in]fortune,[786] the native will be wealthy and praised in all of his works.

If Venus were direct and outside of the rays of the Sun, in the triplicity of Jupiter,[787] and she possessed some one of the angles, the native will be somewhat wealthy.

If the Moon were in the triplicity of Jupiter without the aspect of the infortunes, and Jupiter, being fortunate, possessed a good place in the figure, the native will have many riches, and he will be fortunate everywhere.

---

[784] Reading with Jag.
[785] That is, that Jupiter aspects *both*.
[786] Reading *infortunae* for *fortunae*.
[787] I believe that this means she is configured by a whole-sign trine with Jupiter, here and in the next sentence.

If Jupiter were in the domicile of the Moon, direct and appearing from out of the rays of the Sun, and free of the infortunes, the native will earn money on a journey, and he will always be wealthy.

If Jupiter were direct, with the Moon,[788] in some one of the angles, and free from the infortunes and burning up, the native will be wealthy and will live in importance from [his] good status.

If Jupiter, appearing in some one of his own dignities, were made fortunate in some one of the angles, the native will be wealthy, high and famous, and his mastery [will be] fine, and he will live a praiseworthy life.

If the Sun were with Venus and Mercury, [and] Saturn and the Moon in the Midheaven aspected them, the native will be wealthy, and [his] gain will not be removed from him, and his deeds will be beautiful.

If[789] Jupiter and Venus aspected the Moon by a good aspect, with the infortunes being cadent from them, the native will be wealthy, and he will commingle himself with kings and lofty men.

If Jupiter were in his own exaltation and in the Ascendant, and Saturn, appearing in Capricorn, aspected him from the west, the native will have money and substance.

If the Sun, appearing in his own exaltation, aspected the Moon by a trine aspect, and both were free of the infortunes, the native will be wealthy, and always overflowing with goods, not to mention conducting a decorated life, especially if the nativity were diurnal.

If the Sun were in a masculine sign and free from the infortunes, and the fortunes aspected him from their own domiciles by a good aspect, the native will be wealthy.

If the Sun and Venus were with the Moon in the Midheaven, and Venus [were] direct and in the good aspect of Jupiter, the native will be wealthy, of sound body, and honored by lofty men.

If the Sun were with Jupiter, and he aspected the Moon by a good aspect from out of the Midheaven, the native will be wealthy, of ample money, not to mention of great dominion and reputation.

If the Sun and Mercury were with Jupiter in his domicile, or they aspected Jupiter in his own domicile or exaltation, and the infortunes fell away[790] from

---

[788] Jag. reads "in the domicile of the Moon," which would put him in his exaltation in Cancer.
[789] Reading with Jag. for clarity.
[790] I.e., "were cadent," which undoubtedly means by whole-sign aspect.

them, the native will have much money, and will have honor and advantage in the city where he stays.

If the Sun, appearing in some one of his own dignities, aspected the Moon from out of the Ascendant or the 4th house by a good aspect, and the infortunes fell away from him, the native will be famous and fortunate.

If the Lot of Money and its Lord were free from the infortunes, in a good and strong place, and the fortunes aspected them, the native will be of ample money through his whole life, rejoicing and honored.

If[791] the Lord of the house of money were bound to the Lord of the Ascendant, the native will earn money without labor, and it will come to him from out of a place for which he does not hope.[792] And if the Lord of the Ascendant were bound to the Lord of the house of money, the native will acquire money with labor. And if some planet would be bearing away the light between them, the native will have money according to the nature of the one bearing it away. If the Lord of the Ascendant were separated from the Lord of the house of substance, the native will not acquire substance, and he will leave his mastery. And if the Lord of the house of money were separated from the Lord of the Ascendant, he will labor much in order to acquire money, but he will earn nothing or little.

Chapter II.3.2: On the administrators of kings, and their fortune[793]

If Jupiter were with Saturn in his[794] own domicile, the native will be an administrator[795] of kings or royal houses or lofty men, and thence he will obtain wealth and monies.

If Saturn were in the 3rd house, and he had dignity and strength in it, the native will be an administrator of kings, and other administrators will render accounts[796] to him.

If Saturn (it being a diurnal nativity) were in his own domicile and in the Ascendant, and Jupiter aspected him from out of the Midheaven, the native

---

[791] Cf. *JN* Ch. 11.
[792] I.e., either from an unexpected place, or from sources in which he does not have explicit hopes or efforts invested.
[793] The rest of the following chapters on wealth correspond to prosperity topic [5] from II.2.0, and I have organized it as best I could according to that list.
[794] I take this to refer to Jupiter. Jag. does not mention this.
[795] *Dispensator*. This word refers generally to administrators, but can also include treasurers.
[796] *Computum reddent*.

will be an administrator of kings or lofty men, and thence he will assemble many riches.

If Venus were in a domicile of Jupiter, and Jupiter aspected her[797] in the Midheaven by a good aspect, the native will be an administrator of queens or lofty ladies.

If an oriental Mercury, appearing in his own domicile or exaltation, possessed the 2nd house, and Venus aspected him by a good aspect, the native will be the administrator of some powerful and noble lord or lady.

If Venus (it being a nocturnal nativity), appearing in her own exaltation, possessed the 3rd house with Jupiter, the native will be an administrator of lofty lords. Which if Venus aspected the Moon from the 4th house [domicile], the native will be a greater lord.

Chapter II.3.3: On natives who are wise, and their fortune

If Mercury were with Venus in the Ascendant or the Midheaven, the native will be wise and a good writer,[798] and on the occasion of these things he will be elevated to status and honor; and by how much more he lived, by that much more will the honor and dignity be increased.

If Jupiter were with Mercury in the Midheaven, and the Sun aspected them by a good aspect, the native will be a famous speaker, and he will have the same dominion in the houses of kings.

If the Moon were in the square aspect of the Sun, and free of the infortunes, and appearing in the aspect of Jupiter, [and] she aspected Mercury, and Mercury were made fortunate, the native will be the greatest and renowned writer, and because of this he will be fortunate and wealthy.

If Jupiter aspected Mercury from out of the Midheaven, the native will be a writer. If Mercury, appearing in his own domicile, were joined to Jupiter (he appearing in the Midheaven), the native will be the king's writer, and he will be famous because of this.

If Mercury (it being a nocturnal nativity) were in the Ascendant and in his own exaltation, the native will be the secretary of kings or princes, and a wise

---

[797] Reading *eam* ("her") for *eum* ("him"). This condition is omitted in Jag.
[798] *Dictator*, here and below. This word has to do both with dictating to others, and composing texts oneself. But it also refers here to those in a high advisory role.

writer, and thence he will have good fame and fortune, he will assemble monies, and thus he will persist to the end of life.

If Mercury [were] the Lord of the house of substance, and Jupiter [were] with him or aspected him by a good aspect, and [from] a good and fortunate place, the native will be fortunate in writing, and he will have good from thence, and he will earn much money.

If Mercury were in the 5th house, and appearing in his own face, not to mention appearing from under the rays of the Sun, and cadent from the infortunes, and the Lord of his domicile aspected him by a good aspect with reception, the native will be fortunate in writing and legal assistance, and an assembler of many monies.

If Mercury, appearing oriental from under the rays of the Sun, not to mention appearing in his own domicile or exaltation, possessed the 9th house, and Jupiter (being free from the infortunes) aspected him by a good aspect, especially from out of the Midheaven, the native will be the king's writer, and wise in great secrets, and fortunate, with a fine appointment, faithful, famous, of good memory, and sufficient in all things.[799]

Chapter II.3.4: On the native's fortune from commerce

If Jupiter, appearing in some one of his own dignities, possessed the 10th house, and Mars aspected him by a good aspect, the native will a great merchant of goods.

If Mercury [were] direct and made fortunate in a domicile of Venus, and Venus aspected him from the 10th house by a good aspect, the native will be a great merchant.

If Mercury were made fortunate in a good place, the native will earn his substance from commerce, writing, or computation.

If Venus [were] in the Ascendant or in a common sign, especially appearing in her own exaltation, and free from the infortunes and retrogradation and burning up, the native will be a merchant of good memory, not to mention acquiring monies in many ways, and fortunate in commerce.

---

[799] A version of the 15° eminence rule for triplicity Lords originally appeared here, and seems to have been the result of a mixup between *Carmen* I.26.3 (which appears above in II.2.2) and I.26.4. I have deleted it here.

If Mercury were in the 2nd house (it being a nocturnal nativity), and in some one of his own dignities, [and] oriental, and he were free from the rays of the Sun, the native will trade in foreign money, and he will earn much, and he will have fortune in these things.

If Mercury were made fortunate in the 6th house (it being a diurnal nativity), and in the good aspect of Jupiter, and the infortunes fell away from him, the native will be fortunate in selling and buying. [And if Mercury is in the ninth sign and the infortunes do not aspect him, and he will be with one of the fortunes, oriental, he will be a merchant of fine goods, clinging to money.]

If Mercury were direct in the domicile of the Moon, and free from the rays of the Sun, and [he were] the Lord of the 2nd house, and the Moon in Virgo aspected him by a good aspect, the native will be fortunate in commerce.

If Mercury were the Lord of the 10th house and appearing direct in a domicile of Saturn, and Saturn [were] direct and safe from mixing,[800] [and] aspected [Mercury] from out of Libra, the native will be wise in commerce. [And if Saturn will be in a domicile of Mercury or in {*missing*} sign, the native will rejoice in commerce and he will have fortune.]

If Mercury were direct in a domicile of Jupiter, and Jupiter (being direct) even aspected him from out of Pisces, the native will be a strong and fortunate merchant.

If Jupiter were the Lord of the 10th house, appearing in some one of his own dignities, and a fortunate Mars aspected him by a trine aspect, the native will be fortunate in commerce from the middle of life up to the end [of it].

If[801] Jupiter were made fortunate in the Midheaven, and Mercury (being oriental and free from the infortunes) possessed a house with some one of the fortunes, the native will be a fortunate merchant, and have much money.

If the Moon were increased in light and number, and free from the infortunes, and Mercury (appearing in the good aspect of Jupiter) aspected her[802] from out of the 10th house by a good aspect, the native will rejoice in commerce, and will have fortune from it.

---

[800] *Confusione.* I assume this means, "safe from mixing *with Mars.*"
[801] These last two paragraphs are not in Jag.
[802] Reading *ipsam* for *ipsum*.

Chapter II.3.5: On the native's fortune from slaves and servants[803]

If Mercury were in some one of his own dignities and in a good sign [and good] place, not to mention free from the infortunes, and the fortunes aspected him by a good aspect, the native will obtain fortune and wealth from slaves.

If the Lot of Slaves were free from the infortunes, in the Midheaven, elevated over the Ascendant,[804] and the fortunes aspected [the Lot], the native will have many slaves and will get wealth and fortune from them.

If the Lord of the 6th house [were a fortune], made fortunate in some one of the angles, and[805] Venus were appearing [safe] from the [in]fortunes, the native will have fortune and wealth from slaves.

If Saturn were in some one of his own dignities and in a good place of the figure, and the fortunes aspected him by a good aspect, and the Lord of the Ascendant were bound to him, the native will have male and female slaves.

If Jupiter, in the 6th house and in some one of his own dignities, and the Lord of the 3rd house [were] with Mercury in some one of the angles, [and] they were also free from the infortunes, the native will have slaves, and will be successful[806] with them.

If Mercury were in the 12th house, and the fortunes aspected him, the native will sell slaves, and men will obtain profit from that selling.

If Venus, appearing in some one of her own dignities, were in the Midheaven, and the Moon aspected her from out of the house of slaves, the native will have slaves and will be successful with them.

If the Lord of the 6th house were in the 7th house, or made unfortunate under the earth, the native's slaves will die. Likewise, if the Tail of the Dragon were in the 6th house, the native will lose [his] slaves.

If Saturn were made unfortunate in the 2nd, 6th, or 12th house, the native will have sorrow from slaves. If Saturn were made unfortunate in the 6th house (it being a nocturnal nativity), the native will incur harm on the occasion of slaves.

---

[803] Cf. *JN* Ch. 22, *TBN* III.7, and II.12.32 below.
[804] That is, by definition the tenth sign from the Ascendant is in a superior square from it or "overcoming" it. Jag. reads, "elevated in the heaven."
[805] Jag. omits this part about Venus.
[806] *Proficiet*, here and below. This verb can also mean "to make money, be profitable."

If Mercury, appearing in some one of his own dignities, were in the Ascendant or Midheaven, and made unfortunate in a common sign, the native will hire servants.[807]

If the Lord of the house of children were in the 6th house, the native will sell his own children (so they become slaves), or he will make them available[808] to serve others. If the Lord of the 6th house were in the 5th house, the native will give his permission for his own slaves to generate other slaves for himself.[809] If the Lord of the house of children were in the 6th house, and he were bound to the Lord of the Ascendant, the native will sell or lease out his own children.

If the Lord of the house of slaves were in the 10th house, or were in the 10th house from the Lord of the Ascendant,[810] the native will elevate his own slaves.

Chapter II.3.6: On the native's fortune from beasts[811]

If Saturn were made fortunate in his own triplicity (it being a diurnal nativity), especially in a quadrupedal sign, the native will buy beasts, and will have wealth from them.

If Saturn were in the western angle and in a quadrupedal sign, direct, and appearing safe from the rays of the Sun, in some one of his own dignities, and Jupiter aspected him by a good aspect,[812] the native will obtain fortune from beasts. And judge the same if Saturn were not in the sign of a beast, and Jupiter aspected him from the sign of a beast.

If Mars (it being a nocturnal nativity) were in the 4th house and in a quadrupedal sign, and especially in a fiery sign, appearing in the 10th or 11th house, made fortunate, and the Sun and Jupiter aspected [him], the native will be a master of four-footed beasts, and be made fortunate because of them.

---

[807] *Conducet servientes.*
[808] *Exponet.* In its most traditional sense, this means he will expose or abandon them as infants for someone else to take.
[809] That is, by procreation.
[810] This is a clear instance of "overcoming."
[811] Cf. *JN* Ch. 23.
[812] Jag. adds, "from a quadrupedal sign."

If Mars were made fortunate in some one of his own dignities and in a quadrupedal sign, and the Lord of that sign, received by Jupiter, pushed to him, the native will buy many beasts.

If the Lord of the 12th house, appearing in a quadrupedal sign, were joined to Jupiter or Venus, the native will be made fortunate because of beasts, and will have profit from thence. If Sagittarius were the Ascendant, and Jupiter [were] joined to Mars, or [Mars] himself were in a quadrupedal sign, and he aspected Jupiter ([Jupiter] being in Cancer), the native will profit from beasts.

If the twelfth-part of the seven planets (especially that of the Sun, Moon, and of the Lord of the Ascendant), fell into[813] a quadrupedal sign, the native will be a rider of beasts.

If the Sun and Moon, Ascendant, Lot of Fortune, the Lord of the conjunction or the prevention of the nativity, were in a quadrupedal sign, the native will buy beasts.

If Mars were the Lord of the Ascendant [or] of the conjunction or the prevention of the nativity, not to mention in a good place of the figure and in some one of his own dignities, and the fortunes aspected him from a strong place by a good aspect, the native will buy beasts for riding.

If Mars were in a fearful place from the Ascendant and in a fiery sign, and Jupiter aspected [him] by a good aspect, the native will buy great beasts. And if it were in Capricorn, the native will have diverse beasts (as are horses, camels, sheep and cows).

If the sign of the 12th house were watery, and a peregrine Saturn [were] in it, the native will let his beasts go, because they will die on him.

Chapter II.3.7: On masters of soldiers, and their fortune

If the Moon were with Venus, and Jupiter and Mars aspected her by a trine aspect, the native will be a master of soldiers who take up others' matters with force, and he will be renowned for killing and disputes, and on account of this he will have honor and dignity among kings.

If Mars were in the Midheaven, and he aspected Jupiter and the Moon, the native will be a master of soldiers, fortunate in killing and a famous victor, [and] on account of this he will have honor from kings.

---

[813] Reading *in* for *ex*.

If Saturn were with Jupiter and Mercury, the native will be a master of soldiers and a victor over enemies, and defended by God.

If Mars, appearing in the Ascendant, were in his own domicile or exaltation, the native will be the head of soldiers and a lord of wars, and perfecting great matters.

If Mars were in the angle of the earth, and Jupiter in the Midheaven, the native will be a great master of soldiers, and subtle, and a victor over many cities, and he will be fortunate in disputes and in killing.

If Jupiter aspected the Moon and Mars by a trine aspect,[814] the native will be a lord of horses and the head of soldiers, not to mention honored by all, particularly if Jupiter were in a masculine sign. If the Sun were in a masculine sign, and he aspected the Moon and Mars by a trine aspect, the native will be famous in killing, and will be said to be bold and clever, and he will be an organizer of wars and always conquering, and he will have what he wants from [his] enemies.

If Jupiter, appearing in the 5th house in his own face, were the Lord of the house of life and of the Lot of Fortune, and Mars aspected [him] by a good aspect (it being a diurnal nativity), the native will be great and of far-reaching reputation among men, and flags or swords will be lowered before him; he will even be a lord of wars and perfecting great matters. But he will rule over men by force and iron.

If Saturn (and Mars)[815] were in the 9th house, and appearing from under the rays of the Sun, and he aspected the Lot of Fortune (it being in the Ascendant), the native will be great and powerful, and the head of many soldiers, and a victor over many things, but he will not fear God—rather, he will do things which are prohibited by God.

If Mars, in a nocturnal nativity, were in his own domicile or exaltation, and in the Midheaven, the native (even if he should be of a minor lineage) will still be elevated by kings or powerful men, and he will be wealthy, and the head of the king's soldiers.

---

[814] Here and in the next paragraph I wonder if Abū Bakr has a certain Persian theory in mind. In *BOA* (p. 253) Bonatti explains that the Moon and Mars signify endings and changes of state; if there is a connection here, then Jupiter and the Sun signify renown in relation to wars and changes in rule.

[815] Parentheses mine, since the verbs used are in the singular and seem to refer primarily to Saturn's being in this condition, with Mars as another possibility.

If some one of the *biyābānīya* stars of the second magnitude and of the nature of Mars and Jupiter[816] were in the Ascendant or the Midheaven, or with the Sun or Moon, the native will have a great heart, and of a high place and appointment, and he will be a lord of soldiers who will win villas and fortresses as profit; his commands concerning acts of war will be perfected, [and he will be] a victor and of good memory.

And if some one of the *biyābānīya* stars of the first magnitude, and of the nature of Mars and Mercury,[817] were in the above-said places, the native will be a lord of soldiers and wars, putting himself into great deeds; his command will be perfected, and he will be made fortunate in his own affairs and wars; he will be a victor over his enemies; he will organize wars with deliberation and knowledge. He will have good sense, and will look to the status of his life and [its] final end long before [his own] death, especially if the nativity were a nocturnal one. But if it stood [as a] diurnal one, the native will be fearful, frenzied, of little piety, and observing evil in his heart.

If the Lot of Fortune were between Mars and Jupiter, and its Lord in a good and fortunate place, the native will be a master of soldiers, and he will have fame and a name, and a role in slaughter and strength, by the command of God.

Chapter II.3.8: On natives who are soldiers, and their fortune

If Mars, appearing in his own domicile or exaltation, and in the Midheaven, were the Lord of the Ascendant, and aspected the Moon in its[818] place, the native will be a strong and famous soldier, and will have reputation that he would freely expose himself in dangerous places.

If the Moon were in the Midheaven, or the Sun[819] in the Ascendant, the native will be strong and quick in his business matters.

And we have already said enough concerning this material, where we have recently handled the mastery or masteries of soldiers: judge therefore according to that what was written in that same place.

---

[816] See *BA* III.2.1, p. 78; Rhetorius Ch. 58 p. 102. The stars of the second magnitude in this group are: Antares (α Scorpio), Menkalinan (β Auriga), and Altair (α Aquila).

[817] See *BA* III.2.1, p. 79; Rhetorius Ch. 58 p. 105. The stars of the first magnitude in this group are: Bellatrix (γ Orion), Procyon (α Canis Minor), and Betelgeuse (α Orion).

[818] *Suo* (Jag.). I am not sure whether this is the Moon in a domicile of Mars, or in her own domicile.

[819] Jag. has the Moon.

Chapter II.3.9: On the native's fortune on the occasion of money in the earth or found elsewhere

If Saturn, appearing in some one of his own dignities, were in the 4th house, and made fortunate in the good aspect of Jupiter,[820] the native will find great wealth hidden under the earth, especially if Saturn were slow in his motion.

If Jupiter is appearing in the angle of the earth, and Venus aspected him by a good aspect, and both were free from the infortunes, the native will find great wealth or money underground.

If the Lord of the 2nd house were in the 4th house, and it pushed light and strength[821] to a planet appearing in the Ascendant or the 4th house, secret monies[822] will be uncovered for the native, and he will find underground money.

If the Lord of the Ascendant were in the Ascendant, and Jupiter pushed to him from out of the angle of the earth, the native will find underground money.

If Venus, as the Lady of the 2nd house, were in the angle of the earth, and the Sun and Moon (being in signs elevated over Venus)[823] aspected[824] her, the native will take silver from the earth and find underground money.

If Mercury, appearing as the Lord of the 2nd house, were made fortunate in the angle of the earth, the native will take heavy things [from out of the ground] by his own understanding,[825] and he will understand the secrets of the sciences, and something which he wants to devise or arrange will not be concealed from him.

Chapter II.3.10: On the native's fortune coming about from the inheritances of the dead

If the Moon, filled with light and increased in number, were in the 8th house (it being a nocturnal nativity), and Jupiter, made fortunate and

---

[820] Jag. omits this part about Jupiter.
[821] Reading *fortitudinem* for *ordinatio[nem]*.
[822] Reading *secretae pecuniae* for *secreta pecuniae*.
[823] This sounds like the Hellenistic "overcoming."
[824] Reading *aspexerint* (pl.) for *aspexerit*.
[825] *Sensu*: plan, intent, sense.

appearing in some one of his own dignities, aspected her from out of the 11th house,[826] the native will be wealthy and will inherit the money of the dead.

If the Lord of the 8th house were with the Sun, not burned up but made fortunate in the Midheaven or the 11th house,[827] the native will have money from the direction of the dead, but he will lose or consume it quickly.

If Jupiter, increased in number, or appearing in some one of his own dignities, possessed the 8th house, the native will have good and fortune from the direction of the dead, especially if Jupiter were free from the conjunction or aspect of the infortunes.

If the Lord of the 8th house were a fortune, and the Lord of the house of substance were bound [to him], the native will have something from the dead.

If Saturn were in the 8th house (it being a diurnal nativity), and some one of the fortunes aspected by a good aspect, the native will obtain money from the dead.

If the Lord of the 8th house, appearing in some one of its own dignities, were made fortunate in the Midheaven, the native will have good fortune, and he will obtain money from the dead. And if some one of the infortunes aspected by a good aspect, his father will die and he will have the paternal inheritances and dignities, and he will be a good heir in the father's stead.[828]

If the Lot of Possession[829] were in the 8th house, and its strength [were] greater than the Lord of the 2nd house, the native will have money and inheritances.

If the Lord of the Lot of Fortune were in the 8th house, and the Lord of the Ascendant aspected him, the native will live on the things of the dead.

If the Lord of the 8th house, being a fortune, were in the 8th house, not burned up nor retrograde, the native will have the substance of inheritances.[830]

If the Lord of the 2nd house gave his power to the Lord of the 8th with reception, from out of a bound,[831] and he were in the domicile of a fortune,

---

[826] Jag. reads, "2nd."
[827] Jag. reads, "2nd."
[828] *Loco patris.*
[829] Probably the Lot of Money/Substance.
[830] Reading *haereditatum* for *haeredum*. This sentence does not appear in Jag.
[831] *Ex termino.* Meaning uncertain. This sentence does not appear in Jag.

the native will inherit the substance of inheritances;[832] and judge likewise if the Lot of Fortune were in the 8th house, joined to some fortune.

Chapter II.3.11: On the native's fortune from fields and gardens

If Venus, appearing in some one of her own dignities, were in the angle of the earth, and free from the infortunes, the native will have many fields.

If Saturn were in a good place and in his own domicile or exaltation, and he aspected the Ascendant by a trine aspect, the native will be rich from lands, gardens or fields. If Saturn were the Lord of possession and in the Ascendant or in the second, conjoined or bound with it[833] or aspecting it from a strong place, the native will have fortune from fields and vineyards. If Saturn, appearing direct and in his own exaltation, were in the Midheaven, the native will be a lord of fields, lands, vineyards, and he will value the populations [on them] and the buildings, and will be made fortunate in them.

If some one of the *biyābānīya* stars of the second magnitude (and also of the nature of Mars and Venus)[834] were in the Ascendant or the Midheaven with the Sun or Moon, the native will be rich, and fortunate in lands or fields, and he will build houses and palaces. And if some one of the *biyābānīya* stars of the first magnitude (and of the nature of Jupiter and Saturn)[835] behaved thusly with each other, the native will be rich and moneyed, not to mention overflowing in real estate, lands, and vineyards, and thence he will obtain fame and dominion.

If the Moon were separated from the Sun, in the domicile of the Sun,[836] and she were bound to a fortunate Saturn, the native will have profit from lands, and he will build houses.

If Saturn were in the angle of the west and in a domicile of Jupiter, and Jupiter (appearing in the angle of the earth)[837] were bound to him, the native will possess many lands, and will be made fortunate in building, the populace [on it], and the like.

---

[832] Reading *haereditatum* for *haeredum*.
[833] Reading with Jag., but it is unclear who is meant here.
[834] This must be the two stars of the first magnitude from *BA* III.2.1 p. 80, and Rhetorius Ch. 58 p. 107: Aldebaran (α Taurus) and Antares (α Scorpio).
[835] The stars of the first magnitude in this group are from *BA* III.2.1 p. 78, and Rhetorius Ch. 58 p. 103: Rigel (β Orion) and Capella (α Auriga).
[836] These references to the Sun are not in Jag.
[837] Omitting "and Pisces" (1540).

If Saturn were made unfortunate in the western angle, the place where the native is will be destroyed: that is, it will go to ruin. And if Mars were made unfortunate in the west, and he aspected the Moon by a square aspect, the destruction of the said place will be by fire. And if it were the Sun, Mars, and the Head of the Dragon,[838] and an infortune aspected them, the native's home will be destroyed.

---

[838] *Jawzahirr* (Pahlavi).

[Chapter II.4.0: Siblings]

The ancient sages look at the matter of brothers from many places, namely: from [1] the 3rd house and [2] its Lord, and from [3] the Lords of its triplicity, from [4] the Lot of Brothers and [5] its Lord, from [6] the Lot of Fortune and [7] its Lord, and also from [8] Saturn, Jupiter, Mars, the Sun, Venus, Mercury, the Moon, and [9] a planet appearing in the 3rd house. For through the 3rd house and its Lord we will know whether the native will have more siblings, or whether he will be alone. The Lot of Fortune and its Lord[839] indicates the siblings' fortune and their misfortune, being raised up or being pressed down. The Sun and Saturn indicate older brothers, Jupiter and Mars, middle ones, Mercury younger ones; the Moon, older sisters, and Venus younger ones.

[Chapter II.4.1: Multiple siblings]

If you wished to know whether the native will be the first-born or not, if the Lord of the triplicity of the Ascendant were in the Ascendant, the native will be first-born. And if it were in the Midheaven, he will be the first or fourth; and if it were in the 7th, he will be the first or seventh. Likewise, if you did not find one of the planets between the Ascendant and the Midheaven, the native will be the first one. If the Lord of the triplicity of the Ascendant in a diurnal nativity were in the Ascendant, the native will be first one, [and] one who will be relieved concerning siblings, because those who were [born] before [him] will die. If the Sun were in the Ascendant, the native will be the first one, and he will see the diminution and scarcity of [his] siblings.

If the Lord of the house of siblings were in the Ascendant, the native will be alone, without siblings. And if it were in a sign of many children, and a fortune aspected it, the native will have many brothers and sisters. If the Head of the Dragon[840] were in the 4th house, and Jupiter, the Sun and Venus were with the Moon, or they aspected her, the native will have many siblings and will rejoice with them.

---

[839] But cf. *BA* III.3.6, which combines the Lot of Fortune with the Lot of Brothers.
[840] *Jawzahirr* (Pahlavi).

If the Lot of Brothers were strong and made fortunate in some one of the angles, the native will have siblings of great power. If the Lord of the Lot of Brothers were in a sign of many children, the native will have many siblings. And if it were strong under the earth, the native will have siblings older than himself. If Jupiter, Venus and Mercury were in a good and strong place, and in feminine signs, the native will have sisters. If the Lord of the house of siblings were in a good place and oriental, and a fortune aspected him, the native will have siblings.

If[841] the Lord of the triplicity of Mars were in a sign of many children, the native will have many siblings.

If the Moon were the Lady of the 3rd house, the native will have many sisters.

If the Lord of the 3rd house and the Lord of the Lot of Brothers were in the Ascendant or in the Midheaven, the native will have siblings. And if it were in sterile signs, the native will lack siblings. And if one part of them were in watery signs, and the other in sterile ones, it signifies a middling number of siblings. And one must judge concerning this [matter] according to the proportion of the planets.

If the Lot of Brothers were in a masculine sign, and Mars in the Ascendant, the native will have brothers without sisters. And if it were the other way around, you will judge to the contrary. And if one part would be in a masculine sign, and the other in a feminine one, the native will have brothers and sisters.

If Venus were the Lady of the 3rd house and in a feminine sign, the native will have sisters younger[842] than himself. And judge [older ones][843] if the Moon were separated from Mars. And if it were Venus (just as I said concerning the Moon),[844] the native will have sisters older than himself.

If the planet who is conjoining the testimony of the planets, and who signifies brothers and sisters, were in a good and strong place, and it were ascending in its own circle, it indicates the addition and multitude of brothers and sisters.

---

[841] *BA* III.3.3 item 1.5.
[842] Reading *minores* for *maiores*.
[843] Reading *sorores maiores* for *idem* ("the same"). The Moon signifies older sisters, Venus younger ones.
[844] That is, with the Moon separating from Venus. Cf. *JN* Ch. 13 p. 267.

Chapter II.4.2: On the scarcity of siblings

If the first and second Lords of the triplicity of the Ascendant were in the 3rd house, the native will lack siblings; and if he had them, they will die before him.

If Saturn, Mars and the Sun were in feminine signs, and in cadent places, it signifies the death of the siblings. If Mars and the Lord of the 3rd house, and the Lord of the Lot of Brothers, were under the rays of the Sun, all the native's siblings will die before him. And if all three were not [placed] in this manner, one part of the siblings will live and the other will die, especially if it were made unfortunate in this place.

If the Lot of Brothers were joined with Saturn, or in his square or opposite aspect, and the fortunes did not aspect [the Lot], it signifies the death of the native's siblings.

If powerful [in]fortunes[845] made the Lot of Brothers unfortunate, there will be death in the sisters. If Venus, appearing as the Lady of the 3rd house, were made unfortunate, the native's younger sisters will die. And if it were the Moon instead of Venus, the older sisters will die.

If[846] Saturn or the Sun were made unfortunate, the native's older siblings will die. And if Jupiter were made unfortunate, the native's middle siblings will die. And if some were made unfortunate, and others not, one part of the siblings will die and the other will be healed.

If the infortunes were between the Ascendant and the 4th house,[847] made unfortunate, the native will lack siblings, nor will [another] child be born to the mother except a dead one. If the Lord of the triplicity of the Ascendant were under the earth, and the infortunes made it unfortunate, the native's siblings will die. And judge the same if there were infortunes in the Ascendant and the Midheaven. If Venus were with Saturn below the earth, the native's sisters will die.

If the Lot of Brothers were in a domicile of Mars, and infortunes aspected [the Lot] by a bad aspect, the native's younger siblings will die. And if the Sun or Saturn were the Lord of that Lot, the older ones will die. And if Jupiter or Mars were the Lord of that Lot, or the Lot [were] in their domiciles, the native's middle siblings will die.

---

[845] Reading more with Jag. for *pars fortunae* ("Lot of Fortune"). The parallel text seems to be *BA* III.3.2, item 3.1, but the Lot of Brothers plays no role and so is of no help.
[846] Cf. *BA* III.3.4 and *JN* Ch. 13 p. 267.
[847] Reading *et quartam domum* for *secundae et quartae domus*. Cf. *JN* Ch. 13, p. 267.

If the Moon, separated from Saturn, were bound to Jupiter, the native's older siblings will die. And if it were Venus instead of the Moon, the younger ones will die.

If the Lord of the house of siblings, appearing oriental, were in the 2nd house and in the aspect of a fortune, the native will inherit his siblings' things.

If the Lord of the Lot of Brothers were in its own dignity and in the 2nd house, and its Lord [were] strong, and the Lord of the Ascendant made unfortunate, the native's siblings will inherit [his things].[848]

Chapter II.4.3: On the native's fortune with the siblings

If the Lord of the 3rd house, appearing from under the rays, were in a good place and in some one of the Moon's dignities, and the Moon [were] in the same sign, and the infortunes [were] separated from the Lord of the 3rd house, and even from the Moon, the native will have profit from the siblings, and they from him, because [they will be] of one status, and one will have good and honor from the other.

If a planet of much testimony were the indicator of the siblings, and it aspected the *hīlāj* by a good aspect, it signifies the agreement of the native's siblings, and esteem between them.

If the Lord of the 3rd house were in a good place, and some one of its own dignities, the native will have joy from the siblings, and they will love him.

If the Lot of Fortune were in the 3rd house, and the Lord of the said Lot of Fortune in a good place,[849] it portends the esteem of the siblings and advancement for the native.

If the Lot of Brothers were in the 3rd, 9th, or 11th house, and the fortunes aspected it, it indicates kindness between the siblings, and the advancement of one with the other.

If the Lord of the Lot of Brothers pushed its own power to[850] the Lord of the Ascendant, the native's siblings will honor him, and will prefer him, and they will be in his obedience and protection.

---

[848] *Ipsum.*
[849] Omitting *ac.*
[850] Reading *ad* (and the accusative case) for *a.*

If the Lot of Brothers were made fortunate in the house of children, the native will have[851] younger siblings, and they will be under his protection.

If the Lot of Brothers were made fortunate in the 2nd house, the siblings' life will come from the native, and he will bestow [things] freely to them from his own goods.

If the Lord of the house of substance pushed power to the Lord of the Lot of Brothers, the native's siblings will have money on the occasion of him, especially if the said Lord of substance, a fortune, were made fortunate, and he received the Lord of the house of siblings.

If Mars were made fortunate in his own domicile or exaltation, and he aspected the Lot of Fortune by a good aspect, the native will have advancement from the direction of his siblings.

Chapter II.4.4: On the siblings' enmity

If the Lord of the house of siblings were peregrine and made unfortunate in the 12th house, the native's siblings will be enemies to him and he to them, and they will do evil to him, and he to them.

If Saturn were peregrine in the 3rd house, and Mars aspected him by a good aspect, there will be enmity between the brothers and sisters, and the native will be inimical to them.

If Jupiter, appearing retrograde, were in the 3rd house with the Tail of the Dragon and Saturn, the native will have evil on the occasion of the siblings.

If the Lot of Brothers were with an infortune in the 7th house, the native's siblings will plot against him, and will strain to destroy him.

If Saturn, Mars, the Sun, and the Moon aspected each other by a bad aspect, the native's siblings and he will kill each other.

If[852] Taurus or Libra were the 3rd house, and Mars aspected that place by a bad aspect, and the Lord of the 3rd house were separated from the Lord of the Ascendant,[853] losses will come to the native, and his siblings will seek to kill him, unless he[854] were protected by a fortune. [If Mars and Venus were in the third, the native will find loss and evil from the brothers, and they will be inimical to him.]

---

[851] Omitting *se* with Jag.
[852] Reading this sentence with Jag.
[853] 1540 reads: "made unfortunate and in a bad place."
[854] This probably refers to the Lord of the 3rd.

If the Lord of the 3rd house were made unfortunate and peregrine in the 6th house,[855] he will receive evils and losses from the siblings.

If the Lord of the 3rd house were in the Ascendant, or it aspected the degree of the Ascendant by a good aspect, there will be perfect friendship between the native and his siblings; and if it aspected it from a bad aspect, there will be hatred and anger between them.

If Mars, appearing peregrine, aspected the degree of the Ascendant or its Lord by a bad aspect, the native will do battle with his siblings.

If Cancer or Capricorn were ascending, the native will squabble[856] with his siblings. And if Aries or Libra were ascending, the native will be the occasion of their death, and disputes will be renewed for him in a foreign land, or with men staying as guests [in his land]. And if Taurus or Scorpio were ascending, the native will have a dispute with women, and obtain substance from lands, but more of his friends will die. And if Gemini or Sagittarius were ascending, the native's siblings will destroy his substance, and more of his children will be his enemies.

Chapter II.4.5: On the misfortune and fall of the siblings

If the Lord of the house of siblings were an infortune, and in addition it appeared retrograde and in a bad place, and the Lot of Brothers [were] in the 2nd house under the rays of the Sun, made unfortunate, the native's siblings [will be] unfortunate, and certain ones of them will be incarcerated or suffer a chronic illness. And if the said Lot is in the [second from the Ascendant and made unfortunate by a bad one, the native's brothers will suffer a chronic illness and many evils. And if the Lot were made unfortunate in the sixth from the Ascendant, and {the place} is made unfortunate by Saturn, certain brothers of the natives will kill their slaves, and {others} will be just like slaves].[857] [The Lot of Brothers in the sixth, free from the bad ones, the brothers will be poor and do all evil things, and they will be in need. And if the Lot is in the 12th and its Lord had testimony there, and it aspects its own place, {the brothers will do the bad works of kings?}.][858] If the Lot of

---

[855] Omitting 1540's "and made unfortunate in the 3rd house."
[856] *Litigabit.* Or, "litigate."
[857] Adding a paraphrase of Jag. 1540 combines the two sentences but leaves key points out.
[858] Adding a paraphrase of Jag.

Brothers were made unfortunate in the house of travel, and even its Lord made unfortunate, it signifies the foreignness[859] of the native's siblings, and separation from him.

If the Lord of the Ascendant and the Lord of the Lot of Brothers did not aspect [each other], and the Lord of the Lot of Brothers likewise did not cast a ray at the Lot,[860] the native's siblings will be separated, and they will not be conjoined.

If the Lot of Fortune were joined with an infortune in the 3rd house, or it aspected an infortune by a bad aspect, it portends the native's siblings' labor, and their fall,[861] and misery.

If a planet having many testimonies in the matter of siblings were made unfortunate, and in a bad place, the native's siblings will be full of labor.

And if you wished to know the number of the siblings, look at the Lord of the triplicity of the Ascendant: and if you found it above the earth, count from it up to the Ascendant, and how many[862] were between them, the number of the siblings will be that much; and count two siblings for every common sign. And if the said Lord of the triplicity were under the earth, count from the Ascendant up to the sign in which he is, and what came out will be the number of siblings. Which[863] if the sign of siblings were common, and its Lord in a common sign, the native will have siblings who will not be from one father and one mother, but they will be only from his own father or from his own mother.

Look even at the Lords of the triplicity of the house of siblings: if they were with the Lot of Fortune, and the Lord of the said Lot [were] strong, and in a good place, then the native's siblings will have a good reputation, being raised up, and loftiness. But you should know that the first Lord of the triplicity signifies older siblings, the second one the middle ones, and the third the younger ones. Therefore, judge concerning the siblings' status according to the strength or weakness, good fortune or misfortune, of the said Lords.

---

[859] *Extraneitatem.* This seems to mean simply that they live in foreign places, not that they have an estranged relationship.
[860] Jag. has the Lords of the Ascendant and of the Lot aspecting the Lord of the third.
[861] Omitting a redundant *laborem.*
[862] I take this to mean "planets." Cf. *BA* III.3.3, *JN* Ch. 13, *TBN* III.3, and *Carmen* I.17.
[863] *BA* III.3.4 item 3.3; Rhetorius Ch. 106.

[But Antir[?]calt says:][864] if the Lord of the house of siblings fell in the degree of the house of fathers, and the Lord of that place were a masculine planet, and in a masculine sign and degree, it signifies siblings on the part of the father.[865] And[866] if that planet were Venus, and in a feminine sign or degree, it indicates sisters on the part of the father.

Albucaic[867] said: [in his profit, loss, and fortune and misfortune, according to what that same planet signifies, concerning which he spoke, with an aspect and strength and elevation and depression and goodness and malice of his place, and were his aspect good {the brother will be} proven, praised, true, etc., if God wills.]

---

[864] Adding with Jag. 1540 attributes this statement to Albucaic or Almizut below.
[865] Reading *ex parte patris* with Jag. (and the next sentence) for *ex parte fratris*. This might mean something like a half-sibling through the father.
[866] This sentence is not in Jag.
[867] Jag. seems to read something like Almizut.

Chapter II.5.0: Parents

The father's status is known from eight significators, namely: from [1] the 4th house and [2] its Lord, from [3] the Lot of the Father and [4] its Lord, and [5] Saturn and the Sun, and [6] the planet appearing in the 4th house, and also from [7] the place of the conjunction or prevention preceding the nativity.

But [you will know] the mother's status from [1] the 10th house and[868] [2] its Lord, from [3] the Lot of the Mother and [4] its Lord, from [5] the Moon and Venus, and from [6] the planet appearing in the 10th house, and also from [7] the place of the conjunction or prevention preceding the nativity.

Therefore if the planet conjoining the testimonies and significations in the matter of the parents were in a strong place, made fortunate and received, judge good and fortune for the parents from that nativity. And if it were different from this, you will judge the contrary.

Chapter II.5.1: On the parents' exaltation

If the planet having dominion with respect to the Lot of the Father[869] were in an angle or a succeedent, and also in its own domicile or exaltation, it signifies the exaltation of the father and his honor, and the elevation of his status. If the Lot of the Mother were situated just as I said regarding the Lot of the Father, it signifies the mother's elevation and [her] honor.

If Jupiter were in the 4th house, with him appearing in his own domicile or exaltation, the native's father will be high, famous, rich, and someone who will have some dignity or dominion.

If the Lord of the Lot of Fathers were made fortunate [and] strong, in some one of the angles, and free from the aspect of an infortune, the native's father will be famous, and high in his kin.

If the Lord of the 4th house were in an angle, the native's father will have great standing.

---

[868] Omitting "and the Ascendant," to stand in parallel with the father's significators.
[869] Reading *parte patris* for *parentibus*. It might also be the "Lot of Parents," as this is sometimes used in *BA*, although in Valens the Lot of the Father and the Lot of Parents are distinct.

If the Lot of the Father were in the 3rd, 9th, or in the 11th house,[870] the native's father will have great status, [and] the native's parents will be famous and praised in their own city.

If the Sun were in his own domicile or exaltation, and in a good place (it being a diurnal nativity), the native's father will have a high name and a great voice in his city. And if Saturn bore himself thusly in a nocturnal nativity, you will judge the same.

If planets [relevant to] the signification of fathers were conjoined[871] in the Midheaven, and in their own domiciles or exaltations, and fortunes (being free of the infortunes) aspected them, the native's father will be a great lord. If the aforesaid planets aspected the degrees of the conjunction or prevention preceding the nativity, and the fortunes likewise aspected, the native's parents will have a high and good name.

If the Sun aspected[872] the angle of the earth, and also Saturn and Jupiter,[873] by a good aspect [and] with reception, the native's father is of those who will have dominion and power.

If the Moon and Venus aspected the 4th house, there will be fame and praise for the mother. If Venus were in the Ascendant, and made fortunate in a feminine sign, the native's mother will be more noble than the father.

Chapter II.5.2: On the parents' fall or being pressed down

If[874] the Sun were peregrine in the 12th house, and the Lord of the house of substance (the 2nd) [and] of the 4th [were] in bad places, and likewise the fortunes[875] appeared in bad places, the native's parents will be pressed down.

If the planet having greater testimony in the signification of the parents were peregrine in the 12th house, the native's parents will have a small status, [a bad background], and their wealth [will be] from wages.[876]

---

[870] Jag. lists: the second, fifth, ninth, and third.
[871] Reading *coniuncti* for *coniunctiones*.
[872] Reading *aspexerit* (sing.) for *aspexerint* (pl.).
[873] Jag. adds, "and Venus." But it is unclear whether the Sun must be aspecting all of these, or these other planets are also aspecting the angle of the earth.
[874] In Jag., this sentence applies only to the Sun in the 12th, with no further conditions given.
[875] Omitting *in-*.
[876] *Mercede*.

If the Moon were diminished in light and number in Scorpio and in the 4th house, and the Lord of the 4th house [in this case] appeared in a bad place, wild and retrograde, and also lacking the aspect of a fortune, the native's mother will have a small status and substance. [And likewise if the Sun is in Libra in the fourth, the native's father will be the lowest, bad, and falling down. And if the Lord of Libra will be receding from the angles, the native's father will be a slave.][877]

[And if the Moon is in the 12th from the Ascendant, and especially if the Sun aspected her, the native's mother will be a slave, infirm, a servant.]

If the Lord of the domicile of the Sun, or the Lord of the Lot of Fathers, or the twelfth-part of the Sun, or the Lord of the triplicity of the Sun, were in the 6th house and in the aspect of an infortune, the native's father will be greedy, have a bad background, and be falling down. If the twelfth-part of the Moon were in the 6th house with an infortune, or in the bad aspect of an [in]fortune, the native's father will be a slave and in need.

If the Lord of the Lot of Fathers were peregrine in a blameworthy place, without the aspect of a fortune, the native's father will be full of labor [but] have little or no success.[878]

If the Lord of the domicile of the Sun were with the Lord of his triplicity in cadent places, and in the bad aspect of an [in]fortune, the native's father will be a slave.

[And if the Lord of the twelfth sign is with the Sun, the native's father will be a slave.]

If the infortunes made the degrees of the conjunction or prevention preceding the nativity unfortunate, the native's father will be falling down from his status.

If the sign of the conjunction or prevention were made unfortunate, and both infortunes [were] in the angle of the earth, or they aspected the angle itself by a bad aspect without the fortunes sending rays, the native's parents will be from a bad lineage, and conceived in servitude.

If the Lord of the domicile of the Sun, or the Lord of the conjunction[879] of the nativity, or the Lord of the Lot of Fathers, were made unfortunate,[880]

---

[877] Adding and slightly paraphrasing from Jag.
[878] Reading *profectum* (as something generically good) for *labor*. See a parallel passage in *BA* III.4.3, item 2.2.
[879] Omitting "or prevention," as that pertains to the mother.
[880] For both the mother and father, Jag. also allows the sign of the prenatal syzygy to be made unfortunate.

it portends the father's fall or being pressed down. If the Lord of the domicile of the Moon, and the Lord of the domicile of the[881] prevention, or the Lord of the[882] Lot of Mothers were made unfortunate, it signifies the mother's evil and fall.

If the Sun were wild, with the Tail of the Dragon, in a feminine sign, the native's father will be falling down or be a slave.

If the Sun[883] and the Moon were bound to infortunes in the conjunction or prevention of the nativity,[884] and the fortunes were cadent from the places of their joys, the native's parents will not be of the same status nor of the same estate[885] nor city.

Chapter II.5.3: On the native's friendship and enmity with the parents[886]

If the Sun were in the bound of Mars (it being a diurnal nativity), or the Moon in the bound of Saturn (in a nocturnal nativity), and both infortunes aspected [the luminary by a bad aspect] without the aspects of the fortunes,[887] there will be enmity and hatred between the native's parents and the native himself.

If the Lot of the Father and the Lot of the Mother were [in the 12th from the Ascendant], the native's parents will be inimical to the native himself, and he will have oppression and labor from them.

If the Lord of the Ascendant, appearing peregrine, aspected the Lord of the 4th house and the Sun in a diurnal nativity (or Saturn in a nocturnal one), and also [aspected] the Lot of Fathers in an opposite aspect without reception, the native will be contrary to the parents. [And when there is an aspect of Venus and the Moon or the Lot of Mothers,[888] there will be hatred and contrariety with the mother.]

---

[881] Omitting "conjunction or," as that pertains to the father.
[882] Omitting *domus*.
[883] Jag. has only the Moon.
[884] I take this to mean that the *malefics* are in the signs of the pre-natal lunation, not the luminaries.
[885] *Villa*.
[886] Like the parallel passages in *BA* III.4.5 and Rhetorius Ch. 99, this chapter deals only with enmity.
[887] Reading *sine aspectu fortunarum* with *BA* III.4.5 and Rhetorius Ch. 99 for *sine infortunarum aspectu malo*.
[888] This should probably be combined with the other conditions earlier in the paragraph.

If the Sun were peregrine [in one of the angles, and especially] in the 4th house, and Mars aspected with the opposite aspect without reception, and likewise Saturn[889] sent a ray to the same place by an unfortunate aspect,[890] the native's parents will be inimical to the native himself.

If the Sun and the Lords of his triplicity were in a bad place and in a diurnal nativity, and the infortunes made them unfortunate without reception, by a conjunction or bad aspect, there will be enmity between the native and the parents.

[And if Saturn is elevated over Jupiter, or Jupiter is in the succeedent to the angle of the tenth, the native's parents will kill the child, and they will not care about him.][891]

[And if the planet which is conjoining the significations of the planets of his parents will be aspecting the significator of the native or the Lord of the Ascendant, when it has many and strong testimonies, by a square or opposite aspect, it signifies the {*unclear*} of that which the planet signified regarding the parents and the native.]

If the Sun, appearing wild[892] in the 4th house, appeared corporally joined to the planet having many testimonies in the native's nativity (and the Lord of the 4th house were peregrine [and] made unfortunate from the bad aspect of an infortune in the 8th house),[893] the father will bury the native alive, or he will deny that the native is his own [child].

If the planet which is the *mubtazz* of the parents were separated from the native's signification [whether] by a conjunction or aspect, the heart of the parents will be separated from the native, and they will hate him.

---

[889] Omitting *quartae domus*. But perhaps it should read, "Saturn *as the Lord of* the fourth house." The parallel sentences in *BA* III.4.5 and Rhetorius Ch. 99 do not mention Saturn.
[890] This sentence about Saturn is missing in Jag.
[891] Adding with Jag. In this case, Saturn would be overcoming Jupiter from the 8th house.
[892] Jag. omits this.
[893] My sense is that the malefic is supposed to be in the 8th, not the Lord of the 4th. Everything in the parentheses is missing in Jag.

Chapter 157: On the native's fortune with the parents

If Venus were in the second from the Ascendant, and that sign [were] the domicile of the Sun,[894] [and she were] direct and safe from burning up, and also in the good aspect of the Lord of the 4th house, the native will be made fortunate because of the father's money. And if Venus bore herself thusly in the domicile of the Moon, the native will be made fortunate from the mother's money.

If[895] the Sun were in a domicile of Jupiter and in the angle of the earth, joined with Jupiter by one minute, and the Lord of the 4th house aspected them with reception by a good aspect, the native will have money from the parents, and will be made fortunate because of that.

If Saturn were in his own domicile or exaltation, and in the Midheaven, and the Lord of the 4th house aspected him with reception from out of the angle of the earth, the native will be made fortunate by his father, and will have money from him.

If the Lord of the 4th house pushed from out of the 8th house, the native will inherit the parents' money.

If the Lord of the house of money gave its own power to the Lord of the 4th house, the parents will inherit the native's money.

Chapter II.5.5: On natives squandering the parents' money

If the twelfth-part of the Sun fell in the 12th house, and the infortunes aspected [the twelfth-part][896] by a bad aspect, the native will consume the parents' money, and he will make them sad.

If Saturn were peregrine in the 12th house, with the Lord of the 4th house,[897] the native will squander the parents' money.

If the fortunes were in the 4th house, and the Lord of its house were made unfortunate,[898] the native will lose the parents' money.

---

[894] Reading with Jag. for "as the Lady of the Ascendant, were in Leo and in the 2nd house." Some of the extra conditions here (such as the aspect to the Lord of the 4th) are missing in Jag.
[895] These conditions are very elaborate compared with Jag, which only has Jupiter conjoined to the Sun; the next paragraph is likewise much simpler in Jag.
[896] I take this to mean the 12th house, i.e., the house corresponding to the twelfth-part. Jag. omits the aspect from the infortunes.
[897] Jag. omits this clause about the Lord of the 4th.

[If the Sun by night is in the fourth from the Ascendant, the native will lose his parents' money, and he will be poor and needy. And if an infortune is in the second from the Sun, it signifies{he will waste his money and be in need and his life and status impeded}].[899]

[And if Saturn aspected the Moon from the seventh,[900] the native will lose his father's money and will live badly, and will be infirm in his life.]

[And if Saturn is being conjoined to the Sun, the father's money will recede and be harmed...until nothing remains.][901]

And[902] if the Sun will be with Mars, and the Moon aspected them from a square, it signifies that the money of the native's father will be diminished, and his life and status harmed. And if the Sun will be in the sixth or twelfth from the Ascendant, and Mars aspected him, the native will dissipate the father's money, and he will be in need. And if instead of the Sun it is the Moon or Venus, he will harm the mother's money and will throw away all of it.

Chapter II.5.6: On the fortune of the native's parents

If the Lord of the 4th house were in its own domicile or exaltation, made fortunate in a good place, and the Lord of the house of substance [were] in its own dignity and in the 4th house, and the Lot of the Father and its Lord appeared fortunate, the native's parents will be fortunate, and also they will see good and increase in their matters.

If the Sun, being the Lord of the 4th, were in the bound and in the face of a fortune (it being a diurnal nativity), and in the good aspect of Jupiter, it indicates the goodness of the native's parents.

---

[898] Omitting "with the Lord of the 5th house." Jag. has the infortunes aspecting the fourth instead of its Lord.
[899] Adding and paraphrasing with Jag.
[900] That is, from the opposition.
[901] Adding and paraphrasing with Jag.
[902] Reading with Jag. for the following: "If the Sun and Mars, being wild, were joined together, and the Moon diminished in light and number, [and] likewise should Saturn be joined to it in a bad place, and Mars aspected with a bad sending of rays without the aspect of a fortune, and the Lord of the house of substance appeared unfortunate in a bad place, the money will be diminished by the native." 1540 is probably right to want to emphasize the condition of the Moon.

If the Sun were joined corporally with Jupiter, in a domicile of Jupiter, and the Lord of the 4th house aspected them by a good aspect, it portends a good status and fortune for the native's parents.

If[903] Saturn in a nocturnal nativity will be in the Midheaven or in the place of the [Lot of] Fortune, or in some good place, the native's father will be fortunate [and] rich.

If the Lot of the Father were in the good aspect of the Lord of the house of substance, and he and the said Lot [were] made fortunate, and they appeared free from the infortunes,[904] it indicates forward movement, salvation, and fortune for the native's parents.

[And if Saturn is in the trine aspect of the Sun, the native's parents will find good and success, and better than that if it will be in a diurnal sign, received by the Lord of his own house.][905]

If[906] the Lord of the domicile of the Sun, appearing in his own domicile or exaltation with the Lord of the Lot of Fathers, were made fortunate in some one of the angles, the native's father will have a dignity or dominion.

If the Moon, conjoined to Venus in Taurus, possessed the Midheaven, and Mars, appearing in Scorpio, aspected her from out of the angle of the earth, the native's parents will obtain fortune and joy, by the command of God.[907]

Chapter II.5.7: On the labor and impediment of the native's parents[908]

You[909] should know that the Lord of the bound of the Sun and Moon, if they will be under the rays or in a bad place, receding, and the fortunes

---

[903] Reading with Jag. for "If Saturn, appearing in his own domicile or exaltation, were in the Midheaven, and Jupiter were the Lord of the 4th house, and he aspected with a good aspect, the native's father will be fortunate and rich."
[904] In all of this, Jag. has simply the Lot being strong and free of the infortunes.
[905] Reading with Jag. for "If Saturn, being in a diurnal [birth], were received by the Lord of the house of substance, and the Sun, being the Lord of the 4th house, aspected him by a trine aspect from out of Aries or Leo, the native's parents will find good and advancement and fortune." This reading does have merit, though.
[906] Missing in Jag.
[907] Jag. reads: "And if Mars will be aspecting the Moon from a sinister square, and the Moon is in the Midheaven, conjoined to Venus, it signifies the native's {*unclear*} and fame and joy."
[908] This chapter is exceedingly short in 1540 compared with Jag., and I have added the missing paragraphs in brackets.

cadent from it, the infortunes aspecting, it signifies the poverty of the native and of his parents.

If there were a wild infortune in the 7th house, and it aspected the Sun or Moon by a bad aspect, [it signifies that the native's parents have evil and poverty and fall and labor.]⁹¹⁰

[And if the Sun will be in the angle of the 7th, [and] the infortunes aspected him, the natives parents will go down from fortune to misfortune and a fall in their status.]

[And if the Moon will be in the 7th, made unfortunate, impeded, the native's mother is poor and needy.]

[And if Saturn will be in the opposition of the Sun, the native's father will have evil and labor. If the Moon will be with Mars and Saturn, the native's mother will become infirm and evil and neediness will conquer her.]

[And if the Sun will be conjoined to Mars or in his opposition or square, and more powerfully so if this is in diurnal nativities: it signifies the impediment of the father's status.]

[And if the Sun will be in the seventh with an infortune, it signifies the father's sorrow and grief, and he will have {bad thoughts because of money}.]

[And if the Moon will be in the bound of an infortune or in the third sign from the Ascendant, and that she is with the Head or Tail, it signifies that the mother was of noble stock and fine status; and especially with the Tail, but she fell and {she will live by labor and sweat}.]

[And if the infortunes will be in Leo (which is the domicile of the Sun), it signifies the father's impediment and misfortune, and the loss of money, and the changing of his life. And likewise if the infortunes will be in Cancer (which is the domicile of the Moon), it signifies the impediment and labor and neediness of the mother. And worse is if it is Saturn by night in the domicile of the Moon, and Mars by day in the sign of the Sun. And if the Tail will be in some one of the aforesaid places, evil is signified by that sign, and descending and a bad life. And if the Moon is being conjoined to Saturn, the native's mother will be weak and dry.]

---

⁹⁰⁹ Reading with Jag. for "If the Lord of the 4th house were in a falling house, burned up or retrograde, the native will not buy lands."
⁹¹⁰ Reading with Jag. for "and the Lot of Fathers and its Lord appeared unfortunate in a bad place, and the fortunes retrograde or uncivilized in cadent places, the native's parents will have evil and impediment on the occasion of him."

If the Sun and the Lord of his triplicity were in the 6th or 12th house, made unfortunate, and in the aspect of an infortune, evils and a chronic illness will befall the native.

[If Mars and Saturn will be with the Sun or aspecting from the square or opposition or trine from one of the angles, the native's father will have chronic and strong illnesses in his body.]

If the Moon were conjoined to Saturn,[911] the native's mother will be weak [with chronic illnesses].

[And if the Moon will be decreasing in light, and Saturn in an angle, and that he is made unfortunate under the rays, it signifies evil and chronic illness, and laborious and bad worries for the native's parents.]

[And if the Moon is being conjoined to Mars and {she is increasing in light} the native's mother will have evil and illness in her body. And if Saturn will be above the Sun and in the western angle, the native's father will have evil and a defect in his body.][912]

Certain people said that if Mars and Saturn were in the 4th house, and the said house is not the domicile of some fortune, nor [were] there some fortune in it, the native will be dragged out of his burial place.

Chapter II.5.8: On the death of the native's parents[913]

If the Sun, Saturn, Mars and Mercury were in the 4th[914] house, the native's father will die quickly. If the Moon bore herself just as was said regarding the Sun, the native's mother will die quickly enough after his nativity.

If the Lord of enemies were in the 8th house, and the infortunes aspected him by a bad aspect, the native's father will live [only] a little bit.

[If Mars were in the {*illegible*} or in the second from the Ascendant, the native's father will have little life.] If Mars were elevated over the Sun,[915] the native's father be killed by the sword.

If the Sun and the Lords of his triplicity were made unfortunate, the native's father will be killed.

---

[911] Jag. adds, "in her/his orientality."
[912] 1540 reads: "If the Sun were peregrine in the western angle, and in the bad aspect of an infortune, and the Lord of the 4th house burned up, and the Lord of the Lot of Fathers unfortunate, the native's parents will incur evil and labor and falling down."
[913] For many statements in this chapter, cf. *BA* III.4.6-7 and III.4.9.
[914] Reading with Jag. for "6th."
[915] This must refer to "overcoming."

If Mars were in the domicile of the Sun, the native's father will leave the world behind by means of a sudden death, especially if the nativity were diurnal; but if it were nocturnal, he will live [only] a little bit. [If Mars will be in the domicile of the Moon in a nocturnal nativity, it signifies the mother's death.]

If Saturn were in the opposition of the Sun, the native's father will die a bad death.

If the infortunes aspected the place of the conjunction or prevention preceding the nativity without a fortune sending rays, it portends a bad death for the native's parents; but the conjunction especially signifies the father, but the prevention the mother.

[And if the Moon, after the separation of the Sun {in the conjunction}, will be bound to an infortune, it signifies the bad death of the father; but if the prevention, it will be the mother's.]

If Saturn and Mars were in the house of fathers, and they aspected the Lord of the said house,[916] the native's father will die by an abscess or another illness leading to a quick death.

If the Lord of the Lot of Fathers, being in a bad place, aspected the Ascendant and the place of the said Lot, and in addition the said Lord were made unfortunate, the native's father will die in a place where he will not be known.

If the Lord of the Lot of Fathers, appearing in a bad place, [and will be burned up or] in the bad aspect of the infortunes, and [worse than this if the bound of the Lot is made unfortunate],[917] it indicates death and loss for the father's life.

If the Lord of the house of fathers were bound to the Lord of the 8th house in the 4th house,[918] and both were made unfortunate, and the Sun and the Moon [were] in cadent and bad places, it signifies the parents' death.

[If Mars aspected the Sun from the Ascendant in a diurnal nativity, and the fortunes did not aspect the Sun, the native's parents will die a bad death. And if Mars is being conjoined to the Sun in one sign, the native's father will die a bad death. And if the Moon will be in the west and is setting, the native's mother will die.]

---

[916] Jag. has the malefics in the fourth or aspecting it.
[917] Reading with Jag. for "likewise the Lord of life appeared as the Lord of the Father."
[918] Jag. seems to read, "with the Lord of the 8th [or] the 4th."

If the Moon and Saturn were joined in the same degree, and Mars aspected them, the mother will die from [giving] birth. [And if the Moon is being conjoined to the Sun in one sign, the native's father will die a bad death. And if the Moon is will be conjoined to Mars, and she decreasing in light, and she were in a bad place, it signifies a fall and illness and the death of the mother just like the father. And if the Moon will be conjoined to the Sun in a masculine sign, it signifies the[919] death of the mother before the father.]

If the Lord of the Lot of Fathers were in the Midheaven and the Lord of the Lot of Mothers were in the angle of the earth, the mother will die before the father.

If the Sun and Saturn were joined in the same degree, the father will die before the mother. [And if the Moon will be conjoined with Saturn, the mother will die first.]

If Mars were in the fourth sign from the Sun, and Saturn on the left side, the father will die first.

[And if the planet which has greater signification for fathers will be made unfortunate by Saturn or Mars, from the opposition or square, the father will die before the mother. And if the planet which has the signification for mothers were as I said about the father, the mother will die before the father.]

[Chapter II.5.9: Primary directions for the parents]

You could even know this through the *tasyīr* of the two significators[920] to the conjunction, square or opposite aspect of the infortunes: for the one of them which was bound to one of the infortunes first, that one will die before the other.

[And in a certain place I saw proof {of this} by al-'Anbas] in the twenty-third year:[921] a certain person came to me having a page on which the nativity of a certain [male] native had been written down, and he asked me if I would judge something about the nativity. Then I asked of him whose nativity it was: he responded that it was that of his own son. Therefore I took the page and I put it before myself, considering the figure of the nativity and the

---

[919] Jag. also seems to read "the height of the father."
[920] That is, the significators of the mother and father.
[921] This is probably Abū Bakr's own age at the time.

places of the planets. Then al-'Anbas, seeing this, received the page from my hand, and he looked in it, and he said that the son for whom the figure had been made, was conceived from adultery. And I asked whence he knew this. He responded, "this old man believes that the native is his own son, but it was already four years from the year in which the native was a boy, that the father died."[922] I asked again whence he knew this, to which he responded, "In this figure, I looked to the Lot of Fathers, and I found it in the opposition of Mars, and I did not find but one degree between them. Likewise I looked to the Lord of the said Lot, and I found it in the 11th house from the Ascendant, which is the 8th house from the 4th house,[923] and there was not but one degree between him and Saturn. Therefore I said that the father of the native died in a year in which the son was a boy." And the old man said, "When you said that I am not the father of this native, you spoke truthfully, because I took him in and nourished him, and his father died in the year named by you."

[Chapter II.5.10: The father, according to 'Umar al-Tabarī][924]

Al-Khasībī[925] said that he saw al-Tabarī[926] look to the sign of the 4th house[927] and its Lord, from the Lot of Fathers and its Lord, and also from the Sun and Saturn, and [he saw him] take the *mubtazz* over these places. And likewise he used to look to the planet appearing in the 4th house, and he used to make it a significator of fathers. Afterwards he used to look at the significator so that through it he would know the length and shortness of the native's life, according to what I have explained in the beginning of this treatise.[928] Then, after the Lot of Fathers he used to look at the Sun and the degree of the house of fathers, to see which of them was more fit to be the

---

[922] This does not quite make sense, as al-'Anbas is about to say that the father died after one year. But perhaps he means the native's father died four years ago.
[923] Actually the 12th is the 8th from the 4th. Jag. has the Lord of the Lot in the 2nd from the Ascendant, which makes even less sense.
[924] See *TBN* III.4.1-2. That 'Umar is treated separately is a signal that Abū Bakr knows there are differences between him and the sources like *BA* or its Hellenistic antecedents which he has used so far.
[925] Lat. *Alksibit*. Illegible in Jag.
[926] Lat. *Tabarium*.
[927] Jag. reads "fourth sign."
[928] That is, 'Umar treated the chief significator as a *kadukhudhāh* and combined its years with the direction of the Lot of the Father, the Sun, and the IC (see the next sentence).

hīlāj, and then he used to make a *tasyīr* of the parents' life to the places of the infortunes, and he used to judge according to what he saw.

And likewise,[929] in order to know the status of the parents in any year, ['Umar] used to make a *tasyīr* from the Lot of Fathers to the places of fortunes and infortunes, and he used to judge concerning the status of the father according to its quality and its place in that year.

Likewise, in a diurnal nativity ['Umar] used to make a *dustūriyyah* of the Sun and the planets, and in a nocturnal one a *dustūriyyah* of Saturn and the Moon: and if the native had a *dustūriyyah*, his father will be great and will have honor, riches, and good.

And ['Umar] even used to judge (in the matter of status) by the first and second Lords of the triplicity of the Sun in a diurnal nativity, and in a nocturnal nativity by the first and second Lords of the triplicity of Saturn.

Moreover, ['Umar] used to claim that the native was [conceived] from adultery, and that his father feared concerning him that he was not his own son, if the Sun will apply to Mars by a conjunction or square or opposite aspect in a diurnal nativity, or to Saturn in a nocturnal nativity. Likewise, if he found the Moon impeded by Mars in a diurnal nativity, and by Saturn in a nocturnal nativity, he used to judge that the native's mother was not honest, or at least he had doubts regarding her.

But certain ones of the sages said that if the Lord of the house of fathers does not aspect its own domicile[930] (and likewise the Sun did not even aspect his own domicile, and the Lord of the Lot of Fathers its own Lot), the native's father will be [only] thought to be [so], because the father believes him to be his own son, and he will not be.[931]

[Chapter II.5.11: The mother, according to 'Umar al-Ṭabarī][932]

Look at the Moon and Venus, the Midheaven and its Lord,[933] and [the Lot of the Mother and its Lord], also the planet which will be the *mubtazz* over these places, and make that one the significator of life.

---

[929] That is, for the father's "greater condition," he profected the natal Lot of Fathers by 30° increments and took note of what bodies and aspects fell into that year's region: see *TBN* III.4.1, paragraph 4.
[930] 'Umar reads "house of children," but I suspect Abū Bakr is correct.
[931] 'Umar adds: "but if one of them aspected, he will be legitimate."
[932] Again, a parallel account of *TBN* III.4.2.
[933] See footnote to this passage in *TBN* III.4.2.

Then look at the *tasyīr* of that planetary [significator], and see what it would signify in terms of addition or diminution according to what I said regarding the native's years.

Then look at the status of the mother[934] from the *dustūriyyah* of the[935] [nocturnal planets from the Moon in the night, and from the *dustūriyyah* of Venus from the Moon in the day], and judge regarding the status of the mother according to the quality.

Moreover, look at the Lot of Mothers and the Moon; and the one of them which was the *hīlāj* of life, you should make a *tasyīr* with it to the fortunes and infortunes. For whenever an infortune were joined there, it will impede the native's mother. And if the Moon or the Lot of Mothers were not the *hīlāj*, and you wished to know the place from which you should make the *tasyīr* for the mother, make it from the degree of the Moon. And when she reaches an infortune, death will fall upon the mother.

Likewise[936] you should make a *tasyīr* for the mother from the Midheaven to the infortunes, by giving one year for each sign; and when it is bound up with an infortune, judge just as you will see it.

Afterwards, you could weigh carefully the life of the mother and her status (both in a diurnal nativity and a nocturnal one) from the Lords of the triplicity of the place of the Moon. For the first Lord of the triplicity signifies the beginning of life, the second one the middle, the third the last period of life.

Then you would look into the oppression of the mother's life, or its lightness, from Venus and her Lord,[937] from the Moon and her Lord, from the Lot of Mothers and its Lord: for if these were impeded by an infortune, they signify a bad death.[938]

---

[934] Reading *matris* for *Martis*.

[935] The text reads "of the planet of the triplicity of the Moon," which accidentally combines two similar paragraphs in 'Umar (see the reference to triplicity Lords of the Moon below). In brackets I reproduce 'Umar's statements. But cf. *BA* III.4.1 and *JN* Ch. 16: neither Māshā'allāh nor Abū 'Ali mention using Venus in the night.

[936] This sounds like a misguided attempt to find the "greater" condition of the mother by profection; but 'Umar clearly states that this is found using the profection of the Lot of the Mother.

[937] 'Umar only mentions the Moon; Abū Bakr seems to want to distinguish diurnal (Venus) and nocturnal (Moon) charts.

[938] 'Umar seems to treat this as a purely natal delineation, but I could see using this with profections and primary directions.

And[939] in the hastening of the mother's or father's death, you will be judging through the luminary (according to Dorotheus)[940] which more quickly enters [the pivot] under the earth.[941]

[Chapter II.5.12: The method of pseudo-Ptolemy][942]

But Ptolemy said that, concerning the status of fathers we ought to look first, in a diurnal nativity, from the Sun and its Lord, [then] from the Midheaven and its Lord. And in a nocturnal nativity, from Saturn and his Lord, then from the Sun and his Lord, and afterwards from the 4th house, and to seek the *mubtazz* over these places: for that one will be the significator of the father's life.

[The significator] having been found, you should do a *tasyīr* [of it] by looking at the Sun in a diurnal nativity, if he were in the Ascendant or the Midheaven, or in the 11th, 9th, or 7th[943] house, and some one of the planets which had some dignity in the place of the Sun aspected him.

And if the Sun were not in some one of the aforesaid places, look to Saturn by [his] traversing through the said places, and that [if] some planet having dignity there would aspect him, then you will do a *tasyīr* from him to the rays of the fortunes and the infortunes.

And if Saturn were not in the said places, you should make a *tasyīr* from the degree of the Midheaven, and afterwards distribute that which it signifies in its years, until it would come from the Midheaven to that [number of years] in which the *kadukhudhāh* will come; and if it were equal [to the years of the *kadukhudhāh*], the father will die in that year.

---

[939] As with 'Umar, I have moved this paragraph to the end of the section.
[940] See *Carmen* I.15.5: the one which goes more quickly according to the diurnal rotation of the heavens, not by motion in the zodiac.
[941] Reading *quod citius [angulum/ cardinem] sub terra intrabit* (with *Carmen* I.15.5) for *quod Venus sub terra iudicabit.*
[942] This is not the Ptolemy of the *Tetrabiblos*. But in fact Jag. does not seem to attribute this to anyone.
[943] Reading with Jag. for "2nd."

But in a nocturnal nativity [according to pseudo-Ptolemy], you will start from Saturn if he were in some one of these seven places: namely in the 11th, 7th, Midheaven, 9th, 5th, 4th, or 3rd.[944]

And if he were not in some one of these seven places, and the Sun were in the Ascendant, the 3rd, 4th, 5th, or 7th (namely from the degree of the Ascendant up to five degrees appearing under the earth), then you will make a *tasyīr* from the Sun.

And if the Sun were not in some one of the said places, then you will make a *tasyīr* from the degree of the house of fathers, whether a planet having dignity there should aspect it or not. Afterwards, see what came out of the years of the *tasyīr*; and if it were equal to the years of the *kadukhudhāh*, or around that, the father will die in that year.

[Chapter II.5.13: The method of Dorotheus][945]

But Dorotheus said that in a diurnal nativity we ought to look to the Sun, and in a nocturnal one to Saturn, and to the Lot of Fathers and its Lord in each:

If therefore the Sun were in some one of the angles or the succeedents (it being a diurnal nativity), and some one of the planets having dignity in the place of the Sun (and principally a domicile, exaltation, triplicity or bound) [aspected him],[946] make [the Sun] the *hīlāj* and the planet aspecting him the *kadukhudhāh*.

And if the Sun is not fit to be the *hīlāj*, look at Saturn: and if you will find him in some one of the angles or succeedents, and some one of the planets having some dignity in his place aspected him, Saturn will be the *hīlāj*, and [make] the planet aspecting him the *kadukhudhāh*. Then you should make a *tasyīr* from that place of killing.[947]

---

[944] All of these places are considered "good" in that they are configured with the Ascendant.
[945] See *Carmen* I.12-14.
[946] Adding *ipsum aspexerit* in accordance with the usual report of this procedure, and its appearance in the instructions for Saturn below.
[947] Reading *occisionis* for *occasionis*.

And if it happened that Saturn is cadent, take the Lot of Fathers: which if it were in some one of the angles or the succeedents, and some planet having dignity in its place aspected it,[948] the said Lot will be the *hīlāj* and the planet aspecting [it is] the *kadukhudhāh*. Therefore, make a *tasyīr* from it to the fortunes or the infortunes.

And if the said Lot were not fit to be the *hīlāj*,[949] take the degree of the 4th house. [And if some {planet} which has dominion there aspects it, it will be the *hīlāj*. And you should make the *tasyīr* to the fortunes and infortunes, and the one which aspects will be the *kadukhudhāh*.]

And it must be known that in the night we should begin for the father from Saturn, then from the Sun, after that from the Lot of Fathers, and finally from the degree of the 4th house.

But for the mother in a nocturnal nativity, we should start first from[950] the Moon, then from Venus, then from the Lot of Mothers, and finally from the degree of the 10th house. But Ptolemy[951] begins (in both a diurnal and nocturnal nativity) from Venus and her Lord, then from the Moon and her Lord, and he takes the *mubtazz* of the said places, and makes it the *kadukhudhāh*. But in a diurnal nativity he makes the *tasyīr* from Venus to the place of killing;[952] and in a diurnal nativity, from the Moon.

Which if the Sun[953] were the *hīlāj*, it signifies the father's life, and the native's life, so that sometimes it happens that the father and native die at one [and the same] hour. But if the native had a bad life (that is, if the Sun were the *hīlāj* and it were weak and impeded), [the significator of the father][954] will give its own lesser years, unless it were strong in the nativity of the father—because then it confers its own middle years. And if it were retrograde, and in an angle, free from the infortunes, and its retrogradation crossed over [past] the opposition of the Sun, it will give its own lesser years. And if it were retrograde in a succeedent, it will subtract one-third of its own

---

[948] *Eum*, indicating either the degree or the sign.
[949] Jag. specifies that it is cadent.
[950] Omitting redundant "Venus, then from."
[951] Cf. *Tet.* III.5.
[952] Reading *occisionis* for *occasionis*.
[953] Reading with Jag. for "Moon."
[954] Reading with Jag. My sense is that we are still directing the *hīlāj* for the father in the native's chart, but this significator is the *kadukhudhāh* of that *hīlāj*. Cf. *JN* Ch. 19.

lesser years. And if it were retrograde in a cadent, it will subtract two-thirds of them. And if it were retrograde and burned up or made unfortunate, it will turn its own lesser years into months. And if it were retrograde, burned up, unfortunate, and in its own fall, the father will die at the hour of the nativity.

[Chapter II.5.14: Comment on 'Umar's method]

But 'Umar[955] expressed a general and abbreviated statement, saying: look first for the father at the 4th house and its Lord, at the Lot of Fathers and its Lord, at Saturn and the Sun, [and planets in the fourth], and you will know the *mubtazz* over these places: for the father's life will be according to its strength and weakness. But for the mother, you would look at the 10th house and its Lord, the Lot of Mothers and its Lord, the Moon and Venus, and take the *mubtazz* over these places, and judge concerning the mother's life according to the status of this.

Al-'Anbas[956] said that he had found the *mubtazz* according to what 'Umar[957] said, by giving 5 dignities to the Lord of the domicile, 4 to the Lord of the exaltation, 3 to the Lord of the triplicity, 2 to the Lord of the bound, and 1 to the Lord of the face; and the planet who had more dignities in the said places, will be the *mubtazz*.[958]

---

[955] Lat. *Ubelides*. Again, *TBN* III.4.
[956] Jag. reads, "And al-'Anbas said, however, that he errs in this place, *ubi fuit* [?] Asemczael [probably al-Hasan bin Sahl, 782-851 AD], that he used to find...". Without further research we cannot be sure whether this view belongs to al-'Anbas or "Asemc-zael." See my Introduction.
[957] *Ubelides*, but *Aomarides* or *Uomarides* according to Jag.
[958] This method is the familiar weighted *mubtazz*, and seems to have been partly inspired by the parallel comments in *Tet.* III.5 pp. 17-18. At this point Jag. seems to have Abū Bakr supporting the older view of the *mubtazz* which does not grant points, but the text is hard to read.

[Chapter II.6.0: Children]

It[959] must be known that sometimes nativities are related back to the nativities of fathers, and that the signification which [a child] has in the nativity of [his] father is a firmer significator than that of the native [himself]. If, in the nativity of a father, the [significator of] the child were an infortune, the child will be full of labor, and likewise his life; therefore it will not signify [anything] except for what was signified in the father's nativity, even if there are many [children]. And if there were fortune [signified] for some one of [the children] in the nativity [of a father], it will be little and weak [in itself, although one child] will be elevated over his own brothers, and first and greatest among them. And likewise for natives, it will be reverted back to the nativity of those of their own faith, but the nativity of those of his faith are reverted back to the type of him who has greater power in the native's type.

And the sages looked, in the matters of children, from many things: namely from [1] the 5th house and [2] its Lord, from [3] the Lot of Children and [4] its Lord, from [5] Jupiter and [6] the Lords of his triplicity, from [7] Mercury and Venus, and also from [8] the planet appearing in the house of children.

If therefore you wished to know the manner of the native in terms of children, look at [9] the planet which has power in the stated places, and which one conjoins their testimonies. And if you should find it binding with the Lord of the Ascendant, or with a planet having great dominion in the Ascendant, judge for the native that he will have children, and their manner will be according to the strength, weakness, fall, elevation,[960] fortune, and misfortune of that planet.

[Chapter II.6.1: Multiple children]

If Jupiter, Venus, and Mercury were sound and strong in the nativity, the native will have many children, and he will see their multitude and [their] riches.

If Saturn aspected Jupiter by a trine aspect, the native will have children.

---

[959] Correcting this paragraph a bit with Jag. The point of this paragraph is to suggest that the significations in a nativity are not absolute: that one must also look at the context of one's own parents and social and ethnic group.
[960] Reading *elevationem* for *electionem*, to match *casum*.

If Saturn were direct in the Midheaven, and Jupiter aspected without the aspect of the infortunes, the native will have many children [and he will rejoice with them].

If the first and second Lords of the triplicity [of Jupiter][961] were strong, and free from burning up and the infortunes, the native will have children, and he will rejoice with them.

If the Moon and Mercury were in the Midheaven, the native will have children and also good and joy with them. And if the Moon and Mercury were in the 5th house, and their Lord [were] strong, and free from all impediment and the infortunes, the native will have many children.

If Jupiter were in the Ascendant and Mars in the west the native will have children, and he will live with them in honor and a good [status].

If the sign in the Midheaven[962] were one of many children, and in it [there were] a fortune having signification over these things (like Jupiter, Venus, and Mercury), the native will have many children.

If Jupiter were in the Ascendant, and Mercury in the west, the native will have many good and just children, and happiness with them.

If the Lot of Children were in some one of the angles, or in a good place from the Ascendant, the native will have many [good and just] children.

If the sign of the 5th house were made fortunate, and its Lord in an angle, and a fortune aspected [the sign], the native will have many children.

If Mercury were in the Ascendant and the Moon in the west, and the fortunes aspected them, and the infortunes [were] cadent, the native will have [many] children and will rejoice with them.

If Mars were in the Midheaven in a nocturnal nativity, and the fortunes aspected him, the native will see a multitude of children, and will have joy with them.

If the significators of children, or the planet which conjoins the testimonies, were in the Ascendant or the Midheaven or in the house of trust,[963] the native will have children in his youth. And if in the 2nd, 4th,[964] or 7th house, the native will have children in old age or around the end of life.

---

[961] Adding "of Jupiter" because those were the only triplicity Lords mentioned above.
[962] Reading with Jag. for "8th."
[963] The 11th.
[964] Jag. reads "4th, which is probably correct.

If the planet of children were [in a masculine] sign in the fourth and a masculine[965] degree, it signifies sons; if in feminine ones, daughters. [And if it is mixed, you should say that it will be mixed.][966]

Chapter II.6.2: On natives lacking children, or having few children

If Jupiter or the Sun were in the 7th house, the native will be without children, or will have few.

If the Lord of the house of children were in a sterile sign (or one of few offspring), the native will lack children or will have few offspring, especially if that Lord were impeded or made unfortunate.

[And if Jupiter will be aspecting Mars from the square or opposition, and he will be with one of the infortunes, he will have few offspring, and the majority of them will not have children.]

If an infortune were in the 5th house, and its Lord impeded by burning up or descension, or by the conjunction or bad aspect of an infortune, the native will lack children, or will have few [of them].

If Venus were with Saturn, it portends the diminution of children, and that they will be bad.

If Jupiter aspected Saturn by a bad aspect, and he were with the other infortune, the native will have few offspring.

If the Moon were in Aries or Libra, the native will lack children.

If the Lot of Children were made unfortunate, the native will have few offspring or none. [And likewise if it will be in the twelfth, he will have no offspring or few.]

If Saturn aspected Venus by an opposite aspect, the native will lack children and his reputation will be destroyed.

If Jupiter, Venus, and Mercury were in bad places, and the infortunes had dominion over them, the native will have few children, or they will die, and he will incur sorrow or impediment.

If the Lord of the house of children were in the third sign from the angles, and the infortunes aspected, [and the fortunes were cadent from him], the native will have few children; and if he did have them, they will die.

---

[965] Reading *masculino* for *masculinis*.
[966] Adding with Jag., and reading *mixtus* for *magis*.

If Saturn were in the Ascendant and Venus in the west, and Jupiter did not aspect Saturn, the native will have few offspring or none.

If the Lord of Jupiter's triplicity were burned up in the third sign from the angles, the native will be without children.

If the Lot of Children were in the 6th or 12th house, the native will lack children.

If Saturn were with the Lot of Children, the native will have few or no children.

Chapter II.6.3: On sterile natives[967]

If a peregrine Saturn were in the Ascendant, and a retrograde[968] Venus aspected him from the western angle, the native will lack offspring.[969]

If the Moon and Venus were in sterile signs (that is, in Gemini, Leo and Virgo), and Mars and Saturn aspected them by a bad aspect, a [male] native will not generate offspring, nor even a female [native].

If a peregrine and retrograde[970] Saturn were in the western angle or the Midheaven, and an unfortunate Jupiter and a Moon diminished in light and number aspected [Saturn] from under the rays of the Sun, a male native will lack offspring, and a female one will be sterile.

If Venus were retrograde and in the 2nd house (through which the womb of a woman is signified), and besides that in a sterile sign, and Saturn aspected her by a bad aspect, the native will be sterile.

If Saturn were elevated over Venus,[971] and the Moon is being made unfortunate in the 6th or 12th house, a male native will not have offspring, and a woman will not be impregnated.

If[972] Mars and Saturn were retrograde in the 6th house and in a movable sign, without the aspect of a fortune, and both aspected Venus by a bad

---

[967] Many of these indications in Jag. mention only female fertility.
[968] Jag. does not make her retrograde.
[969] *BA* III.5.3 p. 117 and *Carmen* II.12.5 have something very close to this.
[970] Again, perhaps a worst-case scenario, as Jag. does not make him peregrine and retrograde.
[971] Again, "overcoming."
[972] For this whole paragraph, Jag. reads: "And if Mars and Saturn will be in the sixth from the Ascendant, and the sixth will be a movable sign, the native will be sterile and impeded in the place of his seed; and if it will be in the domicile of Saturn, the native will be sterile."

aspect, a male native will be sterile, and impeded in the place of seed; and judge thus with regard to a female one. If Venus were burned up in a domicile of Saturn, without the aspect of a fortune, and Mars aspected her by a bad aspect, a male native will not have offspring, and a female one will be made sterile.

Chapter II.6.4: On the number of children

Dorotheus said in [his] fifth book:[973] look at the Lords of Jupiter's triplicity, and if they were in one sign, reckon from them up to the Ascendant: and the number of the signs appearing between them will be the number of children.

Other sages[974] looked at the first and second Lord of Jupiter's triplicity, and from the stronger one and the one made more fortunate, and appearing in a better place: reckon, and how many signs there were between it and the Ascendant, the native will have so many children. And if there were a common sign among them, give them two children.

Al-Andarzaghar said:[975] reckon from the place of the Lord of the Lot of Children up to the said Lot, and how many signs there were between them, the native will have so many children.

[And he said that you should][976] look at the planet which aspects the Lord[977] of the house of children, and the number of children will be according to the number of the signs appearing between them, by giving two children to every common sign (if they were there). And whichever of the planets aspected the Lord of [the house of][978] children from a masculine sign and quarter, it proclaims sons; and from a feminine sign and quarter, daughters.

---

[973] Cf. *Carmen* II.8-9. II.8 begins with the triplicity Lords being in one place, but the material on counting signs is in II.9. That Abū Bakr calls this Dorotheus's fifth book suggests that he was working with the 11-volume Pahlavi version.
[974] *Carmen* II.9.1-2.
[975] Al-Andarzaghar would have been drawing on *Carmen* II.10.1-2, as does Māshā'allāh in *BA* III.5.4 item 3.2.
[976] Adding with Jag.
[977] Jag. simply says, "the house of children."
[978] Again, Jag. uses only the house of children, not its Lord.

Chapter II.6.5: On the hour or time[979] in which the native will have children

If[980] the year or revolution reached Jupiter or the Lot of Children,[981] and there were either a binding of the Lot of Children to the Ascendant or the house of children, or to one of the angles, or a binding of the rays of Jupiter with the Lot of Children,[982] or a binding of Jupiter with the Lot of Children to the 5th house, or to the Ascendant or the twelfth-part of Jupiter, the native will have children at that hour, year, or time.

Chapter II.6.6: On the native's happiness with children

If Saturn aspected Venus by a trine aspect with reception in a diurnal nativity, the native will be glad because of children, and he will have good and fortune because of them.

If Jupiter aspected Venus by a trine aspect, the native will obtain good and joy from the children.

If Jupiter were in the Midheaven, [direct],[983] the native likewise will have good and fortune on the occasion of children.

If Venus were in the Ascendant, and Jupiter in the west, the native will have children with whom he will rejoice, and will lead a happy life.

If the Lot of Children were in the Ascendant, and its Lord appeared free from the infortunes, strong and made fortunate, the native will have children honoring him, and on the occasion of them he will obtain fortune and elevation.

---

[979] *Tempore.* In Latin, this word can also mean "season," which suggests the possibility of a broader expanse of time.

[980] Jag. is very terse and not very helpful here (though it does seem to involve profections of or to the Midheaven). Abū Bakr seems to be combining two sets of information: prediction by transit and profection, and the love between the native and his children. The two primary predictive methods mentioned here are [1] the transit of Jupiter to the angles or stakes of the Lot of Children (see next footnote) and [2] the profection of the Ascendant to the place of Jupiter. Both of these can be found with more detail in *BA* III.5.5 and *JN* Ch. 21. The relationship between the native and the children is described in similar ways in *JN* Ch. 21 p. 278.

[981] According to *Carmen* II.11 and *BA* III.5.5, this is the Mars-Jupiter Lot for the time of children, not the generic Lot of Children (the Jupiter-Saturn Lot).

[982] Reading partly with Jag.

[983] Adding with Jag.

Chapter II.6.7: On the native's labor with a child or children

If Saturn were in his own triplicity and Mars aspected him by a trine aspect, the native will labor with the children, and sorrow and worries will be multiplied.

If Saturn were in the opposite of Mars, the native will not rejoice with children, but his worries will be multiplied.

If Saturn were in the western angle in a nocturnal nativity, the native will labor with his own children.

If Saturn were in a domicile of Venus, the native will incur worries and a fall on the occasion of the children.

[And if Mars will be in the western angle, especially if the Moon aspected him, the native will worry about his children, and worries will be multiplied, and a fall.]

If Saturn were in the Ascendant and the Moon in the west, and an infortune aspected him without the aspect of a fortune, the native will have little joy with his wife and children, and for the whole of his life he will be full of labor with them.

If Venus were in the Ascendant and Saturn in the west, the native will feel pain on the occasion of children.

If[984] the Lot of Children were without the conjunction [or] aspect of the planets, the native will be sad with the children, and his first child will die quickly and perhaps be aborted; and evil and sorrow will be multiplied for the native with them.

If an infortune [were] joined to the Lot of Children or appeared in its bad aspect, the native will have few children, and middling joy with them.

If the Lot of Children were in the 7th house, the children will hate the father and will do evil to him.

If the Lord of the 5th house were in the 12th house, and the Lord of the 12th house in the 5th, the native will have an impediment on the occasion of children, and he will see what does not please him concerning them.

If the Lord[s] of the 5th and of the 11th house, and the Lot of Fortune,[985] were in the 2nd house, the native will nourish strange [children];[986] and judge

---

[984] Reading with Jag. for the first part of the sentence, for clarity.
[985] Not the Lord of the Lot, but the Lot itself.
[986] That is, others' children.

the same if the Lord of the 5th house were in the 2nd house, and the Lord of the 2nd in the 5th.

If Venus and Mercury were in the 4th house, and the sign of the 4th house were the exaltation or domicile of Jupiter, the native will nourish the children of great men or of some princes.

Chapter II.6.8: On the fortune of the native's children

If Jupiter were in the Ascendant and in some one of his own dignities, the native will have high and famous children, so that few in the estate will be more noble.

If the Lot of Children were in the Ascendant, the native's children will have good and honor, and the native will be honored on the occasion of them.

If the Lot of Children were strong in the 2nd house, and had some dignity in it,[987] the native's children will have an acquaintance with kings and high men, and there will be a great reputation concerning him in his parts [of the country], especially if the Lord of the said Lot were a fortune, and free from the infortunes.

If the Lot of Children were in the 3rd house, strong and made fortunate, the life of the native's children will be beautiful [and he will have good and profit from the native's brothers].[988]

If the Lot of Children were in the 4th house, and the fortunes aspected it, and the infortunes appeared cadent from it, the native's children will possess the money and substance of the grandfathers, and thence they will obtain fame and height.

If the Lot of Children were in the 5th house, and Jupiter and Venus aspected it, or they were joined with it, the native's children will have fortune and fame, and they will be renowned in their own offspring.

---

[987] Lots do not rule anything, and so cannot have dignities. I am not sure what Abū Bakr means here.
[988] Adding with Jag. Perhaps it means the *child* will have good from the native's brothers.

If the Lot of Children were in the 6th house and in the aspect of the fortunes, the native's children will obtain substance from female and male slaves, or beasts, or they will be the medical doctors for men or beasts.[989]

If the Lot of Children were made fortunate in the 8th house, the native's children will inherit his money.

If the Lot of Children were in the 9th house, and its Lord free from the infortunes, the native will have good, frank, and religious children. [990]

If the planet conjoining the testimonies of children were in some one of its own dignities, and also strong and made fortunate, and the infortunes [were] cadent from it, the native's children will be famous and wealthy. If the significator of children were in a good place, and the Lord of the Ascendant [were] made unfortunate in the 10th house, the native's children will be more noble than the native himself, but they will always obey him.

Look even at the Lots of Masculine and Feminine [Children], and judge concerning the elevation and strength of the children according to their strength and weakness.

Chapter II.6.9: On the labor of the native's children

If Mars and Venus were with the Moon or they aspected her, the native's child will incur labor, stupidity, and shamefulness.

If Mars were in the Ascendant and the Moon in the west, the native will have shameful and sad children.

If Jupiter and Saturn were in the Ascendant and Mars, Venus, and Mercury in the [west or the] Midheaven, the native will have shameful children.

If the Lot of Children were in the 4th house (which is the house of the children's enmity),[991] the native's children will be in labor and have many enemies. And if in addition the Lord of the Lot of Children were made

---

[989] The Lot in the 7th missing.
[990] The Lot in the 10th—12th missing.
[991] I.e., because it is the 12th from the 5th. In the Persian and early Arabic period, the 12th was the house of enemies generally.

unfortunate by Mars, the native's children will have many worries, and also they will incur prisons and things which they do not want.

If the Lord of the Lot of Children were made unfortunate in the 6th house, the native will have children ill with a chronic illness, and they[992] will live in poverty and need.

If the Lot of Children were made unfortunate in the 10th house, the native will have the worst children,[993] and he will nourish them foully and in debauchery, and they will do evil deeds, and he will speak badly about them.

If the Lord of the Lot of Children were made unfortunate, the native's children will be slaves or do the works of slaves.

If the Lot of Children were in the 11th house, the native's children will be enemies to each other,[994] and have bad morals. And if the said Lot were made unfortunate and impeded, they will be fornicators.

If the Lord of the 5th house and the Lord of the Lot of Children were under the rays of the Sun, the native will have concealed children, or from adultery.

If Saturn and Mars aspected the Moon by a trine aspect, the native will sell[995] his own children, nor will he want to acknowledge that they are his children.[996]

If the *mubtazz* or significator of children were made unfortunate, and appearing in a bad place, peregrine and in its own descension, it portends a fall and labor and also the poverty of the children.

Chapter II.6.10: On the death of the children

If Saturn and Mars were in the house of children, or they aspected it[997] by a bad aspect, the native's children will die [a bad death].

If the Lord of the 11th house were in the 5th house, and the Lord of the Lot of Fortune in the 8th, all of the native's children will die.

If the Sun were joined to some[998] infortune,[999] the native's children will die before him, and not one will remain to him.

---

[992] Reading *qui* for *quae*.
[993] The 10th is the 6th from the 5th.
[994] This must be because the 11th is the 7th from the 5th, so the children's behavior will be characterized by enmity.
[995] Jag. reads, "abandon."
[996] Correcting the text with Jag.
[997] Reading *ipsam* for *ipsa*.

If the Sun, Saturn, and Mercury aspected the Moon from out of the Midheaven, the native's children will die.

If Mars aspected Jupiter by the opposite aspect, the native's children will be killed or die a bad death. If Saturn were in the opposite aspect of Jupiter, the majority of the native's children will die.

If Mercury were in the Ascendant and Saturn in the west, the native's children will live only a little.

[If Saturn is with Mars in the Ascendant or fourth, the native's children will not live.]

If the Lord of the house of children and the Lot of Children were in the 8th house, the native's children will die before him.

If Mars and Mercury were in the west or in the Midheaven, the native will see the death of his own children.

If Jupiter were in the 4th or 7th house, [and] he applied to some infortune by conjunction or a bad aspect, and [especially if] he were burned up or descending,[1000] it portends the death of the children.

If the infortunes were conjoined to the Lord of the house of children, or they aspected him by a bad aspect, it signifies the death of the children and the cutting off of their reputation.

If the Lord of the house of children were being bound to the Lord of the 8th house, the native's children will die, and their[1001] reputation will be cut off.

If the Lords of Jupiter's triplicity were burned up or descending,[1002] or they appeared in the conjunction or bad aspect of the infortunes, they indicate the death of the native's children.

If Venus were cadent from the fortunes, and the infortunes aspected her, the native's children will die.

If the Lot of Children were in a domicile of Saturn, and the infortunes aspected it,[1003] it pronounces the death of the majority of the native's children.

---

[998] Reading *alicui* for *alicuius*.
[999] Jag. reads only "If the Sun were in the 5th."
[1000] *Descendens*. I am not sure whether this means descending in the circle of the *awj*, or in his fall, or what.
[1001] Reading with Jag.
[1002] See footnote above.
[1003] *Ipsam*. Grammatically, this could indicate either the Lot or the domicile. Based on other things Abū Bakr has said, it probably refers to the domicile.

[Chapter II.7.0: Illness][1004]

[You should know that God, who made the world and will destroy it when it pleases Him, created the lesser world to be like the greater one.

Being above the earth pertains more to visible ailments, the head and upper parts of the body, being below the earth signifies internal ailments and the lower parts. of the body. The Sun and Moon are attributed to the eyes because of their clarity and prominence; the nostrils to Mars and Venus because they are the next planets on either side of the Sun; the Sun signifies the brain; Saturn and Jupiter signify the ears, which discern things nearby or far away; Mercury signifies the tongue, and this is related to his lightness and quickness, orientality, occidentality; but he can also indicate some internal organs.[1005]

Aries signifies the head; it is the exaltation of the Sun, who signifies the brain, thought, and intellect, and the brain is able to distinguish good from evil and profit and loss.

Taurus signifies the neck and throat, and is the exaltation of the Moon; her domicile rules the chest which produces the air from the lungs which comes through the throat.

Gemini is the exaltation of the Head of the Dragon; it signifies the hands.

Virgo is the exaltation of Mercury.[1006]

Libra is the exaltation of Saturn and domicile of Venus. It signifies the spleen (among other things), and is a domicile of sexual intercourse and appetite.

Scorpio is the domicile of Mars; it signifies the liver.[1007]

Sagittarius is the exaltation of the Tail of the Dragon.[1008]

Flesh is like earth, blood is like water.[1009]

Finally, Abū Bakr gives general advice on looking at the planets with respect to diseases.]

[1004] This entire chapter was missing in 1540. I have paraphrased from Jag., but it is rather hard to read and I am uncertain about many details.
[1005] I am somewhat uncertain about this.
[1006] I cannot read most of this sentence, but it does mention bad thoughts and envy, which perhaps were thought to be related to the belly.
[1007] I cannot understand most of the rest of this sentence.
[1008] This whole long sentence is opaque or unreadable to me.
[1009] I have omitted the rest of this opaque sentence.

Chapter II.7.1: Illnesses according to planetary signification[1010]

If[1011] the Sun were impeded by some one of the infortunes in a diurnal nativity, the native will have an illness in his right eye, or perhaps he will be one-eyed or a squinter. And if it were a nocturnal nativity with the Sun so disposed, the native will have an illness in his stomach or brain.

And if the Moon were made unfortunate above the earth, the native will suffer an illness in his left eye. But if she were made unfortunate under the earth, it signifies a pain of the neck or throat, or of the lung, because of coldness and moisture.

If Mercury were made unfortunate above the earth, an illness of the tongue is presented. And if he were made unfortunate under the earth, the illness will be in the internal fleshy[1012] places.

If Venus and Mars were made unfortunate [above the earth], it signifies an illness of the nostrils, so that the native will not sense odor, nor will he have an appetite, and perhaps he will suffer dripping from them. And if they were made unfortunate below the earth, the illness will be in the liver or veins or kidneys, and the paths of urine, with the appetite for sexual intercourse.

If Saturn and Jupiter were made unfortunate above the earth (like if they were burned up or in opposition to their own *awj*es, or in bad places, or in dark degrees), it signifies an illness in his ears or their [internal] channels. And if they were made unfortunate under the earth, there will be a pain in the spleen or spirit, like those who believe they will die suddenly.

Certain sages said that if the Moon were above the earth in a nocturnal nativity, her signification will be regarding the right eye, and the Sun in a nocturnal nativity regarding the left eye.

[1010] Jag. reads differently in details and procedure, including brief comments about the planets' ascension and descension (though whether this is in latitude or in the circles of their *awj*es, I do not know.
[1011] For this sentence, cf. *Carmen* IV.1.103.
[1012] *Fisculis* or *visculis*. This can refer particularly to sack-shaped places such as the scrotum. But translation is somewhat uncertain.

[Chapter II.7.2: Chronic illness]

If the infortunes were in angles, nor did fortunes aspect them, nor did they have some dignities in that same place, they signify chronic or inseparable illnesses.

If the Moon is being separated from some planet and a fortune did not aspect her, it portends illnesses.

If the Moon were in the 6th house without the aspect of a fortune, and the infortunes did aspect her, it portends chronic illnesses.

If the Lord of the 6th house were in the Ascendant and [the Ascendant is] a movable sign, and the fortunes [were] cadent from him, the native's illnesses will be chronic and inseparable.

If Mars were in Libra without the power of Jupiter, it signifies chronic illnesses.

If the Moon were in the Ascendant and the infortunes aspected her, it signifies illnesses and pains.

If the infortunes were in angles and they aspected the luminaries, the native will have an inseparable illnesses in his body.

If the infortunes were oriental,[1013] they signify illnesses; and if they were occidental, he will have misery and weakness.

If the Moon were bound up with an infortune, it signifies chronic illnesses and the weakness of the body.

If[1014] the sign of the 6th house were impeded by the aspect or rays of an infortune, it signifies illnesses. If the sign of the Ascendant were movable, the said illnesses will be in the eyes. And if the sign of the 6th house[1015] were movable, and its Lord in a movable sign, the native's illnesses will be from phlegm. And if Mars aspected the Lord of the 6th house, they will be from heat or fire. And if Jupiter[1016] aspected the said Lord, they will be of the nature of hotness and moisture.

And if Venus were the Lady of the 6th house, the native's illnesses will be around the kidneys and private parts, or from excessive sexual intercourse. And if Mercury were the Lord of the 6th house, the native's illnesses will be in the tongue or hearing. And if the Moon were the Lady of the 6th house, the native's illnesses will be in the genitals and the lower parts.

[1013] Omitting "under the rays" with Jag.
[1014] Cf. *BA* III.6.1, item 1.1.
[1015] Jag. reads: "if the Lord of the Ascendant is in a movable sign."
[1016] Omitting "Saturn and," with Jag.

And we have stated these things about illnesses in a general way; but since the sages put the particular significations in their books, we have proposed to make them clear in what follows.

Chapter II.7.3: On blindness and illnesses of the eyes

If[1017] the Sun and the Moon were besieged by the infortunes, and the Ascendant made unfortunate, and its Lord in a bad place, and besides that the fortunes cadent from the Ascendant, the native will be blind or he will have an inseparable illness in the eyes.

If the Moon, decreased in light and number, were in the 6th house, and especially [if] she aspected Mars[1018] by the square or opposition, it signifies blindness.

If[1019] the infortunes were in [the second {sign} from the luminaries or in] the same degree with the luminaries, or they aspected the luminaries by the square or opposite aspect without the aspect of a fortune, the native will lose his sight.

If[1020] the Sun were the Lord of the 6th house, and he were made unfortunate through the aspect of some infortune without the aspect of a fortune, it signifies an illness in the eyes. If the Moon, appearing as the Lady of the 6th house, were in the degree of the Ascendant, made unfortunate by the bad aspect of the infortunes, and the fortunes did not aspect her, the native will have an illness in the eyes.

If the Tail of the Dragon were in the degree of the Ascendant, and the luminaries made unfortunate, the native will lose one of his eyes, unless the fortunes aspected that same place with a good aspect.

If Mars were the Lord of the 6th house, and the Ascendant a movable sign, [and the fortunes did not aspect him, it signifies blindness.][1021]

If Mars, appearing above the Moon in the 7th house, were burned up,[1022] it signifies an illness of the eyes.

[1017] Cf. *BA* III.6.2, item 1.2.
[1018] Adding with Jag.
[1019] Cf. *BA* III.6.2, item 1.4.
[1020] Cf. *BA* III.6.2, item 1.4.
[1021] Adding with Jag. Instead of the material in brackets, 1540 reads: "and the Moon diminished in light and number with the Tail of the Dragon, and in the square or opposite aspect of Mars, the native will lose his sight."
[1022] Jag. omits combustion.

[And if the Sun and Moon were in the second from an angle, and Mars in the Ascendant, it signifies blindness and the loss of vision.]

If an infortune were in the 3rd house, and Mars made unfortunate in the Ascendant, the native's eyes will become ill.

If the infortunes were with the luminaries in cadent places, they signify illnesses of the eyes.

If the luminaries were in signs signifying chronic illnesses, and the infortunes aspected them by a bad aspect, and the fortunes were cadent from them, the native will have illnesses in the eyes.

If the Sun and Moon were in the 7th house, and Mars ascends immediately after the Moon, they signify illnesses of the eyes.

And if the Sun were in the second from the Ascendant, and its Lord were Saturn, and the Sun were the Lord of the Lot of Fortune or of the Ascendant, the native will be blind and lose his sight.[1023]

And it must be known that in some signs are some degrees which destroy vision:[1024] in Taurus, the place of *Thurayyā*,[1025] the sixth, ninth, and tenth degrees.[1026] In Cancer, from the ninth degree up to the fifteenth.[1027] In Leo, the place of *Ḍafīra*,[1028] the eighteenth degree, the twenty-seventh, and twenty-eighth.[1029] In Scorpio, the nineteenth and twenty-eighth. And according to Dorotheus,[1030] in Scorpio the eighth degree, the ninth, tenth, and twenty-second.[1031] In Sagittarius, the first, seventh, eighth, and ninth degree.[1032] In Capricorn, from the twenty-sixth up to the twenty-ninth.[1033] In Aquarius, the sixth degree, tenth, and nineteenth.[1034]

[1023] Reading with Jag. for clarity.
[1024] Cf. *BA* III.6.2, item 1.5. This is the same list as Mash'allah's.
[1025] Taurus (Lat. *alchorade*).
[1026] The Pleiades.
[1027] The nebula in Cancer.
[1028] Lat. *Alephereph*. Adhafera, ζ Leo.
[1029] The stars in Coma Berenice near Leo's tail.
[1030] *Drocheum*. See *BA* III.6.2 p. 126, and *Carmen* IV.1.108.11.
[1031] These stars are meant to indicate the face and sting of Scorpio.
[1032] Primarily the point of the arrow in Sagittarius.
[1033] The spine of Capricorn, the stars Epsilon and Kappa.
[1034] Primarily the Pitcher in Aquarius.

Chapter II.7.4: On the loss of one eye

If the Moon, waxing in light, were made unfortunate by Mars, or with [her in] diminished light [and made unfortunate] by Saturn, and the Sun [were] in a good place, it signifies the loss of the left eye or an inseparable infirmity.

If the Sun in a diurnal nativity were [above the earth], made unfortunate, and the Moon [were] free from the infortunes, it portends blindness for the right eye.

If the Moon in a nocturnal nativity [were] made unfortunate above the earth, and the Lord of the 6th house appeared with the Tail of the Dragon,[1035] and the Sun [were] unfortunate, the native will be blind, or will lose one eye.

If the Sun were eclipsed in a diurnal nativity, it signifies the loss of the right eye.

If the Sun were the Lord of the 6th[1036] house in a nativity,[1037] the native will have an illness in his right eye, unless the fortunes aspected him.

[And if Mars will be the Lord of the sixth, and he will be in the Ascendant, and Jupiter or Venus did not aspect him, it signifies blindness or the loss of one eye and badness in vision.]

Chapter II.7.5: On cloudiness in the eyes

If some one of the planets were under the rays of the Sun, particularly Mars or Mercury, the native will have a cloudiness or defect in the eye, so that his vision will be impeded by it.

If the Moon were with Mars in the same sign under the rays of the Sun,[1038] it signifies cloudiness in the eye.

If Venus were the Lady of the 6th house [and] in the Ascendant, and the infortunes aspected her by a bad aspect, the native will suffer weeping of the eyes, and moisture, or he will have a scar or cloudiness in his eyes.

[1035] Omitting a redundant *fuerit*, unless a specific planet is supposed to be the Lord of the 6th.
[1036] Reading with Jag. for "2nd."
[1037] This is probably in a diurnal nativity.
[1038] Jag. simply says, "with Mars in one degree."

Chapter II.7.6: On one-eyed people or squinting eyes

If the Moon were joined to an oriental Saturn, and [with Saturn] appearing under the rays of the Sun, the native will be a squinter or one-eyed.

If the Sun and Moon were joined in a movable sign, and cadent from the Ascendant, and in addition being bound up by the infortunes with the aspect of a fortune, the native will be one-eyed.

If the Sun were impeded in a diurnal nativity, and in a sign ascending crookedly, and Mars aspected the Sun, the native will be one-eyed, especially if the Sun were in a dark degree.

Chapter II.7.7: On dark eyes

If[1039] the Moon were in the middle of Taurus, or were in the sixth, ninth, or 10th degree,[1040] or in the ninth or nineteenth degree of Cancer,[1041] or in the first, seventh, ninth, or in the eighteenth degree of Sagittarius,[1042] the native will have a cloudiness in an eye, or his eyes will be dark.

If the Moon were in the Ascendant and in the burnt path or in a dark degree, or in a degree signifying the destruction of vision, it signifies the darkness of the eyes.

If the Sun were under[1043] the earth in the square aspect of Saturn, the native will have dark eyes.

If the Moon were in some one of the degrees signifying the destruction of vision, it signifies the darkness of the eyes, particularly if the Moon were diminished in light.

And you must know that in the signs there are some dark degrees:[1044] namely in Taurus, the ninth and twentieth; in Leo the fifth, twelfth, fourteenth and sixteenth; in Virgo the thirteenth, nineteenth, and twenty-first; in Libra, the nineteenth, twentieth and twenty-first; In Scorpio the

---

[1039] See Rhetorius Ch. 61 p. 114 and al-Qabīsī I.51. These degrees are azemene or *zamin* degrees (of chronic illness). At least some of these overlap with nebulas.
[1040] The Pleiades. See above.
[1041] The nebula in Cancer. See above.
[1042] Primarily the point of the arrow in Sagittarius. See above.
[1043] Jag. reads "above."
[1044] Jag. reads "in signs having degrees of chronic illnesses," viz. the *zamin* degrees. The list above corresponds somewhat to the degrees injurious to the eyes in Rhetorius Ch. 62. But they do not really match the standard welled or dark degrees.

twenty-first, twenty-second, and twenty-third; in Capricorn, from the eleventh degree up to the fifteenth; in Aquarius, the second, third, and fourth.

Chapter II.7.8: On weak vision

If the Moon, diminished in light, were in a bad aspect of Saturn and Mars, it signifies weakness of vision.

If[1045] Saturn and Mars were in the second sign from the Sun, and the Moon (made unfortunate and diminished in number and light) aspected him from the west or the Midheaven, the native will have weak vision.

If the Moon were besieged by the infortunes, and a fortune aspected her by a square or opposite aspect, it portends weakness of vision.[1046]

If the Moon, diminished in light and number, aspected Saturn (appearing in Sagittarius) by a square or opposite aspect, the native will have weak vision.

If the Moon, at the hour of the separation from the conjunction or prevention of the Sun, were bound to Saturn or Mars, the native will be weak of vision, or the native will suffer an inseparable illness in his eyes.

If the Moon appeared from under the rays of the Sun,[1047] and the infortunes aspected her by a bad aspect, the native's vision will be weakened.

If the Moon, under the rays of the Sun,[1048] is being joined to Saturn, with her not aspecting Jupiter in that same place, it signifies weakness of vision and a chronic illness of the eyes.

If Mars and the Sun were in the western angle, and Mars were strong and oriental, there will be weakness in the native's vision, or a chronic illness in his eyes.

If[1049] the Sun and Moon were in dark degrees and under the rays of Saturn, descending in their circle, they signify a weeping of the eyes,

---

[1045] Jag. reads: "And if it were in the second sign from the Sun, and the Moon aspected him from the opposition or from out of the Midheaven, the native will be weak of sight." Between 1540 and Jag., it is unclear to me who is where, and whether the aspect is from the opposition and the superior square, or from out of specific houses.

[1046] Presumably the fortune prevents the blindness suggested in the besieging of the Moon in Ch. 54.

[1047] Or, "adding in light" (Jag.).

[1048] Jag. says, "in Sagittarius."

especially if Saturn appeared above them[1050] in moist signs—and a worse thing which could be in the illness of the eyes, is that the Sun, made unfortunate by Mars, should suffer eclipse: for this signifies the destruction of the eyes.

Chapter II.7.9: On illnesses of the ears

If Mercury, being the Lord of the 6th house, were in a bad place from the Ascendant, and Saturn aspected him or the 6th house from the square aspect,[1051] the native will be deaf.

If the Moon, filled with light, encountered Mars in the 6th house, the native will hear practically nothing.

If Mercury (it being a nocturnal nativity) were appearing from under the rays, and in addition retrograde and in a bad aspect of an infortune[1052] in the 6th house, the native will be hard of hearing.

Mercury even appearing in a domicile of Saturn, being made unfortunate, [the native will be hard of hearing]. If it were in the 10th house, [the native will be hard of hearing]. And if Mercury [is the Lord of the Ascendant and] the infortunes aspected him, the native will lack all hearing, especially if the fortunes were peregrine from him.[1053]

Chapter II.7.10: On the native's speech

If Mercury were under the rays of the Sun, and appearing in the aspect of the Moon in some one of the signs lacking a voice (like Cancer,[1054] Scorpio or Pisces), the native will be mute.

If Mercury were in Scorpio and in the bound and face of Mars, and the Moon aspected in the opposite aspect, the native will be a stutterer or impeded a little bit in his speech.

[1049] Jag. reads "If the Sun and Moon will be in the angles and they will be in dark degrees under the rays of Saturn, and Saturn descending in his own circle, and if [he were] above them and in moist places, it signifies a weeping of the eyes…".

[1050] Probably overcoming them in the tenth whole sign from their position.

[1051] Jag. reads "aspecting Mercury from the square or the sixth sign from the opposition."

[1052] Reading *infortunae* for *fortunae*.

[1053] This probably means "cadent from him," not aspecting the sign he is in.

[1054] Reading *Cancro* for *Tauro*. Taurus is not a mute sign.

If Mercury were the Lord of the 6th house, appearing in the Ascendant, the native will speak with difficulty.

If Mercury were the Lord of the 6th house, and in a sign lacking a voice, and the infortunes aspected him by the opposite aspect, the native will be mute.

If Mercury were in the conjunction and bound of Mars, and Mars aspected him by a bad aspect, the native will have an impeded tongue and practically mute.

If the Moon were filled in light, bound to Mars from the Ascendant, the native will have a chronic illness in his tongue.

If Mercury were in the domicile and bound of Saturn, the native will speak with labor.

If Venus possessed the 10th house, being in a domicile of Saturn, retrograde, and in the aspect of Mars, and Mercury were cadent from her, the native will be a stutterer, or much impeded in his tongue, so that he would hardly be able to speak.

Chapter II.7.11: On hunchbacked natives

If[1055] the Moon were at the beginning or end of a sign, and Saturn aspected her, the native will be a hunchback.

If the Moon were in the 3rd house, and Saturn, descending toward her and being in a movable sign, is elevated[1056] above her, the native will be a hunchback.

If Saturn (descending to the earth) and Mars ([as] Lord of the Ascendant[1057] and ascending[1058] in a crooked sign), and having little latitude, were joined, the native will be a hunchback, especially if Mars were in the third part[1059] of that sign.

[1055] For this paragraph, cf. *BA* III.6.7 and *Carmen* IV.1.135, and II.7.28 below.
[1056] This must refer to the Hellenistic "overcoming," which would put Saturn in the 12th.
[1057] Jag. has "And if the Lord of the Ascendant is being conjoined to Saturn and Mars..."
[1058] I believe this means ascending in the circle of the *awj*, not in the rising sign (*ascensus*).
[1059] I.e., in the third face.

Chapter II.7.12: On leprous natives

If the Moon, separated from the conjunction of the Sun, were bound to Saturn, and the fortunes did not aspect her, the native will be leprous.

If the Moon were with Saturn and Mars in Aries or Taurus [or Cancer], the native will have a filthy body, and be practically leprous.

If Saturn, Mars, the Moon, and Venus were in Cancer, Scorpio, or Pisces, they signify morphew[1060] or cancer or an abscess corroding the flesh and making it stink.

If[1061] Jupiter were retrograde, and the Lord of the 6th house peregrine, and in the aspect, domicile or bound of an infortune, the native will have redness in the face, or a scar or abscess. Likewise Venus, being disposed just as was said about Jupiter, portends an abscess and redness in the face.

If Mars or Saturn were peregrine and wild in the 7th house, and ascending fortunes aspected Mars and Saturn, the native will have a redness in the face, tending towards leprosy.

If[1062] Jupiter were made unfortunate in the 6th house, it signifies a bad liver, and windinesses, and besides that an illness in the face, which is called "rose" or "rust."[1063]

Chapter II.7.13: On natives having white morphew

If Venus and the Moon were made unfortunate[1064] in a watery sign, the native will suffer white morphew.

If the Moon were with an infortune in the one sign, under the rays of the Sun,[1065] the native will have white morphew with bloody foam, and the falling out of the hair [on the body].

If the Moon were made unfortunate by Saturn in Aries, Cancer, Scorpio, Capricorn or Pisces, it signifies morphew.

[1060] A kind of skin lesion with hardened skin and a colored halo.
[1061] Jag. reads "And if Jupiter were the Lord of the 6th house, and the infortunes aspected him, the native will have a chronic illness and this from a redness, and he will have an abscess on his face."
[1062] This seems like it might be an alternative version of the statement above.
[1063] Probably the reddening of the nose and cheeks associated with heavy drinking.
[1064] Or "with the infortunes" (Jag.).
[1065] Jag. omits this part about the Sun.

If some one of the aforesaid signs were ascending, and the Lot of Absence[1066] or of Fortune were in it, morphew will invade the native.

Chapter II.7.14: On those born lunatics, fools, or one-eyed

If Mars were in the angle of the earth, and the Sun aspected him by a square or opposite aspect, the native will be a lunatic or of bad sense, or practically stupid or a fool.

If Mercury were with Saturn in the Ascendant, and Mars aspected him by an opposite aspect, the native will be a lunatic, unless the fortunes aspected them with a good aspect.

If the Moon were joined to Saturn in the Ascendant, and an unfortunate Mercury aspected them, the native will incur stupidity, especially if the fortunes did not aspect there.

If Mars were between the Sun and Moon in the same sign, the native will be made a lunatic or one-eyed.

If[1067] Mercury or Mars were in the Ascendant, and Saturn above him in the angle of the Midheaven,[1068] and Mercury in the opposition of the Moon from the 7th house, the native will be a fool or one-eyed.

If the Moon, [full of light], separated from Saturn, were joined to Mars without the aspect of a fortune, the native will be a lunatic or of little sense.

If the infortunes aspected the Ascendant and its Lord by a bad aspect, and the fortunes did not cast rays there, the native will be of little sense.

If the Moon, separated from the conjunction of Mars, were under the rays of the Sun, and the fortunes did not aspect that same place by a good aspect, the native will be a lunatic.

If the Lord of the triplicity of the Sun in a diurnal nativity were in the opposition of the Sun (and the Lord of the triplicity of the Moon in a nocturnal nativity were in the opposition of the Moon), the native will be a lunatic.

[1066] I do not understand why the Lot of Spirit is relevant here. This should probably be the Lot of Illness.
[1067] Jag. reads "And if the Moon will be in the Ascendant, and Saturn above her in the angle of the Midheaven, and Mercury will be in the opposition of the Moon from the seventh…"
[1068] I.e., the relationship of "overcoming."

If Saturn aspected the Lord of the conjunction or the prevention, and the Moon were diminished in light, the native will be a lunatic, especially if the fortunes did not aspect that same place.

If the Moon, waxing in light, were in Sagittarius or Pisces, and she aspected Mars by a bad aspect without the aspect of a fortune, the native will be made a lunatic.

If the Moon and Mars were in the Ascendant, and Saturn in the 7th house aspected them, the native will be a lunatic, especially if the fortunes did not aspect the Moon.

If Mercury and Saturn were wild, and they aspected each other by the opposite aspect, and the Moon aspected Mars in one of the angles, and the Lord of the Ascendant were in the 7th house, the native will be a lunatic.

If Mercury were separated from the Lord of the Ascendant, the native will sometimes express strange words.

If the Sun (through whom sense is signified), were made unfortunate by both infortunes, and besides that in the opposition of the Ascendant, and in the bound of an infortune, and his Lord did not aspect[1069] him, the native will be melancholic or stupid.

If the Moon and the Lord of the Ascendant were made unfortunate by Mars, and Mercury would be joined with them, the native will be a lunatic and practically stupid.

If the Sun and Moon were peregrine or in the 6th house,[1070] and conjoined in the same degree, and the infortunes aspected without the aspect of the fortunes, the native will be made a lunatic or stupid. [And if they were conjoined in the same degree in the seventh sign from the Ascendant, the native will be stupid.]

Chapter II.7.15: On epileptic natives[1071]

If the Sun and Venus were in the Ascendant, and Saturn, [being] occidental, aspected them from out of the angle of the earth, the native will

---

[1069] Reading with Jag.
[1070] Jag. reads "if the Sun and the Moon will be conjoined in the same degree and in the sixth sign…"
[1071] Chapter missing in Jag.

be an epileptic or diminished in sense, or of those who are said to be "star-struck."[1072]

If the Sun were in the Ascendant, and [Pisces or Virgo] ascending,[1073] and the Moon in Pisces, and Saturn in Sagittarius, and Mars in Gemini or Virgo, it signifies those falling epileptic.

If[1074] the Moon, in a diurnal nativity, is not complected [with] Mercury, nor is she being unified with the Ascendant, the native will be an epileptic.

Chapter II.7.16: On paralytic natives

If the Moon were peregrine, not far from Saturn, it signifies illness in the nerves and limbs from coldness, or a paralytic pain.

If the Moon, diminished in light, were with Saturn in a phlegmatic sign under the rays of the Sun, without the aspect of a fortune, the native will incur a paralytic illness. If the Moon, appearing peregrine, were with Saturn in some one of the angles, under the rays of the Sun, without the aspect of a fortune, the native will be a paralytic.[1075]

If the sign of the 6th house and its Lord were made unfortunate by the Ascendant,[1076] and Saturn aspected it without the aspect of Jupiter, the native will incur a cold and moist illness.

Chapter II.7.17: On natives with heart problems[1077]

If the Sun, being the Lord of the 6th, were made unfortunate, and the fortunes cadent from him, it signifies the weakness of the heart and its illness.

If Jupiter were made unfortunate in the angle of the earth, and especially by Saturn, the native will have anxiety and pain in his heart.

[1072] *Stellatici*.
[1073] Extrapolating from Rhetorius Ch. 65 p. 20 for 1540's *ascendens signum nonum*.
[1074] Cf. Rhetorius Ch. 65 p. 120.
[1075] For these two sentences, Jag. reads "And if the Moon were with Saturn in some one of the angles, and Saturn burned up under the rays, it signifies an illness of much moisture of the body, and paralysis and immobility from phlegm."
[1076] This is obviously an error.
[1077] *Cordiacis*. Normally, *cardiacus* means "heartburn," but clearly something more serious is meant.

If, in a diurnal nativity, Saturn, Jupiter and Mars were in the 4th house,[1078] it signifies anxiety, and that the native will feel a motion of the heart when he hears some rumors.

Chapter II.7.18: On natives with liver problems

If the sixth sign from the Ascendant were a domicile of Jupiter, and [the sign was] made unfortunate[1079] from the square or opposite aspect of the bad ones, the native will have pain in his liver, and will incur fever easily.

If the Moon were the Lady of the 6th house, and the infortunes aspected her without the aspect of the fortunes, and the aspect of Mars were stronger in misfortune, it signifies a pain in the liver and a chronic illness proceeding from the liver.

And[1080] if Mars will be impeded in diurnal nativities it signifies a pain of the liver if he were in the fourth or if he were in the nocturnal boundary—that is from the Ascendant to the seventh.

If the Moon and the Lord of the Ascendant were made unfortunate by Mars, the native will have a pain in the liver and hot illnesses, and perhaps that blood will go out of his body through an incision or blow.

If the Sun were in Scorpio (it being a diurnal nativity), the native will suffer pain in his joints.

Chapter II.7.19: On natives with spleen problems

If the Moon were the Lady of the 6th house, and the infortunes (especially Saturn without the aspect of some fortune)[1081] aspected her, the native will have pain in his spleen.

If the Lord of the Ascendant were in the seventh,[1082] and the infortunes aspected [the Lord], the native will incur a pain in the spleen [or moisture].

[1078] Jag. reads "ninth," but 1540 is probably right.
[1079] Reading with Jag., which makes it clear that the sign (not Jupiter) is made unfortunate.
[1080] Reading with Jag. for 1540's continuation of the previous sentence: "especially if Mars were in the nocturnal bound[ary] and in the 4th or 7th house."
[1081] This condition is not in Jag.
[1082] Reading with Jag. for "in its ascending."

If the Lord of the Ascendant (in a diurnal nativity) were burned up or impeded or in a bad place, and Mars (being in the angle of the earth)[1083] impeded him, it signifies a pain in the spleen.

If Saturn (being the Lord of the Ascendant) were made unfortunate by a peregrine infortune, the native will have an illness [of the spleen and moisture], and incurable abscesses.

If the Moon, diminished in light and number, were in a domicile of Saturn, especially in a nocturnal nativity, the native will be feverish, and will have a tumor or hardness in his spleen.

Chapter II.7.20: On natives with lung problems

If the Moon were made unfortunate under the earth, [the native will suffer in his lung. And if the Moon were conjoined with Mars in the same place], the native will have an abscess in his lung; and this will be worse if the Moon were in the angle of the earth, because the native will have a serious cough based in his lung, and he will spit phlegm with frothy blood.[1084]

If Venus (being the Lady of the 6th house) [were] made unfortunate[1085] by Saturn (being in a fiery sign), the native will suffer heat with dryness, and pain in the lung.

If the Moon were under the earth, made unfortunate by Saturn from a square or opposite aspect, the native will have suffocation with panting.[1086]

Chapter II.7.21: On natives with stomach problems

If Mars and Saturn were in the 6th or 12th house, the native will suffer in the stomach, and he will have cancer and external[1087] pains.

If the Sun in a diurnal nativity were impeded and made unfortunate, the native's illnesses will most often be in the stomach.

If a weak and unfortunate Moon were in the 6th house, the native will become ill with many illnesses existing in the heart or stomach.[1088]

[1083] Jag. reads "and it was in the bound of an angle" (*termino anguli*, for 1540's *terrae angulo*).
[1084] This sounds like tuberculosis.
[1085] Reading with Jag.
[1086] This sounds like asthma.
[1087] *Extraneos*. This might also mean "strange" pains, or pains in the extremities.

Chapter II.7.22: On natives having pain in the belly and intestines

If Mars were in the 7th house and in Scorpio,[1089] without the power of Jupiter and Venus, it signifies flaying[1090] and pain in the intestines.

If Mars in a diurnal nativity were in the 3rd[1091] or 4th house with the Tail of the Dragon, without the aspect of a fortune, it signifies an ulceration of the intestines.

If Saturn and Mars were in the 6th or 12th house without the aspect of a fortune, the native will be consumed by pain and ulceration in the intestines, and he will have rottenness in the blood.

If Saturn were with the Tail of the Dragon in the 7th house (which signifies the belly), it portends a pain of the intestines with windiness, coldness and dryness, and besides that suffering a pain of the guts and colic.

If the Lord of the 6th house were in the Ascendant and in a movable sign, and likewise the Lord of the Ascendant in a movable sign, and Saturn aspected him, it signifies a chronic illness from moisture and blood, and a pain of the belly.

If a peregrine [and] burned-up Saturn were in the bound of Venus, the native will have illnesses in the belly.

If the sign of the 6th house were made unfortunate, and its Lord in the 6th house or 7th under the rays of the Sun, the native will incur a pain and inflammation of the belly.

If the Lot of Fortune, or the Moon, or the Lord of the Ascendant, were made unfortunate in the 7th house, the native will suffer pain in the belly, and the pain will be according to the nature and quality of the sign of the 7th house.

Chapter II.7.23: On illnesses of the genitals

If the Moon were separated from Saturn (he being in one of the angles, under the rays of the Sun), the Moon decreasing in light, the native will have pain of the belly and coldness of the genitals. If the Moon, waxing in light

---

[1088] This sounds like digestive complaints, heartburn, and perhaps even anxiety disorders which cause such symptoms.
[1089] Jag. reads "Taurus."
[1090] *Excoriationem.*
[1091] Jag. omits the 3rd.

and diminished in number, aspected Mars in a diurnal nativity, it portends pain in the genitals and a chronic illness in them.

[And if the infortunes were in the angles, and the luminaries falling in the cadent places, they signify a pain of the testicles and coldness.]

If a peregrine Venus were in the Ascendant, and Saturn aspected her, it signifies pain in the genitals.

If the Moon, diminished in light, were in the 2nd[1092] house and in a moist sign, and she applied to Saturn by conjunction (he being in the opposite of his *awj*), the native will have inflammation, or an opening, or a rupture, in the genitals.

If a retrograde Venus were with Mars in the 8th house (especially in Scorpio), the native's genitals will be large.

If the Moon, Venus, and Mars were in the same place, and Saturn aspected them without the aspect of Jupiter, the native will have an illness in the genitals.

Chapter II.7.24: On stones and grains of sand[1093]

If Saturn were the significator of illnesses, with him being unfortunate, and the Moon would be bound to him by conjunction or aspect, it signifies a stone and sand in the kidneys or bladder, and besides that pain and dryness in the genitals and penis.[1094]

If the Lord of the Lot of Infirmity aspected the 6th house, and the Lord of the 6th and 7th house were made unfortunate, the native will suffer pain in the kidneys and bladder according to the nature of the 6th house.

Chapter II.7.25: On natives having much sexual intercourse

If Venus were in a wanton sign,[1095] the native will have an appetite for sexual intercourse. If Venus were peregrine in the third fortune or face of Gemini,[1096] the native will be lacking in self-control and sterile.

[1092] This should probably be the 12th.
[1093] That is, kidney-stones and other kinds of stones and deposits.
[1094] *Virga*, lit. "stick, rod, cane."
[1095] Probably the lecherous signs of Rhetorius Ch. 76: Aries, Taurus, Leo, partly Capricorn, Pisces, and Libra.

If Venus were in the first face of Leo[1097] and in a bad place, the native will be openly lacking in self-control.[1098]

If Venus were in Aquarius and in the good aspect of Mars, the native will be lacking in self-control.

If Venus were in Pisces, and Mars aspected her from his own exaltation, the native will have much sexual intercourse and be a fornicator, and thence he will procure death for himself.

If Venus, being the Lady of the 7th domicile, were made unfortunate by Mars in a bad place, the native will be lacking in self-control.

If Venus were in the domicile of the Sun, and in the bad aspect of Mars, the native will be lacking in self-control, and a great fornicator.

If Venus were with the Tail of the Dragon in Libra, without the aspect of Jupiter, the native will be lacking in self-control and a sodomite.

Chapter II.7.26: On natives having little sexual intercourse

If Venus and Saturn were made unfortunate and peregrine, joined in the 10th house, the native will be impotent for sexual intercourse.

If the Moon were in the 2nd[1099] house with Saturn, and Venus, being retrograde, aspected him by a square aspect, it portends impotence in sexual intercourse.

If a retrograde Saturn were in the 6th or 12th house and in a moist sign, it signifies the impediment and coldness of [his] seed.

If a peregrine and retrograde Saturn were in the bound of Venus, it signifies the impediment of seed and pain in the genitals.

If the Moon, separated from Venus, were bound to Mercury (he being in the 7th house),[1100] it signifies the impediment of sexual intercourse, but still it will not be totally destroyed.

[1096] This face belongs to the Sun.
[1097] This face belongs to Saturn.
[1098] Jag. next has Venus in the third face of something, but the text is unclear.
[1099] This should probably be the 12th.
[1100] Jag. reads, "in their setting," which suggests they are both going under the rays.

Chapter II.7.27: On natives [who are] eunuchs and hermaphrodites

If Saturn were in the angle of the earth, and he and Venus, being made unfortunate, aspected an eclipsed Sun, the native will be castrated.

If Venus and Moon were made unfortunate in the 6th or 12th house, and Saturn [were] elevated over them,[1101] the native will be castrated.

If Saturn were elevated over the Moon and Venus,[1102] and Mars aspected him by a bad aspect, a limb of the native will be lopped off by iron, or the native will be castrated.

If the Sun were peregrine in some one of the angles, and Saturn, Venus, and Mercury [were] with him, and Mars aspected him by a bad aspect, the native will be castrated.

If Leo were ascending in a diurnal nativity, and Venus, Mars, and the Sun [were] in it, the native will be castrated.

If Saturn, the Sun, Venus and Mercury aspected the 4th house from the angles, and Mars were in it, making them unfortunate, the native will be castrated.

If a male planet were in a female sign and direction, and a shining star of the nature of Mars [were] with him, occidental from the Sun by 19°,[1103] the native will be a hermaphrodite, and he will have each sex (namely, of a man and of a woman).

Chapter II.7.28: On the illness of the anus

If the Head of the Dragon were in Libra, the native will have hemorrhoids or another defect in his anus.

If Saturn were peregrine in the 11th house, and a retrograde Mars aspected him by an opposite aspect,[1104] it signifies hemorrhoids.

If Mars were in the place of the conjunction or prevention preceding the hour of the nativity, the native will suffer dry hemorrhoids, or he will have a fistula in his anus, and he will be weak.

[1101] This probably means he is "overcoming" them, being in the 9th house or domicile.
[1102] I.e., overcoming.
[1103] Reading with Jag. for 1540's "198," putting Mars on the edge of the Sun's rays, thus partaking in a sense of both "sides" as hermaphrodites take part in both types of genitals. See *Carmen* III.1.5, *BA* II.1 p. 19 and I.3 p. 14.
[1104] Jag. reads "If Saturn is in the second from the Ascendant," with no mention of Mars.

If the Lord of the Ascendant were with Mars in the 7th or 4th house, it signifies pain in the anus, and hemorrhoids with a flowing of blood.

And[1105] if Mars were in Scorpio without some dignity of Jupiter and Venus, and especially if he were ascending, it signifies bloody froth trickling from the anus, and pains of the intestines.

If a peregrine Saturn were in the Ascendant without the aspect of a fortune, and Mars aspected him from the west, pain in the anus will invade, with windiness and hemorrhoids, and it will project blood with froth from the anus.

If the Lord of the Ascendant were an infortune, and in the 7th house without the aspect of a fortune, the native will suffer pain in the lower part of the belly and anus.

If Saturn, in a diurnal nativity, were retrograde in the 7th house, without the aspect of an infortune, and Mars aspected him with a bad aspect, the native will suffer a pain in the lower part of his anus, and will project blood with froth from his anus.

Chapter II.7.29: On natives of short stature

If the Moon[1106] were in the latter part of the sign of the 4th house, and Saturn aspected her, the native will be short in stature.

If the Moon will be in a sign of crooked ascension, and in the aspect of Saturn (he being in the opposite of his own *awj*), the native will be short in stature, having short and diminished limbs, and perhaps he will be missing some limb.

If the Moon were under the rays of the Sun, and she aspected Saturn,[1107] the native will be short of stature.

[1105] Reading with Jag.'s fuller account.
[1106] Cf. *BA* III.6.7, and above Ch. II.7.11. This chapter probably emphasizes the Moon because her cycle of waxing and waning is often made analogous to the growth and diminution of the human body. Note that she is always connected to Saturn in these cases, as he is a very cold and dry planet, contrary to the heat and moisture we normally associate with conditions of growth.
[1107] Jag. omits Saturn.

Chapter II.7.30: On natives of tall and even stature

If the Moon were made fortunate in the Midheaven, and the Lord of the Ascendant in the same sign with her, it signifies beauty of stature with evenness.

If the Lord of Ascendant were made fortunate in the Midheaven, and free from the bad aspect or conjunction of Saturn, and Mars aspected the Lord of the Ascendant, the native will have a beautiful stature.

If a sign of direct ascension were ascending, and its Lord in a sign of direct ascension, it likewise signifies the tallness of [his] stature, and more strongly than this if the Moon were not burned up, nor descending in her circle.

Chapter II.7.31: On natives with weak bodies

If the Moon, diminished in light, is being separated from an infortune, and were burned up in an angle, the native will have a weak body and be lazy in his matters.

If the Sun, peregrine in the Ascendant, were [in] some bound of an infortune, and Saturn aspected him by a square or opposite aspect, the native will be weak and lazy.

If the Moon were in the Ascendant and in the sign of Aries, and she were bound to Saturn from a movable sign, the native will be weak and short of motion.

If the Sun were cadent from the Ascendant, and Mars (descending in his own circle) aspected him from a succeedent to an angle, with the Moon being in the square or opposite aspect of Saturn, the native will be weak and short in motion.

Chapter II.7.32: On bald natives

If Leo, Virgo, or Scorpio, or Sagittarius were ascending,[1108] [the native will be bald and his hair will fall out.]

[1108] Reading with Jag. 1540 adds "and Mars in them."

If Cancer were ascending, and Mars or the Moon in it, or that Mars would aspect [Cancer] by a square or opposite aspect, the native will be bald.

If the Lot of Fortune and the Lot of Faith,[1109] and their Lords, were in Aries, the native will be bald.

Chapter II.7.33: On natives having a sparse beard

If Aries, Cancer, Scorpio or [Capricorn or] Pisces were ascending, and the Lot of Fortune in the same place, with Mars aspecting the said Lot, the native's throat will be plucked, and his beard small and sparse.

Chapter II.7.34: On natives having sweat and stinking breath

If Venus were retrograde in a domicile of Saturn, and in his bad aspect, the native will have sweat and stinking breath; and more strongly than this if Venus possessed the sign of Capricorn.

If Mercury, being the Lord of the 6th house, were [made unfortunate][1110] by a bad aspect of Saturn, the native's sweat will be stinking and his mouth will stink.

If Venus, being the Lady of the 6th house, retrograde in the domicile of the Moon, and she aspected in the bad aspect of Saturn, the native's mouth and his buttocks[1111] will stink.

If Venus were burned up in a domicile of Jupiter, and Saturn aspected her without a good[1112] aspect of Jupiter, the native will be wholly stinking.

If Venus were in a movable sign in the bound[1113] of Saturn, and in his aspect, the native will have a stink in his mouth and buttocks.

If the Moon were with Saturn in Aries and in the Ascendant, the native will have a strange and stinking breath.

[1109] This does not make sense, and is not in Jag. Perhaps it is the Lot of Illness?
[1110] Addition mine, but Jag. omits anything relating to Saturn.
[1111] *Asellae*, here and below (translation somewhat uncertain). Normally this indicates a donkey or jackass.
[1112] Reading *bono* for *malo*.
[1113] Jag. reads "domicile," but that would limit it to Capricorn (see above).

Chapter II.7.35: On the illness of the joints,[1114] and the breaking of limbs

If the Moon and the Lot of Infirmity were in the 2nd house, and Mars aspected them by the opposite aspect, the native's body will be broken and his joints will be impeded.

If the Moon were in a sign of crooked ascension[1115] and burned up under the rays of the Sun, and a retrograde Mars aspected [the sign][1116] by a bad aspect, with the Moon not aspecting Jupiter, the native will suffer a chronic illness, so that some limb will be cut off him.

If the Moon were joined to Mars in the Ascendant, or she (being peregrine in the Ascendant without a good aspect) aspected Mars from the opposite aspect, some one of the native's limbs will be lopped off.

Chapter II.7.36: On illnesses of the hands and feet

If Saturn and Mars were with Jupiter, with Venus being made unfortunate, in the 4th house, the native will have an impediment in his hands and feet.

If the infortunes aspected Jupiter[1117] from out of the 6th house or the 12th, the native will be bent over.

If Saturn and Mars and the Dragon[1118] and the Sun were in the 6th house, it signifies a chronic illness in the feet.

If the Lot of Fortune and the Lot of Courage,[1119] and the Lords of their domiciles were in Sagittarius, Capricorn, Aquarius, or Pisces, the native will suffer gout and cancer in the feet.

If the Moon were in the opposition of the Sun, and in the 6th house, and she were bound to Mars by a bad aspect, it signifies a chronic illness in the feet, so that the native will not be able to go [somewhere] without the aid of men or a cane.

[1114] *Nodorum.* This can also denote the tendons.
[1115] Jag.: "in a cut-off sign," the so-called defective or maimed signs, such as Aries and Taurus.
[1116] *Ipsum.* It is possible this refers to the Sun.
[1117] Reading with Jag. for "Saturn," and omitting "without the good aspect of Jupiter."
[1118] *Jawzahirr*, "Dragon" (Pahlavi), reading "and the" with Jag. for "or their."
[1119] *Animositatis.* Undoubtedly the Hermetic Lot of Courage or Boldness, though I do not understand its role here.

If Saturn, the Moon, and Mars were peregrine in the 12th house, and Jupiter did not aspect them with a good aspect, it portends a chronic illness in the feet.

If the Lot of Infirmity were in a movable sign, or in the aspect of an infortune, and the fortunes did not aspect it,[1120] the native will have crooked legs and feet.

If the Lord of the Ascendant were in the 12th house with an infortune, or an infortune aspected [the Lord] by a square or opposite aspect, it signifies a chronic illness in the feet.

If the Sun and Moon were in the 6th house, and the infortunes aspected them, the native will suffer gout in the feet, or surgery in the hands.

If a retrograde and peregrine Mars possessed the 6th house, the native will have some impediment in his feet.

If the sign of the 6th house were movable, and its Lord in a movable sign, the native will have crooked feet.

If Saturn were peregrine and impeded in the 6th house, the native will be distressed by gout or arthritis, especially if the nativity were nocturnal.

[Chapter II.7.37: In what part of the body the illness will be]

Then look to the infortunes which [signify] imped[iment], [to see] over which limb their rulership is,[1121] and judge that the illness will be in the part of the sign in which the infortune is,[1122] by counting from Aries up to the place in which the [in]fortune is.[1123]

Dorotheus says[1124] that you will know from the Midheaven in which part the illness will be, for if some one of the planets were in the Midheaven, the illness will be from the right side; and if none were there, from the left side. [And certain people said if a malefic were above the earth, it will be on the right side]; and if it were under the earth, it will be from the left[1125] side.

[1120] Reading *eam* for *ea*, indicating the Lot.
[1121] Reading with Jag.
[1122] Reading with Jag. for "in accordance with how the illness was in the part of the sign receiving the said infortune."
[1123] Perhaps we are supposed to mix the significations of the limbs indicated by the planet, with that indicated by the sign.
[1124] Cf. *Carmen* IV.1.79-80.
[1125] Reading with Jag.

[Chapter II.7.37: On the time of illness]

You[1126] would be able to know the time of the chronic illness in this way: for if the Lot of Infirmity, and an infortune signifying illness, were from the Ascendant up to the 10th house,[1127] the illness will be in the time of infancy. And if it were from the 10th house up to the 7th, the illness will be in childhood. And if it were from the 4th house up to the 7th, it will be in youth.[1128] And if from the Ascendant up to the 4th house, it will be in old age, and around the time of death. Likewise, if the significator of infirmities were in the bound of the earth,[1129] you should divide that bound according to the above-stated distribution.

And these statements should suffice regarding illnesses, both generally and in particular.

[Chapter II.7.38: On the greatness of the native's testicles][1130]

If the Moon were in the twelfth from the Ascendant in a moist sign, and is conjoining herself to Mars and Saturn in the opposite of her angle, the native will have large testicles.

And if Venus were with Mars in the 8th, and especially if it were in Scorpio, and Venus were [*unclear*], the greatness of the testicles is signified.

And if the Moon and Venus and Mars were in the same place, the native will have a great illness in his testicles, and especially if [Saturn?] aspected that place and Jupiter were cadent from their aspect.

[1126] See *BA* III.6.8 and *JN* Ch. 24 pp. 282-83.
[1127] That is, to the degree of the Midheaven.
[1128] Or rather, adulthood. In Abū Bakr's text the last two quarters have been switched, so I have corrected their order here.
[1129] This probably means "in the same bound as the IC."
[1130] Adding this chapter from Jag.

[Chapter II.8.0: Slaves][1131]

Look at [1] the 6th house[1132] and [2] its Lord, and also at [3] the Lord of the triplicity of the 6th house,[1133] and at [4] Mercury,[1134] and at [5] the Lot of Slaves and [6] its Lord, and see [7] which planet is the *mubtazz* over these places. For if there were a binding between the said *mubtazz* and the *mubtazz* of the native, the native will have slaves (otherwise, not); and you will judge the quality of these [by means of] the *mubtazz* of slaves, and their standing toward the native, and of the native toward the slaves.

And we have already determined sufficiently regarding the significations of this house in what has preceded.

[1131] Cf. *JN* Ch. 22.
[1132] Jag. says "sign."
[1133] Reading with Jag. for "2nd."
[1134] Jag. says "Mars," who does have his joy in the 6th.

Chapter II.9.0: Marriage

For a marriage-union and its status, look from [1] the 7th house and [2] its Lord; from [3] Venus and the Moon; from [4] the Lot of Marriage-Union and [5] its Lord, and also from [6] a planet appearing in the 7th house.

For if [7] the planet which had more testimonies in the said places were appearing in an angle or a succeedent, free from the infortunes and retrogradation and burning up, and it applied to the Lord of the Ascendant, the native will obtain a good and praiseworthy marriage-union. And if the said planet, or the Lords of the triplicities of the said places, were weak and impeded and made unfortunate, they portend the impediment of the marriage-union, and its imperfection,[1135] and also trouble and sorrow.

[Chapter II.9.1: Good and bad sexuality]

Which[1136] if Venus were made unfortunate by Mars, it signifies fornication. And if Venus were in a masculine sign [in the nativity of a man], the native will be a common[1137] fornicator or sodomite. And if Venus were made unfortunate by Mars in the nativity of a woman, and in a masculine sign, the [female] native will be a prostitute. And if she were [in a feminine sign in a male nativity], he will be [soft and passive and] a sodomite; [but in a feminine sign in a female nativity, the female native will be lascivious and shameless].

If Venus were made unfortunate by Saturn,[1138] the native will be of bad sexual intercourse and have hidden children.[1139] And if he did take a wife, she will be a little old woman or a slave-girl. Which if Venus were joined to Jupiter,[1140] it will decree the goodness of sexual intercourse, and also joy and fortune in the marriage-union.

[1135] *Imperfectionem.* This might also mean its "incompleteness," in the sense that the marriage will never be finalized.
[1136] I have reconstructed this paragraph based on *Tet.* III.15 pp. 66-67 (whence it originally derives) and Jag.
[1137] *Publicus.*
[1138] Reading *infortunata* for *in.* Cf. *Carmen* II.4.13.
[1139] Reading with Jag., for "concealer of children."
[1140] Reading with Jag.

Chapter II.9.2: On natives who will not be loved by women[1141]

If Venus were made unfortunate in the domicile of the Sun, women will abhor the native, because the native will have bad sexual intercourse.

If Venus were in a movable sign (apart from being in her own domicile), retrograde, and in the bad aspect of an infortune, the native will be abhorred by women.

If the Moon were burned up in a domicile of Venus, and in the bad aspect of an [in]fortune, and Venus (being peregrine and retrograde) were besieged by the two infortunes, women will abhor the native in sexual intercourse.

If Venus were made unfortunate in the 7th house, and the Lord of the Ascendant aspected her from the Ascendant by an opposite aspect, and the Moon were joined with Saturn in the 4th house and in the aspect of Venus, the native will be abhorred by women, and will be disparaged on account of the stink of his seed.

Chapter II.9.3: On natives lacking a wife

If the planet which [had] the testimonies of planets signifying marriage-union were not bound to a planet having many testimonies and a role in the Ascendant,[1142] the native will not have a marriage.

If the Lot of Marriage-Union were in a bad place, and Venus in a masculine sign and quarter, the native will lack a wife. If the Lords of the triplicity of Venus aspected [neither] Venus nor the Midheaven, the native will not have a wife. If the Lords of the triplicity of Venus (and especially the first one) were[1143] in the bound of infortunes, or peregrine and made unfortunate in the 4th house, the native will not have an appetite for women, nor will he take a wife.

If Venus, being made unfortunate, [did not][1144] aspect the Moon nor the Ascendant, and a peregrine Saturn were cadent from the aspect of Jupiter, the native will lack a wife. If the Lot of Marriage-Union were in the 12th house, and the infortunes aspected it without the aspect of the fortunes, and

---

[1141] This chapter is missing in Jag.
[1142] Reading with Jag. for "nativity."
[1143] In the rest of the sentence the verbs referring to the triplicity Lord are all singular, underscoring that the first one is preferred.
[1144] Adding *non* with Jag.

its Lord did not aspect [the Lot], but [the Lord] would be burned up or descending[1145] or impeded by one of the infortunes, the native will be without a wife and his seed [will be] impeded.

Chapter II.9.4: On marriage with charming[1146] and good women

If the Lord of the 7th house were in the 7th house, the native will take an honest and frank wife. If Jupiter, Venus and Mercury were in the 7th house, the native will have a beautiful and notable wife, and also [have] good and happiness on the occasion of her.

If the Lord of the 7th house were in the 9th, the native will take a foreign but good and religious wife. And if the fortunes aspected [the Lord, while he was] appearing in some one of his own dignities, and the infortunes were cadent from him, the native will be good and famous, and will take a noble wife.

If Venus were in the Midheaven, and a fortune aspected her without the aspect of an infortune, the native will take noble wives. If the Lord of the domicile of the Sun [were] without burning in the 7th house, and in its own domicile, and fortunes aspected it from out of the angles or succeedents, the native will have beautiful wives, and ones big in body. And if Jupiter aspected there, they will be noble and honest.

If the Lot of Marriage-Union were in the 3rd house, [and there will be a strong fortune {there}],[1147] and its Lord free from the infortunes, the native will take a foreign wife, and he will have good and success on the occasion of it.

If the Lot of Marriage-Union were in the 10th house and free from the infortunes, the native will take a good, famous and respectable wife. And if the Lord of the said Lot were made fortunate in the 10th house, the native's wife will be the daughter of great and lofty men.

If the Lot of Marriage-Union were in the 5th house, free from the infortunes and made fortunate, the native will take a wife from his own kin,[1148] [and] who will have a good and beautiful manner, and riches in her

---

[1145] Reading with Jag. for "ascending." This could indicate going under the rays.
[1146] Reading *venustarum* for *venustatis*.
[1147] Reading with Jag. and adding *ibi* ("there") for "and it were strong and made fortunate." I assume the benefic planet may also aspect it.
[1148] *Propinquis*.

own lineage;[1149] and she will be younger than the native and delicate[1150] in her own life.

If Jupiter aspected the Moon by a trine or square aspect, and Venus were in the 8th or 12th house, the native will take a wife from a good lineage, and he will see her death. If Jupiter were in the 7th house, appearing as the Lord of the Lot of Marriage-Union, the native will take a wife with happiness, and he will be drunk.[1151] And if it were Mercury instead of Jupiter, the marriage will be [filled with] laughing and astuteness.

Chapter II.9.5: On marriage to wicked women and prostitutes

If Mercury were with Venus in the fourth angle, and Mars aspected them, the native will have a bad and mischievous[1152] wife.

And if Venus were in an angle, appearing in Cancer or Capricorn, the native will take a prostitute and bad wife.

If Venus were in the angle of the earth and in Aquarius, and the Moon aspected her by a bad aspect, the native will take a prostitute as wife. If Venus were in the 6th house, the native will lie with a prostitute, and will have evil and sorrow because of women. If Venus were in the 12th house, the native will take a bad wife, and one inferior to him.

If Mercury were in the 7th house, the native will take a mischievous wife. If the Sun were in the 7th house, the native's wife will be disobedient to him,[1153] an adulterer, not caring whether people speak well about her, and she will go around many places.

If the Lord of the 7th house aspected the Lord of the 8th, the native will take a wife without a root.[1154]

[And][1155] especially if the sign of the 7th house were fixed, [he will have one wife]; [and if] common, he will have two wives; and if movable,[1156] many.

[1149] *Progenie.*
[1150] *Delicata.*
[1151] I take this to mean he will be "drunk with happiness."
[1152] *Malefica*, lit. "evil-doing."
[1153] That is, the Sun will make the wife arrogant.
[1154] *Radice*, a questionable lineage or background.
[1155] Treating this as a separate sentence. The text seems to blend the notion of her background with the number of wives altogether, but traditionally these are distinct considerations.

If the Head of the Dragon were with Saturn and Mercury in the 7th house, the native will take a widow as wife, or one who had many men.

If the Lot of Marriage-Union were in a blameworthy place, the native will take a disgraced or stained wife, or one having an inseparable illness.

Chapter II.9.6: On the native's marriage with little old women, foul[1157] ones, or sterile ones

If Capricorn were the sign of the 7th house, and Saturn and Mars [were] in it or aspected it, the native will take an aged (but beautiful and wealthy) wife.

If the Lords of the triplicity of Venus were in strong in[1158] the angles, made unfortunate or burned up or impeded, they signify the oppression of the marriage, and sorrow; and that the native will take a little old lady as a wife, or a slave-girl, or a sinful[1159] one, and he will have little love with regard to her.

If[1160] Venus were with Saturn in his own bound, or Saturn aspected her, the native will take a wife that is a little old lady, corrupt, and having an evident deformity.

If Jupiter or Venus were under the rays of the Sun, in a sterile sign, the native will have a little old lady as wife.

If Saturn, appearing [as] the Lord of the Lot of Marriage-Union, were in the 7th house, the native will take an aged wife. If Saturn were the Lord of the 7th house, the native will take a wife from his own lineage.

If some one of the two superior planets were in the western angle, and it had testimony [and were sinking],[1161] the native will take little old ladies and sterile women.

If Saturn conjoined the testimonies of the planets of marriage-union, and he were occidental, it signifies a marriage-union with little old ladies and sterile women.

[1156] Reading *mobilia* for *nobiles*.
[1157] *Turpibus*. This can also mean "filthy" and "ugly."
[1158] Reading with Jag. for "in front of."
[1159] *Peccatricem*.
[1160] See *Carmen* II.4.13.
[1161] Reading *et occidit* with Jag. for "in the marriage-union." I have also deleted the following redundant material after "sterile women": "especially if the said planet, appearing in the 7th house, were occidental."

Chapter II.9.7: On the native's marriage-union with slave-girls

If Venus were in the 12th house and Saturn and Mars aspected her, the native will take slave-girls or prostitutes as wives. If the Lord of the Ascendant were in the 12th house, the native will have a slave-girl or prostitute as a wife.

If the Lord of the 2nd house were in the west, the native will take a slave-girl as a wife. If the Lot of Marriage-Union were in the 2nd house, and its Lord free from the infortunes, [and] it had some dignity in its own place, the native will lie with the slave-girls of noble people, and he will have riches from thence.

If the Lot of Marriage-Union were made unfortunate in the 6th house, the native will lie with slave-girls and captives.

If the Lord of the 7th house were in the 12th house, and the Lord of the 12th in the 7th, the native will have and take a slave girl as a wife.

If Saturn were with Venus in his[1162] domicile, and in the Ascendant, the native will copulate with a woman who is a slave and bad. If Venus, appearing in her own domicile, were with Saturn in the Ascendant, the native will copulate with many women, or with slave-girls, or with foul and low-class women.[1163]

If Saturn were in the western angle or the Midheaven, and also in Leo, Capricorn or Aquarius, and Jupiter or the Moon did not aspect him, the native will take a slave-girl or prostitute as a wife. If Mars aspected that same place, the native will incur detriment on account of this.

If Venus were in a domicile of Mercury, the native will take a slave-girl or one of low-class lineage as a wife. If Venus were in the domicile of the Moon, the native will lie with prostitutes and slave-girls.

Chapter II.9.8: On natives marrying against the law, or lying with prohibited women[1164]

If Venus and Mercury [were] appearing in the Ascendant, and Saturn or Venus were the Lord of the Ascendant, the native will lie with his sisters or

---

[1162] I take this to mean Saturn, since the next sentence has Venus in her own.
[1163] This sentence does not appear in Jag.
[1164] Cf. *BA* III.7.7.

daughters. Judge the same if Venus and Saturn were in the Ascendant, and, of them, Venus were the Lady of the Ascendant.[1165]

If the sign of the 3rd house were Aries or Scorpio, and Venus and Mars aspected it, the native will lie with his brothers' wives, or those of his own friends.

If the Lot of Marriage-Union were in the 3rd house, the native will take some one of his blood-relatives as a wife, or he will lie with the wives or sisters of his brothers, or with those prohibited by law. And if the said Lot were made fortunate in that same place, the native will lie with his own daughters.

If the Lot of Marriage-Union were made unfortunate in the 4th house, the native will lie with his mother or grandmother, or with his father's girlfriend.

If the Lot of Marriage-Union were joined with an infortune, and the Moon appeared in the 7th house or aspected there, the native will lie with his maternal aunt—that is, with the sister of his own mother.

If the Lot of Marriage-Union were made unfortunate in the 5th house, and the fortunes [were] cadent from it, the native will lie with his own daughters or granddaughters.[1166]

And likewise if the Lot of Children were in the 7th house, the native will lie with someone who will be just like a daughter to him.

If the Moon aspected the Lot of Marriage-Union, and the Lord of the said Lot were with the Lot,[1167] the native will lie with maternal aunts or relatives of his mother. If Mars aspected without the aspect of Jupiter, his deed will be revealed, and on account of this he will be defamed.

If[1168] the Sun were in a domicile of Jupiter, the native will fornicate with the wife of his son, or with sisters of his own brothers or relatives. [And if the Moon were in a domicile of Jupiter, the native will have sex with the wife of his father and brothers. And if it were the nativity of a woman, she will have sex with the {brother?}] of her father, or the brother of her husband, or {other male relatives}.]

[1165] But see above, where this is given a different delineation. But clearly we are talking about socially-disapproved-of sexual relations.
[1166] *Neptibus.* This can also refer generally to female descendants.
[1167] Reading with Jag. for *ea.*
[1168] Through the rest of the chapter, some of the sentences between 1540 and Jag. have criss-crossing overlaps, and there may be material missing or garbled in each.

If Venus were in a domicile of Saturn (and especially in Capricorn), he will fornicate with the girlfriends of his father, or those of his own brothers, or with his own mother.

If the Moon were in a domicile of Venus with Mars, and the Lot of Marriage-Union in the square or opposite aspect of them, the native will lie with the girlfriends of his father or those of his own brothers.

If the Sun were in the bound of Venus, the native will take a slave-girl or prohibited woman as a wife.

If Venus were in the domicile or exaltation of the Moon, the native will take his own blood-relative as a wife. And speak thusly if Venus were in her own domicile or exaltation.

If the Moon were in the 7th house, and in a feminine sign, and Venus and the Sun aspected her by a bad aspect, the native will have two wives at the same time.[1169]

Chapter II.9.9: On natives' fornication[1170]

If Venus were in the west or the Midheaven,[1171] and Mercury with her in a bound of Mars, the native will be a fornicator, and he will have offspring in the fornication.

If Venus and Mars were in the Midheaven or in the west without the aspect of Jupiter, the native will be a fornicator and have a bad reputation.

If Saturn,[1172] Venus, and Mercury were in the domicile or exaltation of Venus, and besides that in the west or Midheaven, without the aspect of Jupiter, the native will be a fornicator, and it will reveal whatever he will have in fornication.

If Mars and Venus were in the Midheaven or in the angle of the earth, without the aspect of Jupiter, the native will be a fornicator, and will rejoice in this.

If Venus were in the Midheaven, and the Moon aspected Saturn, and Saturn Venus, the native will be a pimp, and partial to prostitutes.

[1169] Jag. seems to say he will marry two sisters or his daughter-in-law.
[1170] Cf. *BA* III.7.6 and 7.8.
[1171] Jag. adds the Ascendant as well.
[1172] Jag. omits Saturn.

If Saturn and Mars were in the 6th house, and Venus aspected them with a good aspect, without the aspect of Jupiter, the native will be a pursuer of prostitutes.

If Venus, in a diurnal nativity, were in her own domicile, and Mars sent rays to her with a good aspect from his own domicile, the native will frequent prostitutes.

If Venus were in a domicile of Mars, and Mars in a domicile of Venus, the native will be an open fornicator, and without shame.

If Venus were joined with Mars, or in the square or opposite aspect, the native will commit bad and dirty fornications.

If Mars and Venus were in a masculine sign, the native will be a fornicator.

If Venus were made effeminate, the native will be very effeminate, and he will love fornications beyond nature.[1173]

[And if Venus will be in an unfortunate place, aspecting Jupiter and Mars, and the Lord of the triplicity of Venus in the Midheaven, a female native will be a prostitute, and be famous in her prostitution. And since the Lord of the triplicity of Venus is in the Midheaven, and Jupiter with Mars, her prostitution will be disclosed.]

Chapter II.9.10: On the sodomy of male and female natives

If the sixth sign were male, and Mars and Venus [were] in it without the aspect of Jupiter, the native will be a sodomite; and you will judge likewise if Venus were made unfortunate in a domicile of Mercury, and in a cadent sign.

If Mercury were the Lord of the Lot of Fortune,[1174] the native will be a sodomite; and you will judge likewise if the Lot of Fortune were with Mercury in some one of the angles and in a masculine sign, [and he aspects the house of marriage-union].[1175]

[1173] The Latin is ambiguous. It could mean he has excessive love for fornicating, or else that he enjoys fornication which is "beyond" or contrary to nature (i.e., sodomy). See next chapter.
[1174] Reading with Jag.
[1175] Moved from the next sentence, with Jag., and omitting the next sentence as being a reworking of the following one.

If Mercury were bound to the Lot of Marriage-Union, or the Lord of that Lot [were] masculine, and it were in a masculine sign or place, the native will be a sodomite.

If the Moon were in a masculine sign, [and][1176] the Sun and Venus aspected him from a masculine sign, the native will be a sodomite.

If Mercury and Venus were joined in the 7th house, the native will be a master of gigolos and a sodomite.

If Mercury were in the 7th house, and Venus cadent from him, and in addition [she were] appearing as the Lady of the Ascendant, the native will be a sodomite.

If Mercury were in the 7th house with Mars, and[1177] Venus (appearing peregrine) aspected them by a bad aspect from a masculine sign, the native will be a sodomite.

If Venus were in a domicile and bound of Mars,[1178] and in a bad place, the native will be a sodomite.

If Mercury, Mars, and Saturn were in the house of his body, the native will be a sodomite,[1179] particularly if Venus were[1180] with Mercury in a masculine sign.

If the Lot of Marriage-Union were in a domicile of Mercury and in a masculine sign, and in some one of the angles, the native will be a sodomite.

If Venus and the Moon, in the nativity of a woman, were in the 4th[1181] house, the female native will be a sodomite. If Venus were in the 7th house and in a masculine sign, and the Moon in the Ascendant, the female native will be a sodomite. If feminine planets were in masculine signs, degrees, and places, the female native will be conceived in adultery, and she will have an appetite for sleeping with women.

[1176] The rest of this sentence is not in Jag.
[1177] The rest of this sentence is not in Jag.
[1178] Jag. reads "Mercury."
[1179] The rest of this sentence is not in Jag.
[1180] Reading *fuerit* (sing.) for *fuerint* (pl.).
[1181] Reading with Jag. for "8th." But cf. *BA* III.7.13, item 13.4.

Chapter II.9.11: On the innocence[1182] of natives, or the prohibition of sodomy

If Venus were in a domicile of Jupiter, and free of the bad aspect of Mars, the native will have a good complexion, and innocent[1183] of the sodomitical sin.

If Venus were in the Ascendant or Midheaven with Jupiter, or will bind to him from out of places from which she received him, and Mars did not aspect Venus, the native will be restricted and free from the sins against nature.

If one of the *biyābānīya* stars[1184] of the first magnitude and of the nature of Jupiter and Venus were in the Ascendant or in the Midheaven, the native will be innocent and free from every sodomitical crime; [and he will be] generous, pious, good, and of good reputation.

Chapter II.9.12: On the womanliness of natives

If Mercury or[1185] Saturn were with Venus in the Ascendant or in the Midheaven, the native will be womanly.

If the Sun and Moon were in the 3rd house, the native will be womanly and his manners will be like the manners of a woman; and he will acquire a livelihood from that womanliness.

If[1186] Venus were in Aries, Taurus, Leo,[1187] or Capricorn, and Mars and the Sun projected their own rays upon Saturn, the native will be womanly, and will have an appetite for men.

If the Moon were in a domicile of Saturn, and Saturn in a domicile of Venus or in Scorpio, and in the angle of the earth, or in the 6th or 12th house, the native will have womanly manners.

If Venus were with an infortune appearing in a feminine sign, the native will be practically like a woman, and will do womanly things, not to mention

---

[1182] *Castitate*, which also has connotations of chastity.
[1183] Omitting *quantum*.
[1184] *BA* III.2.1 p. 80, Rhetorius Ch. 58 p. 106: Toliman (α Centaurus) and probably θ Eridani.
[1185] Reading *aut* with Jag.
[1186] Cf. *BA* III.7.13, item 13.3.
[1187] Jag. reads "Pisces."

that he will have an appetite for men (and [this will also be so] if [the native] *is* a woman).

Chapter II.9.13: On the native's fortune regarding women

If Mercury, appearing in the Ascendant and in a feminine sign (especially in Virgo), were free of the infortunes, the native will have good and usefulness from women; and speak thusly if the Lot of Fortune were in the 3rd house, joined with Venus and in her face.

If Venus were in the 3rd house in some one of her own dignities (it being a nocturnal nativity), and she aspected the Lot of Fortune by a trine aspect, the native will take a wife, he will be the master of his wife's money, and he will have good on the occasion of her.

If Venus [were] appearing in the 4th house and in a fixed sign, and Jupiter aspected her by a good aspect, and the infortunes were cadent from her, the native will obtain fortune and riches because of women.

If the Lord of the 7th house were in the 5th house, strong and made fortunate, the native will have success with women.

If Venus were in the 5th house (which is the house of her joy), made fortunate, the native will obtain good on the occasion of women, and he will rejoice with them.

If Venus were in Taurus and in the western angle, made fortunate, and free from the bad ones, the native will have a good marriage-union, and will rejoice with his wife.

If Mercury were made fortunate in the 7th house (it being a nocturnal nativity), the native will rejoice with women and he will have good and success from them.

If Venus were joined with Jupiter in the 9th house or in his trine aspect, the native will be fortunate in the marriage-union, and will have dominion and riches and a [good] reputation on the occasion of women.

If the Head of the Dragon, Venus, and Mercury were in the 11th house, the native's fortune will arrive on the occasion of women.

If the Lot of Marriage-Union were in the 7th house, the native will take as a wife a woman whom he esteemed. And if the Lord of the said Lot were made fortunate, the native will have good and joy with her.

If the Lot of Fortune were in the 7th house, made fortunate by Jupiter, and the infortunes cadent from [the Lot], the native will be fortunate in the marriage-union, and will have success and honor from the wife.

If Venus were in her domicile, free from the infortunes, the native will obtain good and fortune from women, and will be rejoicing with them. If Venus were in a domicile of Jupiter, free from the infortunes, the native's honor will proceed on the occasion of women, and he will be fortunate with them.

Chapter II.9.14: On the native's misfortune regarding women

If Venus were in the 12th house, the native will have a bad wife, and he will suffer sorrow and detriment and much evil on the occasion of her.

If Venus were in the 2nd house (it being a diurnal nativity), and the infortunes aspected her, the native will obtain evil, sorrow, and detriment on the occasion of women.

If Venus were in some one of her own dignities and in the 3rd house (it being a nocturnal nativity), and Saturn and Mars were joined with her or they aspected her by a bad aspect, the native will not be able to stand firm with just one woman, and thence he will have evil, sorrow and detriment, especially if Venus were in a movable sign.

If Venus were in the angle of the earth and the infortunes aspected her, the native will have bad sexual intercourse and will rejoice little with women.

If the Moon, filled with light, were joined to Mars in a domicile of Venus or in the 6th house, the native will incur evil and sorrow and labor on the occasion of women.

If Venus were in the 9th house and in some one of her own dignities, and the infortunes aspected her, the native will obtain evil and sorrow and pain on the occasion of women, and he will take a wife lower than himself.

If the Lot of Marriage-Union were impeded and made unfortunate in the 7th house, the native will suffer evil and detriment from the direction of women.

If the Lot of Marriage-Union were made unfortunate in the 9th house, women will not seek out the native, but they will hate him, and he will have evil and pain from them.

If the Lot of Marriage-Union[1188] were made unfortunate in the 12th house, the native will labor with women or wives, and thence he will have evil and sorrow.

If the Lot of Fortune[1189] were made unfortunate, the native will incur worry[1190] and sorrow because of women.

Chapter II.9.15: On natives who fornicate secretly with women[1191]

If the Lord of the 7th house were in the angle of the earth or under the rays of the Sun, the native will fornicate secretly with women. If the Lord of [the Lot of][1192] Nuptials were in the house of nuptials, the native will conceal his fornication.

If Mars were the Lord of the Lot of Nuptials and in the 7th house, the native will fornicate secretly with someone from his own lineage.

If Saturn and Mars were in the 6th house, the native will conceal his own marriage-union or fornication, especially if they did not[1193] aspect the Lot of Marriage-Union, nor even the 7th house and its Lord: the native's fornication will be concealed. But if they aspected the said places, it will be made public.

If Venus, appearing in the 3rd house and occidental, were in her own bound or in a bound of Jupiter, the native will take a wife secretly, but he will have good from her, and also riches and fortune.

Chapter II.9.16: On natives whose wives die first

If the Moon were in the 4th house, the native's wives will die and he will be in pain from that.

If Venus were in the angle of the earth, and Saturn and Mars aspected her, the native's wives will die and their death will be concealed. And if that sign were movable, many wives of the native will die before him.

[1188] Reading with Jag. for *fortunae*.
[1189] Both texts say this, but my sense is that something else involving the Lot of Marriage-Union is required.
[1190] *Cogitationem*.
[1191] Jag. treats this as a secret marriage, not secret fornication.
[1192] Reading with Jag.
[1193] Adding *non*, to contrast with the next sentence in which they *do* aspect.

If the Lord of the 7th house were in the 8th house, the native's wives will die before him, and he will remain alone.

If the Moon, separated from Mars, applied to Venus (she being in the west), the native will have many wives, but they will die before him.

If Saturn were in the 7th house (it being a nocturnal nativity), and Venus and the Moon are being conjoined to him, they signify the death of the native's wife, and also an impediment to the marriage-union—and the destruction of the home in which the native is.

If Venus were in the 7th house, and the fortunes aspected her without the aspect of the infortunes, the native will see the death of his wives. If the Lord of the 7th house were burned up or descending[1194] or made unfortunate in the 2nd house, the native's wives will die before him (because the 2nd house is the 8th from the 7th).

If one of the infortunes were in the 4th or 7th house, the native will see the death of the wife.

If Venus, being occidental, were joined to an infortune, it portends the quick death of the wife.

If the Lord of the 7th house were made unfortunate by the aspect of Mars and Mercury, and Jupiter did not aspect, the native will kill the wife on account of jealousy.

If the Lot of Marriage-Union and Mars were in the same degree, and an unfortunate Mercury aspected them, the native will suffocate his own wives, or will kill and deceive them in betrayal.

If Mars and Venus were in the 12th house, the native will kill the wife.

If Venus were in a domicile of Mars, the native will have evil from women, and will kill them because of fornication and jealousy.

Chapter II.9.17: On the number of the native's wives

Dorotheus said:[1195] the number of planets appearing between the Midheaven and Venus signifies the number of the native's wives. And if it were the nativity of a woman, reckon from the Midheaven up to Mars. Which if Mars were in the Midheaven, reckon from Mars up to Jupiter: and

---

[1194] My sense is that this means going under the rays.
[1195] *Carmen* II.5.1-3. *BA* III.7.9 counts signs in imitation of the rules for children, but Abū Bakr has Dorotheus correctly.

the number of the female native's (or woman's) men[1196] will be according to the number of planets appearing between them.

Chapter II.9.18: On the time at which the native will take a wife[1197]

If Jupiter applied by *tasyīr* to the degree of the Lot of Marriage-Union, or the Lot of Marriage-Union to the degree of Jupiter, or the Lord of the 7th house to the degree of the Lord of the Ascendant, or if Jupiter applied to the degree of Venus, all of this signifies a marriage-union will come to be at that time (by giving one year to every degree).

If the year of the revolution from the Ascendant reached the seventh[1198] sign, the native will take a wife in that year. And if that sign were movable, the native will make many marriage-unions [over the course of his life].[1199] And if it were common, he will have two wives; and [if] a fixed one, only one.

[1196] *Virorum*, a standard synonym for "husband" (*maritus*).
[1197] This chapter not in Jag.
[1198] Reading with *JN* Ch. 26 for "second."
[1199] Added by Dykes.

Chapter II.10.0: Death

The[1200] places of the significators of death are these:[1201] [1] the Ascendant and [2] its Lord; [3] the sign of the 8th house and [4] its Lord; and [5] infortunes appearing in that same place; [6] the Lot of Death and [7] its Lord, [8] the first Lord of the triplicity of the angle of the earth, [9] the eighth sign from the Sun [in a diurnal nativity, and] the eighth sign from the Moon [in a nocturnal nativity], [10] the Lord of the bound of the degree of the 7th house; [11] the Moon and [12] the Lord of her domicile. Therefore you should know these places and look at [13] the planet which conjoins the testimonies of these places, and just as you saw their manner and nature, so judge concerning the native's death.

[Chapter II.10.1: Types of death]

It must be known that men's deaths are of many kinds:[1202]

[a] There are some who wish for death and fear it;

[b] And some who love death and do not fear it.

[c] And some are fortunate in death (that is, having a beautiful death);

[d] And others who have bad pain and labor in death.

[e] There are even those who kill themselves.

[f] And [there are] certain ones who die a bad death;

[g] And some end life elegantly in their own bed;

[1200] This paragraph was appended to II.10.3 immediately below, but I have replaced it here to parallel the other general instructions for other topics.
[1201] It is worth comparing this with the significators listed in Jag.: the seventh [sign], the eighth [sign] and its Lord, the Lot of Death and its Lord, Saturn, and the first triplicity Lord of the fourth sign. Some of these items have been drawn from other sources.
[1202] I have labeled the chapters below as best I can, according to the list here.

[*h*] And certain ones die in a foreign land;

[*i*] And others in their own homeland.

And we will distinguish concerning this by particular [items] in what follows.

[Chapter II.10.2: Death according to an Ascendant template]

If Aries were the Ascendant, Mars (who is its Lord) will be the significator of death, because Scorpio will be in the 8th house, of which Mars is even the Lord. Therefore, on account of Mars the native will die in his own home; and likewise on account of Mars he will be litigious, one who, because of his death will have great strength, not to mention he will cause lawsuits, wars, and robberies leading the native to [his own] death.

Likewise if Libra were the Ascendant, Taurus will be the sign of the house of death, and Venus the Lady of the 8th—who, as the Lady of death and life signifies that the native will cause death to himself. Likewise, women in whose nativities Libra was the Ascendant, will cause death to themselves by fornication, adulteries, and other troubles:[1203] and perhaps that sexual intercourse will be the cause of their death: [because] if Libra [were] in the Ascendant, [then] they desire this more.[1204]

[*c*] If Sagittarius (whose Lord is Jupiter) were the Ascendant, the sign of his exaltation (namely Cancer) will be in the 8th house; and since Jupiter signifies religious and faithful men, and clerics, hermits, and men praying to God, it is a sign that the native's death will be good and honorable, and also that his soul will be arranged in the bosom of Abraham, by the command of God.

[1203] *Molestia.*
[1204] *Hoc magis appetunt.*

Chapter II.10.3: On natives fearing death

[*a*] And they are Mercurial ones, [that is, if Gemini or Virgo were the Ascendant], because the house of his death is that of Saturn and Mars,[1205] which signifies dread and laborious and bad deaths.

Chapter II.10.4: On natives who will die by some illness

[*d*] If Mars or the Sun were the Lord of the 8th house, appearing in a moist sign, the native will die from a hot and moist illness, like from a flowing[1206] of the belly and the like.

If Mars were the Lord of the 7th house, appearing under the rays, the native will die from a pain in the belly or some limb in his body.

If the Sun were eclipsed in the 7th house, and the Lord of that angle in its own station or retrograde, the native's death will be from a chronic illness.

If the Moon were made unfortunate in the angle of the west, the native will die from a hot and moist illness, or from cancerous and stinking abscesses.

If the Sun were in the Ascendant and the Moon in the west, and Mars in the Midheaven or in the angle of the earth, and Jupiter did not have testimony there, nor did he aspect Mars,[1207] the native's death will be from scorching humors.

If the Moon were with Mars in the 7th house, the native will die from a flowing of blood through the anus or another place.

Chapter II.10.5: On natives who will die a bad death

[*f*] If the Moon were in the 7th house and the infortunes aspected her, the native will die a bad death. If the Moon were in the 12th house, and the infortunes aspected her, the native will die a bad death, and this signification will be stronger if one of the said infortunes appeared as the Lord of the 7th house.

[1205] The eighth sign from Gemini is Capricorn (ruled by Saturn); from Virgo, Aries (ruled by Mars).
[1206] *Ex fluxu.*
[1207] Reading *Martem* for *mortem*.

If Saturn, Mars and Mercury were with Jupiter and Venus in the 4th house, the native will die a bad and stinking death.

If Mars were in the 7th house, and the Moon aspected him, the native will die a bad death.

If the infortunes were descending after the 7th house, and the Moon aspected from out of one of the angles, they signify the native's bad death.

If the Lords of the triplicity of the 4th house were in bad places, and the infortunes aspected them, the native will be burdened over the exit of [his] soul.

[And if Jupiter and Venus will be in the 8th from the Ascendant, the native will die a bad death.][1208]

If Saturn were in the 8th house (it being a nocturnal nativity), and the fortunes did not aspect him, the native will die a bad death.

If[1209] the Head of the Dragon, the Sun, the Moon and Mercury were in the 12th house, they signify great and strong infirmities, or the breaking of bones, or blindness, or burning up, and that the native will die a bad death, or will be killed malignly by the hands of his own enemies, especially if Saturn were with the same [planets] in the 12th house.

Chapter II.10.6: On natives who will die a sudden death

If the Head of the Dragon, Saturn, and Mars were in the 4th house, the native will incur a sudden death.

If the Moon were in the 8th house (it being a nocturnal nativity), and the infortunes aspected her, the native will die a sudden death.

If the first Lord of the triplicity of the angle of the earth were outside of its own domicile, and the 8th house were made unfortunate, and the fortunes cadent from [the 8th], the native's death will be sudden.

If Mars were in the domicile of the Moon, the native will die suddenly by iron or the outpouring of blood.

[1208] One would think perhaps they would improve the death; but perhaps their being in the 8th is understood to rob them of their benefic character.

[1209] This sentence originally appeared at the end of II.14.0 below (on enemies), probably because it includes a reference to the 12th.

If[1210] the Lord of the conjunction or prevention preceding the nativity were in the 12th house, the native will die suddenly.

Chapter II.10.7: On natives who will die in water

If Saturn were in the 4th house, occidental and in a movable sign, and Mars aspected him, the native will die in water.

If the sign of the 4th house, the Lot of Death and its Lord, and also Saturn and the first Lord of the triplicity [of the angle of the earth] were in watery signs, or[1211] the majority of them, the native will die in water.

If the planet which is conjoining the testimonies of the said significators were in a sign of water, the native's death will be in water.

If the Lord of the 4th house were in the 7th house and in a watery sign, the native will die in water or on account of the excessive drinking of water.

If Saturn, Mars, and the Moon[1212] were in the Midheaven and in a watery sign, the native's death will be in water or from the clouds of the sky.

Chapter II.10.8: On natives who will die by fire

If the Lord of the 4th house were in the 7th house and in a fiery sign, and the fortunes aspected him from out of fiery signs, the native will die by fire.

If the Moon were with Mars in the 8th house, the native will be burned up.

If all planets signifying death were in a fiery sign, the native will die by fire.

If the planet which is conjoining the testimonies of the planetary significators of death [were] in a fiery sign, the native will be burned.[1213]

If the Moon were the Lady of the 7th house, and Mars and the Sun aspected her from out of the 7th and 10th house, the native will be burned up.

If the Moon were in a sign of the angles or succeedents, and in a fiery sign, and the infortunes aspected from out of fiery signs without the aspect of Jupiter, the native will die by fire.

[1210] This sentence originally appeared at the end of II.14.0 below (on enemies), probably because it includes a reference to the 12th.
[1211] Reading *aut* for *et*.
[1212] Jag. omits the Moon.
[1213] This can include burning alive (*cremabitur*).

Chapter II.10.9: On natives who will die by falling from high places

If the Sun were in the 8th house, peregrine and made unfortunate, and the infortunes aspected the Lord of the 8th house, the native will tumble or die from a high place.

If the Moon were in some one of the angles or succeedents, and a peregrine Jupiter appeared in the 2nd or 12th house and in an earthy sign, the native will die by falling from a height.

If Saturn were the Lord of the 8th house, he will fall headlong[1214] and die.

If Jupiter and Mars were in the west, and they did not aspect the angle of the earth, the native will die by falling from a height.

If the Moon were in the Midheaven, and the infortunes in her opposition, a house or wall or tree above the native will tumble down and he will die.

Chapter II.10.10: On natives who will die by a poison or toxin

If the Lord of the 8th house were peregrine, and made unfortunate by Mars or Saturn, and it appeared in Cancer, Scorpio or Pisces, the native will be struck by a serpent, or will die by a poison or toxin.

If Venus, being the Lady of the 8th house, were impeded, the native will die by poison given by women or he will take medicine which will make him die.

If Venus, being the Lady of the 8th house, were made unfortunate, and likewise the sign of the 8th house made unfortunate, the native will die by drunkenness or the excessive drinking of wine or accepting poison.

If Venus were the ruler of death or of the above-written places signifying death, and also free from all harm, the native will die by a pain in the belly. And if she were impeded, the native will perish on account of an excess of medicine or of sexual intercourse.

If the Head of the Dragon were in the 4th house with Mercury, the native will end his life by a deadly drug, or by black magic.

If the Moon were in the 8th house with the Tail of the Dragon, the native will die by poisonous purgatives or a lethal drink.

[1214] *Ruet.*

Chapter II.10.11: On natives who will be eaten or killed by beasts

[¶] If the Lord of the 12th house were with Saturn in the Ascendant, beasts will eat the native, but he himself will love the hunt and dogs.

If the Lot of Fortune were in the 2nd house, and an infortune aspected the Ascendant and the said Lot, the native will be eaten by wild animals or dogs.

If Mars, being the Lord of the 8th house, were joined with the Moon in the sign of a beast, animals will eat the native and kill him.

If the Moon were in some one of the angles or the succeedents, and a Jupiter peregrine [were] in an angle and in a quadrupedal sign (especially in Leo), the native will be eaten or killed by wild animals.

If the Moon were joined with Saturn and Mars in the Midheaven, and in a quadrupedal sign or in Virgo, wild animals will eat and kill the native.

If[1215] Saturn or Mars, being the Lord of the 12th house, were in the Ascendant, the native will have a great desire to hunt, and perhaps he will be killed by a wild animal or torture.[1216]

Chapter II.10.12: On natives who will die by the sword or be hung

[¶] If the Lord of the house of life were in the 7th house, and Mars [were] the Lord of the 7th house, the native's neck will be cut off.

If Mars were in the 10th house and the Moon in the 7th, and the fortunes did not aspect her, the native will be killed by enemies or robbers.

If the Moon, being the Lady of the 7th house, were bound to the infortunes or were impeded by burning up, and the Sun made unfortunate in the 6th house, the native will be killed by command of the king.

If one of the infortunes were in the Midheaven, and the other in the angle of the earth, the native will be killed or hung.

If the Moon were in the Ascendant, and Saturn in the Midheaven, and Mars in the angle of the earth without the aspect of some fortune, the native will be killed or decapitated, and after that he will be hung.

If Mars were with the Head of the Dragon in the 8th house, and the Lord of the 8th impeded [them], the native will die in prison.

[1215] This sentence originally appeared at the end of II.14.0 below (on enemies), probably because it includes a reference to the 12th.

[1216] Reading *tortura* for *tarte*. Another meaning, "extortion," would be appropriate for the house of enemies.

If Mars were in the 8th house, and he impeded the Lord of the 8th, the native's death will be by iron.

If some one of the infortunes were in the eighth sign from the Sun (it being a diurnal nativity), or in the eighth sign from the Moon (it being a nocturnal nativity), it signifies the same thing which it signified in the 8th house from the Ascendant.

If the degree of the 7th house were impeded, and likewise its Lord, it signifies the worst death.

If the luminaries were with *Caput Algol*, and Mars[1217] aspected that same place by a bad aspect, the natives will be hung, with his hands and feet lopped off.

If the Sun were eclipsed in the 7th house after the conjunction of the Moon, the native will be killed by looters and plunderers.

If Mars were in the Midheaven (it being a diurnal nativity), and the Moon in Scorpio, and none of the fortunes aspected there from out of the angles, nor were bound there, the native will be killed by enemies or robbers.

If the Tail of the Dragon, Jupiter, Venus and Saturn were in the 8th house, the native will be killed, and perhaps he will be decapitated or hung without cause.

If Saturn were in the Ascendant, and the Moon in the west, and Mars aspected them from out of the 4th house, the native will be killed or hung.

If Saturn were with Mars in the west or in the angle of the earth, the native will be killed by the sword.

If Saturn, Jupiter and Mercury were in the west, the native will be killed in a war.

If the infortunes aspected the Lot of Death without the aspect of the fortunes, the native will be killed.

If the Lord of the Lot of Death were in the opposite of the Lord of the 8th house, and in a sign inimical to himself, the native will be killed.

If Saturn and the Moon were in the west, and Mars in the angle of the earth, the native will be killed or hung.

If Mars were in the 8th house, or he impeded the 8th house, the native will die by iron.

[1217] Reading *Mars* for *natus*, following *Tet.* IV.9 p. 40.

Chapter II.10.13: On natives who kill themselves

[*e*] If the Sun and Moon, Jupiter and Venus were in the Midheaven, and Saturn and Mars aspected them, while however one of [the malefics] was the Lord of the 2nd house, the native will hang himself.

If the 7th house[1218] and its Lord were made unfortunate, and the said Lord were in the Ascendant, the native will kill himself.

If the Lord of either the Ascendant or[1219] of the 7th house did not aspect the Moon, the native will kill himself.

If the Lord of the Ascendant applied to the Lord of the house of death, or the Lord of the house of death or the Lord of the 7th house were in the Ascendant, and they did not aspect the Moon, the native will kill himself.

If Saturn and Mars were in the 10th house, and the Lord of the Ascendant [were] made unfortunate, and the Moon (being separated from the Lord of the Ascendant) did not aspect the Ascendant, the native will hang and kill himself.

If Mars were in the Ascendant and the Moon in the west, and the fortunes did not aspect them, the native will kill himself.

Chapter II.10.14: On natives who will die on the occasion of women

If the Lot of Nuptials were in the 8th house, and its Lord were made unfortunate, the native will die on the occasion of women.

If Venus, being the Lady of the house of nuptials, were made unfortunate in the 6th house, the native's death will be because of a slave-girl.

If Venus were in the 7th house, the Moon being peregrine, and the infortunes aspected her, the native will die on the occasion of women. And if it were Jupiter instead of Venus, the native's death will be because of his offspring. And if it were Mars instead of Venus, the native will die on the occasion of brothers. And if it were Saturn instead of Venus, the native's death will be on the occasion of the father. And if it were the Moon instead of Venus, the native will die on the occasion of the mother.

[1218] Jag. has "the Ascendant."
[1219] Reading *ascendentis vel* for *ascendens*.

Chapter II.10.15: On natives whose death will be secret

If the Lord of the triplicity of the 4th house were in the 4th or 7th house, the native will die in a secret place, and nothing of him will be found.

If the Lord of the 8th house were made unfortunate, or the tenth sign made unfortunate, the native will die secretly on the occasion of friends and relatives.[1220]

If the Lord of the 8th house and the Lord of the Lot of Death, and the common significators in death, and also the planet which is conjoining their[1221] testimonies, were in the 4th house under the rays of the Sun (or [if] the majority [of them] were), the native will die secretly.

If the Lord of the Ascendant applied to an infortune appearing in the angle of the earth, none will have acquaintance of the native's death.

Chapter II.10.16: On natives who will die in their own land or homeland

[*b*] If the Lord of the 8th house were in the 8th house and in his own house,[1222] the native will die in his own home or homeland.

If the sign of the 8th house and its Lord were [not][1223] made unfortunate, nor impeded, the native will end his life in his own home or homeland.

If Jupiter and Venus aspected Mars[1224] by a trine aspect without the aspect of Saturn, the native will die in his own land or homeland.

If Mars were in the Ascendant, and Jupiter aspected him by a trine aspect, the native will die in his own land or homeland.

If the Lot of Death were in some one of the angles, safe from the infortunes, the native will end his days by a natural death in his own land or homeland.

[1220] This might be because the eighth is the tenth sign from the eleventh (signifying friends), and the tenth is the tenth sign from the first (signifying the native, but here standing for people from his own background).
[1221] Reading *ipsorum* for *ipsi*.
[1222] Following Jag. It is redundant to say that the Lord of the 8th in the 8th is in his own domicile, unless one uses a quadrant house system.
[1223] Adding *non*.
[1224] Reading *martem* for *mortem*.

Chapter II.10.17: On natives who will die outside their homeland, or in a foreign place

[¶] If the Lord of the 8th house were in the 12th house, the native will die on a journey, and he will have impediment on the occasion of dead people.

If the Lord of the 4th house were naturally inimical to its house [in which it is],[1225] and it possessed the 6th or 12th house, the native will die in a foreign land.

If the Lot of Death were in one quarter,[1226] and its Lord in another, the native will die outside of his own land. If the Lot of Death were in the 3rd or 9th house, the native will die outside of his own land. If the Lot of Death and its Lord, and the Lord of the 7th house, were in the Ascendant or in signs in which the Lord of the Ascendant has no dignity, the native will die outside of his own land.

If the Lord of the angle of the earth were in the 8th house, the native will die outside of his own land.

If the Lord of the 8th house were in the 3rd house, the native will die outside of his own land.

If the[1227] Moon were in the 7th sign by day, under the rays, and binding itself with some infortune, the native will die in a foreign place.

If Saturn were in the 4th house,[1228] and Mars (being peregrine) aspected him, the native will die outside of his own land.

If Jupiter were the Lord of the 8th house, and also peregrine and made unfortunate, the 8th house likewise being made unfortunate, the native will die in a foreign place because of kings or princes.

If the Lord of the 8th house were in the 2nd house, the native will die in a foreign place.[1229]

If Venus, Saturn, Mars and the Moon were in the 9th house,[1230] the native will die in a foreign land or by the bite[1231] of a beast.

[1225] Following Jag. and adding the clarification in brackets.
[1226] *In una 4*. This material on the Lot does not correspond to the section in Jag.
[1227] Reading with Jag. for "If the Moon were in the 5th house (it being a diurnal nativity), and she were bound to an infortune, the native will die outside of his own land."
[1228] Jag. reads, "the 8th."
[1229] This draws on an old notion of the sign of detriment signifying being away from home.
[1230] Jag. reads, "8th house."
[1231] Omitting *siti vel* (corresponding to an illegible word in Jag.), which seems to be a synonym for "bite."

If the Lord of the 8th house were peregrine, the native will die outside of his own land.

If the Sun were in the Midheaven, and Mars aspected him by a bad aspect, the native will die in a foreign land.

Chapter II.11.0: Travel

For the native's travels, we should look to [1] the sign of the 9th house and [2] its Lord, to [3] the sign of the 3rd house and [4] its Lord, to [5] the Lot of Travel and [6] its Lord, and [7] Mars and Mercury, and also to [8] a planet which is in the 9th house, or [9] which gathered together the testimonies of the said places: and you will judge just as you find [them].

[Chapter II.11.1: Successful travel]

If the Lord of the 9th house were in the Ascendant, strong and made fortunate, and the infortunes did not have testimonies with him,[1232] then travel will be agreeable to the native, and [he will be] rejoicing in it, clever and wise, and his standing and his body will be put in order[1233] on the journey.

If the Moon were in the 3rd house, oriental and appearing from under the rays of the Sun, the native will love journeys, and will have success from thence, with joy.

If the Moon were in the 5th house, and Jupiter and Mars aspected by a good aspect, the native will have joy, fortune and usefulness on a journey.

[If the fortunes will be in the ninth, the native will obtain profit from travel, and good fortune, and he will not go on a journey] without joy, especially if the Lord of the 9th house were in a good place and in some one of its own dignities, and the infortunes were cadent from it.

If the Sun, Venus and Mercury were in the 9th house, the native will obtain joy and success on a journey, and will undertake what he loves in it.

If the Moon, appearing in a [nocturnal] nativity, were in the 9th house and in a feminine sign, the native will make many journeys, and he will obtain riches and honors on the occasion of them, and he will be fortunate in them.

If the Moon and her Lord were in the place[1234] of travels, the native will love travels, will rejoice on them, and will have success from thence, especially if the Moon and Venus were made fortunate: for then he will obtain great good and honor from his travels.

[1232] This probably refers to aspects.
[1233] *Dirigetur.*
[1234] I say "a" place instead of "the" place, because we have seen the 3rd be relevant for journeys. But of course the 9th is the most important place for this.

If the Lord of the Ascendant were in the 9th house, and the Lord of the 9th house in the Ascendant, the native will love travels or rejoice in them.

If the Moon were bound to a fortune on the third day from the nativity,[1235] and that fortune were [pertaining-to-arising], outside of the rays of the Sun, the native will be fortunate on a journey, and will have good from his travels. And if the said planet were made fortunate[1236] and oriental, and [in its own bound, and the infortunes aspected it],[1237] the native will make long journeys, and he will go[1238] from place to place, with middling exploits.[1239]

If the Lord of the 9th house were in some one of the angles, strong and made fortunate, and the infortunes[1240] cadent from him, the native will be fortunate on his journeys, and he will find good and fortune from them, and also honor from it, and honor will not be removed from him while he is on his journey.

Chapter II.11.2: On natives who will die on their journeys, or never come back from them

If Jupiter and Venus were in the 5th house, the native will have children on a journey, and he will not return [to them].[1241]

If Mercury, appearing from under the rays of the Sun, were in the Midheaven with Mars, the native will go out from his own land and never turn back to it.

If Saturn were in the domicile of the Moon, the native will jump at the chance to take a long journey, from which he will hardly or never will come back to his own land.

[1235] Cf. Dorotheus Excerpt XX, which has the Moon with Mars or in his square or opposition (or in his domicile) on the third day: this also grants life abroad.
[1236] Reading *fortunatus* for *infortunatus*.
[1237] Reading with Jag. for "also in the aspect of bound of a fortune."
[1238] *Incursor erit*. In classical Latin this means he will be an "attacker," but I follow the milder medieval senses.
[1239] *Cum modico facto*.
[1240] Reading *infortunae* for *fortunae*.
[1241] Reading with Jag. for "the native will have children who will never come back on their journeys and wanderings."

Chapter II.11.3: On natives who come back on their journeys

If Saturn were in his own domicile, the native will jump at the chance to take a long journey, but he will come back to his own land.

If Mars were in the Ascendant and had some dignity in the house of travels, the native will make long journeys and will come back from them into his own land.

If Venus were with Jupiter, Mercury and Mars, and the Moon aspected them, the native will jump at the chance to take many journeys, from which he will come back to his own land.

Chapter II.11.4: On natives who incur losses and misfortunes on the occasion of journeys

If the infortunes were in the 3rd house, and its Lord impeded and in a bad place, the native will have evil and detriment on the occasion of a journey.

If the Moon were in the 3rd house (it being a diurnal nativity), and in a feminine sign, and the infortunes aspected her, the native will have little success and much evil because of his travels.

If Mars and Venus were in the 5th house, and the Moon aspected them by a good aspect, the native will make many journeys, and will have many [worried] thoughts and sparse good from them.

If the Moon were in the 7th house (it being a diurnal nativity), the native will become ill on his journeys.

If Saturn, Mars, Venus, and the Moon were in the house of travel, the native will obtain much labor and little wealth from his journeys, nor will he see what would please him on them.

If Mars aspected the Ascendant by a trine aspect, and the Moon were joined with him, the native will make many journeys, and obtain more evil than good from them.

If Mars were in a domicile of Mercury, the native will jump at the chance to take many journeys, and will incur losses on the occasion of them.

If the Lord of the house of travel, being in a watery sign, made the Lord of the Ascendant unfortunate, the native will make a journey by sea in which he will suffer many evils and fears.

If Mars were the Lord of the house of travel, and he aspected the Lord of the Ascendant [by a] bad aspect, without [the aspect] of the fortunes,[1242] the native will suffer many evils on his journeys, so that he will be the neighbor of death.

If the Lord of the triplicity of the Sun (in a diurnal nativity) or the Lords of the triplicity of the Moon (in a nocturnal nativity) were cadent from the angles and made unfortunate, nor did they aspect the Ascendant,[1243] the native will not be fortunate on his journeys, even if he went on the journeys willingly.

If the planet conjoining the testimonies of the planets signifying journeys were in a bad and blameworthy place, the native will be blamed because of his journeys, and he will be in much evil and labor on them.

If the Lord of the house of travel and the Lord of the Lot of Travel were made unfortunate in a watery sign, the majority of the native's journeys will take place on water, and thence he will obtain evil and labor, especially if the infortunes aspected him, the fortunes were cadent from them, or that Saturn was the infortune. But if Mars were the infortune, evil and the fear of robbers and warriors will befall the native. And if the aforesaid significators were in an earthy sign, the majority of the journeys will be by land, or by groves and deserted places.

If the Lord of the Ascendant went to the Lord of the house of travel, the native will jump at the chance to take a journey [that has been] devised.[1244] If the Lord of the Ascendant were separated from the Lord of the house of travel, the native will hate journeys, nor care about them. If the Lord of the house of travel were separated from the Lord of the Ascendant, the native will seek journeys and will quickly get a start at them, but he will get little or no good from them.

[1242] Reading with Jag.
[1243] Reading *ascendens* for *ascendentes*.
[1244] *Excogitatus* also means things which are *carefully* or *thoughtfully* devised.

Chapter II.12.0: Dominion and mastery

[Chapter II.12.1: Indications of lasting dominion]

Look therefore, for the native's dominion and honor, to [1] the Midheaven and [2] its Lord, and also to [3] [the Lot of the Kingdom and] [4] the Sun (in a diurnal nativity) and Saturn (in a nocturnal nativity). And you should know [5] the *mubtazz* over these places: for if there were a binding between that *mubtazz* and the *mubtazz* of the Ascendant, the native will have a kingdom and dominion; otherwise not.

But[1245] others say, look at the significator of the aforesaid places: for if the stronger of them were in its own domicile, and it also applied to the Lord of the Ascendant, or it had some agreement with it, the native will reach a kingdom or dominion, and will obtain honor and glory through it. But if there were no application or agreement between them, the native will lack a kingdom or dominion, and his estate[1246] will be middling.

[But] 'Umar[1247] and Vebinus said, look at the Midheaven and its Lord, also the *mubtazz* of the mastery, and its Lot[1248] and its Lord. Then look at the *mubtazz* over these places, whether they were one or more. Then look at its nature and mingle [it] with the *mubtazz* of the Ascendant, and judge according to [their] manner and agreement. And if it were one of the ways[1249] which we have named, the native will be of much mastery and dominion, and he will not be removed from it.

Likewise, look at the Sun: for if he were in some one of the [eastern quarters, his kingdom will be early in life; but in][1250] western quarters, the native's kingdom or dominion will be at the end of his life.

And if the Lords of the triplicity [of the Sun] were strong, his dominion or exaltation will not be removed. But if they were impeded, he will be impeded on account of what he does[1251] [in the corresponding time of life]: because the first Lord of the Sun's triplicity signifies a dominion or kingdom around

---

[1245] This paragraph does not appear in Jag. The unnamed source here may be based on *JN* Ch. 32 pp. 296-97.
[1246] *Possessio.*
[1247] *Ubelius et Vebinus.* Jag. has one long garbled name. See *TBN* III.9.
[1248] The Lot of Work, per *TBN* III.9.
[1249] Omitting *obliquis* as a misread for *aliquibus* (Jag.).
[1250] Adding from *TBN* III.9.
[1251] *Quod faciendum.*

the beginning of life, [but] the [second and third Lords] confer [it around] the middle [and end of life].

Certain people[1252] even said that if Saturn were in an angle (it being a nocturnal nativity), and likewise Mars in an angle (it being a diurnal nativity), and especially in the Ascendant or the Midheaven, the native will remain in that exaltation or dominion until the lesser years of Saturn or Mars were completed; and after that time, he who had the exaltation from Mars will incur persecutions and reproaches; but after that time, he who had the exaltation from Saturn will be imprisoned or he will be made an exile or die in hunger or misery.

Chapter II.12.2: On the native's mastery

You should know that the Lords of masteries are three: namely Mars, Venus, and Mercury. Mars was made one Lord of masteries on account of his lightness, mobility, hotness, happiness and strength. But Mercury was made a Lord of masteries with Mars since he has the intellect, subtleness, judgment, speech, and writing. But Venus, since she has the operations of the hands, and wondrous forms, and besides that matters perfected with lastingness and slowness,[1253] took up the dominion of masteries with the others. Nor should we wonder if no mastery can rightly come to be without the assistance of the aforesaid planets. For a mastery does not come to be without wit and skill,[1254] and wit cannot be without intellect; and intellect cannot be without organization and deliberation, and organization and deliberation cannot come to be without knowledge and effort; but knowledge and effort cannot be without lastingness.

Therefore the ancients did not bestow the dominion of the masteries upon the aforesaid three planets without reason; but Saturn, Jupiter, the Sun and the Moon signify nothing in masteries without the partnership of the aforesaid three planets—and no wonder, for:

[1252] Namely 'Umar (*TBN* III.10.9), who likely draws on *Carmen* I.23.
[1253] I find this unusual, but Jag. seems to agree (adding "subtlety").
[1254] Or, "trade" (*artificium*).

The Sun signifies kingdoms and kings, and high and lofty men, and those who rule over others, nor do they become slaves, but they have slaves and tradesmen under them.

Saturn is the master of laziness, greed, heaviness, misery, foulness and sorrow: and for this reason, if the native had a peregrine Saturn in his nativity (and especially without the good aspect of some of the three aforesaid ones signifying masteries, or he aspected the said lords of masteries by a bad aspect), the native will suffer injuries and reproaches on account of [his] mastery, and he will seek to be at rest—not by his own goodness but on account of his misery. And if some planet aided Saturn by aspect and power, the native [will be] digging lands, will empty channels and pits, bury the dead, and change[1255] from place to place; or he will work in fields and vineyards (like slaves and miserable people do), getting commerce from thence.

Jupiter is the lord of religion, oration, and frankness. And therefore if he were peregrine or made unfortunate in some nativity, without the aspect of some one of the said lords, the native will be freed from these secular things, and will meditate on those things which are of God; he will leave the world behind, and will be made to be of a poor life.

The Moon is the mistress of weakness, hastening, quickness, of little intellect and quick response, and her greatest work is to go and come back. Therefore, if the Moon were badly disposed in some nativity, the native will be of fruitless motion.[1256] And if she were strong, it signifies the carrying of lumber and bags, and working with the hands, and criers,[1257] and besides that those who sow discord among others, by saying about them that "such a person has said bad things." And she signifies every work in which one labors with the hands and feet, and this according to the aspect and reception with the aforesaid three lords and the other planets.[1258]

[1255] Omitting *eos*.
[1256] Or perhaps, of fruitless *motives*, i.e., that he will be changing and inconsistent in his motives, coming to nothing.
[1257] Or, "heralds" (*praecones*).
[1258] See below.

Moreover,[1259] one must know that men have four manners of masteries: [1] there are some who have masteries in speech, voice, and language, and [2] some who work with the hands: like a sculptor, mason, carpenter, pelter, a sewer, common laborer, and every worker of the hands. And [3] others who operate in merchandizing, sales and purchases. And [4] there are others who are lazy, without a mastery of the hands or tongue or wit or merchandizing. And I will organize this according to the nature of the planet and the mastery and the work of the planet conjoined to it, and its aspect to it.

[Chapter II.12.3: Fortune and misfortune in masteries]

And[1260] if you looked well in the chapter on chronic illnesses,[1261] and you wished to speak to the native about mastery, speak like this:[1262] look in the four angles: the Ascendant, the tenth, seventh, and fourth. And after these, the four which are after the angles: namely the 8th, 11th, 5th and 2nd. And the sixth sign from the Ascendant and its Lord, and the Lot of Fortune and its Lord, and the orientality of the Moon and [her] occidentality after seven days from the nativity. And look to see where you found the planet of the mastery, with respect to its domicile.

And[1263] if you found only one of the lords of masteries in its own domiciles, give the native a higher mastery. [And if it were in its own domicile and bound, or its own domicile and face, give him a higher mastery. And if it were strong and fortunate, and in its own exaltation, give him the highest mastery which he could have, because the native will be famous and a renowned master in the said mastery. And if the said lord were only retrograde, subtract one-half of the mastery. And if it were retrograde and peregrine, subtract three-fourths of the mastery. And if it were retrograde, peregrine, and burned up, subtract the whole mastery, because the native will not have [anything] from that, except for fame and a name.

And you should know that the significator of the mastery signifies work and masteries, in terms of what agrees with the nature of the sign in which it

---

[1259] Reading this paragraph from Jag.'s fuller version.
[1260] This paragraph is from Jag. In a few places I have paraphrased.
[1261] This is probably a reference to the original ordering of the text, which placed masteries after illnesses, in the 1st house.
[1262] What follows seems to be the approach of Paul of Alexandria, Ch. 26.
[1263] Omitting the redundant first part of the sentence, and adding throughout with Jag.

is, if it is in its own domicile. Which if the said lord were not in its own domicile, but in a sign in which it did not have dignity, conjoin the nature of the sign and the planet which is in it.

Therefore if the significator of the mastery were made fortunate in a domicile of Jupiter, it signifies a good and high mastery.

And if it were in a domicile of Saturn without the aspect of a fortune, it will signify a bad and miserable and low-class mastery.

And if it were made fortunate in a domicile of Mars, a mastery with wit and talent[1264] is signified, in which joy and happiness stick together.

And if it were made fortunate in the domicile of the Sun, it portends a mastery in the matters of lords and princes, with honor.

And if it were in the domicile of the Moon, it shows a foreign[1265] mastery which a man will do with his own cleverness and skill.[1266]

If[1267] the significator of the mastery were made fortunate in the Ascendant or by 5° before the Ascendant, the native will be fortunate in his mastery, and adding in his own fortune. And if it were in the 2nd,[1268] his work will be fortunate and elevated. And if it were in the 12th, worry and malice will commence in his work.

If the significator of the mastery were in its own sign, free from impediments, the native will have happiness and fortune in his mastery.

[1264] *Artificio*: skill, talent, a trade.
[1265] *Extraneum*, which might also mean "strange."
[1266] *Ingenio*.
[1267] Reading this paragraph with Jag., which does not use the 5° rule or indicate the use of quadrant houses, unlike 1540, although it does speak of the significator being "in front of" or "before" the degree of the Ascendant. 1540 also treats the rising degree as separating the 1st and 12th houses.
[1268] Remember that *ii* or "eleven" can sometimes be mistaken for the Roman numeral II in manuscripts, so this might indicate the 11th.

And if it were made[1269] unfortunate in a strong place, it will be unpleasant in his work according to the quantity of the strength of that planet (and its weakness), and according to the goodness and malice of the place.

And if the said significator were in its own descension, it will give the native a mastery of great labor and little wealth.

And if it had some dignity in that place, it will give the native a middling mastery.

Which if the said significator [were] appearing in the house of its descension, and peregrine,[1270] the native will not care about his own mastery.

Which if the fortunes aspected it,[1271] it will make a mastery which he esteems and he will not remove his mind from it.

And if the infortunes (especially Saturn) aspected the said significator, it will give the native a mastery with pain and serious labor, and because of this fact the native will crave to leave it behind. And if Mars aspected the said significator instead of Saturn, it will impose upon the native (regarding the mastery) infamy and cunning and greatness of mind. Which if Mars were then made unfortunate, the native will easily leave his mastery behind, and perhaps the mastery will be unuseful for him.

[Chapter II.12.4: Masteries by type of sign]

You should even know that the fiery signs signify fiery masteries (as are masteries of blacksmiths, craftsmen, bakers, glass-makers and the like). And the earthy signs signify masteries which come to be by means of earth or

---

[1269] Reading with Jag. for "fortunate in a strong place, the native will be unpleasant in his mastery."
[1270] Reading with Jag. for *descensus*.
[1271] Reading with Jag. for *fortem ipsum aspexerit*.

from the earth, as are the masteries of potters,[1272] masons, diggers, and the like. But the watery signs signify fishers, launderers, fullers, and those like these. But the airy signs signify singers, jokers,[1273] birdcatchers, and those like these.

If the significator of the mastery were in a sign of wild beasts, the native's mastery will have to do with wild beasts (as are lions, bears, and apes, and those like these). And if it were in a human sign, the native will be a natural philosopher[1274] or barber[1275]—and thusly with the other masteries which have to do with men. And if it were in Aries, it signifies shepherds and butchers, makers of church-bells,[1276] and those like these.

[Chapter II.12.5: Venus, Mars, and Mercury as significators]

If Venus were the significatrix of the mastery, appearing in a human sign, and one of the superior planets aspected her by a good aspect from a human sign, the native will be a happy singer and joker,[1277] and thusly with other like [masteries]. And if some [planet][1278] aspected her [in a sign of wind], the native's mastery will have to do with good-smelling things, and [good]-smelling fruits, and thusly with the others. And if it aspected her from an earthy sign, the native will be a seller of gems or glassware, and of things like these. And if it aspected her from a watery sign by a good aspect, he will be a seller of pearls and white and lucid stones, and of like things which are found in the sea. And if it aspected her in the same way from a fiery sign, the native will be a goldsmith, and thusly with other precious masteries which come to be through fire. And if it aspected her from a quadrupedal sign, the native will be a seller of horses, swine[1279] and wild asses, or cows from the mountains, and thusly with other like things.

[1272] Or, "bricklayers" (*figulorum*).
[1273] Probably medieval jesters, but modern-day comedians (*ioculatores*).
[1274] What today we would call a scientist.
[1275] Traditionally, barbers also performed minor surgeries.
[1276] *Campanarum*. Perhaps because the ram (or rather, lamb) was associated with Christianity.
[1277] *Lusor*.
[1278] Reading and adding with Jag. for *infortuna*.
[1279] *Cirogrillorum*. In medieval Latin this is a hedgehog, but given the other animals here it must derive from the Greek for "swineherd."

If Mars were the significator of the mastery, and some one of the planets signifying masteries aspected him from a fiery sign, the native will be a craftsman, or founder of metals, and thus with the rest. And if it aspected from an earthy sign, the native will be a potter[1280] or glass-maker, and thus with other masteries which come to be out of earth and fire. And if it aspected him from a watery sign, the native will be a bathing-attendant or shopkeeper,[1281] or a maker of cheeses or distiller of waters, and thus with other masteries which come to be from out of water and fire. And if it aspected him from an airy sign, and it were peregrine in it, the native will project stones by clever devices or machines, or he will be an archer or bird trapper, and thus with other masteries which come to be with air as a medium or in the air. And if it did have some dignity in the said sign, the native will be a natural philosopher. And if it were descending[1282] peregrine and unfortunate in the said sign, it signifies barbers and dancers.[1283] And if it aspected him from out of a sign of a beast, and it had dignity and fortune in it, the native will be a medical doctor of beasts. And if it were peregrine and in its own fall in the said sign, the native will be a bearer of dead beasts outside of estates, and a skinner of them, or a preparer of hides, and thus with other foul masteries.

If Mercury were the significator of the skill,[1284] appearing in a human sign, and some one of the planets signifying masteries aspected him by a good aspect, it signifies the teaching of words and the recollection of holy men, of beautiful [deeds] and of histories, not to mention it indicates philosophy and the knowledge of poetry.[1285] And if it were made fortunate in a fiery sign, it signifies bankers and minters. And if it were in an earthy sign, a sower of lands; and it signifies their measurement, number, and computation, and geometry. And if it were in an airy sign, it portends bird-catchers. And if it were in a watery sign, it signifies a pilot[1286] of waters and rivers.

[1280] *Figulus.* See above.
[1281] *Tabernarius.* But this is probably closer to "bartender" or "bar owner," to account for the relation to liquids.
[1282] This probably does not mean that it is in its own descension, but either it is descending in the circle of its *awj* or it is "dismounting" in that sign: dismounting is an Arabic term occasionally used to mean a planet is "in" a sign.
[1283] Reading *saltatores* with Jag. for *significatores.*
[1284] *Ingenii.*
[1285] *Dictaminis.*
[1286] *Ductorem.*

[Chapter II.12.6: Other points to look at for the mastery]

You even ought to look (in the native's mastery) at [1] the Lot of Mastery[1287] and [2] its Lord, to [3] the Moon's binding, and [4] her separation in the sign in which she is, not to mention [5] the bounds of the Sun and [6] of the Moon, and [7] the Lords of their domiciles, and [8] which planets would be aspecting the said significators. For if a planet made fortunate aspected them by a good aspect, it will give strength to the native, joy, and good fortune in his mastery, especially if the aspecting planet were a fortune; and if it aspected them by a bad aspect, the native will despise his own mastery, especially if that aspecting planet were an infortune: for then the native's mastery will be of little wealth and much labor and much sorrow.

[Chapter II.12.7: The Moon with other planets signifying masteries][1288]

[The Moon with the Sun and other planets]

If[1289] the Moon were in her own domicile or exaltation, or, were she appearing in some one of her own dignities [and] bound to the Sun from out of the 10th house, and one of the [lords of] masteries aspected her by a good aspect, it signifies a mastery around kings, and the native's exaltation. And if Mars aspected a Moon so disposed, by a good aspect, the native will be a master of soldiers and an arranger of wars, not to mention a [man of] fornication and robbery. And if Mercury aspected her instead of Mars, it signifies the organization of monies and of things collected together.[1290] And if Jupiter aspected her instead of Mercury, the native will be a judge and preserver of the king's justice. And if Saturn, appearing in a place signifying mastery, aspected her instead of Jupiter, and Jupiter were with Saturn through dominion and power, the native will be the master of the king's house, or of some great man.

[1287] This is probably the Lot of Work.
[1288] See the Introduction for my commentary on the next few sections.
[1289] Jag. reads differently: "if the Moon will bind with the Sun from the tenth sign, and she were in her own domicile or exaltation, *or* she would have a power, and a planet of mastery aspected her..."
[1290] By "things," Abū Bakr might mean "goods."

[The Moon with Venus and other planets]

And if there were a binding of the Moon[1291] with Venus by conjunction, and both [were] in the Ascendant or the 10th house,[1292] and in a human sign, it signifies song, liberality and joy. And if Mercury aspected them, it portends the putting together of musical instruments. And if Mars aspected them, it signifies jokers and the sculptors of images, and the quickness[1293] of games. And if Jupiter aspected them instead of Mars, it indicates books of the law and their study, not to mention sweet songs in matters of faith, and voices like those crying and praying to God. And if Saturn aspected them instead of Jupiter, it signifies the beating of the breast and pain of the dead.

[The Moon with Mercury and other planets]

And if the Moon were bound to Mercury in a quadrupedal[1294] sign, it shows teaching. And if the Moon aspected the Sun by a good aspect, it portends the papers of the king, and their writing. And if she aspected Jupiter instead of the Sun, it signifies the writing of books, frankness, and famous deeds, and perhaps that the native will be a writer of judgments, or an attorney or accountant. And if she aspected Venus instead of Jupiter, it indicates the writing of verses by women, and their teaching, and wisdom. And if she aspected Mars instead of Venus, the native will be a blacksmith of horses, or a pilot of beasts,[1295] or a medical doctor. And if she aspected Saturn instead of Mars,[1296] the native will be a sculptor of images of black magic.

[The Moon with Saturn and other planets]

And if there were a binding of the Moon with Saturn, and Saturn [were] in an earthy sign, it portends building and the masteries of buildings. And if the Sun aspected Saturn, it signifies building from large stones. And if Jupiter aspected her instead of the Sun, it indicates the building of churches and of places in which there are prayers and the material of idols. And if Venus

---

[1291] Reading "Moon" for "Saturn."
[1292] Reading with Jag. for "11th."
[1293] Reading with Jag. for "skirmishers."
[1294] This does not make sense to me, but Jag. is practically illegible.
[1295] This must mean someone who leads beasts to market and pasture.
[1296] Reading "Mars" for "Venus."

aspected her instead of Jupiter, it portends all building that has a beautiful look. And if Mars aspected her instead of Venus, it shows the building of ovens or of stoves or furnaces. And if Mercury aspected her instead of Mars, it signifies building the foundations of houses. And if Saturn were in a watery sign, it indicates the putting together of embankments,[1297] not of baked bricks, and of bridges or walls from mud.

[The Moon with Mars and other planets]

And if her binding were with Mars, and Mars [were] in a fiery sign, it signifies a mastery of fire. And if the Sun aspected her, the native's mastery will be around kings, or the native will be a producer of arms and of swords. And if Jupiter aspected her instead of the Sun, the native will be a master of air[1298] or of copper or metal. And if Saturn aspected her instead of Jupiter, the native will be a craftsman. And if Venus aspected her instead of Saturn, the native will be a craftsman of gold. And if Mercury aspected her instead of Venus, the native will be a banker or minter or a sculptor of sigils.

[The Moon with Jupiter and other planets][1299]

And if there were an aspect of Jupiter alone to the Moon,[1300] the native will be a craftsman of lead. And if there were an aspect to Mercury, the native will be a master of boys or a judge. And if Mars aspected her from a human sign, the native will be a natural philosopher, especially if Mars were made fortunate. And if he were retrograde or made unfortunate, the native will be a barber. And if Mars aspected her in a sign of a beast, the native will be a butcher. And if he aspected her[1301] from the last part of Sagittarius, the native will be a medical doctor of beasts. And were there an aspect of Venus, the native will be a *barifaldus*.[1302] And if there were an aspect of Saturn, and

---

[1297] *Laterum*, which indicates coasts and the sides of things.
[1298] *Aeris*, which can also indicate atmosphere and weather. It could indicate someone good at managing winds (as in sails) or perhaps even predicting the weather.
[1299] The heading of this section is tentative, but Jupiter is the only planet left.
[1300] Reading with Jag. for "of the Sun and Moon to Jupiter."
[1301] Reading *eam* for *eum* ("him").
[1302] Uncertain. Jag. seems to read *lamfaldus* or *lanifaldus* (which suggests working with wool). Latham has a *berefellarius* (a clerk wearing a bear-skin collar), and Niermeyer *barigildus*, a court official.

Saturn [were] in a human sign, the native will be a digger. And if he were in the sign of a beast, the native will be a preparer of hides.

[Chapter II.12.8: Other points to consider]

And it must be known that if some planet received the lord signifying the mastery in an aspect, and it aspected agreeably, it will give subtlety to the native in the mastery. And if many planets aspected the significator of the mastery, the native will have many masteries. And[1303] if some one of the said planets were received, the native will esteem that mastery before all other words. And if it were not received, he will reject it and will not esteem it.

And if the significator of the mastery were under the rays of the Sun, the native will hate his mastery, and he will be lazy and leisurely in it, unless Mercury were the significator of the mastery: because then it will make the native a writer of books or a craftsman of masteries with more height.

And let us move from these general statements about the masteries of natives, to the particular ones.

Chapter II.12.9: On natives who are weavers[1304]

If Mercury, appearing as the significator of the mastery, were descending or retrograde, the native will be a weaver. And if the Sun aspected him, he will be a weaver of tapestries and the like. And if Venus aspected him, he will be a weaver of *bocaxini*,[1305] and of other things which come to be with silk. And if Saturn aspected him, [the native] will be a weaver of velvet and *surianorum*[1306] and the like. And if Jupiter aspected, him, he will be an *alkisons*[1307] of fine cloths made of wool. And if the Moon aspected him, he will be a weaver of straw mats. And if Saturn were in Gemini, he will be a weaver of cloths of linen.

[1303] Reading the rest of the paragraph with Jag.
[1304] The rest of the individual trades correspond to category [6] in Chapter II.2.0 above.
[1305] Unknown (Jag.: *buchatum?*), but Niermeyer has a *bucheramun* for buckram, a cloth nowadays used to cover books, but in the medieval period it was of softer cotton; if so, perhaps it was also made with silk.
[1306] Unknown, but probably *storiorum*, "mats," which is more Saturnian than velvet.
[1307] Jag.: *alkisses?* Probably "clothier" or "profiteer," both of which would be related to Ar. *kuswah* (clothing) or *kassb*, "profiting."

Chapter II.12.10: On native who are sewers

If Mercury were made unfortunate in the 4th house, just as was said,[1308] the native will be a sewer. If Jupiter aspected him from out of a sign of a beast, the native will be a pelter. And if the Sun aspected him, the native will be a sewer of flags and tents and the like. And if Venus aspected him, the native will be a sewer of curtains and wool. And if the Moon aspected him, the native will be a sewer of cloths of linen or silk. And if none of the planets aspected him, the native will be a worker and sewer of silk.

Chapter II.12.11: On natives who are common laborers or tawyers[1309]

If Mars showed support to Jupiter in some one of the angles, and Venus [aspected one] of them in a fiery sign and the other in a sign of a beast, the native will be a maker of slippers.[1310] And if Saturn aspected them, the native will cut and sew hides. And if Mercury mingled himself with Mars, the native will be someone putting together the instrument or ornament by which men work in the land of the Moors, and they carry it on their heads with the fruits of *Saziph*.[1311] And if Saturn mingled himself with Mars, the native will be a preparer of hides or a maker of instruments from leather for fighting. And if Venus aspected Mars from a domicile of Saturn, the native will be a common laborer and a sewer of hides. And if the Sun showed support to Venus, the native will be a sewer of reins and shoelaces, that by which beasts are beaten, and sheaths.

Chapter II.11.12: On natives who are carpenters

If Mars aspected Mercury from out of the house of mastery, and the sign of that house were of the signs of seeds and of things born of the earth, the native will be a carpenter, or of that mastery which come to be from lumber and iron. And if Venus aspected them, the native will be a maker of trumpets

---

[1308] Perhaps this means "descending and retrograde," as in the previous chapter.
[1309] *Alutariis*, processors of goat skins, especially turning the leather into purses or shoes (*alutae*).
[1310] Or, "shoes" (*sotularium*).
[1311] Jag.: *saziph* or *sariph*. I am not sure whether this is a place or kind of fruit.

and pipes, or of citheras and of like instruments. And if Saturn aspected them, the native will be a carpenter of houses, and of all things of which builders are in need, so far as lumber goes. And if the Sun aspected them, the native will be a carpenter of shields and of other instruments which are put together on account of kings and battles. And if Jupiter aspected them, the native will be a worker of instruments which pontiffs and abbots use in churches, or of instruments by which stones are lifted up on high. And if the Moon aspected them, the native will be a worker of ships and bridges. If Saturn, Mars, and Venus were [*missing verb*] toward one another in a masculine sign[1312] (and especially in Aries, Leo or Sagittarius), the native will be a carpenter or a merchant of lumber.

Chapter II.12.13: On natives who are painters and sculptors

If the Moon, in the bound of Mercury, aspected him from the moist signs, the native will [be a writer or painter and the like. And if Venus aspected her, it signifies that he will][1313] work with various [and] gentle colors in his paintings, for looking at them.[1314] And if Mars aspected her, the native will be a sculptor of wood. And if Saturn aspected her, the native will be a sculptor of obscure stones,[1315] or of gypsum.[1316] And if the Sun aspected her, the native will be a painter or sculptor in gold or gems. And if Jupiter aspected her, the native will be a painter or illuminator of books of faith, or a sculptor of images by which prayers and bendings of the knee to God come to be. Which if it were the Moon instead of Jupiter, the native will be a sculptor of ships or of vessels in which water or wine is put. Likewise if Venus were joined with [Mercury] [in] the angles or succeedents, and appearing from under the rays of the Sun, the native will be subtle in the works of his hands. And you should know that Mercury signifies painting or

---

[1312] Omitting "of Mars."
[1313] Again the text reads throughout as *eam* or *ipsam*, suggesting the planets are aspecting the Moon. But it must be that they are aspecting Mercury (who is a significator of sculpture and painting), especially since the Moon is brought in as an aspecting planet near the end of the paragraph.
[1314] *Natus in picturis suis variis coloribus et ad videndum placidis utetur.* Jag. simply speaks of paintingi n diverse colors.
[1315] That is, with dim or dark colors.
[1316] *Gipsi.*

sculpture in homes, and in everything made from hollowed-out wood, not to mention the sculpting of coins.

Chapter II.12.14: On natives who are dyers

If Venus and Mars [were in the place of mastery or][1317] had firmness, binding, or an aspect there, the native will be a dyer, especially if they were in fiery and watery signs. And if Saturn aspected them, the native will be a dyer of black cloths. And if the Sun aspected them, he will be a dyer of bright cloths and of all things in which there is gold, not to mention beauty and light, such as are the banners of kings and their tents. And if Mercury aspected them, the native will be a dyer of *abbassenus*[1318] and of every green thing or one colored in a medium color, such as are *suriani*.[1319] And if Jupiter aspected them, the native will be a dyer of cloths or things of an orange color. And if the Moon aspected them, the native will be a dyer of wool with which *ventagii*[1320] come to be.

Chapter II.12.15: On natives who are diggers

If Mars were appearing as the significator of the mastery, made unfortunate or peregrine, and in an earthy sign, the native will be a digger of the earth. And if the Sun aspected him, the native will dig up gold and silver and precious stones from the earth. And if Jupiter aspected him by a bad aspect, the native will be a digger of diggings which come to be on account of wars and the protection of some place. And if Saturn aspected him, the native will be a digger of latrines, and of stinking and dark places. And if Venus were with Saturn, the native will be a digger of wells or fountains. And if it were Mercury instead of Venus, the native will be a digger of gardens or places in which water would be put.[1321] And if it were the Moon instead of Mercury, the native will be a digger of lakes or swamps.

[1317] Adding and reading the rest of the clause with Jag.
[1318] Jag.: *abissi*. Unknown.
[1319] See above.
[1320] Unknown, but perhaps a cloth used in winnowing (*ventagium*).
[1321] Reading *ponatur* for *pontatur*.

Chapter II.12.16: On natives who are sailors

If Saturn or Mercury were in the Midheaven, the native will be a sailor or a master of sailors. And if the Sun aspected them, the native will be a sailor with lofty men and ships, which come to be in the service of kings and lofty men. And if it were Jupiter instead of the Sun, the native will be a sailor of ships which go to war on the occasion of faith, especially if Mars were made firm with them. If it were the aspect of Mars instead of Jupiter, the native will put together instruments with which sailors cast forth fire. If it were Venus instead of Mars, the native will be the master of a ship, yelling and encouraging [his] servants to sail. And if it were the Moon instead of Venus, the native will be a sailor of ships, of the profession of boatmen.[1322]

If the Moon, appearing in the west, were bound to Saturn (he appearing immovable), especially from the left side, [he will be] a famous sailor and practically a master of them.

Chapter II.12.17: On natives who are craftsmen

If Mars (and Saturn)[1323] were in some one of the angles, especially in the Midheaven, and in a fiery sign, the native will be a craftsman. And if the Sun aspected them, he will craft swords and breastplates and the iron for spears. And if Jupiter aspected them, the native will be a craftsman of mirrors or keys, or of the locks of books, and of every work which comes to be from alloys [of silver and lead].[1324] And if the Moon aspected them, the native will be a craftsman of instruments which come to be for taking out water from wells. And if it were Venus instead of the Moon, the native will be a craftsman of portfolios[1325] and of instruments pertaining to women. And if it were Mercury instead of Venus, with him appearing in a domicile or bound of Mars, the native will be a craftsman of little knives or of other instruments of iron which craftsmen need.

[1322] *Nauta batelorum magisterii navium.*
[1323] The text reads in the singular, so it seems that either Mars or Saturn would be relevant. But the Latin could contain a misprint for the plural, so perhaps one needs both in angles.
[1324] *Stagno.*
[1325] Or other decorative cases (*scriniorum*).

Chapter II.12.18: On natives who are jokers

If the Moon and Mercury were with Mars and Venus, and one showed its own power to another, the native will be a player of the cithara or the *rota*.[1326] And if the said planets were receding from the angles, the native will dance while making jokes. And if Mercury and Venus were in their own bounds, the native will be a dancer, especially if one of them were in Capricorn. If Mars and Mercury were in the angle of the earth, the native will be of those who makes his way with musical strings.[1327] If Venus were with Mercury in his[1328] own domicile, and in the angles, the native will be a mime or a joker, such that he will play an instrument with the hands or tongue. If[1329] Mercury and Venus firmed themselves up in the angles or in the 4th house, and [Mercury and] Venus appearing in the bound of another or oriental,[1330] [and] they were in their own domicile, exaltation or triplicity, the native will be a joker of the voice, and a dancer, and clapping his hands.

Chapter II.12.19: On natives who are medical doctors and surgeons

If Mars and Venus were joined, or they aspected each other by some aspect, or they would be receding, the native will be a medical doctor, and a master of men's natures.

If Mars and Mercury (or one of them) were in the domicile of Venus, the native will be a medical doctor and a black magician, and he will deceive men by his experiments.

If Mars were the significator of the mastery, and the Moon were bound to him from the sign of a beast, the native will be a medical doctor. And if no planet aspected Mars, he will be a surgeon, and someone who makes his cures with fire. And if Venus aspected him, the native will be a cutter of veins or a giver of medicines. And if Saturn aspected him, he will give injections, and he will inspect hemorrhoids and other sufferings of the anus. And if Jupiter aspected Mars,[1331] he will heal sick people by means of songs

---

[1326] This is probably a hand-held harp resting on the knee, but a similar instrument was shaped like a wheel with bells on it.
[1327] *Vadunt super chordas*. This might be a medieval idiom.
[1328] I take this to mean Mercury because of the connection to the tongue and hands.
[1329] Reading the first part of the sentence with Jag.
[1330] Jag.: occidental.
[1331] Reading *Juppiter* with Jag. for *in ipso*.

and the expression of words. And if Mercury aspected him, the native will be an enchanter and a medical doctor of words, or of medicines made by means of an art. And if the Sun aspected him, he will be a surgeon of the eyes. And if the Moon aspected him, the native will be an extractor of teeth, and a surgeon of the mouth. And if the Lords of masteries were in the Midheaven and in the sign of a beast, so that one would be bound to another, the native will be a surgeon of broken limbs.

Chapter II.12.20: On natives who are fishermen or trappers or hunters

If Saturn were in the Ascendant and Mars aspected him in the angle of the west, the native will be a hunter or fisherman.

[If Mercury is in the third from the Ascendant and Mars in the ninth, the native will be a hunter or fishermen. If Mercury and the Moon will be in Gemini or Sagittarius or in the first degree of Pisces, the native will be a hunter and fisherman and *parsator*.][1332]

If Mercury and the Moon (in her fullness) were in Taurus,[1333] the native will be a rearer of falcons or hawks or sparrowhawks, or he will catch birds with skill and cleverness. If the Moon were with Mercury in a watery sign, the native will be a fisherman.

Chapter II.12.21: On natives who are ropemakers

If Saturn were in the house of mastery and in a common sign, and some one of the lords of masteries aspected him, the native will be a maker of ropes. If Mars aspected him, he will make them for torturers. If Venus aspected him, the native will make ropes from hemp. If the Sun aspected him, the native will one who puts together the bridles and halters of horses. If Jupiter aspected him, the native will put ropes together by hand. If Mercury aspected him, or Mars were the sole significator, or in the sign of a beast, the native will put together ropes or bridles or halters from the hair of animals. If the Moon aspected him, the native will make cords or ropes for whipping men or beating horses. And if the Sun aspected him from a

---

[1332] *Parsator* is unknown to me.
[1333] Omitting an extra *et Mercurius cum ea*.

domicile or bound of Mars, the native will put together cables or ropes which powerful men use in wars.

Chapter II.12.22: On natives who sell good-smelling commodities

If Venus were in the Ascendant and in a movable sign, not to mention in some one of [her own] dignities, the native will be a seller of good-smelling commodities. If Venus were the significatrix of the mastery, and arranged in a sign signifying a mastery (such as, should she be located in Libra), and Saturn aspected from Capricorn, the native will be a seller of musk or amber. If Venus [were] appearing in her own domicile or in the exaltation of Saturn, it signifies good and handsome merchandise, and of good odor. And if Venus aspected Saturn from out of Taurus, the native will be a seller of odiferous ointments and olives, like *sambac* or *keiri*,[1334] and one who puts together like things. And if Venus were the significatrix of work, appearing in a human sign, the native will be a seller of commodities which men use, like ginger,[1335] cinnamon,[1336] and the like.

Chapter II.12.23: On natives who are shopkeepers

If the ascending sign were watery, and Jupiter and Saturn in the 4th house, the native will be a shopkeeper.

And if Mars and Venus were the significators of the mastery, and one aspected the other by a square aspect, the native will be a shopkeeper. And if Mars were in the place of mastery, and Venus aspected him[1337] from out of a watery sign, the native will be a seller of ointments or noodles, and the like.

And if Mars, appearing as the Lord of the mastery, aspected Saturn from out of Taurus or Gemini, the native will be a seller of colors and dyes.

And if the Sun were with a burned-up Saturn in Capricorn, the native will be a merchant of gall-nuts[1338] and bark or roots from which dye comes to be.

[1334] Unknown at this time.
[1335] *Zinziber.*
[1336] *Cinamomum.*
[1337] Reading with Jag. 1540 has both of them in watery signs.
[1338] *Gallarum.*

Chapter II.12.24: On merchants of fruits

If Saturn were in Capricorn, and Jupiter aspected him from out of Cancer, the native will be a merchant of many grains, or of other notable fruits. And if Jupiter aspected him from out of Pisces, the native will be a merchant of sweet fruits. And if he aspected him from out of Taurus, the native will be a merchant of *dyarac*[1339] fruits. And if Mars aspected a Saturn appearing in Capricorn, from out of Cancer, the native will be a merchant of small fruits having hard rinds.

Chapter II.12.25: On merchants of herbs or roots, and of seeds

If Saturn were in Capricorn, and the Moon aspected him from out of Cancer, the native will be a merchant of herbs. And if Mercury were in a watery sign, and the Moon aspected him, or she were bound to him from a fertile sign, the native will be a merchant of melons[1340] and of other like seeds. And if the Moon aspected a Mercury appearing in the Ascendant, from out of the angle of the earth, the native will be a merchant of turnips and of other like roots.

Chapter II.12.26: On natives who are farmers

If Mercury and Venus were in the Midheaven and in an earthy sign, and Saturn aspected them from an earthy or watery sign, the native will be a farmer. If the significator of the mastery were bound to Saturn from a movable sign, it indicates the native will be a farmer. If Venus were the significatrix of the mastery, and Mars (being cadent from the Sun) made her [un]fortunate,[1341] the native will be a farmer. If Saturn made the significator of the mastery unfortunate through his aspect, and the Moon were bound to him[1342] from a movable sign, the native will be a farmer and even a gardener. If Saturn were in Taurus, the native will be a sower and cultivator of lands.

[1339] Unknown at this time.
[1340] *Melonum*.
[1341] Adding *in-*.
[1342] I believe this refers to Saturn.

Chapter II.12.27: On merchants of *rethau*[1343] and of things smelling nice

If Venus [were] the significatrix of the mastery, and Saturn aspected her from Cancer or Scorpio, the native will be a merchant of *rethau*, and of every thing smelling nice. If Saturn were in Taurus and Venus aspected him in Virgo, the native will be a merchant of *rethau*, and of things which smell nice. If Venus were in Virgo and Saturn aspected her from a watery sign (especially from out of Pisces), the native will be a merchant of *rethau* and of other like things.

Chapter II.12.28: On merchants of cloths of linen or silk

If Venus were in the Ascendant or Midheaven and in a fixed sign, the native will be a merchant of cloths of linen. If Venus were the significatrix of the mastery, appearing in a fertile sign, and another of the significators [were] in the sign of a beast, the native will be a merchant of linen and silk. If Saturn were in Capricorn and Mercury aspected him from out of Virgo, the native will be a merchant of cloths mixed from linen and silk.[1344] For if Mercury were in his own domicile or exaltation, it signifies a good and reputable commerce. And if Mercury aspected him from out of Taurus, the native will be a merchant of very fine linen cloths. Likewise if Saturn were in Taurus and Mercury aspected him from out of Virgo, you will judge the same. And if Mercury were with Saturn in Capricorn, the native will be a merchant of cloths of coarse linen. And if Saturn aspected Jupiter from out of Libra, the native will be a merchant of cloths of coarse silk. And if Saturn aspected the Moon from out of Libra, the native will be a merchant of coarse cloaks,[1345] because every linen cloth [belongs to the Moon].[1346] And if Saturn were in Aquarius and Mercury aspected him from out of Libra, the native will be a merchant of cloths of precious silk, such as are velvet and like clothes. If Jupiter were with Saturn, the native will be a merchant of old cloths. And

---

[1343] Unknown at this time. Jag. seems to read something like *rituam*. My best guess is that this is aromatic resin, and by extension perfumes and incenses.
[1344] But perhaps, "thick hair" (*setae*).
[1345] *Mandalium* (1540) or *mantalia*.
[1346] Reading with Jag. for "is a profit of little value."

likewise if Saturn were in Taurus and Jupiter aspected him from out of Virgo, the native will be a merchant of coarse and old cloths.

Chapter II.12.29: On merchants of wool

If the significator of the mastery were in the sign of a beast, and [were also] the Lord of the house of death, the native will be a merchant of wool. And if Mars aspected there, the native will be a merchant of hides with wool. And if Jupiter aspected there, the native will be a merchant of cloths made of hair. And if Mercury aspected the significator of the mastery, and that significator were Venus, the native will be a merchant of precious carpets.[1347] And if Saturn were in Aquarius, and the Moon aspected him from a domicile of Mars, the native will be a merchant of wool or of *alluscorum*[1348] cloths.

Chapter II.12.30: On merchants of bread-grains[1349] and of other seeds

If Mercury were the significator of the mastery, appearing in a fertile sign, and Saturn aspected him from out of a fertile sign, the native will be a merchant of wheat. And if the Moon aspected him from out of Virgo, the native will be a merchant of seeds. And if Saturn were in Taurus, and the significator of the mastery aspected him, the native will be a merchant of seeds. And if Jupiter were there, and the significator of the mastery aspected him, the native will be a merchant of diverse seeds. And if he aspected him from out of Virgo, the native will be a merchant of bread-grains. And if Mars aspected Saturn from out of Virgo, the native will be a merchant of small and moist seeds. And if Mars were with Saturn in Taurus, the native will be a merchant of fine and sharp seeds, such as the mustard seed and the like. And if Saturn aspected the Sun and Virgo, the native will be a merchant of bread-grains and of fruits. And if the Moon were with Saturn, the native will be a merchant of soft seeds. And if the Moon aspected Saturn from out of Virgo, the native will be a merchant of bread-grains and of other seeds. And if the Moon aspected Saturn and Venus and Capricorn, the native will be a

---

[1347] Or, tapestries.
[1348] But Jag. has *abissas*, as above.
[1349] *Bladi.*

merchant of bread-grains. And if she aspected Venus by a good aspect, the native will be a merchant of wheat.

Chapter II.12.31: On merchants of leather [or hide]

If Saturn were in Aquarius, and Mars aspected him, the native will be a merchant of the hides of mules and cows. And if Jupiter aspected Saturn from out of the house of mastery (particularly from an airy sign), the native will be a merchant of sandals—that is, of new shoes. And if a retrograde Mars aspected Saturn from out of an airy sign, the native will be a merchant of old shoes. And if Mars aspected Saturn from out of the sign of a beast, the native will be a merchant of the hides of dogs or yew [trees][1350] or foxes. And if the Sun aspected the place of Mars, the native will be a merchant of the hides of *alkumae*.[1351] And if the aspect of the Sun to Mars were from out of the sign of Gemini, the native will be a merchant of new shoes and of the hides of yew [trees].[1352] And if the Sun aspected Mercury from out of Gemini, or were with [Mercury], the native will be a merchant of carpets made out of hide. And if Mercury aspected Saturn from out of Gemini, the native will be a merchant of books covered in leather. And if Jupiter were in the domicile of the significator of the mastery and in the sign of a beast, and the Moon aspected him from out of the sign of a beast, the native will be a merchant of the hides of rams, she-goats and cows, especially if Mars were made firm with the Sun.

Chapter II.12.32: On the merchants of slaves

If Jupiter were the Lord of the house of mastery, and the Lord of the 6th house aspected [him], the native will be a merchant of slaves. If Venus were the Lady of the 6th house, the native will be a merchant of slaves [of good] reputation and of those singing well. And if it were Mars instead of[1353] Venus, the native will be a merchant of Christian slaves, and he will sell them to Moors and other foreigners who are not of the law of Christ. And if it

---

[1350] *Taxorum*, but this does not really fit in. Jag. seems to read *caxorum*.
[1351] Unknown Arabic transliteration.
[1352] *Taxorum*, but this does not really fit in. Jag. seems to read *caxonis*.
[1353] Adding *in*.

were Saturn instead of Mars, the native will be a merchant of black slaves. And if it were Mercury instead of Saturn, he will be a merchant of boys and girls. And if it were the Moon instead of Mercury, the native will be a merchant of those who are slaves by nature. And if it were the Sun instead of the Moon, the native will be a merchant of captives: because the Sun does not signify slaves, but those who can be freed from servitude.

Chapter II.12.33: On merchants of quadrupeds

If Jupiter were in the house of the significators of mastery, and the Lord of the 6th house aspected him from out of a quadrupedal sign, the native will be a merchant of beasts by which men aid themselves. And if Venus were the Lady of the 6th house, the native will be a merchant of camels and dromedaries. And if Mercury were the Lord of the 6th house, the native will be a merchant of donkeys. And [if] the Moon were the Lady of the 6th house, the native will be a merchant of cows. And if the Sun were the Lord of the 6th house, the native will be a merchant of horses and courier horses. And if Saturn were the Lord of the 6th house, the native will be a merchant of goats and horses. And if no planet aspected Jupiter, the native will be a merchant of sheep and rams.[1354] And if it were the Lord of the 3rd or 9th instead of the Lord of the 6th house,[1355] and in a quadrupedal sign, the native will be a merchant of rams, sheep and cows, or a merchant of milk or cheeses.

And if the Lord of the 7th house were bound to Jupiter, or were with him or with the Lord of the 4th house, the native will be a merchant of dogs or cats or wild animals.

Chapter II.12.34: On merchants of birds

If Mercury[1356] were the Lord of the house of mastery, and Jupiter aspected him from out of the signs of a beast, the native will be a merchant of birds. And if Mars aspected him, the native will be a merchant of falcons,

---

[1354] The typesetter mixed two sentences together: omitting the redundant *et si in loco domini sextae domus dominus 6 fuerit, natus erit mercator ovium*.
[1355] Note that the angles of the 6th are related to the 6th.
[1356] Reading *Mercurius* for *Iupiter*.

hawks, eagles, and of all other birds living by pillage.[1357] And if Venus aspected him, the native will be a merchant of hens, chicks, and capons. And if the Moon were in a watery sign, the native will be a merchant of birds living in water or next to water. And if the Sun aspected them, the native will be a merchant of cranes and of other birds flying high. And if Saturn aspected him, the native will be a merchant of ravens, and of all low-class birds and those eating stinking things. And if Mercury were the sole significator of the mastery or [were] under the rays of the Sun, the native will be a merchant of small birds, as are sparrows, wagtails,[1358] and the like.

Chapter II.12.35: On merchants of fish

If Mars were the significator of the mastery, and Saturn aspected from out of Cancer, the native will be a merchant of fish. And if the significator of the mastery were in a watery sign, and Mars aspected from out of a watery sign, the native will be a merchant of fish. And if Mercury [were] the significator of the mastery, and the Moon aspected him from out of a watery sign, the native will be a merchant of small fish. And if Mercury were with Saturn in Pisces, and the Moon aspected him, the native will be a merchant of small[1359] fish. And if Jupiter aspected him [instead of the Moon], the native will be a merchant of large fish. And if the Moon, occidental and diminished in light, were in the domicile of the significator of the mastery, and Jupiter aspected her from out of the sign of a beast by a good aspect, the native will be a merchant of salted fish.

Chapter II.12.36: On natives who are potters

If Saturn were in Taurus, and Jupiter or the Sun aspected him from out of Cancer (or Mars from out of a fiery sign), the native will be a potter. And if Mars aspected him from out of Cancer, the native will be a merchant of vessels made from earth. And if the Moon aspected him from the contrary, the native will be a potter. And if Jupiter aspected him from out of

---

[1357] *Rapina.*
[1358] *Cauda tremula*, a long-tailed bird in the sparrow family.
[1359] *Insipidorum*, which actually means "foolish." But I take it to mean "small" as opposed to the large fish in the next sentence.

Capricorn, the native will be a cooker or maker of gypsum or *palustri*.[1360] And if Mars aspected him from out of Aries, the native will be a cooker of limestone. And if Saturn were in Aries, and Venus aspected him from out of Capricorn, the native will be a potter of beautiful vessels. And if Mercury aspected Saturn from out of Aries, the native will be a digger of quicksilver.[1361] And if Saturn were in Aries, and the planets did not recede[1362] from him, or if the lord of the mastery were in a fiery sign, and Mars aspected him from a watery[1363] sign, the native will be a potter.[1364] And if Jupiter aspected him, the native will be a potter.

Chapter II.12.37: On those turning and putting together bowls

If Venus were with Saturn in Aries, the native will put together bowls and other wine vessels. If Venus aspected Saturn from Leo, the native will repair wine vessels. If Saturn were in Taurus, and Venus aspected him from out of Cancer, and Mars did so from out of a fiery sign, the native will make glass vessels. And if Mercury aspected him from out of Cancer, the native will make sculptures or writings on the said vessels. And if Venus aspected him from a fiery sign, the native will put together many beautiful works of glass.

Chapter II.12.38: On merchants or preparers of pearls

If Venus, as the significatrix of the mastery, were with the Sun, the native will be a preparer or merchant of pearls. And if Mars aspected her, the native will be an alchemist. And if the lord of the mastery were in a watery sign, and Mars aspected it from a fiery sign, the native will be a merchant of pearls. And if Saturn were in a watery sign, and Venus aspected him, the native will be a merchant of small pearls. And if Venus were the significatrix of the mastery, appearing in Gemini with Saturn, the native will be a merchant or preparer of middle-sized pearls. And if Saturn were outside of Gemini [in a watery sign], the native will be a merchant of small pearls. And if Saturn were

---

[1360] Unknown at this time, but Jag. omits this.
[1361] *Argenti vivi*.
[1362] Jag. has the planets being in aversion to him ("*falling…from him*").
[1363] Adding from Jag.
[1364] Reading with Jag. for "digger of metals."

without the aspect of some planet in a watery sign, and [he were] in the house of mastery, the native will be a merchant of marine stones of little value.

Chapter II.12.39: On natives who are moneychangers[1365]

If the Sun were the significator of the mastery, and the Lord of the 2nd house (appearing in a fiery sign) pushed to him from the Ascendant, the native will be a moneychanger. And if the Moon, appearing in her own domicile or exaltation, aspected from the 10th house by a good aspect, the native will be a moneychanger of kings. And if Saturn were in Aries, and the Sun aspected him from Sagittarius, the native will be a preparer[1366] of gold and silver, or [will be] a gold-worker or minter. And if the Lord of the 2nd house were with Saturn in Aries, the native will be a digger of gold and silver. And if he aspected him from Leo,[1367] the native will extract gold and silver from other things. And if he aspected him from Sagittarius, the native will be a minter.

Chapter II.12.40: On natives who are butchers and bakers

If Mars, the significator of the mastery, were in the sign of a beast, the native will be a butcher, or the master of a place in which blood is made to flow. And if Jupiter aspected him from out of the sign of a beast, the native will be a butcher [for] churchmen. And if Venus aspected him from out of Taurus, the native will be a grocer[1368] or butcher of cows. And if she aspected him from out of Sagittarius, the native will be a medical doctor for beasts. And if she aspected him from out of a human sign, the native will be a barber of beasts or men. And if Mercury aspected him, the native will be a cutter of veins. And if the Sun aspected him by a bad aspect, and [Mars] were with *Caput Algol*, the native will be a torturer and one who cuts off heads. And if the luminaries were with *Caput Algol*, and Mars aspected them by a

---

[1365] Or, "bankers" (*campsoribus*).
[1366] Jag. reads, "bearer."
[1367] Reading with Jag. for "Jupiter."
[1368] *Macellator*. Technically this is a medieval word for butcher, but the text already uses *carnifex* (butcher); a similar word, *macellarius*, means a grocer.

bad aspect, the native's head will be cut off, or he will be hung with his hands and feet cut off. And if Mars aspected Saturn from a fiery sign, the native will be a breadmaker or baker. And if he aspected from out of a watery sign, the native will make curds.

Chapter II.12.41: On merchants of dates and apples[1369] [and] olives

If the Sun were in the domicile of the significator of the mastery,[1370] and he aspected Saturn from out of Taurus,[1371] the native will be a merchant of dates. If Jupiter were in the domicile of the significator of the mastery, in a producing[1372] sign, and Venus aspected him from out of a producing sign, the native will be a merchant of dates. And if the Sun aspected Saturn from out of Virgo, the native will be a merchant of apples [and] olives. And if Saturn were with Mars in Capricorn, the native will be a merchant of red fruits, and small ones (as are *hoasor*).[1373] And if Venus aspected Saturn from out of Virgo, the native will be a merchant of coriander and of like seeds. And if the Moon were with Saturn in Capricorn, the native will be a merchant of breads[1374] and of seeds. [And if Venus aspected them from a sign of a beast, he will be a seller of {small seeds?}]

If Jupiter were in his own exaltation, the native will be a merchant of sugar, especially if he aspected the Sun and Saturn.

Chapter II.12.42: On merchants of bread and wine

If Saturn were in Capricorn, and Mars and Venus aspected him from out of a watery sign, the native will be a bar-owner[1375] or a merchant of wine. If the Sun aspected Saturn from out of Taurus, and Venus were with Mars in

---

[1369] *Pomellorum*. Technically this word means the pommel of a sword or similar ball-shaped thing.
[1370] Jag. has the Sun as the significator himself.
[1371] This would be so only if Venus were the significatrix of the mastery, *unless* Abū Bakr means that the Sun is in the *same* domicile *as* the significator, which in this case would happen to be in Taurus. But the mention of Venus in the next sentence suggests to me that Venus is the key planet here.
[1372] Reading *nascenti* with Jag. for "sterile."
[1373] Unknown (Jag. has *hoafor*), but probably an Arabic transliteration.
[1374] Or grains, reading *colliriorum* as a variant of the medieval *collyridium*.
[1375] *Tabernarius*.

the Ascendant, the native will be a merchant of wine made from the juice of fruits.

And if Jupiter aspected the Moon and Saturn from out of a sign of a beast (they appearing in Capricorn), or the Moon [aspected] Saturn (he being in Capricorn), the native will be a merchant of bread. And if Mars and Venus were in the western angle, and the Moon aspected them from out of the angle of the earth (or from out of the house of mastery), the native will be an innkeeper, bar-owner, or pimp.[1376]

Chapter II.12.43: On merchants of sugarcane, arrows, spears, or lumber

If the Moon were in the domicile of the significator of the mastery,[1377] or in a watery sign, and Mercury aspected her from out of a watery sign, the native will be a merchant of sugarcane. And if Mars aspected her, the native will be a merchant of spears. And if Mars were under the rays of the Sun, and Mercury were bound to him, the native will be a merchant of arrows. And if Jupiter were made firm with them, the native will be a merchant of sugarcane. And if Mars were in a watery sign, and Mercury (appearing under the rays of the Sun) aspected him[1378] from out of a fertile[1379] sign, the native will be a merchant of lumber. And if Mercury aspected Saturn from out of Cancer (or the Moon [aspected Saturn] from out of Scorpio), and Saturn were in Capricorn, the native will be a merchant of lumber or arrows. And if Mercury aspected her from out of Pisces, the native will be a merchant of chaff or stalks or herbs.

Chapter II.12.44: On natives who are heralds

If the Sun were in the house of mastery,[1380] and the Moon aspected him, the native will be a herald or messenger. And if the Sun aspected Mars (with [Mars] appearing in his own descension), the native will be a liar on his

---

[1376] Specifically, someone running a brothel.
[1377] Again, Jag. has the Moon as the significator herself.
[1378] Reading *ipsum* with Jag. for *ipsam*.
[1379] Again, Jag. has "producing" (*nascenti*).
[1380] Again, Jag. has the Sun as the significator himself.

journey or legation. [And if Mercury aspected, the native will be a courier. And if Mercury is in a quadrupedal sign, and especially Sagittarius, he will be a contractor for another work. And if Jupiter aspected him from a quadrupedal sign], he will be a bearer of burdens. And if the Moon were with him, he will be a bearer of water. And if the Sun aspected the Moon (she appearing in her own exaltation), the native will be a messenger from morning until evening. And if he aspected Saturn, the native will be a messenger.

Chapter II.12.45: On diverse masteries of natives

If Saturn were [the significator of work], in Cancer, and Mars aspected him with a good aspect, the native will be a washer of cloths. And if it were thus in Virgo, he will be a maker of gypsum. And if Saturn were in Aquarius, he will be a baker. And if he were in Gemini, he will be a weaver. And if he were in Taurus, he will be a sower.

If the Moon were with Mars, or she aspected him from the opposition, the native will likewise be a merchant of oil. And if Venus [were] appearing as the significatrix of the mastery, and Jupiter aspected her from out of a fertile sign, the native likewise will be a merchant of oil.

And if Saturn were with Jupiter, and Jupiter [were] made unfortunate, burned up or retrograde, the native will be a bar-owner, innkeeper, or pimp. And if the Moon were in the domicile of the significator of the mastery, and in the angle of the earth, the native will be a dealer in wine.

And if Mercury were in Capricorn, with Mars appearing over him,[1381] the native will be [*missing word*].[1382]

And if Saturn were in Aries, the native will be the modifier of a house. If Saturn aspected the Moon or her twelfth-part,[1383] and the Moon were in the bound of Saturn or in one of the angles or the succeedents, the native will be the stone-worker[1384] of a house.

And if the Tail of the Dragon were in the Ascendant, the native will be a reciter of famous deeds and lands.

[1381] *Super eum*. This could refer to "overcoming," i.e., being in the tenth sign from Mercury.
[1382] Missing in both texts. Jag. has a lacuna of about three or four words.
[1383] *Duodenariam*. This probably means her sign, *viz.*, Cancer.
[1384] *Lapidator*, which classically means a stone *thrower*.

And if the planet ruling the native were Mercury, the native's mastery will be from wisdom, unless Mercury were retrograde. For if he were retrograde, the native will be a shoemaker, or a repairer of old clothing.

Chapter II.12.46: In order to find the lord of the mastery[1385]

You will recognize the planet ruling in the mastery, thusly: consider the place of Mars, Venus, and Mercury. For the planet which had dominion in the said places,[1386] is said to be the one ruling in the mastery.

And if Saturn would be commingled with the ruling planet, the native's mastery will be low-class, like preparing hides and fitting harnesses.[1387] And if both were in earthy sign, the native will be a burier of the dead.

And if Jupiter aspected the one ruling in the mastery, the native will acquire great profit and riches from his mastery, and more often the native's mastery will turn around matters of the law and judgments.

And if the Sun aspected it by a good aspect, the native's mastery will be around kings or their matters.

Hermes said:[1388] if the planet ruling in the mastery were burned up or retrograde, or in the 6th or 12th house, and none of the planets aspected the Moon, the native will strive or search for his livelihood among hostile people.[1389]

Ptolemy says:[1390] one must always look into the planet oriental from the Sun, and the native's mastery will be according to its nature (and the nature of the sign in which it is, and according to the nature of the aspect of the planets).

[1385] This chapter originally appeared at the end of the list of trades. Like the previous chapter, it seems to present a miscellany of information. It is not in Jag.
[1386] This sounds like the domicile Lord of such places.
[1387] Reading *straturas* for *stratas*.
[1388] Source unknown at this time.
[1389] *Hostitatim*.
[1390] Cf. *Tet.* IV.4.

But Hermes says[1391] that whenever the planet ruling in the mastery possessed the sign of Scorpio, the native will be a robber; which if the Moon were in the opposite of Mercury, and Mars aspected them from some one of the angles, the native's mastery will be in robbing.

[1391] Source unknown at this time.

Chapter II.13.0: Friends

Look, therefore, for the native's friends and friendship, to [1] the 11th house and [2] its Lord, to [3] the Lot of Friends and [4] its Lord, to [5] Venus, Jupiter and Mars, and to [6] the planet appearing in the 11th house,[1392] and also to [7] the planet which conjoins the testimonies of the said significators; and judge concerning the native's standing as far as friendship goes, according to its status in its strength and weakness, strength and non-strength,[1393] moving direct and retrogradation, and thus concerning the other statuses or manners of the planets.

Chapter II.13.1: On the friendship of kings or lofty men toward the native

If Venus were in the Ascendant and in some one of her own dignities, the native will have friendship with powerful men and noble women, and he will be great and honored among them.

If the Lord of the 3rd house[1394] were in a good place from the Ascendant and in some one of its own dignities, and the fortunes aspected it, but the infortunes were cadent from it, the native will have friendship with kings and powerful men, and he will obtain success and honor from them, and even from his friends.[1395] If the sign of the 3rd house were Leo or Cancer, and Jupiter [were] in it or aspected it,[1396] the native will be esteemed by lofty men, and thence he will procure good and fortune.

If Sagittarius or Pisces were in the 4th house in a diurnal nativity, and the fortunes (especially Jupiter) aspected that same place, but the infortunes were cadent from the said house, the native will have friendship with kings or powerful men, and he will be honored by them. If Jupiter were in the 4th house and in some one of his own dignities, the native will have friendship with kings or illustrious men on the occasion of his parents, and thence he will obtain good and fortune. If Venus were made fortunate in the 4th house,

---

[1392] Reading *11* for *2*. In the Latin manuscripts it is sometimes unclear whether the scribe is using Roman or Arabic numerals, and I take Abū Bakr to be referring to the 11th.
[1393] Reading *fortitudine ac infortitudine* for *fortitudinis ac infortitudinis*.
[1394] Perhaps because the 3rd is in a trine to the 11th, and the trine is an aspect of complete friendship.
[1395] Reading *amicis* for *amici*.
[1396] *Eum*, the sign.

the native will have friendship with kings or powerful people in his old age, and he will receive good and fortune from them in the end.

If the Sun were in the 5th house and in his own face, the native will acquire the friendship of kings and lofty men, and they will prefer him in doing things. If Mars were in the 5th house, strong and free from the infortunes, and a fortune (especially Jupiter) aspected him, the native will be much honored by kings or illustrious men. If Venus were in the 5th house, made fortunate and strong, and also free from the infortunes, the native will be a friend of kings or princes, and esteemed and honored by powerful women.

Chapter II.13.2: On the friendship of bad and low-class men, and of certain others, toward the native

If the Lot of Friends and its Lord were made unfortunate in the 2nd, 6th, 8th, or 12th house, the native will be a friend of evildoers or fornicators.

If the Lot of Friends were made unfortunate in a blameworthy place, the native will be a friend of bad and low-class men, and thence he will obtain infamy for himself.[1397]

If the Lord of the house of friends pushed to the Lord of the Ascendant from the 3rd house, the native will have friendship for brothers and relatives.[1398] Which if the said pusher were made unfortunate, the native will incur evil and immodesty through that friendship.[1399] If the said pusher were in the 4th house, the native will have the friendship of old men. Which if it were in the 5th house, he will be the friend of younger people and minors, and thence he will obtain infamy.[1400] And if in the house of slaves, he will have friendship with slaves and miserable people. And if it were in the house of travel, the native will acquire friends in a foreign land, and will have wealth from thence. And if it were in the 12th house, his enemies will come to be friends to him. And if the Lord of the house of friends were in the 8th house, the native will see the death of his brothers or friends.

[1397] Reading *sibi infamiam consequetur* for *sibi infamia consurgetur*.
[1398] *Propinquis*, which can also refer to people in the neighborhood or those one meets casually on a daily basis.
[1399] Reading *amicitiam illam* for *amicitia illa*.
[1400] This suggests a kind of sexual suspicion among the public with regard to this friendship.

Chapter II.13.3: On the native's faithful and good friendship

If Aries were the sign of the house of friends, the native will be of good friendship and be a faithful friend, and he will honor his brothers and aid them in all things.

If the house of friends were [*missing word*],[1401] the native will be looking for and associate with friends, and he will esteem them and will be of good counsel with them.

If a fortune, being the Lord of the Ascendant, were in the 11th house, the native will profit from his friends, and he will have good and honor from them.

If Pisces were the sign of friends, the native will have many friends and the native's friendship will profit them.

If the Lord of the house of friends were bound to or applied to the Lord of the Ascendant, the native will have many associates and friends who will procure his love, and he will be a necessary person in their business matters.

If the Lord of the Ascendant applied to or were bound to the Lord of the house of friends, the native will acquire the friendship of many who will be necessary to him, and he will be happy and rejoicing in the business matters of friends.

If the Lord of the 11th house were made fortunate, and in a good place and status, and being also free from the infortunes, [and] applied to the Lord of the Ascendant with reception, the native will have love and agreement with his friends and associates, and he will get usefulness from them, and they from him.

If the Lot of Friends were in some one of the angles, and in a fixed sign, and the fortunes aspected [the Lot], and the infortunes were cadent from [the Lot], the native will have firm friendship, and be of great success to his brothers,[1402] and also rejoicing with his friends, and they with him.

If the Lot of Friends and its Lord were of good condition and in good places, the native will have many friends and associates. And if the said Lot and its Lord were made fortunate, the native will have usefulness from the friends, and they from him. And[1403] if in addition they were received by the fortunes, the native will be esteemed by them.

[1401] Jag. reads *natus*, but I believe it may be Taurus.
[1402] *Profectus fratribus suis*. This probably means that he benefits his brothers.
[1403] Omitting a mistaken sentence that repeats the beginning of this sentence and the end of the previous one.

Chapter II.13.4: On natives who will have discord with friends

If the planet which gathers or conjoins the testimonies of the significators of friendship, aspected the planet [signifying the native][1404] by a bad aspect, the native will destroy the friendship of friends, and he will be hateful to them, and he will change his friendship into enmity.

If the Lot of Friends were in a movable sign, the native will be unfaithful, and he will destroy the friendship which he will first have with associates or friends, and he will turn himself around to enmity and betrayal.

If the Lord of the Ascendant were retrograde in the house of friends, and the Lord of [the house of] friends [were] likewise retrograde, the native will betray his friends, nor will he be firm in his friendship.

> And[1405] if the Lord of the house of friends impeded the Lord of the Ascendant, the native will receive evil and burdens from his friends or associates.

> And[1406] if Venus made the other fortunate, the native will receive usefulness and help from his associates and friends, and likewise they from him.

> If the Lord of the Ascendant were separated from the Lord of the 11th house, the native will hate the friends, and will destroy their friendship and love to be alone.

> If[1407] the Lord of the 11th house were separated from the Lord of the Ascendant, the native's friends will hate him, and will cut off friendship from him, and he will also be blamed by them.

> If there were an infortune in the 11th house, it signifies the bad condition[1408] of the friends, and that the native will have few friends.

[1404] Following Jag.; cf. *JN* Ch. 35 and *TBN* III.10.
[1405] This sentence is not in Jag.
[1406] This sentence is not in Jag.
[1407] The rest of this chapter is not in Jag.
[1408] Or, their nature or being (*esse*).

If the Lord of the 11th house did not aspect the 11th house, the native will not have partnership, friendship, [nor] comfort with anyone, and he will love to be solitary, and to be set aside from men.

Chapter II.13.5: On natives who will receive evil from their friends

If the sign of the 3rd house were Taurus or Libra, and an infortune (being the Lord of the 11th house)[1409] aspected that sign, the native will obtain evil and detriment from his own friends.

If Saturn were in the 3rd house, the native will receive powerful evil.

If the Lord of the 3rd house were in the 6th house, the native will have detriment from his friends or relatives.[1410]

If the Lord of the 12th house were in the 12th house, and the Lot of Friends in the 12th house, the native will receive oppression and labors from the friends.

If Virgo were in the house of friends, the native will have little friendship, so that his friends will not care about his friendship. And if an infortune were there, and he made the Lord of the Ascendant unfortunate, the native will incur evil and detriment on the occasion of friends.

[1409] By whole signs, if Taurus were the 3rd, then Capricorn (ruled by Saturn) would be the 11th. But if Libra were the 3rd, then Gemini (not ruled by a malefic) would be the 11th.
[1410] *Propinquis*: again, this could mean casual associates.

Chapter II.14.0: Enemies

For[1411] the native's enemies, look to [1] the 12th house and [2] its Lord, and to [3] the Lot of Enemies and [4] its Lord, to [5] Saturn,[1412] and to [6] a planet appearing in the 12th house, and also to [7] the planet which had greater strength and dominion in the said places.

[Chapter II.14.1: Good and bad fortune with enemies]

And it must be known that if there were a common sign in the house of enemies,[1413] and the Lot of Enemies and its Lord were in a common sign, the native will have many enemies.

If there were many planets in the house of enemies, the native's enemies will be many, and their standing in weakness or strength will be according to the status of the said planets.

If Gemini were the sign of the house of enemies, the native's enemies will be many but weak, so that they will not be able to harm him. If Cancer were the sign of the house of enemies, the native will be humble toward his enemies, and he will fear them much. And if Leo were the sign of the said house, the native will be inimical to those stronger than himself, and he will fear them much. And if Libra were the sign of the said house, the native will have many enemies, and someone will not be inimical to him who does not [also] litigate with him. If Pisces were the sign of the said house, the native will have enemies without guilt, and he will be envious of everyone.

If the planets signifying enemies aspected the Lord of the Ascendant and the planet which has greater dominion in the nativity, the native's enemies and his adversaries will be multiplied, and their standing in weakness or strength will be according to the status of the said planets.

If the planet in the house of enemies were the Lord of the house of brothers, the majority of the native's enemies will be from his own brothers or relatives, or from the men of his own house. And if it were the Lord of the house of fathers, the parents will be enemies to him. [And if it were the Lord of the house of children, the enemies will be from the children. And if

---

[1411] Cf. *TBN* III.11 and *JN* Ch. 36.
[1412] Saturn has his joy in the 12th, so is relevant to enmity in general.
[1413] Omitting an extra "and its Lord" with Jag., but it would be even stronger if the Lord of the 12th were also in a common sign.

it is the Lord of the 6th house, the enemies will be his own slaves. If the Lord of the 10th, his enemies will be those more powerful than he. And if it were the Lord of the house of friends, his own friends will become his enemies. And if the Lord of the Ascendant will be in the house of enemies, the native will be his own enemy, and he will hurt himself more than he will others.][1414] For if the Lord of the house of enemies were in that house, the native will bear grudges, and will have few enemies, who do not reveal their enmity towards him, nor will they harm him in public, but their enmity will be hidden.

If[1415] the Lord of the house of enemies were in the Ascendant, the native will be full of labor, and will have many enemies who will cause anxieties in the beginning of his life. And if it were in the 2nd house, the native will have bad works, and a bad life and status, and bad words will be said about him, and many lies. And if it were in the 8th house, the native will have few enemies, and much substance will be inherited from him.[1416] And if it were in the 9th house, his own brothers will receive oppression from enemies.[1417] Which if the native[1418] jumped at the chance for travel, he will have annoyances on it, and will have a bad law.

If[1419] the Lot of Enemies were free from the infortunes, in some one of the angles, and likewise its Lord, the native will be inimical to powerful men and to those stronger than him, and labor and evil will come to him, and this signification will be stronger if the Lord of the Ascendant would be made unfortunate.

If the Lot of Enemies were in the 3rd, 5th, 9th or 11th house,[1420] the native's enemies will not have good fortune over him, and he will have few enemies.

And this signification will be stronger if the said Lot were in the 3rd or 9th house, for then the native's enemies will be religious or [be only a]

[1414] Filling in with Jag. for 1540's brief "And state thusly about other men, according to that nature and signification." The statement about the Lord of the Ascendant in the 12th originally appeared below, but I have used Jag.'s version here.
[1415] This paragraph does not appear in Jag.
[1416] This does not make much sense to me, unless perhaps it means the enemy will get the native's inheritance. In Māshā'allāh's *On Sig. Planet.* Ch. 19, if the Lord of the 12th is in the 8th, "his enemy will labor to kill him," which makes more sense.
[1417] The 9th opposes the 3rd. *On Sig. Planet.* Ch. 19 says that the Lord of the 12th in the 9th signifies "he will have a bad faith."
[1418] Reading *natus* for *Saturnus*.
[1419] Cf. *JN* Ch. 36 p. 303.
[1420] Reading *ii* for *2*. Jag. has the 7th instead of the 11th.

little obstacle. And if in addition the said Lot were made unfortunate, the native's enemies will be enchanters or those who speak with *daimons*.[1421]

If the Lot of Enemies were in the 11th[1422] house, the native's friends will become enemies to him.

And if it were in the 5th house, the native's children will be inimical to him.

And if it were in the 2nd,[1423] 6th, 8th or 12th house, the native will have few enemies, and they will not harm him, unless the Lord of the said Lot were made unfortunate, and it made the Lord of the Ascendant and the said Lot unfortunate. And it must be known that the enmity will be of the nature of that house in which the said Lot is: for if it were in the 2nd house, the enmity will be because of money; if in the 6th, because of slaves; if in the 8th, because of the inheritances of the dead; and if it were in the 12th house, because of envy.[1424]

Chapter II.14.2: On natives who have their enemies in their own power

If Mercury were strong and fortunate in his own place, the native would be able to resist his enemies and subjugate them.

If Mars and Venus were in the west or in the angle of the earth, the native will be strengthened over his enemies, and they will be humbled before him, and will come to his feet.

If the Lord of the 12th house were burned up or impeded (whether cadent or peregrine, or made unfortunate by some infortune), the native's enemies will be few, and they will come to misery, and dread will enter upon them.

[1421] *Cum daemonibus*. I do not know what the original Arabic word was, and whether it simply meant "spirits" in the older Greek sense or "demons" in the later Christian sense.
[1422] Reading *ii* for *2*. See earlier footnote.
[1423] Jag. reads, "4th."
[1424] The 1540 edition originally contained three further statements which fit into categories mentioned above in the material on death; I have replaced them there with footnotes.

If the [Lord of the]¹⁴²⁵ Ascendant did not aspect the Lord of the 12th house, the native will have few enemies.

If the planet which had greater power in the Ascendant overcame¹⁴²⁶ the planet conjoining the testimonies of the significators of enemies, the native will be strengthened over his enemies, and they will be under this feet, and he will have what he pleases¹⁴²⁷ from them. If one¹⁴²⁸ of these planets did not aspect the other, the native will escape from his enemies, and will live in leisure and peace, without fear [of them].

If the Lord of the house [of enemies or]¹⁴²⁹ of the Lot of Enemies applied to the Lord of the Ascendant by a good aspect, the native's enemies will be made friendly with the native, and they will be humbled publicly before him, if God wills.

If¹⁴³⁰ some one of the two infortunes were in the house of enemies, and the Lord of the house of enemies made unfortunate in a bad place¹⁴³¹ from some infortune, the native will have what he desires from his enemies. [But if one of the fortunes were there, or the Lord of the 12th applied to fortunes, it signifies the strength of the enemies against the native.]¹⁴³²

If¹⁴³³ a fortune (being in some one of its own dignities) were in the 12th house, the native's enemies will be good and just, and he will escape from them. And if were an infortune there, the native's enemies will be evil.

The Book of Nativities of Abū Bakr, son of the great al-Khaṣībī, ends.

---

¹⁴²⁵ Reading with *JN* Ch. 36.
¹⁴²⁶ *Superaverit*. That is, in the tenth sign from it.
¹⁴²⁷ Reading with Jag. for "wants."
¹⁴²⁸ Reading with Jag. for "Venus."
¹⁴²⁹ This sentence originally appeared at the end of 1540 and Jag., after the next two paragraphs.
¹⁴³⁰ This seems to have been inserted later; it is based on *JN* Ch. 36 p. 303.
¹⁴³¹ Reading *in malo loco* for *a malo loco*.
¹⁴³² Adding from *JN*.
¹⁴³³ This seems to have been inserted later; it is based on *JN* Ch. 36 p. 303.

Appendix A: Miscellaneous 'Umar Excerpts

These excerpts have been removed from various points in the Latin text, as they derive from other sources and branches of astrology. The first excerpt gives indirect evidence of a lost electional text by Māshā'allāh, preserved in Sahl's *On Questions*. If it is originally from Māshā'allāh, then his horary work was fully in line with mainstream practice (despite the special rules on choosing a significator in *OR*), and Sahl's work on questions must derive from Māshā'allāh's, just as Sahl wrote his own copy of *BA*.

1. Horary: the journeys of princes and those they leave behind[1434]

Māshā'allāh said: if the king or prince moves himself [from place to place], and Mars were in the second from the Ascendant, it indicates for him that he will have loss in those things which pertain to him[1435] [and are left behind]: namely in his relatives and children, or kingdom and substance. For this detriment will enter upon him from the contention of wars or burning. If however it were Saturn, what I said will be from robbers or shipwreck or infirmity.

But if the bad one were received, it will not impede this [journey],[1436] and it will be improved. [If it were received but retrograde],[1437] there will be some mention of him, but it will not be perfected.

But if [the bad one] were not received, or it were in its own descension, [the disaster] will be made plain and magnified, until it will be heard by all. And more strongly than that if the planet were retrograde, because it signifies dissolution and destruction.

Likewise a fortune[1438] [in the second] signifies fitness and good praise.

[1434] From near the beginning of Book II. The clearest accessible source for this is Sahl's *On Questions* §9.3. It also appears in *BOA* pp. 547-48. I have used Sahl to clarify the paragraph. Note that since 'Umar's version attributes this to Māshā'allāh, and we know that Sahl had already made his own copy of *BA*, we can well assume that Sahl's own *On Questions* is based on a work by Māshā'allāh.

[1435] Reading *ad eum* for *ad deum*. Hand retains *ad deum*, which means "to God," which has a theological ring to it. But it is better understood as yet another error in the typesetting.

[1436] Moving "there will be some mention of him, but it will not be perfected" below.

[1437] Adding from *BOA*, p. 548.

[1438] Reading *fortuna* for *fortunae*.

2. Elections: the establishing of princes in their rule[1439]

Moreover, Māshā'allāh said: for the choosing and establishing of princes, if the Lord of the domicile of the Moon were retrograde, it signifies the hatred of the soldiers and the cities of the region toward him who is chosen when the prince enters his work.

3. Horary: whether a woman is pregnant, and the status of the fetus[1440]

For pregnancy, look to the Ascendant and its Lord, and at the Moon and the Lord of her domicile, also the fifth and its Lord, and, of the planets, at the *mubtazz* over these places, and at Jupiter. The *mubtazz* over these places is even looked at, and in this signification the eleventh [sign] is introduced, and its Lord, and whatever of the planets were in the eleventh, and the place of Venus.

If therefore you were asked, about a pregnancy, whether there is one or not, look at the *mubtazz* over the Ascendant, and at the *mubtazz* over these places: if there were a conjunction or transfer [of light] or a collection [of light] between them (in any of the fourteen concordant complexions), and it were with the soundness of the receiver and the received, this signifies that there will be a pregnancy here. And if the pushing one were impeded by the receiver, and the receiver were impeded, it signifies that the child will be destroyed and [the pregnancy] will not be perfected. And were there nothing of these complexions between them, it signifies that the pregnancy will not be [at all].

But if you were asked (concerning a pregnancy) whether it already existed or not, look at the *mubtazz* over the aforesaid places, and at the *mubtazz* over the Ascendant [and] the Moon:[1441] if there were a separation between them (out of the fourteen ways and the coming-together) between them, this signifies that the pregnancy already existed. But if there were a conjunction, it signifies that it was not yet, but it will be.

Then look to see whether the child will be saved or not, from the soundness of the *mubtazz* and of the house of children: which if they were then safe, the child will be saved; and if they were impeded, the child will be destroyed.

[1439] From near the beginning of Book II. Source currently unknown.
[1440] From near the end of Book III. Source(s) unknown, but cf. *BOA* pp. 407-08 and the *Book of the Nine Judges* p. 17v.
[1441] Reading *et lunam* for *a luna*.

4. Horary: whether a woman is pregnant, and the status of the fetus[1442]

Look even at what Ptolemy (and the generality [of the astrologers]) says about a woman, whether she is pregnant or not: [look at] the Ascendant and its Lord, the fifth, and Jupiter, the 11th[1443] and its Lord, also Venus and the Sun.[1444] If the [*mubtazz*] of these or the planets of them were joined[1445] in common signs, and by the aspect of many planets in signs of many ascensions,[1446] it signifies that the pregnancy is true. And if the *mubtazz* of the significators were impeded, and the fifth and its Lord,[1447] the child will be destroyed. But if it were impeded by Saturn, this will be because of the coldness of the mother.[1448] And if it were [impeded] by Mars, it will be from an overflowing of heat and dryness, or from the flowing of blood, or from bearing a heavy thing, or a fall. And if by Mercury, from managing or working with the hands. And if it were by the Sun, from heat and an excess of foods, and from the corruption of the complexion of the stomach, or the impediment will be one of the nerves or because of a master and the husband.

5. Horary: when a pregnant woman will give birth[1449]

The way in which one looks to see whether the pregnancy is longer or closer. Look at the significator: if it were in eastern quarters and the planets were oriental from the Sun, the woman was recently pregnant. And if it were in western quarters, and the planets were occidental from the Sun and in[1450] places receding from the angles, the pregnancy is already perfected.

After this, look at the hour by means of the ten[1451] ways of meeting, namely of each of the significators: that is, from [1] their conjunction, and [2] the entrance of any one of them into an angle, and from [3] the conjunction of the two fortunes in an angle, or from [4] a changing of the figures of the significators (that is, from retrogradation to direct motion), or from [5] the

---

[1442] From near the end of Book III.
[1443] Reading *xi* for *xii*.
[1444] I find it odd that the Moon is omitted.
[1445] Reading *fuerint iuncti almuten horum vel planetae* for *fuerit iuncta horum vel planeta*.
[1446] That is, of long ascensions.
[1447] Reading *dominus* for *dominum*.
[1448] Reading *frigore matris* for *fulgore Martis*. Note the similarity to *frugi* which appeared in relation to Saturn in Ch. 7 and indicated dryness.
[1449] Fron near the end of Book III. Source unknown at this time.
[1450] Reading *in* for *a*.
[1451] Reading *decem* for *decimam*. These are not really ways of "meeting," but rather types of "times," as described in works like Sahl's *On Times*.

entrance of the significator into the house of children or the 12th[1452] or the Ascendant, or from [6] the entrance of the significator of the Ascendant and of the Moon to the aforesaid places, or from [7] the degrees which were from each of the significators[1453] by rays, and by [8] the number of the signs and planets which were in the signs which were between them, or from [9] the planets' boundary-determination,[1454] and [10] [their movement from] under the earth toward the upper parts of the earth. Here are joined together the [ten] things signifying the native's nativity.

6. Horary: whether she would give birth to twins:[1455]

Whether the children would be twins or not, look at these significators. If you found them in common signs and in the aspect of many planets, and it came about that the Moon in particular is in a common sign, it signifies that the ones born are twins, if God wills.

[1452] In this case I have retained *xii* instead of translating it as *xi* (11th), because what is at stake here is not so much a matter of fulfilled hopes (11th), but childbirth, and the 12th has a relation to the moments before birth. See *TBN* III.1.2 and Abū Bakr I.1.7.
[1453] Reading *significatorum* for *significatores*.
[1454] *Terminatione*. Meaning unclear.
[1455] From the end of Book III (heading mine). This is a horary question, and seems to be a truncated version of that attributed to 'Umar in the *Book of the Nine Judges*. The fuller version there reads: "For if one would be asked about one [child] or twins, you will note the house of children and what kind of signs its Lord is traversing; no less must the Lord of the hour and the Moon be consulted. Which if their testimonies especially favor the common signs (namely Gemini, Virgo, Sagittarius and Pisces), they are good for twins. But in the rest, they generate only one."

Appendix B: Alternative Text for the *Firdāriyyāt* of the Nodes

The following two paragraphs originally appeared at the end of IV.7 in *On Rev. Nat.* (now IV.8), but I have replaced them by the fuller version which was incorrectly incorporated into the material on transits near the end. The fuller version parallels Māshā'allāh's own use of al-Andarzaghar in *BA* IV.24-25, which also allowed me to correct the Latin text of Abū Ma'shar.

"Then the Head of the Dragon alone disposes 3 years, and it signifies that in a distribution of this kind he will be prospering, and will befriend princes and will rule over many, he will even buy male and female slaves, and he will have friendship with women.

"Then the Tail disposes 2 years. In a distribution of this kind he will become inimical to his friends, and he will be fined and saddened about his wife, and he will be defamed because of her, and he will be sick with a vicious illness."

APPENDIX C: THE TRUTINE OF HERMES (ABŪ BAKR I.4.1)[1456]

The Trutine of Hermes, which apparently goes back to Petosiris, is used to rectify charts and determine the date of conception for tracking transits and events during pregnancy. It is based on the theory that the Ascendant and the Moon at birth are in each other's places at conception: thus the Moon at birth was the Ascendant at conception, and the Ascendant at birth was the Moon at conception. The standard presentation is based on the idea that the standard length of gestation is 9 sidereal months (the number of days in a year divided by 12 months), which is also equivalent to 10 lunar returns.[1457]

> Length of year: 365.2425 days
> Length of sidereal month: 30.436875 days
> 9 month average gestation: **273.931875** days
>
> Average daily course of Moon: 13.17638889°
> Length of lunar return (360°/avg. course): 27.32159798 days
> 10 lunar returns average gestation: **273.2159798** days

The average gestation is usually taken to be 273 days before fine-tuning the time. By definition, if the gestation was of exactly average length, then the Moon and Ascendant would coincide both at conception and birth. In all other cases, we need to calculate how much longer or shorter the gestation was, depending on where the Moon was at birth. If she is above the horizon, it was shorter than average; if below it, longer.

Let us take the following chart:

[1456] See Kennedy 1998, article XVIII. I myself have not practiced with the Trutine, and cannot vouch for its accuracy.
[1457] The values given by Kāshī in Kennedy's article derive the months from the lunar motion, rather than from a pre-given length of the year.

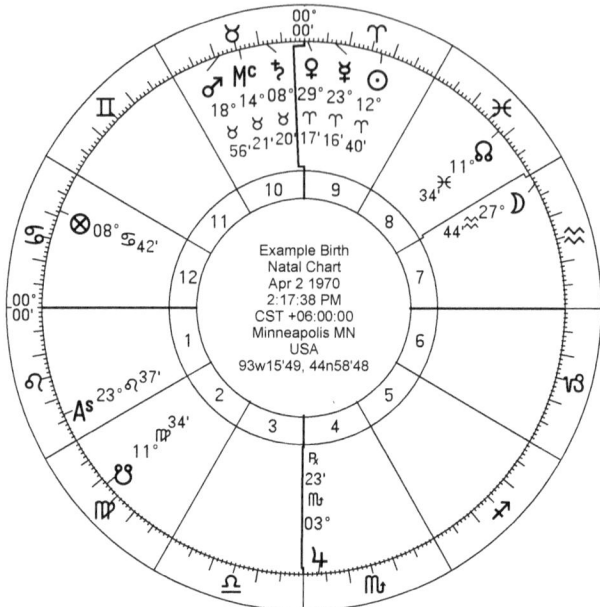

In this case, the Moon is above the horizon, so the birth was less than 273 days ago. We want to convert the Moon's distance from the Ascendant into days, which we will subtract from 273. The distance counterclockwise between the Moon and the Ascendant is 175° 53'. Divide this by the average daily course of the Moon (given above) to get 13.34837145 days. Since the birth was that much earlier than the average, subtract those days from 273 to get 259.6516285 days of gestation.

If the Moon had been below the earth, we would have counted counterclockwise from the Ascendant to the Moon, and divided those degrees by the Moon's average daily course, but *added* it to 273.

Get a calendar and count backwards about 259.6 days, which is slightly over 37 weeks. You should get July 17, 1969. Use a computer program to calculate a chart for this day, and you should see that the Moon's position is very close to the Ascendant at birth. Use your program to move the chart forwards or backwards (depending on the length of gestation), so that the natal Moon's degree is now on the Ascendant of the conception chart. If the Moon in the conception is more than about 6° away from the natal Ascendant, then calculate the same chart for a day later or earlier until the positions match up more closely. According to the theory, the following should be the approximate conception chart:

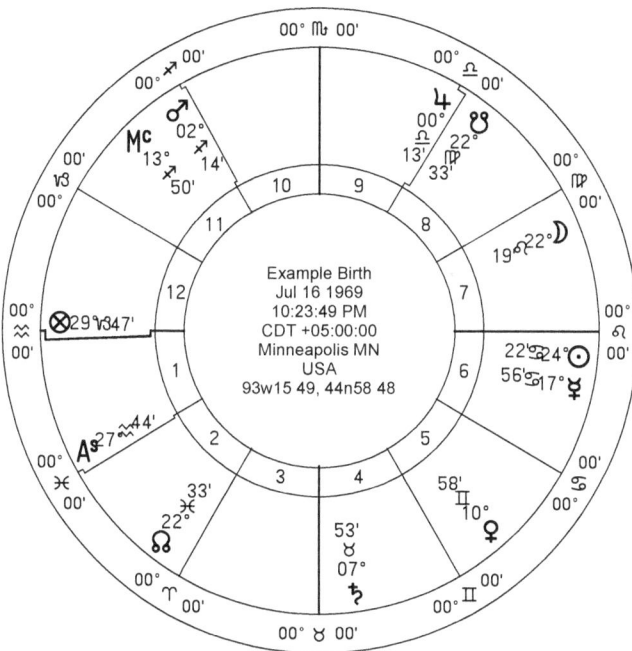

Note that the Moon is not exactly on the natal Ascendant. This means that the natal chart was not precise, and that the natal Ascendant was off by about a degree. This information can be used to re-do the procedure until both charts coincide.

If the gestation was rather premature (7 months), then use an 8-month lunar return cycle as the average gestation; if it was closer to a 10 month gestation, then use an 11-month lunar return cycle.

BIBLIOGRAPHY

Abū Bakr, *Liber Genethliacus* (Nuremberg: Johannes Petreius, 1540)

Abū Ma'shar al-Balhi, *Liber Introductorii Maioris ad Scientiam Iudiciorum Astrorum*, vol. V, ed. Richard Lemay (Naples: Istituto Universitario Orientale, 1995)

Abū Ma'shar al-Balhi, *The Abbreviation of the Introduction to Astrology*, Charles Burnett ed. and trans. (Reston, VA: ARHAT Publications, 1997)

Abū Ma'shar al-Balhi, *On Solar Revolutions*, trans. and ed. Robert H. Schmidt (Cumberland, MD: The PHASER Foundation, Inc., 1999)

Al-Khayyāt, Abū 'Ali, *The Judgments of Nativities*, trans. and ed. Benjamin N. Dykes, in Dykes 2009.

Al-Qabīsī, *The Introduction to Astrology*, eds. Charles Burnett, Keiji Yamamoto, Michio Yano (London and Turin: The Warburg Institute, 2004)

Al-Rijāl, 'Ali, *Libri de Iudiciis Astrorum* (Basel: Henrichus Petrus, 1551)

Al-Tabarī, 'Umar, *De Nativitatibus* (Basel: Johannes Hervagius, 1533)

Al-Tabarī, 'Umar, *Three Books of Nativities*, ed. Robert Schmidt, trans. Robert Hand (Berkeley Springs, WV: The Golden Hind Press, 1997)

Bonatti, Guido, *Book of Astronomy*, trans. and ed. Benjamin N. Dykes (Golden Valley, MN: The Cazimi Press, 2007)

Book of the Nine Judges, in Biblioteca Nacional Madrid, MS Lat. 10009.

Bosworth, Clifford E., *The Medieval Islamic Underworld*: The Banū Sāsān in Arabic Society and Literature (Leiden: E. J. Brill, 1976)

Burnett, Charles, and David Pingree eds., *The Liber Aristotilis of Hugo of Santalla* (London: The Warburg Institute, 1997)

Dorotheus of Sidon, *Carmen Astrologicum*, trans. David Pingree (Abingdon, MD: The Astrology Center of America, 2005)

Dykes, Benjamin, trans. and ed., *Works of Sahl & Māshā'allāh* (Golden Valley, MN: The Cazimi Press, 2008)

Dykes, Benjamin, trans. and ed., *Persian Nativities I* (Minneapolis, MN: The Cazimi Press, 2009)

Gansten, Martin, *Primary Directions: Astrology's Old Master Technique* (England: The Wessex Astrologer, 2009)

Holden, James H., *A History of Horoscopic Astrology* (Tempe, AZ: American Federation of Astrologers, Inc., 1996)

Ibn Ezra, Abraham, *The Book of Nativities and Revolutions*, trans. and ed. Meira Epstein, ed. Robert Hand (ARHAT Publications, 2008)

Kennedy, Edward S., *Astronomy and Astrology in the Medieval Islamic World* (London: Ashgate Publishing Company, 1998)

Māshā'allāh bin Atharī, *Book of Nativities*, trans. and ed. Benjamin N. Dykes, in Dykes 2008.

Māshā'allāh bin Atharī, *The Book of Aristotle*, trans. and ed. Benjamin N. Dykes, in Dykes 2009.

Paulus Alexandrinus, *Late Classical Astrology: Paulus Alexandrinus and Olympiodorus*, trans. Dorian Gieseler Greenbaum, ed. Robert Hand (Reston, VA: ARHAT Publications, 2001)

Pingree, David, "Astronomy and Astrology in India and Iran," *Isis* v. 54/2 (1963), pp. 229-46.

Pingree, David and E.S. Kennedy eds., *The Astrological History of Māshā'allāh* (Cambridge, MA: Harvard University Press, 1971)

Pingree, David, "Antiochus and Rhetorius," *Classical Philology*, v. 2 no. 3 (July 1977), pp. 203-23.

Pingree, David, "Classical and Byzantine Astrology in Sassanian Persia," *Dumbarton Oaks Papers*, v. 43 (1989), pp. 227-239.

Pingree, David, *From Astral Omens to Astrology: From Babylon to Bīkāner* (Rome: Istituto italiano per L'Africa e L'Oriente, 1997)

Ptolemy, Claudius, *Tetrabiblos*, trans. F.E. Robbins (Cambridge and London: Harvard University Press, 1940)

Ptolemy, Claudius, *Tetrabiblos* vols. 1, 2, 4, trans. Robert Schmidt, ed. Robert Hand (Berkeley Springs, WV: The Golden Hind Press, 1994-98)

Rhetorius of Egypt, *Astrological Compendium*, trans. and ed. James H. Holden (Tempe, AZ: American Federation of Astrologers, Inc., 2009)

Sahl bin Bishr, *Introduction*, trans. and ed. Benjamin N. Dykes, in Dykes 2008.

Schmidt, Robert H., trans. and ed. *Definitions and Foundations* (Cumberland, MD: The Golden Hind Press, 2009)

Sezgin, Fuat, *Geschichte des Arabischen Schrifttums*, vol. 7 (Leiden: E. J. Brill, 1979)

Valens, Vettius, *The Anthology*, vols. I-VII, ed. Robert Hand, trans. Robert Schmidt (Berkeley Springs, WV: The Golden Hind Press, 1993-2001)

INDEX

ḥalb 13
ḥayyiz 13, 47
'Uthmān bin 'Affān, Caliph 31
ʾ*idbār* 79, 114
ʾ*iqbāl* 79, 114
Abū Ma'shar .. xiv, xi, xv, xvi, xviii, xx, xxiii, 10, 25, 43, 74, 80, 142, 338, 342
al-'Anbas al-Saimari .... xiii-xiv, xvi, xix-xx, 215-16, 222
al-Andarzaghar .... xvii-xviii, 338
Animals
  benefit/harm 64, 188
Antiochus of Athens 79
Aristotle 72
Birth 102
Body/physiognomy 107
  body type 109, 111
  face 109
  family resemblance 112
Bounds ..... xi, xiii, xvii, 2, 7-13, 17, 20, 22, 24, 27-30, 34-35, 42-43, 46, 65-66, 69-70, 79-80, 84, 94-98, 100-01, 109, 115, 117, 119, 121, 124-25, 127-29, 133, 135-38, 142, 144-45, 151, 157, 159, 162, 169-70, 172-73, 175, 178, 183, 187-88, 193-94, 199, 207, 210-12, 214-15, 218, 220, 222, 233, 236, 240-44, 246, 248-52, 255-56, 257, 259, 262, 265, 268, 270, 274, 277, 283-84, 287, 290, 296, 301-02, 306, 308-12, 316, 321-22, 327
Burning up/combustion . 6, 13-16, 62, 66, 76, 78, 100, 104, 118, 126, 128-30, 132, 155, 158, 169-70, 172-75, 177, 182, 185, 193, 209, 212-14, 222, 224-27, 233, 235, 237, 247, 249, 255-57, 261-63, 265, 275, 280-81, 283, 296, 322-23, 332

under the rays ... 15, 17, 59, 78, 101, 115-16, 118, 130, 134, 143-44, 146, 149, 152, 154, 165, 171, 173, 178, 181, 185, 190, 198-99, 201, 211, 213, 226, 232, 236, 239-42, 244-45, 247, 250, 252, 254, 257, 263, 265, 274-75, 279, 286-87, 289-90, 304, 306, 317, 321
Burnt path/via combusta .. 78, 240
Character
  aggression 143, 144
  beauty 162
  calm/quick 162, 163
  discord 162
  faithfulness 157
  fear 143
  gluttony 161
  happy/sad 145, 159-60
  intellect/knowledge . 150, 153-55
  overview 139
  shame/modesty 144-45, 159
  taking/giving 157-59
  truthfulness 145-46, 155-56
Children 62, 223
  death 232
  fertility 62, 223, 225-26
  love for native 63, 224, 228-229
  number 62-63, 224-25, 227
  sex 225
  status 230-31
  when 62, 224, 228
Conception 85
Conjunction/prevention before birth 2-4, 7-8, 10, 12, 61, 65, 88, 103, 114-16, 125-28, 132, 150, 174, 176-78, 189, 204-07, 214, 241, 246, 253, 281
Death 77, 277
  cause 77, 278-83, 285

easy 278
suicide 285
violent 77-78, 279, 281-83
where 286-87
Dorotheus of Sidon......... ix, xi-xii, xv-xvii, 5, 9-12, 17-18, 21, 23, 26, 47-48, 58-59, 67-68, 114, 118, 126, 219-220, 227, 238, 258, 275, 290
Dustūrīyyah .46-47, 55, 57, 217-18
Elections 29, 335
Enemies 74, 330
    have enemies? 74, 330
    status 74, 330
    who prevails 74, 332
Faith/law 76
    changes 76
    honesty 67, 76, 148
    type 76, 146, 149
    when 76
Fall/descension 13, 16, 48, 90, 116-18, 129, 132, 222-23, 225, 232, 298, 321, 334
Feral/wild ... 49, 155, 157, 171-75, 206-08, 210, 212, 244, 246
Fixed stars 18, 65, 80, 141, 144, 146, 165, 167, 191, 194, 271, 284
    injurious to eyes 238
Friends 71, 325
    strength 71-73, 327-29
    synastry 72
    types 71, 325-26
Gestation 1, 87, 89, 93
God.... ...1, 3-9, 15-18, 20, 25, 27-31, 33-36, 38-39, 41-46, 49-63, 66, 67, 69-71, 73, 75-76, 78, 84, 86-88, 90-91, 93-95, 99, 101, 109, 115, 119, 121-22, 125, 127-28, 131, 133, 146-47, 150, 152, 165-67, 177, 190-91, 203, 211, 234, 278, 295, 302, 306, 333-34, 337

Hand, Robert ..... xvii, 1, 15, 17-18, 25, 27, 29, 33, 35, 45, 48, 66, 76, 334
Head/Tail of the Dragon..... 8, 16, 20, 26, 48, 77, 85, 95, 97, 100, 102, 130-31, 187, 200, 207, 212, 234, 237, 239, 250, 252, 282, 284, 322, 338
Hermes 48-49, 74, 91, 104, 116, 323-24, 339
hīlāj 1, 6-12, 14, 17-27, 33, 55, 57, 80, 84, 125-29, 131, 175, 199, 217-218, 220-21
Horary .... xi, xv-xix, xxi, 29, 334, 336-37
ibn Ezra, Abraham 343
Illness 64, 234
    eyes 65, 237, 239-41
    height 243, 254-55
    indications of 235-36, 258
    mind 245
    sexual 61, 66, 250-53, 259
    various 64, 121-22, 137, 242-44, 246-51, 253, 255-57
    when 259
Incarceration 172
jārbakhtār . xvii, 10, 12, 27, 30, 35, 42, 80, 135
kadukhudhāh 6-17, 22, 32, 84, 115, 119, 125-26, 128-32, 173, 175, 216, 219-21
Lilly, William .... xi, xiv, xix
Longevity . 5, 7, 10, 13, 15, 17, 125
Lots
    of Boldness 142
    of Brothers 53, 196-202
    of Children 62, 223-33, 267
    of Courage 257
    of Death 277, 281, 284, 286-87
    of Enemies 74, 330-33
    of Faith 76, 107, 152, 256
    of Foreign Travel 67
    of Fortune ...3-5, 7, 10, 12, 43, 52, 61, 72, 84, 101, 103-07,

113, 115-16, 118, 120-21, 124-27, 132-33, 144, 150-52, 155, 158, 162, 165-66, 168-70, 173-74, 176-77, 181, 189-91, 193, 196, 198-200, 202, 211, 229, 232, 238, 245, 250, 256-57, 269, 272-74, 283, 296
   of Friends 71, 325-29
   of Infirmities/*Zamīn* 64-65, 251, 257-59
   of Lawsuits or Wars 143
   of Male/Female Children...231
   of Marriage-Union 59-61, 261-68, 270, 272-76
   of Mastery 301
   of Money 175, 183
   of Nuptials 274, 285
   of Possession 170, 193
   of Slaves 171, 187, 260
   of Spirit xxii, 115, 124, 148-49, 154, 245
   of Substance 52
   of the Father 33-34, 55-56, 101, 204-07, 210-17, 220-22
   of the Kingdom................... 293
   of the Mother 33-35, 56-58, 204, 207, 215, 217-18, 221-22
   of Travel 289, 292
   of Work 68-69
Marriage 59, 261
   appropriate/type 59-61, 263-66
   benefit/harm 272-73
   death......................................274
   homosexuality 60, 269, 271
   marry? 59, 61, 262
   number 275
   sexual misbehavior 60, 261, 264, 266, 268, 274
   spouse age 265
   when........................ 59-60, 276

Māshā'allāh ...... ix, xiii, xv-xix, xxiii, 5, 29, 31-32, 34-35, 44, 175, 218, 227, 331, 334-35, 338, 343
Moon
   days of...xix, 120-21, 177, 290
mubtazz... xii-xvii, xxiii, 4-6, 12-13, 50, 52-53, 55-64, 67-71, 74-78, 160, 208, 216-17, 219, 221-22, 232, 260, 293, 335-36
   weighted .... xii-xvi, 222
Muhammad, Islamic prophet 31
Mundane astrology......................30
Myriagenesis 108
Oriental/occidental... 2, 11, 13-15, 17, 46, 52, 55, 59-60, 62, 70, 76, 104, 120, 124, 129-30, 146-47, 151-53, 156, 158-61, 165, 168-69, 173, 175, 178, 181, 184-86, 197, 199, 236, 240-41, 246, 253, 265, 274-75, 281, 289-90, 309, 317, 323, 336
   pertaining-to-arising.. ...11, 70, 290
   pertaining-to-sinking 265
Overcoming 187, 192, 208, 213, 226, 243, 253
Parents......................... 55, 204, 222
   condition 29, 33, 55
   death...55, 57-58, 213, 215-17, 219-20
   inheritance...........................209
   legitimacy...................... 56, 101
   lineage 204
   love between..........................57
   love for native..56-57, 207, 209
   status 55, 57, 179, 204-05, 210-11, 216-17
Peregrination ... 11, 13-14, 46, 117-18, 121, 124, 128, 130, 143, 148, 152, 154-55, 157, 169-75, 178, 189, 200-01, 205-09, 213, 226, 232, 242, 244, 246-47, 249-55, 257-58, 262, 270, 282-

83, 285, 287-88, 295-96, 298, 300, 307, 332
Planets
   above/under the earth.. ...2, 9, 13, 58, 78, 91-92, 118, 187, 192, 197-98, 202, 219-20, 234-35, 239, 249, 258, 337
   years of 133
Prediction 49, 84
   firdāriyyah 133, 338
   primary directions .5, 6, 17-18, 20-31, 33-36, 38, 41-46, 55, 57, 80, 84, 85, 91-93, 122, 124-28, 131, 133, 136, 151, 160, 165-66, 168, 177-78, 181-82, 185-86, 188, 194, 209, 215, 217-21, 224, 228, 255, 276, 325, 336
   profections .. xviii, 5, 6, 18, 22, 29, 30, 32-35, 39-40, 45, 48-49, 55, 218, 228
   triplicity Lords...49, 52, 57, 63, 67-68, 76, 84, 218, 293
Pregnancy 1
Profession/mastery ...... xii, 68, 293
   misc. indications ... 298, 304-22
   Moon's application 70, 301
   success 69, 293, 296, 301, 304
   three significators 70, 294, 299, 323
   when 68
Prosperity....xii, 46, 68-69, 164-65, 167-68, 170-73, 175, 177
Ptolemy..xi-xiii, xvi, 2, 4, 9, 12, 21, 23-24, 43, 46, 50, 59, 63, 70, 72-73, 77-78, 108, 125, 127, 219-21, 323, 336
Ptolemy, Claudius 108
Rearing/nourishment .3, 113, 122, 124
   exposure 124
   monstrous births 4, 103, 105-06

   no survival 114
   type 1 .... 3, 114
   type 2 .... 4, 116
   type 3 .... 6, 118
   type 4 .... 7, 119
Rectification/*namūdār*s
   Hermes 91-92, 339
   others 93
   Ptolemy 2
Retrogradation .. 6, 13-17, 76, 103-04, 118-19, 126, 128-30, 132, 148, 154-55, 157-58, 169-74, 178, 185, 193, 200-01, 206, 212, 221-22, 226, 242-43, 244, 251-54, 256-58, 261-62, 279, 296, 303-05, 315, 322-23, 328, 334-36
Sahl bin Bishr... xiii, xvi, xxiii, 35, 49, 52, 79, 113-14, 129, 155, 222, 334, 336, 343-44
Schmidt, Robert.... xvii, 18, 46, 50, 79, 102, 342
Sect
   of chart...... 14, 47, 90, 97, 104, 118, 121, 124-27, 141-50, 152-53, 156, 158-59, 161, 168-69, 171-72, 174-75, 178-79, 181-84, 186-88, 190-93, 196, 205, 207-08, 210-12, 214, 217-21, 224, 228-29, 235, 239-40, 242, 245, 247, 248-49, 250-51, 253-54, 258, 269, 272-73, 275, 277, 280, 284, 289, 291-94, 325
   of planets... ... 46, 55, 57, 118, 169, 218
   of signs 119, 134, 211
Serapio 50, 102
Siblings 53, 196
   concord 53, 196, 199-200
   death 53
   half-siblings 202
   number 54, 196-98, 202

older/younger 196
sex...53, 197
   status 53, 201
Signs
   bestial...103-04, 188, 283, 299-300, 303-05, 309-10, 313-17, 319-21
   by triplicity........78, 80, 90, 99, 144, 161, 163, 188-89, 197, 244, 249, 281-82, 291-92, 298-300, 302-03, 305, 307-08, 310-13, 315, 317-21, 323
   common 54, 71, 80, 185, 188, 202, 227, 264, 276, 310, 330, 336-37
   fixed 71, 119, 163, 264, 272, 276, 313, 327
   human..100, 103-04, 143, 299-300, 302-04, 311, 319
   injurious to eyes 65
   libidinous 60
   masculine/feminine...9-10, 13, 53, 60, 102, 124-25, 127, 142, 147-48, 151-52, 182, 190, 197, 203, 215, 225, 227, 261-62, 269-70, 289, 306
   movable ....xix, 62, 71, 80, 87, 99, 110, 160, 226, 236-37, 240, 243, 250, 255-56, 258, 262, 264, 273-74, 276, 281, 311-12, 328
   of many children. ... 53, 59, 62, 71, 196-97, 223-24, 227
   quadrupedal...77, 104-07, 188-89, 283, 299, 302, 316, 322
   sterile 62, 197, 226
Slaves 260
   benefit/harm 64, 187, 260
   concord 260
Thābit bin Qurra 131
Travel 67, 137, 289
   benefit 67, 289
   harm 67, 290-291
   whether? 67
Wealth .... xii, 52, 181
   abundance 181
   source....... ...183-85, 187, 189, 191-92, 194
   type/source 52
   when 52

www.ingramcontent.com/pod-product-compliance
Lightning Source LLC
Chambersburg PA
CBHW060450170426
43199CB00011B/1151